Public Sector Organizations

Series Editors

B. Guy Peters, Department of Political Science, Pittsburgh University, Pittsburgh, PA, USA
Geert Bouckaert, Public Management Institute, Katholieke Universiteit Leuven, Leuven, Vlaams Brabant, Belgium

Organizations are the building blocks of governments. The role of organizations, formal and informal, is most readily apparent in public bureaucracy, but all the institutions of the public sector are comprised of organizations, or have some organizational characteristics that affect their performance. Therefore, if scholars want to understand how governments work, a very good place to start is at the level of organizations involved in delivering services. Likewise, if practitioners want to understand how to be effective in the public sector, they would be well-advised to consider examining the role of organizations and how to make organizations more effective. This series publishes research-based books concerned with organizations in the public sector and covers such issues as: the autonomy of public sector organizations; networks and network analysis; bureaucratic politics; organizational change and leadership; and methodology for studying organizations.

More information about this series at
https://link.springer.com/bookseries/14525

Rómulo Pinheiro · Maria Laura Frigotto ·
Mitchell Young
Editors

Towards Resilient Organizations and Societies

A Cross-Sectoral and Multi-Disciplinary Perspective

palgrave
macmillan

Editors
Rómulo Pinheiro
University of Agder
Kristiansand, Norway

Maria Laura Frigotto
University of Trento
Trento, Italy

Mitchell Young
Charles University
Prague, Czech Republic

Public Sector Organizations
ISBN 978-3-030-82071-8 ISBN 978-3-030-82072-5 (eBook)
https://doi.org/10.1007/978-3-030-82072-5

This Palgrave Macmillan imprint is published by the registered company Springer Nature Switzerland AG
The registered company address is: Gewerbestrasse 11, 6330 Cham, Switzerland

Foreword

As sharply illustrated in this book, despite the common ancient root in Latin, the meaning of resilience changes from discipline to discipline, from domain to domain, from perspective to perspective. In recent years, the very term resilience has attracted such increasing scholarly attention that it has acquired centrality in managerial debate, becoming a jargon or portmanteau term; an issue of ambiguity that this book is very clearly addressing, by weaving back and forth in reconstructing the very complex texture of resilience via an exhaustive, cross-sectoral and multi-disciplinary perspective.

In the very days in which this book sees the light, the world is facing the Covid-19 pandemic: an unprecedented jolt and shock to our personal, professional, organizational and communitarian lives. As often happens in times of crisis, politicians and decision-makers are encouraging us to be resilient, and promote the nurturing of resilience at all levels (as citizens, individual workers, teams, organizations and communities). A question legitimately arises, though: Is resilience itself resilient enough to be employed in these troubled days?

To get rid of the potential tautology, some further reflection may be found useful. I like to frame resilience in the light of the Chinese proverb "When the winds of change blow, some people build walls and others build windmills" (Gallo, 2015; Giustiniano et al., 2020), as the capacity to build walls and windmills at the same time, boasting the ability to absorb shocks and endure, to be "sponge and titanium" (Giustiniano & Cantoni,

2018). To do so, one might accept that resilience, however defined, is a complex construct made of opposing tensions (e.g. executing vs. learning, rethinking vs. adapting). As the book unshyly reveals, such tensions are paradoxically intertwined (Giustiniano et al., 2018); hence, resilience has a paradoxical side. To this extent, the practice of resilience can be seen as "paradox work" with managers and policy makers called to resourcing their organizations under tension. The cases presented in the book show that the attempt—and sometimes the achievement—of resilience can be pursued by identifying new scopes of meaning (situational, organizational or institutional) and by extending the very frameworks in which organizational life takes place (see also Schneider, Bullinger & Brandl, 2020).

As organizational life relies on resilience, it's necessary to remember that resilience is not based on individuals but on collectives: entire communities can express resilience, even in the absence of resilient members; on the contrary, a group of resilient individuals does not guarantee a resilient team (for example, if a collaborative atmosphere is lacking).

What's feeding such a resilient life, then? Learning appears to be the main course on the menu, and in particular keeping the capacity of "learning to learn" active and energetic. "Learning to learn" is about nurturing generative doubt (Välikangas & Romme, 2013), by returning to a sense of mission, requalifying and reinventing a new sense of organizational purpose, while asking "why are we doing this?" Resilience emerges as a paradoxical force: Risk factors can destroy, but where they do not, resilience can be energized. While a group of resilient individuals does not guarantee a resilient team (for example, if it lacks a collaborative and socially supportive culture), resilience is based not on individuals alone but collectives; entire communities can express resilience, even in the absence of resilient members. Similar to other related constructs (e.g. grit), therefore, the presence of resilience does not grant the spread of resilience. In fact, for resilience to escalate to higher levels of aggregation (e.g. from the individual to the teams), it must be expressed by individuals, conveyed towards the others and perceived by the receivers (see Rego et al., 2020). Hence, as clearly illustrated in the many cases reported in the book, for organizations and communities to survive and flourish, policy makers, managers and professionals should consider resilience as the achievement and maintenance of "positive adaptation", as reactive organizational experimentation out of the ordinary, building on paradox work and a paradoxical mindset (Miron-Spektor et al., 2018). Nonetheless, as the book gently suggests, "too much of a good thing can be a bad thing". As reality reports, an extreme concern for resilience may induce people to become overly persistent in seeking to achieve unattainable goals or overly tolerant of adversity (like tolerating demoralizing jobs, toxic bosses or dangerous working conditions). Additionally, "unwanted phenomena" (crime, a cancer) can engender resilience.

In synthesis, I believe the construct of resilience can boost resilience even in times of unprecedented uncertainty and ambiguity, both as a construct in the academic debate and as a feature for managerial practice. For that to happen, though, it must be approached from a multi-disciplinary perspective and pursued with a strong-willed agency by organizational leaders, as this book sharply suggests.

November 2020

Luca Giustiniano
Full Professor of Organization
Studies and Director of the
Center for Research on
Leadership, Innovation and
Organisation (CLIO)
Luiss University
Rome, Italy

References

Cunha, M. P., & Putnam, L. L. (2019). Paradox theory and the paradox of success. *Strategic Organization, 17*(1), 95–106.

Gallo, F. T. (2015). *The enlightened leader: Lessons from China on the art of executive coaching*. Emerald Group Publishing.

Giustiniano, L., & Cantoni, F. (2018). Between Sponge and Titanium: Designing micro and macro features for the resilient organization. In Boccardelli, P, Annosi, M. C., Brunetta, F. & Magnusson, M. (Eds.), *Learning and innovation in hybrid organizations* (pp. 167–190). Palgrave Macmillan, Cham.

Giustiniano, L., Clegg, S. R., Cunha, M. P., & Rego, A. (2018). *Elgar introduction to theories of organizational resilience*. Edward Elgar Publishing.

Giustiniano, L., Cunha, M. P., Simpson, A. V., Rego, A., & Clegg, S. (2020). Resilient leadership as paradox work: Notes from COVID-19. *Management and Organization Review*, 1–5.

Miron-Spektor, E., Ingram, A., Keller, J., Smith, W. K., & Lewis, M. W. (2018). Microfoundations of organizational paradox: The problem is how we think about the problem. *Academy of Management Journal, 61*(1), 26–45.

Rego, A., Cavazotte, F., Cunha, M. P. E., Valverde, C., Meyer, M., & Giustiniano, L. (2020). Gritty leaders promoting employees' thriving at work. *Journal of Management*, 0149206320904765.

Schneider, A., Bullinger, B., & Brandl, J. (2020). Resourcing under tensions: How frontline employees create resources to balance paradoxical tensions. *Organization Studies*, 0170840620926825.

Välikangas, L., & Romme, A. G. L. (2013). How to design for strategic resilience: A case study in retailing. *Journal of Organization Design, 2*(2), 44–53.

In Memoriam: Rainer Born (1943–2021)

Acknowledgments

This edited volume traces its origins to a 2018 panel on 'The Surprising Nature of Resilience Organizations' hosted by the European Group for Organizational Studies (EGOS), July 5–7, Tallinn, Estonia. The book is the result of an intense and rewarding 2-year long collaboration involving more than 30 researchers spread across 15 countries. In addition to the (2-day) kick off panel in Tallinn, with 17 papers, a group of researchers met face to face as well as online in Prague for a 2-day workshop (to discuss revised drafts) in September 2019.

First and foremost, we sincerely thank all the participants, including those who, for one reason or another, did not make it in the final volume, for their important contributions in highly engaged and constructive discussions throughout the entire process.

We also wish to give a special thanks to both EGOS and the Faculty of Social Sciences at Charles University for hosting us during 2018 and 2019.

Finally, we would like to thank the following institutions for their valuable financial support in making this entire volume freely available as Open Access:

- Faculty of Social Sciences, Charles University, Czech Republic
- Faculty of Economics and Administration, Masaryk University, Czech Republic
- Faculty of Management and Business, Tampere University, Finland

- Department of Economics and Management, University of Trento, Italy
- Faculty of Economics and Management, Free University of Bozen-Bolzano, Italy
- Wellington School of Business & Government, Victoria University of Wellington, New Zealand
- University of Agder, Norway
- Western Norway University of Applied Sciences, Norway
- KTH Royal Institute of Technology, Sweden

October 2021
Kristiansand, Norway
Trento, Italy
Prague, Czech Republic

Praise for *Towards Resilient Organizations and Societies*

"Resilience is not just a buzzword, but a fundamental ingredient of the cultural shift we need to address the challenges of the 21st Century and take the world onto a sustainable development path. This book provides an excellent framework to design innovative policies and strategies to build a less vulnerable and more resilient socioeconomic system."

—Enrico Giovannini, *Italian Economist and Statistician, University of Rome, Italy, and Italian Minister of Sustainable Infrastructure and Mobility (2021-ongoing)*

"*Resilience in Organizations and Societies* moves forward the notion that organizational and societal resilience are interconnected. An important book that sets the agenda for future thinking and research on the varieties of ways that we think about resilience. Filled with engaging examples and built on a strong conceptual foundation, this is a must read for academics and practitioners interested in the interdisciplinary study of resilience at all levels, individual, organizational, and societal."

—Christopher Kayes, *Professor of Management, The George Washington University, School or Business, USA, and author of* Organizational Resilience: How Learning Sustains Organizations in Crisis, Disaster, and Breakdown (2015)

"This timely book *Towards Resilient Organizations and Societies* adds a much needed cross-sectoral and multi-disciplinary perspective to the field and offers an exciting collection of chapters that examine resilience both at organizational and societal levels. A worthwhile read for academics and practitioners!"

—Martina Linnenluecke, *Director, Centre for Corporate Sustainability and Environmental Finance, Macquarie Business School, Macquarie University, Australia*

Contents

Part I Resilience: Antecedents, Paradigms and Perspectives

1 Resilience in Organizations and Societies: The State of the Art and Three Organizing Principles for Moving Forward 3
Maria Laura Frigotto, Mitchell Young, and Rómulo Pinheiro

Part II Resilience in Organisations

2 Decision Premises, Learning and Organizational Resilience Addressing Novel Adversities 43
Maria Laura Frigotto, Loris Gaio, Alessandro Narduzzo, and Marco Zamarian

3 Installing an Action Space for Resilience in Surprising Situations 65
Johannes M. Lehner, Eva Born, Peter Kelemen, and Rainer Born

4 Building Resilience in Temporary Organizations: Lessons from a Shipyard 91
Anne Russel, Stéphanie Tillement, and Benoit Journé

5 **A Practical Perspective on Resilience in Organizations: The Interplay Between Structure and Action** 117
Anouck Adrot, Oriane Sitte de Longueval, and Alexandre Largier

6 **Growing and Adapting During Continuous Change: Building Employee Resilience in the Public Sector** 143
Esme Franken, Geoff Plimmer, Sanna Malinen, and Jane Bryson

Part III Resilience in Organizational Fields and Societies

7 **The Post-entrepreneurial University: The Case for Resilience in Higher Education** 173
Mitchell Young and Rómulo Pinheiro

8 **Organizational Persistence in Highly Institutionalized Environments: Unpacking the Relation Between Identity and Resilience** 195
Lars Geschwind, Rómulo Pinheiro, and Bjørn Stensaker

9 **Resilience and Change in Opera Theatres: Travelling the Edge of Tradition and Contemporaneity** 223
Maria Laura Frigotto and Francesca Frigotto

10 **Being Resilient Between the Region and the Higher Education System? Views on Regional Higher Education Institutions in Estonia and Finland** 249
Jari Kolehmainen, Heli Kurikka, Anne Keerberg, and Garri Raagmaa

11 **Agency, Institutions and Regional Resilience: An Approach from the Basque Region** 277
Edurne Magro, Elvira Uyarra, and Jesus M. Valdaliso

Part IV Taking Stock and Moving Forward

12 Towards Resilient Organisations and Societies? Reflections on the Multifaceted Nature of Resilience 307
Mitchell Young, Maria Laura Frigotto, and Rómulo Pinheiro

Index 333

Notes on Contributors

Anouck Adrot is an Associate Professor at Paris-Dauphine University PSL, affiliated to the Dauphine Recherches en Management (DRM) research centre. She holds a dual-degree Ph.D. from Georgia State University and Paris-Dauphine University. Her research interests cover collective behaviours, information transmission, organizational collapse and emergence in demanding and critical settings.

Eva Born is an Assistant Professor at the Department of Corporate Economy, Faculty of Economics and Administration, Masaryk University, Brno, Czech Republic, and a Post-Doctoral Research Fellow at the Cognitive Science Research Platform, University of Vienna, Austria. In her research, she mainly focuses on both the identification as well as the development of organizational antecedents and behavioural patterns and skills on team and individual level allowing for resilient dealing with surprise in and around organizations. Her research has been published in journals, such as Journal of Organizational Transformation and Social Change, and in various monographs.

Rainer Born (1943–2021) was an Associate Professor in Philosophy and Theory of Science at the Department of Corporate Economy, Faculty of Economics and Administration, Masaryk University, Brno, Czech Republic and at the Institute of Business Informatics—Communications Engineering at the Johannes Kepler University in Linz, Austria. He was a member of the Scientific Committee of the Austrian Ministry of Defense and Sports. His research centred around the specific practical operationalization of explanatory concepts in applied economics and administrative behaviour, as well as the decision- and action-guiding interplay of these concepts. The second edition of his book *Artificial Intelligence: The Case Against* was published in 2018 by Routledge.

Jane Bryson is a Professor in Human Resource Management and Employment Relations at Victoria University of Wellington. She researches the range of institutional, organizational and individual factors which influence human capability at work. Most recently she has examined the impact of employment law on workplace management practices; and the influence of collective voice on worker access to training.

Oriane Sitte de Longueval works as a Researcher at the University of Geneva, Switzerland. She gained her Ph.D. in Management at Paris-Dauphine University PSL in France and did a post-doctoral fellow at Geneva University. Her research focuses on interactions in tense or risky contexts, following a situated approach and ethnographic method. Her work explores violence between clients and frontline staff, scapegoating in organizations, crisis management professionalization and the negotiation of safety between separate occupational groups.

Esme Franken is a Lecturer in Management at Edith Cowan University in Perth, Western Australia. Her research interests are in leadership behaviours, employee development and resilience.

Francesca Frigotto is a harp Professor at the Conservatory of Music Giovan Battista Martini in Bologna (Italy). As solo-Harpist, and in chamber music groups, she has won several national and international music competitions and recorded for RAI Italian National Radio and Television and Radio France. She has played with the famous orchestras and opera houses, such as Teatro alla Scala in Milano, Maggio Musicale Fiorentino in Florence, Arena in Verona, Teatro La Fenice in Venice and Teatro Comunale in Bologna. She earned her degree in harp at the Conservatory of Music Claudio Monteverdi in Bolzano and her masters at the Scuola di Alto Perfezionamento Musicale in Saluzzo (European Master Music Course). She is also a scholar in Music Studies with a degree in History, Critics and Performance Production from the University of Florence. Her studies address the history of the harp as an instrument and the role of music in the political discourse during fascism in Italy.

Maria Laura Frigotto is an Associate Professor in Organization Theory and Management at the University of Trento (Italy) where she is a member of the Department of Economics and Management, of the Institute for Safety and Security (ISSTN) of the School of Innovation and of the Ph.D. Programme in Economics and Management. She was a visiting scholar at Stanford (SCANCOR) USA, at the University of Alberta, Canada, and at IMT Lucca, Italy. Her research focuses on novelty, especially in its unexpected and emergent form, in relation to resilience and innovation. She has studied emergency management organizations such as civil protection agencies and paradigmatic events such as the 911 terrorist attack in New York, but also very different contexts such as the operatic sector.

Loris Gaio is an Associate Professor in Management at the Department of Economics and Management of the University of Trento (Italy), where he teaches courses in operations and project management. He is a member of the RARE research group and co-director of the Master Programme in Innovation Management. His past and current research interests include topics such as the role of modularity and standardization in the division of labour, the emergence of coordination dynamics in the making of collective knowledge and the evolution of organizational change in the automotive industry.

Lars Geschwind is a Professor in Engineering Education Policy and Management, Coordinator of the research group HEOS (Higher Education Organization Studies) and Head of Division at Learning in STEM at KTH Royal Institute of Technology, Stockholm, Sweden. His main research interests are higher education policy, institutional governance, academic leadership and management and academic work. He is currently involved in a number of projects focusing on change processes in higher education institutions, including, e.g. governance and steering, quality assurance, academic careers and partnership with external stakeholder. Most studies include a comparative component and a historical perspective.

Benoit Journé is a Professor in Management at Université de Nantes (IAE), France, where he carries out field researches and organization studies at LEMNA (Laboratoire d'Economie et de Management de Nantes Atlantique). Specialized in organizational reliability and resilience, he is also an Associate Professor at IMT Atlantique where he heads the

Chaire RESOH, that conducts researches in Human and Organizational Factors of industrial safety.

Anne Keerberg worked as Director of Kuressaare College, a regional unit of Tallinn University of Technology on the island Saaremaa, Estonia (2004–2016). Before that she worked as Deputy Mayor of Kuressaare in the field of education. She currently works as Development Officer at Kuressaare Nooruse School. Anne's research focus is on regional higher educational institutions contributing to regional development and innovation.

Peter Kelemen is a Research Fellow and Doctoral Candidate in Knowledge Management at the Department of Corporate Economy, Faculty of Economics and Administration, Masaryk University, Brno, Czech Republic. He wrote his Master Thesis on the relevance of knowledge in support of resilient organizing. He writes his doctoral thesis on the role of background knowledge in managerial practice. His research results have been published in journals, such as Czechoslovak Psychology (*Československá psychologie*), and Economic Research-Ekonomska Istraživanja and presented at various international conferences, such as the Organizational Learning and Knowledge Capabilities Conference and International Forum on Knowledge Asset Dynamics.

Jari Kolehmainen works as a Research Director at Tampere University, Faculty of Management and Business, Urban and regional Studies Research Group, Sente. He holds Ph.D. in regional studies and he has specialized in knowledge-based urban and regional development. His research interests cover a number of themes, such as regional innovation activities, economic development and innovation policies and strategic urban and regional development.

Heli Kurikka works as a Researcher at Tampere University, Faculty of Management and Business, Urban and regional Studies Research Group, Sente. She is a licentiate of philosophy in geography and has previously worked at the University of Helsinki and at thr University of Oulu. Her research interests include regional development and resilience, strategies and university-society interaction.

Alexandre Largier holds a Ph.D. in Sociology from Paris-Dauphine University PSL, France. He is Deputy Head of the social sciences laboratory at IRSN (Institut de Radioprotection et de Sûreté Nucléaire -

Institute for Radioprotection and Nuclear Safety), which corresponds to the Technical Support Organization of the French Nuclear Regulatory Organization. His research topics concern human activity and safety in both normal and crisis situations. He was formally head of a study department at SNCF (French railway company).

Johannes M. Lehner is an Associate Professor at the Institute of Organization Science, Johannes Kepler University, Linz, Austria. He is researching at the intersection of organization and strategy, with a special focus on collaborative sensemaking processes, by exploring a heterogeneous set of phenomena in organizations, fields and markets, from the military, over financial markets and digital innovation domains. His research appeared in journals, such as Management Science, and in various monographs.

Edurne Magro is a Senior Researcher at Orkestra-Basque Institute of Competitiveness, Spain. Edurne has a long professional career as a Researcher, with 20 years of experience. In the last decade her work has focused in the fields of territorial strategy and smart specialization strategies, regional innovation systems, regional innovation policies and innovation policy-mixes, having published several articles and books chapters. Moreover, she has coordinated and participated in research projects on competitiveness and innovation at European (ESPON, Framework Programme), national and regional levels.

Sanna Malinen is an Associate Professor of Organizational Behaviour and HRM at the University of Canterbury, New Zealand. Her background is in organizational psychology, and she researches in the areas of workplace resilience, employee well-being and disaster management.

Alessandro Narduzzo is a Full Professor in Strategy and Innovation at the Faculty of Economics and Management—Free University of Bozen-Bolzano, Italy. He was visiting scholar at the Department of Management at Freie Universität Berlin and at the Carroll School of Management, Boston College. His main research interest is on organizational capabilities to cope with ill-structured problems, such as unexpected emergencies or contexts dominated by innovation. In his empirical research he applied various methods, including ethnography, computer simulations, field and labs experiments. He has been serving as PI and local-unit coordinator of national and international research projects, granted on competitive basis.

Rómulo Pinheiro is a Professor of Public Policy and Administration at the University of Agder (UiA), Norway, where he is also Deputy Head of Department of Political Science and Management and member of the Centre for Digital Transformation (CeDiT) and for Advanced Studies in Regional Innovation Strategies (RIS) based at UiA. Rómulo's research interests are located at the intersection of public policy and administration, organizational theory, economic geography, innovation and higher education studies.

Geoff Plimmer is a Senior Lecturer at Victoria University of Wellington, New Zealand. His research is centred on how workplace factors affect individual wellbeing and performance. He studies career and organisational development, leadership, psychosocial safety climate and negative workplace behaviours. His work is often focussed on the public sector and he is regularly called in to help address workplace issues. He has participated in and coordinated several large research projects.

Garri Raagmaa (Ph.D., Human Geography), born in Estonia 1966, has published four books and over 70 papers about regional planning and development focusing on regional innovation, entrepreneurship, identity and leadership issues. He has taught regional planning, economic geography and regional innovation systems at several Nordic and Baltic Universities. He has also practised since 1992 as a regional/local development consultant. Garri is a national representative of the Regional Studies Association as well as a member of the Association of Estonian Planners and the Estonian Economic Association.

Anne Russel is a Ph.D. Student in Management at IMT Atlantique, in Nantes and collaborates to the RESOH Chaire that conducts researches in Human and Organizational Factors of Industrial Safety. Her research focuses on the management of complex projects in high-risk industries. She studies the work of multi-skilled workers and technicians in construction sites with a central attention to co-activity, resilience and occupational identity issues. She adopts an interactionist approach.

Bjørn Stensaker is a Professor of higher education and Vice-Rector for Education at the University of Oslo, Norway. He is also a Research Professor at NIFU—the Nordic Institute for Studies in Innovation, Research and Education. Dr. Stensaker has a special interest in studies of governance and change in higher education, including studies of how external and internal quality assurance impacts the higher education sector. He has published widely on these issues in a range of international journals and books.

Stéphanie Tillement is an Associate Professor in Sociology at IMT Atlantique and Researcher at LEMNA: University of Nantes, France. She coordinates the ANR project AGORAS, funded by 'Investissement d'Avenir' and collaborates to the RESOH Chair. Her research focuses on organizational reliability and resilience, on risk management in distributed work context, notably project-based organizations and on decision-making and innovation processes involved in the definition of the future energetic mix. She develops a pragmatist and interactionist approach, with a central attention to symbolic, socio-material and temporal dimensions. She studies various sectors, notably railway and nuclear industries.

Elvira Uyarra is Professor of Innovation Studies at Alliance Manchester Business School (University of Manchester) where she is currently co-director of the Manchester Institute of Innovation Research. She is also Professor II at the Mohn Centre of Innovation and Regional Development at the University of Western Norway, visiting fellow at the Centre for Innovation Management Research (CIMR) of Birkbeck, University of London, and a Fellow of the Regional Studies Association (RSA). Her research focuses mainly on: regional science and innovation policy; spatial dimensions of knowledge and innovation; evolutionary approaches to public policy, universities and regional development and the innovation impact of public procurement.

Jesus M. Valdaliso is a Professor of Economic History and Institutions at the School of Economics and Business Administration of the University of the Basque Country in Bilbao (Spain). He has been Vice President (2001–2008) and President (2008–2012) of the International Maritime Economic History Association and President of the Spanish Economic History Association (2015). One of his research lines in the last years is the historical approach to industrial and innovation policies and strategies for economic development, topic on which he has edited, along with James R. Wilson, Strategies for shaping territorial competitiveness, Routledge, London 2015.

Mitchell Young is an Assistant Professor in the Department of European Studies at Charles University, Czech Republic. His research focuses on knowledge governance and science policy in the EU and Member States both internally as a form of European integration and externally through science diplomacy as a tool in foreign policy. He is a work package leader for the Horizon 2020 project 'Using science for/in diplomacy for addressing global challenges' (S4D4C) and is chair of the ECPR Standing Group on Knowledge Politics and Policies. He teaches courses on EU policies, comparative political economy and European economic integration.

Marco Zamarian is an Associate Professor in Organization Theory and Behavior at the Department of Economics and Management of the University of Trento (Italy), where he is also a founding member of the Institute for Safety and Security (ISSTN). His main research interest is on organizational routines and learning, with a focus on the reproduction of successful practices. Currently, he is working on the relationship between routines and mindfulness in the context of High Reliability Organizations.

List of Figures

Fig. 1.1	Resilience as the overlap or interplay of stability and change (*Source* Authors' own)	14
Fig. 1.2	Resilience realm and types (*Source* Authors' own. Legend: L = Low, M = Medium, H = High)	15
Fig. 1.3	Resilience temporal dimension (*Source* Authors' own, following Fisher et al., 2019; Frigotto, 2020)	23
Fig. 2.1	The challenger of decision premises as a role (*Source* Authors own elaboration)	56
Fig. 3.1	Relationships between types of skill development and resilient action in situations of surprise (*Source* Authors' own work, based on research data)	81
Fig. 5.1	Resilience as a practice: social arrangements between actions and structure, inspired from Schatzki (2002)	121
Fig. 5.2	Resilience as practice in Ral and Fed: interplay between structure and actions (inspired from Schatzki, 2002)	128
Fig. 10.1	Dimensions of organizational resilience. *Source* Denyer (2017, p. 10)	253
Fig. 11.1	GDP per capita in the Basque Country, Spain and the EU-15, 1980–2016 (*Source* Authors' elaboration from EUSTAT and EUROSTAT)	287

Fig. 11.2 GDP variation and unemployment rates in the Basque Country, 1976–2016 (*Source* Authors' own elaboration from EUSTAT and Caja Laboral Popular [1987] for unemployment, and from De la Fuente [2017] for GDP) 289
Fig. 12.1 Mapping and clustering the volume's empirical contributions 316
Fig. 12.2 Fostering interdisciplinarity through an iterative process (*Source* Authors' own, based on MacMynowski [2007, p. 11]) 324

List of Tables

Table 1.1	Resilience papers (title) by disciplinary domain (2010–2020)	5
Table 1.2	Definitions of resilience	6
Table 1.3	Absorptive, adaptive, and transformative resilience	20
Table 1.4	Adversity Triggers in Chapters by Novelty Profile	29
Table 4.1	Data collection summary	100
Table 4.2	Professional occupations and activities	102
Table 5.1	Commonalities and differences between Ral and Fed	126
Table 5.2	Data collection	127
Table 5.3	Overview of the interplay between resilience structure and resilience action	135
Table 5.4	Synthesis of findings	136
Table 6.1	Resilient behaviours and examples	150
Table 6.2	Leadership beliefs and behaviours that foster resilience	152
Table 7.1	Alternative university models	180
Table 10.1	The coevolutionary components shaping the resilience of the RHEI, region and HES	269
Table 11.1	Economic crises, structural changes and policy responses in the Basque Country, 1976–2016	290
Table 12.1	Dimensions of resilience in the chapters of this volume	311

PART I

Resilience: Antecedents, Paradigms and Perspectives

CHAPTER 1

Resilience in Organizations and Societies: The State of the Art and Three Organizing Principles for Moving Forward

Maria Laura Frigotto, Mitchell Young, and Rómulo Pinheiro

The Centrality of Resilience Today

Recent social, political, economic and organizational events (the global financial crisis, the rise of populism, migration, climate change, the COVID-19 pandemic, etc.) have renewed policy and scholarly interest in resilience as a desired feature of modern societal systems. Thus,

M. L. Frigotto (✉)
Department of Economics and Management, University of Trento, Trento, Italy
e-mail: marialaura.frigotto@unitn.it

M. Young
Department of European Studies, Institute of International Studies, FSV, Charles University, Prague, Czech Republic
e-mail: young@fsv.cuni.cz

R. Pinheiro
Department of Political Science and Management, University of Agder, Kristiansand, Norway
e-mail: romulo.m.pinheiro@uia.no

R. Pinheiro et al. (eds.), *Towards Resilient Organizations and Societies*, Public Sector Organizations,
https://doi.org/10.1007/978-3-030-82072-5_1

resilience has become central in various social science domains (Fisher et al., 2019; Linnenluecke, 2017; Williams et al., 2017) and constitutes a suitable concept for tackling contexts or situations that appear to be increasingly volatile, uncertain, complex and ambiguous (VUCA). Resilience emerged out of a general discontent with linear and reductionist perspectives in science and provides a more holistic approach to understanding an increasingly interconnected, dynamic and complex world. So-called 'wicked problems' (cf. Head, 2008) or 'grand challenges' (United Nations[1])—such as climate change, poverty and racial and gender equality—are thought to be impossible to address without resorting to a more holistic view that brings together different disciplinary, theoretical and conceptual perspectives and explores both the social entities in question and the nested systems and interrelationships in which they are embedded. Extant research on resilience from different research perspectives has ascertained that the phenomenon is multifaceted (e.g. Giustiniano et al., 2018; Ruth & Goessling-Reisemann, 2019; Walker & Salt, 2006), making multidisciplinarity both essential to addressing resilience as a phenomenon and a theory.

Resilience has been the target of numerous studies in recent years, and it has gathered momentum (Manyena, 2006). A quick google scholar search (27.05.2020) of the term 'resilience' in the period 2000–2020 yielded 1.27 million results, 97% of which occurred in the last decade alone, attesting to the popularity of the concept/phenomena among scientists. Scholars within the fields of environmental studies/science and psychiatry were rather prominent (Table 1.1).

In a recent literature review, Giustiniano et al. (2018, pp. 18–19) identify 20 influential scientific papers on resilience between 1973 and 2017. Twelve belonged to the management/business/administrative sciences literature, while the rest pertained to the fields of psychology, ecology and cybernetics. Bhamra's (2016, p. 17) analysis of the state of the art of resilience studies (108 papers; 1973–2015) identified the following five key perspectives in descending order of importance/number of influential papers: organizational, socio-ecological/community, individual, ecological and supply chain. Behaviour and dynamics were the most prevalent concepts, featuring in the majority (68%) of the publications, 'possibly due to theoretical and conceptual features of the concept of resilience

[1] Online at: https://www.un.org/en/sections/issues-depth/global-issues-overview/.

Table 1.1 Resilience papers (title) by disciplinary domain (2010–2020)

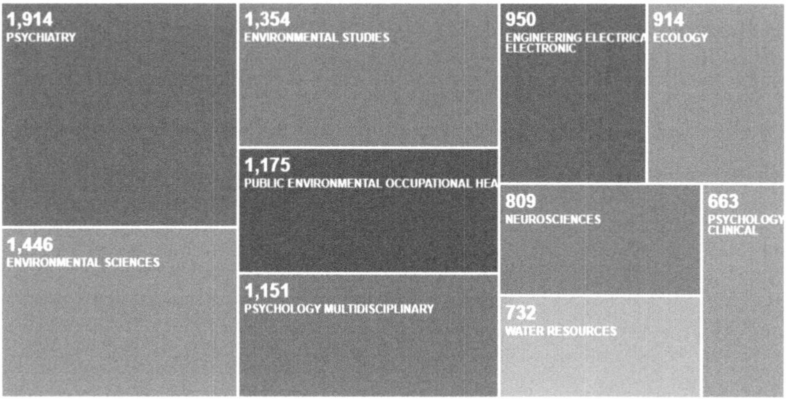

Source Web of Science

being developed' (ibid.). Other topics of significant weight were capability, strategy and performance. This shows that resilience has become highly multidisciplinary, and each discipline has brought forward its own definitions and central bibliographical references. Regarding methodological approaches, theory building and case studies ranked highest, and surveys were the least preferred: 'as the area of resilience-based research has developed, the focus has become increasingly empirically focused' (ibid.), and there is ample room for theoretical elaboration.

The Concept of Resilience

As a scientific term, 'resilience' originates from engineering and physics and denotes elasticity under pressure (Giustiniano et al., 2018, p. 14). The term derives from the Latin verb *salire* (climb or jump) and in particular from its extension, *resilire*, which means to jump back or recoil (Giustiniano et al., 2018; see also Zolli, 2012). Ontologically speaking, resilience thinking pertains to the investigation of complex, interconnected and emergent patterns of relations among entities and their respective sub-entities (Grove, 2018, p. 19). As far as the existing definitions are concerned (Table 1.2), Bhamra (2016) argues that 'regardless of context, the [multifaceted] concept of resilience relates to achieving stability within the functioning of an element or system' (p. 18).

Table 1.2 Definitions of resilience

Author	*Context*	*Definition*
Coutu (2002)	Individual	Resilient individuals possess three common characteristics: an acceptance of reality, a strong belief that life is meaningful, and the ability to improvise
Bruneau et al. (2003)	Disaster management	The ability of social units to mitigate hazards, contain the effects of disasters when they occur, and carry out recovery activities that minimise social disruption and mitigate the effects of future events
Bodin and Wiman (2004)	Physical systems	The speed at which a system returns to equilibrium after displacement, irrespective of oscillations, indicates its elasticity (resilience)
McDonald (2006)	Organisational	Adapting to the requirements of the environment and being able to manage the environment's variability
Zolli (2012)	Socioecology	The capacity of a system, enterprise, or person to maintain its core purpose and integrity in the face of dramatically changed circumstances
Walker et al. (2014)	Ecological systems	The capacity of a system to withstand a disturbance and reorganise itself while retaining function, structure, identity, and feedback
Schaffer and Schneider (2019)	Sociotechnical systems	Protect a system's integrity by strengthening links to other systems and tolerating or even fostering structural changes

(continued)

Table 1.2 (continued)

Author	*Context*	*Definition*
European Commission (2019)	Multi-level governance	The ability to face shocks and persistent structural changes in such a way that societal well-being is preserved without compromising the heritage of future generations

Sources Adapted from Bhamra et al. (2011, pp. 5379–5380), Zolli (2012, p. 7), Schaffer and Schneider (2019, p. 8), European Commission (2019)[2]

In general, resilience is a property of societal systems, individuals, organizations and organizational fields that enables them to survive despite minor or major disruptions (de Bruijne et al., 2010; Ramanujam & Roberts, 2018; Walker & Salt, 2006; Weick et al., 1999; Westrum, 2006; Zolli, 2012). There are two basic perspectives on resilience; they concern: (a) the ability of systems of any kind, including individuals, to bounce back to a state of normality following disruptive and often unexpected events or crises (e.g. how a forest grows again after a fire), and (b) the flexibility to adjust to new, emergent situations without crossing a threshold (e.g. how a forest might adjust to climate change without becoming a quasi-desert).

To some extent, the phenomenon of resilience can be seen as an elaboration of existing theories that frame the interactions between organizations and an increasingly unstable and unpredictable external environment. According to the classic perspective within organizational studies of contingency theory (e.g. Donaldson, 2001) observed outcomes (e.g. striving, survival, etc.) result from a 'fit' or match between environmental imperatives and internal designs or structures. The environment is represented as a list of potential threats that, through the construction of probabilities and scenarios of risk analysis, can be ranked according to risk and uncertainty. This approach allows researchers to focus on the development of effective responses to those categorized situations. A deeper awareness of environmental complexity and volatility, probably due to

[2] Online at: https://ec.europa.eu/jrc/en/research/crosscutting-activities/resilience.

the unprecedented interconnectedness of the world, has recently challenged the possibility of limiting response elaboration to proper actions related to probable contingencies. Systems thinkers have been signalling this interconnectedness since the 1970s (e.g. Meadows et al., 1972), but little attention was paid to indeterminateness until more recent years when researchers started casting doubt on the determinateness of the world and the ability of humans and organizations to understand it—e.g. Weick and Sutcliffe's (2001) 'Expecting the unexpected' and Bazerman and Watkins' (2004) 'Predictable surprises' (Frigotto, 2018). The environment has proved to be hard to classify into precise probable events, because the world is characterized by Knightian 'ignorance', rather than by 'risk' and 'uncertainty' (Knight, 1921). In fact, 'risk' relates to a situation in which probabilities are given, and 'uncertainty' to cases in which states are naturally defined but the translation into probabilities is not; 'ignorance' refers to situations in which states are neither naturally given nor easily constructed (Gilboa & Schmeidler, 1995, p. 622). The concept of resilience has gained momentum in the last decade, as it can capture this change of perspective. This change also implies a shift in the abilities of individuals, organizations and societies to address the shifts in environment: from the ability to classify it to the ability to resist it, with little importance attributed to the definition of the disturbance, and ideally, independently of the source, form and manifestation of the disturbance.

Although resilience embodies a holistic response that is appropriate to the VUCA: (volatility, uncertainty, complexity and ambiguity) world of today, the way in which it has been imported from engineering and physics to the social sciences has brought to the fore some unaddressed issues that, in our view, diminish the potential of the extant literature to serve as a foundation for a thorough resilience framework. In the social sciences, definitions of 'resilience' (Table 1.2) include the ability of a social entity—i.e. an individual, organization, or system—to respond to and recover from disturbances (Linnenluecke, 2017). The concept has been transferred from the realms of physics and engineering to the realm of social action with a metaphorical meaning and, as noted by Carpenter et al. (2001), this has led to an increasing ambiguity in theoretical understandings, operationalizations and measurements (2001, p. 767). The discourse on resilience has typically focused on one level of analysis at a time and has developed within specific disciplines. For example, books on resilience from an organizational perspective tend to have a narrow rather than a systemic or holistic approach, for instance, focusing on topics such as learning and/or the role of leaders (Kayes, 2015; Pirotti, & Venzin, 2016). Other seminal contributions in the field tend to be more conceptual in nature (Giustiniano et al., 2018) or pay considerable attention to certain subsystems such as ecology (Walker & Salt, 2006) and sociotechnical systems (Ruth & Goessling-Reiseman, 2019). Within this landscape of flourishing and diverse literature, this edited volume advances an original perspective on resilience in organizations and societies that combines empirical evidence and theoretical developments at different levels of analysis, from a multiplicity of disciplinary backgrounds and perspectives, as well as, sectors of the economy.

Missing Links on Resilience: Five Key Questions

In this section, we provide a brief overview of five key questions that need to be addressed in order to reach the next step of resilience theory development and empirical understanding.

In physics, resilience refers to a precise kind of disturbance, namely the ability of a system (typically a material) to absorb energy before breaking down when subject to a dynamic perpendicular force (shock) (Kalpakjian & Schmid, 2016). This shock is standardized into the Charpy pendulum, which is used to measure the resilience of materials. Resilience is high when a material has a high level of elasticity. For example, the strings of a tennis racket deform due to the impact of a ball and accumulate potential energy that is released during the return stroke. The opposite of resilience is fragility, which is characteristic of materials with little elasticity and that are close to their breaking point. Unlike resistant materials, resilient materials do not oppose shocks until they break, but absorb shocks due to their elastic properties.

Similarly, resilience in the social sciences represents the ability of a social entity—such as an individual, organization, system, or society—to retain its function while responding to adversity. However, this metaphor is responsible for both the appeal and the opaqueness of the concept in the social sciences (Carpenter et al., 2001), as 'ability' and 'adversity' have been variously understood (e.g. Britt et al., 2016), leading many scholars to ask for further theoretical elaboration (Britt et al. 2016; Duchek, 2020; Fisher et al., 2019; Linnenluecke, 2017; Kossek & Perrigino, 2016; Vanhove et al., 2016). A decade ago, de Bruijne et al. (2010) outlined some of the elements that were lost in translation. This yielded a set of pertinent questions regarding the need for theoretical elaboration, which have been echoed by more recent literature reviews (e.g. Duchek, 2020; Fisher et al., 2019; Linnenluecke, 2017; Kossek & Perrigino, 2016; Ruiz-Martin et al., 2018).

Five questions have remained largely implicit in the understanding of the parallel between materials in physics and individuals, organizations and societies in the social sciences. Here we identify and reframe them to develop *three principles* that both organize our current understanding of resilience and suggest future directions of research.

First, in the social sciences, resilience has been used in quite a broad way. Following a thorough literature review on existing perspectives, concepts and methodologies, Bhamra (2016, p. 24) contended that 'it is essential to understand whether resilience is a measure, a feature, a philosophy or a capability', as in the present literature it refers to all of these. Critics of resilience claim that the concept has been adopted too broadly in the social sciences and provocatively ask: 'At this rate, what isn't resilience?' (Roe & Schulman, 2008, p. 163). To progress with conceptual elaboration, this implies asking: *What is the core of resilience*? Addressing this question clarifies how the concept of resilience can be characterized and better specified to include different conceptual and analytical manifestations while still allowing for the cross-fertilization of concepts, ideas and best practices across the social sciences.

Second, when we say that resilient social entities reach a final state after facing adversities, how should this final state be understood? Answering this question means clarifying when we *can* talk about resilience, and when we *cannot*. Rather than redefining resilience, we aim to define the boundaries and the core of the concept by specifying what 'stable final state' in the social sciences might correspond to the steady states of engineering materials. The fact that a given material finds an equilibrium (i.e. the same state before and after a shock), allows scholars to claim that it is resilient. However, the ways in which individuals, organizations and/or societies respond, recover and return to 'normality' always entails a change—if only because time has passed and experience (learning) has occured. Contrary to physical materials, social systems and the agents that are embedded in them exercise agency, which affects how they adapt to external events. Moreover, it is crucial to clarify whether we can talk of resilience when a 'new normal' is reached in a social system, or if that means that the original system was not resilient and that a new system (with a different state and function) has emerged. So, we ask: *what is the outcome of resilience? Does the recognition of resilience depend upon this outcome?*

Third, *how can disturbances or adversity triggers be qualified in the social sciences?* Recent studies reviewed the following examples of adversity triggers (Britt et al., 2016; Duchek, 2020; Fisher et al., 2019; Kossek & Perrigino, 2016; Linnenluecke, 2017; Vanhove et al., 2016): for the *individual*, the death of a beloved person or a divorce; for *organizations*, a new technology that challenges extant business value propositions; and for *systems*, a new political movement that gains ground. In physics, shocks are precisely defined: they have a certain strength and hit from a certain angle (Frigotto, 2020). In the social sciences, the ability to anticipate, resist and respond to adversity is contingent on knowledge of adversity triggers: when they are well-known and well-defined, they can be anticipated or at least a precise response can be prepared that is activated when they occur; when they are poorly-known and ill-defined, understanding them is part of the challenge (cf. Logan, 2009). Some authors refer to this in terms of the expected and the unexpected (e.g. Weick & Sutcliffe, 2001). While this distinction is intuitive, a more precise elaboration could clarify the impacts of different kinds of adversity and their potential for triggering resilience and its various empirical manifestations.

Fourth, in the social realm, resilience concerns an entity's responses to a shock over time, including before (preparedness), during (recovery) and after (outcome). While a temporal dimension is noticeable in social systems that might take time to show resilience, what some call 'dynamic capability' (Giustiniano et al., 2018, p. 38), others consider a process, as well as, a property and an outcome (Bhamra, 2016) So, the following question arises: *does resilience have a temporal deployment upon which it should be observed and assessed as a whole?*

Fifth, *what is the subject of resilience?* In general, we have referred to system resilience as having a generic subject in the social sciences, and other times and more precisely, we have articulated three main levels of analysis, i.e. individual (micro), organization (meso) and society (macro). This plurality of levels at which it can manifest adds a layer of fuzziness to resilience, as in the same setting, a lower level entity can show resilience, while at a higher level there might be none and vice versa. Carpenter et al. (2001, pp. 765–767) claim that it is always necessary to specify resilience in relation to a social system or a level of analysis by asking: 'Resilience of what to what?' In particular, it is necessary to address if there is a correspondence between lower and higher levels of resilience, and if lower levels of resilience guarantee higher levels of resilience. This has become crucial for policymakers, institutions and citizens in understanding how resilience can be cultivated, especially after the COVID-19 pandemic (e.g. Giovannini et al., 2020).

These five questions, in our opinion, advance the academic debate by allowing us to frame resilience in light of the dynamic nature and complexity and ambiguity inherent to social systems at multiple levels of analysis. This introduction outlines three organizing elements that serve as a starting point for the theoretical and empirical analyses in the chapters that make up the bulk of this edited volume. We argue that resilience needs to be grounded in both stability and change, given that 'becoming' is a characteristic of social entities. We define resilience in terms of change that maintains a continuity of essence, whether self-assessed by those that dealt with the adversity—and that recognize themselves through change—or exogenously assessed when an observer can detect or identify some form of persistence of identity, processes, mindsets, etc.

Organizing Principles for Resilience

Building upon the definitional consistencies and inconsistencies, theoretical missing links and empirical puzzles found in the five questions above, this section introduces three organizing principles for resilience. The first pertains to the core of resilience, which comprises both change and stability. The second principle concerns the novelty profiles of adversity triggers. The third principle regards the temporal deployment of resilience into foresight, mechanisms and outcomes, which take place either before adversities trigger resilience, right after they have occurred and stimulated a response, and/or after they have been addressed. This is followed by a discussion of the temporal, spatial and social scale of resilience, which serves both the advancement of our theoretical understanding and the empirical adoption of resilience.

Stability and Change

Resilience has generally been used to indicate the ability to absorb shocks with a limited impact on stability and functioning (Linnenluecke, 2017; Roe & Schulman 2008; Walker & Salt, 2006; Williams et al., 2017) as well as the ability to recover and learn from the shock (Ramanujam & Roberts, 2018; Ruiz-Martin et al., 2018). In other words, in various definitions and disciplines, resilience entails change from an initial state to a final state via adversity response. *Change* is, therefore, the first fundamental constituent of resilience.

Change can be conceived of as being necessarily entailed by adversity, because if a system does not change, then one could argue that it never faced the sort of adversity for which resilience is needed. Moreover, if it does not change, then it will probably fail, because adversity does not allow systems to remain unaltered over time. If for some reason a system neither changes nor fails, then we would argue that it does not display resilience, but mere survival. Thus, survival is not the key to resilience. Resilience goes beyond mere survival because it requires that the perseverance of being is characterized by change. Likewise, radical change is incompatible with resilience. In fact, we would not call something that changes completely in order to survive resilient, as it would no longer relate to a previous state or function but to something else entirely.

There have been several attempts to theorize about the degree of change that is included in resilience. Like most definitions, the first and more general attempt held that resilience represents either a process of 'bouncing back' or of 'remaining within a threshold' (Table 1.2); 'passing the threshold' was to be understood as *too much change* to constitute resilience. From a complex systems perspective, Walker et al. (2004) note that both resilience and adaptability have to do with the dynamics of a system or a closely related set of systems. For them, transformability refers to fundamentally altering the nature of a system, yet the dividing line between 'closely related' and 'fundamentally altered' can be fuzzy and subject to interpretation. Folke et al. (2010, p. 3) argue that resilience builds on adaptability and transformability, as it is 'the capacity to change [also through transformation] in order to maintain the same identity'. In regional science studies, several authors (Boschma, 2015; Hu & Hassink, 2017; Pike et al., 2010) adopt a distinction between two kinds of change within the context of geographic resilience, 'adaptation' and 'adaptability'; the former relates to maintaining existing economic paths/trajectories or 'exploitation' (March, 1991), while the latter pertains to the creation of new regional growth paths or 'exploration' (March, 1991). In other areas, transformation and transformability are more explicitly mentioned and linked to resilience. The literature on urban ecosystems (e.g. Gotham & Campanella, 2010) explicitly acknowledges transformability among the various types of change; more recently,

Satyal et al. (2017) showed how transformative resilience can consist of regional pathways of evolution.

A second fundamental constituent of resilience that mirrors the first is *continuity of essence*. In all cases, resilience is related to a subject—be it an individual, organization or system—that undergoes some degree of change but, nevertheless, maintains a continuity of essence throughout this evolution. This means that, having changed, either the subject or an external observer can recognize that the same entity is still present following a series of internal and external adversities. Considering both the constituents of resilience together, resilience encompasses both stability and change (Fig. 1.1).

In their conceptual framework aimed at both grounding and triggering a more resilient European society, Manca et al. (2017) proposed a distinction between absorptive, adaptive and transformative capabilities that support resilience. In the field of organizational resilience, Frigotto (2020) specified the following resilience outcomes that result from different levels of change (and as a function of the novelty of adversity triggers): absorptive, adaptive and transformative resilience.

Progressing our theoretical elaboration on the essence of resilience and the different kinds of change that resilience encompasses, we posit the following typology. If we position the combination of stability and change on a continuum where at the extreme ends there are either only stability or only change, resilience concerns only the area in which there is a blend

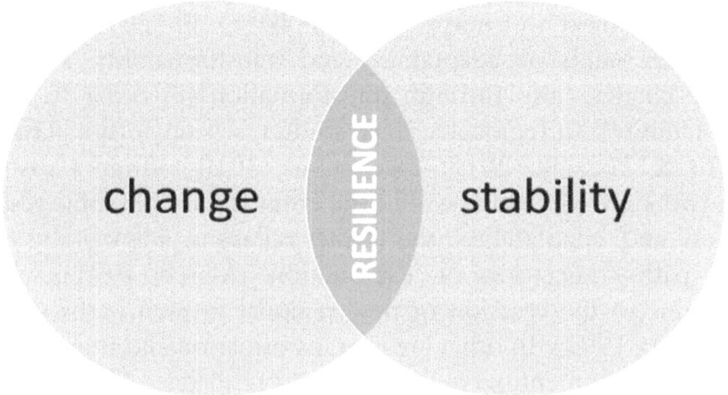

Fig. 1.1 Resilience as the overlap or interplay of stability and change (*Source* Authors' own)

of stability and change. Building on Frigotto's work on novelty (2020), it is possible to define different types of resilience, encompassing not only specific outcomes but also changing processes and antecedents. Along this continuum, we can position three main types of resilience (Fig. 1.2).

Absorptive resilience reflects the fundamental stability of a system and concerns the ability to return rapidly and efficiently to the original state; change is limited in that it is both temporary and produces a near-zero impact (Linnenluecke, 2017). Stability is not challenged; it is refreshed or refined by perfecting competencies, and the previous state is restored. Building upon the work of Folke et al. (2010), resilience in this case can be defined as 'absorbability'. In the metaphor provided by the ball-and-cup model (de Bruijne et al., 2010, p. 17), the cup represents the stability of the system, whereas the ball represents a social entity that is altered by some force. Resilience is then measured by the time the entity takes to absorb change.

Adaptive resilience includes both stability and change at a consistent level; it refers to a system's ability to produce buffer capacity, withstand shock and maintain function during a transition to a new state. In this case, change is persistent and consistent even though it does not challenge the essence of the social entity. In the ball-and-cup model, this type of resilience is represented by the width of the cup, meaning that while persistent change of functioning is necessary, it is still found in the same context. In real-world situations, resilience is measured by robustness, which is the amount of change that an entity can face within the given context. In Folke et al.'s (2010) terminology, this type of resilience is characterized by both adaptability and flexibility.

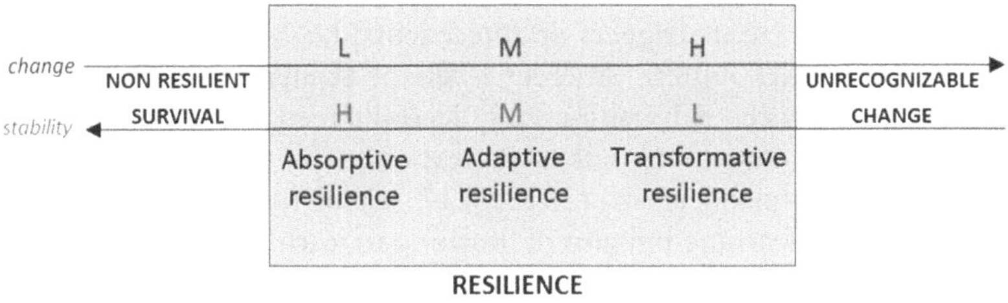

Fig. 1.2 Resilience realm and types (*Source* Authors' own. Legend: L = Low, M = Medium, H = High)

Transformative resilience shows the ability of the social entity to interact with disturbances and impact on the system's change. In this case, the essence of the social entity is challenged; as the context changes dramatically, there is a high risk that it will be thrown into a completely different reality, where points of reference and consolidated functioning are revolutionized. In the realm of organizations, we could argue that in this case, institutional settings are changing. The social entity must undergo a profound renewal while a continuity with the past can be clearly traced at some level. This renewal acknowledges that the entity has also interacted with the changing context (co-evolution takes place) and that the revolutionary potential of the context is scaled back. In complex systems language (Walker & Salt, 2006), this type of resilience would keep the entity away from the dramatic and totalizing change entailed by passing the threshold. It is consistent with the definition of resilience as 'adapting within a threshold'; however, it acknowledges that the threshold might change over time and that resilience occurs when the social entity is able to respond to that challenge by remaining within the renewed threshold. Folke et al. (2010) refer to this ability as 'transformability'. At the organizational or system level, transformative resilience occurs in relation to changes in institutional settings (cf. North, 1990) and is measured by the ability to transform together with the setting in order to maintain a position within the threshold—what systems theorists term 'co-evolution' (for a fascinating account of such processes within the context of organizations and markets, see Padgett & Powell, 2012).

Adversity and Novelty

While change and stability can be used to typify resilience, they can also be used to characterize its triggers or antecedents, i.e. *adversities*. Different kinds of adversities require different levels of change and stability and, therefore, resilience. Adversities vary according to their determinateness, being well-known or unknown, expected or unexpected and/or surprising. Giustiniano et al., (2018, p.17) claim that resilience is 'not only a matter of learning but also of 'learning to learn', including the willingness to continuously engage in experimentation and embrace novelty. According to Kayes (2015, p. 17), novel experiences are characterized by a lack of apparent task constraints, which means that successful resolution must go beyond typical expertise or established routines. In such situations, neither the goal to be achieved ('what') nor the path to solving the problem ('how') are clear, in this way they resemble ill-structured or 'wicked' problems (Rittel & Weber, 1973). Finally, Kayes (2015, pp. 18–20) points to four types of learning mechanisms: direct experience, counter experience, evidence and trial and error or exploration. Studies have ascertained that different organizations adopt and excel at different types of learning (March, 1991) and that context-specific and locally embedded learning styles emerge over time (Powell, 1998). These styles, in turn, enable organizations to develop distinct preferences or habits when it comes to gathering, processing and acting upon different types of knowledge (Kayes, 2015, p. 21). We follow Frigotto (2020) who proposes that the concept of novelty be used to characterize disturbances and to explain different resilience types in relation to triggers.

Defining resilience in terms of novelty produces three main advantages (Frigotto, 2020). First, it allows us to clarify how resilience can be conceived of as a source of stability by ensuring the maintenance of functionality despite adversity, and as a source of change by stimulating positive adaptation and thriving after adversity. Second, novelty is a relative concept that reflects the state of the art of knowledge (Frigotto, 2018); resilience that refers to novelty is not defined as a fixed set of 'must haves' in relation to a closed set of situations but as a changing ability that is renewed continuously according to new challenges. Third, novelty is also relative in a further sense: since knowledge is not homogenously distributed, novelty does not appear equally to every entity because it maps onto one's own knowledge. As a result of differences in their knowledge, entities will perceive different novelty differently. A definition of resilience grounded in novelty articulates that resilience stimulates learning in various forms (e.g. from others that already know) and at different levels (e.g. new knowledge for some or all).

Building upon the work of Levinthal (2008), novelty can be defined as the opposite of knowledge; novelty consists of what is not known. It can be observed in many forms and at many levels; it has been understood as both an ingredient and as an outcome of change (Frigotto, 2018). Novelty is pervasive, appearing in details or in dramatic changes, and thus can be considered a continuous variable rather than a dichotomous one (Frigotto, 2020).

When we assess the novelty of adversity triggers, we consider three different aspects that reflect novelty dimensions (Frigotto, 2018). First, triggers might be novel, meaning that they are not known and vary according to how distant they are from what is already known; this reflects the *degree* of novelty. For example, when New Public Management (NPM) was recommended as the appropriate approach for public administration (cf. Christensen & Lægreid, 2011), it was perceived as having a high novelty degree in relation to public administration theories: it brought principles of management into the public sector that dramatically changed the idea of how public institutions are and should be managed. Conversely, today, the introduction of new efficiency or effectiveness measures represents just an add-on to that framework, which scores lower in novelty degree.

Second, novelty is *spatially and temporally relative*, so the same instance might appear novel to some observers and not to others, and it might appear differently in different times, for example, in Europe, the way we see lockdowns since the COVID-19 pandemic. Before January 2020, the idea of a lockdown was largely seen as an unnecessary measure in the contemporary, developed world: it was perceived as something obsolete, concerning the plagues of past centuries, most recently around 1920, or 'remote' and 'far-away' China. When a lockdown was implemented in Italy in March 2020, it appeared as a major novelty—nobody really knew what lockdown meant or entailed for their everyday behaviour or for the whole economy. Then the lockdown measures slowly spread across Europe, and countries began considering them appropriate and indispensable. A lockdown is no longer a major novelty. When we consider the future (we are writing in June, 2020), a lockdown in the autumn of 2020 seems like a minor or medium novelty. Societies have built up rich knowledge on what the lockdown is and means, and they can also prepare for it in advance. The lesson from this is that novelty should always be assessed in relation to a specific observer at a specific time; otherwise, it is easily misjudged in retrospect. This is what we mean when we refer to novelty's *relativity*.

Third, novelty *awareness* refers to whether the lack of knowledge corresponding to novelty is perceived or not—a 'known unknown' or an 'unknown unknown' (Logan, 2009). Building upon the previous example, the World Health Organization, as well as other institutions, warned the world's governments of the risk of pandemics in previous years. This would lead one to think that the COVID-19 pandemic was something which many should have been aware. While the pandemic might have come as a minor surprise to some, to many it was a remote event, either because they downplayed the warnings or because they thought that the progress of the contemporary world would somehow shield it from catastrophic effects. Awareness reflects the difficulty of addressing something that we do not know but might exist.

Novelty reflects a condition of the observer that reveals one's need for new knowledge by claiming that something is novel to him/her. Thus, *novelty is objectified and transferred to an object*. We typically say 'this product is new' or 'this situation is new', indirectly claiming that we had not experienced that product or that situation earlier. This also applies to characterizing adversity triggers according to their novelty profiles. When someone says that an adversity trigger is novel, this means that he/she is not prepared to handle it with his/her current level of knowledge; further, one either does not know that it exists or that its occurrence is likely.

Building upon these considerations, it is possible to advance three novelty profiles (minor, medium and major). Novelty profiles reflect the amount of knowledge that is necessary to make something novel into something known, predictable and expected, contemplated among possible cases, manageable and controllable. Resilience types refer to these profiles (Table 1.3, column 3).

Absorptive resilience addresses disturbances that display a low novelty profile: they are temporary and concern a narrow range of well-known external conditions (Holling, 1973, p. 1). When triggers are well defined within given knowledge (low novelty profile), they can easily be understood and typically even specified into a list, and it is possible to routinely prepare against them, thus change can be planned and contained. At the individual level, an example of low novelty profile adversity is stress related to an important project; at the organizational level, a delay in sales for seasonal gifts due to a late season; at the system level, the effects of economic growth in regional and national employment patterns.

Adaptive resilience is associated with a medium novelty profile of adversity triggers, meaning that these are not well known but can either be understood and framed using available knowledge or else they require refinement or moderate knowledge development. In the language of James March's exploitation and exploration trade-off (1991), for adaptive resilience, learning takes place through the exploitation of existing knowledge. At the individual level, an example is a job change; at the organizational level, the need for a new product differentiation; and at the system level, the quest for new regional growth patterns based on smart specialization.

Transformative resilience responds to triggers with a major novelty profile. These are challenging triggers, such as 'sharp shifts,' 'regime

Table 1.3 Absorptive, adaptive, and transformative resilience

Resilience type		*Ability and measure*	*Adversities by novelty*	*Change*	*Stability*	*Ball-and-cup model*	
Absorptive Ability to return rapidly and efficiently to the original state	Bounce back	Absorbability = returning time	Minor novelty = temporary, low profile	Temporary change = momentary departure from a stable state	General stability	One equilibrium Resilience = return to earlier stability	
Adaptive Ability to produce buffer capacity, withstand shock, and maintain function	Move within threshold	Adaptability = width of possible change	Medium novelty = persistent, medium profile	Persistent change of functioning within stable context	Stability of contextual elements, e.g. Stable institutional settings	Multiple equilibria within the same basin of attraction Resilience = stay away from threshold (to stay within the basin of attraction)	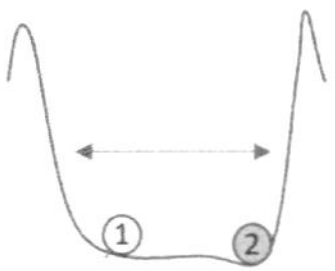

Resilience type	*Ability and measure*	*Adversities by novelty*	*Change*	*Stability*	*Ball-and-cup model*	
Transformative Ability to interact with disturbances and impact on the system's change	Transformability = number and impact of interaction with drivers of change	Major novelty = Durable, major profile/wide range	Profound changethat requires renewal	Major changes in contextual elements, e.g. Changing institutional settings	Changing equilibria within a changing basin of attraction Resilience = evolve with the system	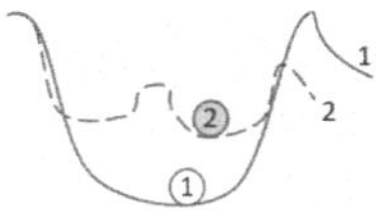

Source Authors' own

shifts,' or 'critical transitions', and concern a variety of adversities that are typically both unpredictable and unexpected (Folke et al., 2010). Building on March's exploitation and exploration trade-off (1991),transformative resilience entails exploration of new knowledge because learning encompasses all aspects of the social entity and entails the acquisition of solutions that are distant from those building the stable response system. At the individual level, an example is divorce, which can challenge people's internal balance; at the organizational level, a change of customers' preferences; at the system level, Brexit.

Temporality

Resilience is only demonstrated over time. Thus, in order to define resilience, we need to take temporality into account. As a complex and dynamics process, resilience encompasses different types of nonlinear interactions among sub-elements, both internal and external. What is more, such interactions are laden with contradictory aspects associated with adaptive and proactive prespectives on resilience (Giustiniano et al., 2018, p. 20), suggesting the importance of approaching the phenomenon from a processual prism. Hence, resilience 'is perceived not as a state of being, a disposition or a structural property, so much as a processual practice (Feldman & Orlikowski, 2011) *of becoming* (Tsoukas & Chia, 2002)' (Giustiniano et al., 2018, p. 20; emphasis added).

Building upon the works of Frigotto (2020) and Fisher et al. (2019), our perspective encompasses adversity triggers, resilience outcomes, and resilience mechanisms and positions them on a timeline (Fig. 1.3). Considering the chronological deployment of resilience, Fisher et al. (2019) distinguished resilience into mechanisms that take place right after adversity triggers have hit and outcomes that take place after recovering from adversity. The authors also talk about 'resilience promoting factors', which are 'characteristics and features of the self or one's environment that can promote the likelihood of successful adaptation' and also specify that they 'serve as valuable targets for interventions aimed at increasing resilience' (Fisher et al. 2019, p. 25). They acknowledge that these factors impact resilience mechanisms while adversity triggers hits, however, they neglect their own temporal dimension. We acknowledge that these factors also have a temporal deployment and that they are put in place deliberately or simply exist before the resilience mechanisms are activated. This form of resilience pertains to 'the potential for adjusting patterns

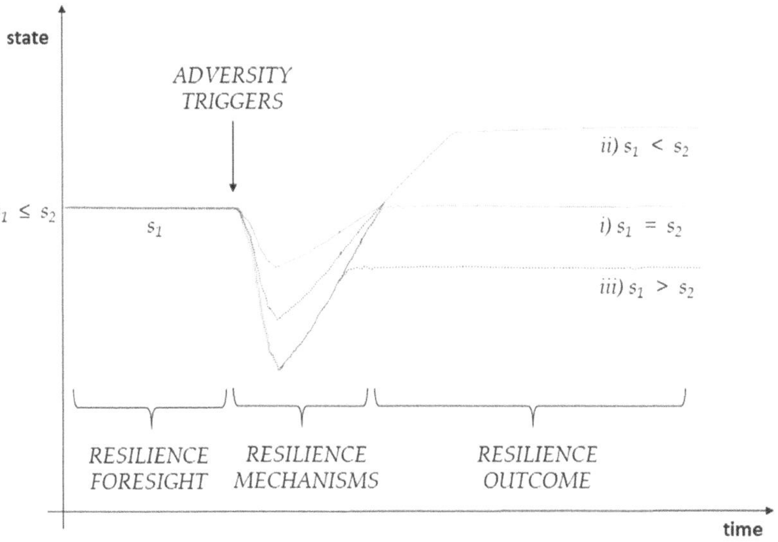

Fig. 1.3 Resilience temporal dimension (*Source* Authors' own, following Fisher et al., 2019; Frigotto, 2020)

of activities to handle future changes in the kinds of events, opportunities and disruptions experienced'; therefore, it exists before disturbances call upon them (Woods, 2019, p. 53). We term the actions that take place before the occurrence of triggers, and that support resilience mechanisms, *resilience foresight*. Thus, our definition of resilience is temporally defined as follows (Fig. 1.3): resilience foresight (*before*); resilience mechanisms (*during*) and resilience outcomes (*after*).

Regarding the 'final state' (s_2) at which resilience outcome stabilizes, there are two main perspectives in the literature (Duchek, 2020). The first states that an entity is resilient if it returns to the initial state; here, the emphasis is on resuming standard performance (Lengnick-Hall et al., 2011). The second understands the resilient entity as one that has coped, thrived and reached another state; this has been interpreted by some as entailing higher performance levels (Burnard & Bhamra, 2011; Hamel & Välikangas, 2003). A further position allows the resilient entity to 'bounce forward', i.e. grow or become stronger for future challenges (Giovannini et al., 2020; Vogus & Sutcliffe, 2007). Some authors subordinate resilience to a stable or increased performance despite adversity. Others associate resilience with a more neutral idea of evolution or a broader conception of development at some level. For instance, for Vogus and Sutcliffe (2007, p. 3418) the concept of organizational resilience entails 'the maintenance of positive adjustment under challenging conditions such that the organization emerges from those conditions strengthened and more resourceful'. Moreover, resilience enhances and emphasizes the ability of systems to resist despite adversity, and, in other words, might seem to suggest survival. Nevertheless, mere survival does not entail resilience. In our perspective, resilience can be associated with any of these three main situations if the system is characterized by both stability and change (Fig. 1.2): (i) the initial and final states, after adversity triggers have hit, are the same; (ii) the final state is better than the initial state; (iii) the final state is worse than the initial state (Fig. 1.3). While resilience has a positive connotation, it is to be interpreted in terms of the maintenance of essence combined with change rather than an assessment of the state based on other criteria—e.g. job satisfaction (individual level), business leadership (organizational level), or economic or social welfare (system level).

Absorptive resilience responds to disturbances with a low novelty profile that can be easily anticipated, making resilience foresight processes consist of risk assessments and contingency plans. Mechanisms enacted in response to adversity could therefore be learned in advance so that during the period of adversity, the depth of the nadir is smaller, recovery is quicker, and the resilience outcome includes the little changes that derive from experiencing and practicing what is known in theory.

Adaptive resilience concerns a medium novelty profile of adversity that can be addressed by leveraging the relativity dimension (looking at available knowledge from others) or by targeting the 'known unknowns'. Resilience mechanisms are somewhat limited in terms of finding, implementing, or including novelty, but the nadir is typically small. The resilience outcome reflects important changes the social entity has implemented while responding to adversities and that persist also in the ex-post phase. These changes might set s_2 at different levels even though it is reasonable to think that it would typically not be the case of $s_1 = s_2$.

Transformative resilience is associated with triggers with a major novelty profile that can be tackled in foresight only through a substantial effort to address the 'unknown unknowns'. Mechanisms that respond to adversities might be very hard to find and implement, so the nadir might be very deep. The resilience outcome might vary substantially but encompasses significant changes that can end into very different outlooks of the social entity being considered.

Scales of Resilience

While clear in principle, when analysing social entities, it is not straightforward to grasp when change and stability are both present or under which circumstances change leads to the abandonment of a previous essence; so that either a red thread between the past and present cannot be detected, or in which change has not occurred at all and the persistence of the entity is simply accidental.[3]

Taking an example from the organizational realm, many corporations go bankrupt as a result of technological and market disruptions, with only a handful being able to survive more than half a century (Peters et al., 1982). In contrast, a handful of businesses have been able to successfully adapt by moving into new markets and by adopting different ways of organizing. Nokia has become a landmark case of resilience. In the 1860s, Nokia was a pulp and paper company. It gradually moved into the rubber and cable businesses, followed by electronics (TV and ICT) and network and mobile technologies in the 1990s and lately the consumer market (Borhanuddin & Iqbal, 2016). Kurikka et al. (2018) present Nokia as a case of regional resilience while Nair et al. (2014) as a case where resilience was missing. Nokia experienced tremendous change throughout its existence, and whether it still preserves a continuity of essence can be debated. Moreover, the outcome of this evaluation might be different depending upon who is assessing it (company members—top management/employees, shareholders, stakeholders, Finnish/global society) and on what level (business competition, innovativeness, societal role). For instance, one could argue that, while it has changed in terms of business, Nokia has remained an important contributor to Finland's GDP and labour market. The Nokia case illustrates the difficulty of setting absolute, clear-cut parameters for assessing the resilience of real organizations, individuals and social systems.

[3] As Walker et al. (2014, p. 3) stated, 'Because of the possibility of multiple stable states, when considering the extent to which a system can be changed, return time doesn't measure all of the ways in which a system may fail—permanently or temporarily—to retain essential functions.' See also Folke et al. (2010, p. 4).

Carpenter et al. (2001) contend that resilience changes depending on the ***temporal***, ***spatial*** and ***social*** scale at which the measurement is made. On the temporal scale, in prehistory, the adoption of iron axes facilitated the emergence of the agricultural economy, as forests could be cut more easily and quickly to create fields. In this sense, the use of iron axes supported resilience at one time. Nevertheless, it also resulted in soil infertility, which demonstrates that resilience at one time may come at the expense of resilience at another (Carpenter et al., 2001, p. 767).

On the spatial scale, resilience can at once take place in one place and not in another. During the COVID-19 pandemic, this point was largely debated when the effectiveness of different national strategies was discussed. Consider two countries with potentially similar contagion incidence: as of the time of writing (summer 2020)—Sweden and Norway. Sweden displayed one of the world's highest mortality levels (4874 deaths) while the nearby Norway recorded 242 deaths (Lindeberg, 2020).

Finally, on the social scale, it is argued that resilience can be analysed at three main levels—i.e. ***individual*** (micro), ***organization*** (meso) and ***system*** (macro)—and that resilient entities (e.g. organizations and societies) can translate or incorporate resilience from one level to the other (Kayes, 2015, p. 16). Giovannini et al. (2020, p. 7) claim that a resilient society is one in which individuals are resilient, and public intervention should enhance and complement people; although societal resilience is not the sum of individual resilience as social ties, community-level capacities and institutions play a role. Conversely, Carpenter and colleagues (2001) stress that these levels do not entail consistency with one another, as smaller systems are nested in larger systems, and as a result, they coevolve and interact in nonlinear and unpredictable ways (Walker et al., 2004), showing that the micro–macro relationship of levels in resilience is complex.

The cases presented in this edited volume lend credence to these scales and demonstrate empirically that it is always necessary to specify which time, space and level of analysis is being referred to when discussing resilience.

Rationale and Scope of the Volume

This edited volume brings together scholars in the fields of human research management, public policy, regional studies and organization theory around the concept of resilience. This is done in an effort to provide a more holistic understanding of this complex phenomenon from a multi-sectorial, cross-national and multidisciplinary perspective. Each chapter brings to the book a contribution on resilience that is built in relation to their area of research and to specific key references on resilience largely adopted in that area. Overall, the volume builds a conversation across the diverse specializations and attentions provided by each chapter. Also, and more broadly, the authors contribute both to theory testing and development and provide key empirical insights useful for societies, organizations and individuals that are experiencing disruptive pressures. Diverse chapters are held together by a clear organization of the volume across levels of analysis (resilience in organizations and the organizational fields and societies in which individuals and organizations are embedded in) and by an original perspective on resilience that we derive from our review of the literature and existing knowledge gaps, according to which we position and connect each of the individual chapter contributions.

In this book, resilience is investigated in cases that display a substantial level of *publicness*. This pertains to the concept introduced by Barry Bozeman. Bozeman and colleagues have long advocated for a move away from the traditional binary distinction public vs. private (e.g. Christensen et al., 2007; Farnham & Horton, 1999) towards the notion that all organizations are in essence public, given that they are all affected by the technical and institutional environments in which they operate (Bozeman, 1984, 2004; Bozeman & Bretschneider, 1994). In short, for Bozeman the key is not whether organizations are public or private, but to what extent their goals, structures and activities are determined by political and economic authority in the form of state regulations and other forms of coercive behaviour. 'Publicness is not viewed as an absolute quality but as a dimension. The dimension is defined by the organization's mix of economic and political authority as a basis of its activity' (Bozeman, 2004, p. 78). The degree of publicness is then defined by the extent to which externally imposed political authority affects organizational activities—goals, mission, funding, strategy, management, etc.

The cases presented in the individual chapters, which span across the public and private sectors, vary in terms of publicness. Yet, because this dimension makes our cases 'revelatory' for the holistic study of resilience (Yin, 2009 [1984]), they 'offer high potential for developing new insight into an understudied phenomenon' (Langley & Abdallah, 2011, p. 118). That said, the majority of the chapters focus on cases that are consistently subject to environmental adversities and disturbances, as they are, by definition, subject to external and highly political drivers. Thus, because of their inherent publicness, not only do these contexts allows us to focus on the effects of external dynamics in resilience, but also enable us to compare cases that cut across a multiplicity of sectors and national contexts. In a nutshell, our argument is that publicness stimulates resilience most, because it entails a higher level of exposure to external requirements for change. Yet, as a downside, it also entails a higher risk of paralysis or inertia if and when resilience is not cultivated.

Presentation of the Chapters

The heart and empirical foundation of the edited volume is structured into two main sections with five chapters each; the first concerns resilience in organizations, and the second concerns within organizational fields and resilience in societies. The case chapters present a variety of adversity triggers that illustrate different novelty profiles (Table 1.4).

In the first section, Chapter 2 addresses the organizational ability to conduct problem solving and learning in the midst of a crisis by exploring the case of a fire brigade's reaction to a novel and unexpected cause of a fire. We see how organizations can face unknown problems that are mistakenly taken as known. Not recognizing the novelty of the problem can lead to failure, as the organization follows rules and norms that are not appropriately adapted to the situation. Hence the ability to rapidly detect novelty and be able to insert new findings quickly and effectively into the problem representation throughout the organization is essential to building resilience. While there are lessons in this case that can help organizations to cultivate resilience, the chapter focuses on resilience in the midst of a crisis. It addresses resilience mechanisms that can be adopted to address major novelty and elaborates on structures and practices that can be developed in advance to support resilience mechanisms.

Chapter 3 brings us to a military context, in which traditional rule-following is the expectation; however, we see that the Austrian military seeks to instil in its soldiers the ability to deal with surprising situations. Drills and rule-following have limits even in highly structured organizations like the Austrian military. Resilience requires the ability to understand when to break rules, and paradoxically, the military has

Table 1.4 Adversity Triggers in Chapters by Novelty Profile

Adversity triggers by	*Chapter*	*Description of adversity*
Minor novelty	5 Adrot, Sitte de Longeval, and Largier	From a practice perspective, adversities are challenges to present practices. They are represented both as increasing vulnerabilities concerning urban regions such as floods, as well as unexpected events such as transportation incidents. From a practice perspective, these adversities challenge the balance between action and structure, displaying various ranges of novelty, and call for minor as well as major changes that range from absorption to transformation of practices
	3 Lehner, Born, Kelemen, and Born	Soldiers in the military must address a wide range of threatening situations. In different kinds of drills, they learn how to deal with adversities with minor, medium, and major novelty profiles corresponding to threats that are standard and threats that appear in new contexts
Medium novelty	3; 5	See description above
	6 Franken, Plimmer, Malinen, and Bryson	Employees in the public sector navigate the complex public management environment with its day-by-day changes, public crises, and institutional reforms. Given the complexity and ambiguity that is intrinsic in a highly political and multifaceted context, even day-to-day adversities incorporate at least a medium novelty profile
	4 Russel, Tillement, and Journe	Occupational groups in a shipyard, such as boilermakers and welders, address adversities consisting of complex safety challenges that emerge during shipbuilding and that cannot be anticipated; thus, they require specific coordination solutions that guarantee resilience

(continued)

Table 1.4 (continued)

Adversity triggers by	*Chapter*	*Description of adversity*
Major novelty	3; 5	See description above
	2 Frigotto, Gaio, Narduzzo, and Zamarian	Firefighters deal with a fire that seems to be standard, while it is actually extraordinary and surprising, and it challenges their cognitive models, rooted in taken-for-granted decision premises
	7 Young and Pinheiro	Over the last decades, the university has addressed adversities such as a mutated dominant logic, pressures to conform to a entrepreneurial archetype, increasing and conflicting missions, and competitive positional objectives
	8 Geschwind, Pinheiro, and Stensaker	Over the last four decades, a higher education institution located in the Nordic region has faced adversities that derive from the institutional setting that seeks to transform it into an institution with higher standards and a distinct identity from colleges
	9 Frigotto and Frigotto	The operatic sector in Italy has undergone significant changes since its birth and, over the 400 years of its existence, has changed with society and institutional settings
	10 Kolehmainen, Kurikka, Keerberg, and Raagmaa	Regional higher education institutions located at the peripheries of Estonia and Finland have been threatened by adversities that derive from changes to the higher education system and the region, i.e. by the focus on research in university mission and the depression of regional peripheries
	11 Magro, Uyarra, and Valdaliso	The Basque Country has addressed adversities such as macroeconomic fluctuations and structural changes over the last forty years

developed a unique form of drill (preadaptive drill) to allow for decision-making in complex situations and to develop resilience foresight. During drills, soldiers learn mechanisms that can be acquired in advance in relation to different novelty profiles of adversities. Drawing on the biological resilience literature, the authors use the concept of 'exaptation'—using old means to achieve new ends (Gould & Verba, 1982)—to explain how this works.

Chapter 4 traces boilermakers in a naval shipbuilding project. The context of temporary organizing under which the boilermakers operate allows the authors to address resilience in situations in which there is not a 'shared culture' of routines and habits, which is what Chapters 2, 5 and 6 presuppose. Concerning mainly resilience mechanisms, Chapter 4 presents how occupational groups working together for the construction of complex products, i.e. ships, build resilience by setting up special coordination mechanisms. The latter bring together the different groups around one priority that is, avoiding coactivity constraints that are related to unexpected events and challenge workers' safety. Adversity, in this chapter, is understood as coming from complex tasks that are undertaken by independent actors, which inevitably do not go exactly according to plan, but which could result in calamitous accidents or a non-functional ship if not addressed. In other words, there is an invisible threat. Treating it this way emphasizes how resilience can be built *ex-ante*.

Chapter 5 looks closely at two public agencies—one dealing with coordination for resilience and the second with public transportation. There is a deliberate attempt to build resilience into these two types of public agency. The authors treat resilience as a practice rather than as a behaviour to emphasize the dynamic interplay between structure and action. Particularly important here is the idea of 'teleo-affective structures', which introduce emotive elements and extend behavioural drivers beyond rules and norms. The chapter distinguishes between cultivating resilience for predictable situations—in which adversity can be anticipated—and those that are the result of a complex environment, in which it cannot. Here again we see the theme of control as a threat, this time expressed not as acting according to norms or micromanagement, but as following prescribed actions. The chapter focuses on resilience foresight and presents organizational arrangements adopted by public organizations to produce resilience before adversity triggers actually occur. The authors show that foresight was triggered in different ways in the two organizations that they studied: one created dedicated crisis management teams to develop the capabilities needed to be resilient, and the other redefined organigrams and engaged in task distribution.

Chapter 6 looks at public managers in New Zealand in a general public sphere context. The authors focus on deliberate attempts to build resilience. Adversity in this case comes as the result of an ambiguous and complex context, one in which an overexertion of control, through micromanagement, can lead to failure. Unlike in Chapter 2, there is no surprise to uncover and 'know' but rather a situation of task complexity in which uncertainty continues to prevail over time. The authors treat resilience as a capability that can be learned and harnessed through leadership. The chapter addresses resilience in foresight: employees prepare their resources to be ready to adapt and flourish at work and when faced with challenging circumstances.

The second section of the volume includes cases that position resilience on a macro level within organizational fields and in society. Chapters in this section are clustered into those that address intra-system resilience and those addressing inter-system resilience. Chapters 7, 8 and 9 belong to the first set, as they analyse one system intended as a whole sector. Chapter 10 analyses several systems that coevolve with each other in a region, and Chapter 11 concerns the whole economic dynamics of the region.

Chapter 7 contributes to the literature on resilience foresight, as it discusses the evolution of universities as institutions, and to mechanisms, as it identifies the archetype of the post-entrepreneurial university as more consistent with threats deriving from general institutional change. In this chapter, the authors demonstrate how the concept of an entrepreneurial university, and the political and economic pressures driving it to become a global archetype, embeds logics that if pursued are likely to undermine the resilience of universities. Drawing on complex systems theory, the chapter looks at how the broad aims of efficiency, diversity and unified actorness are misconstrued in the entrepreneurial university literature and suggests ways to reconfigure universities to be resilient by orienting them to loose coupling, slack and requisite diversity.

Chapter 8 examines the linkage between identity and resilience at a Scandinavian university. By looking at a series of critical junctures in which external adversity coming from the government and the private sector threatened to undermine the university's identity, it explores the possibility of understanding resilience through a dynamic process organization identity formation and evolution that brings together both the internal cultural and teleo-affective structures discussed in Chapter 5 with externally determined possibilities for legitimacy. Addressing both mechanisms and outcomes, it elaborates on the role of organizational identity in resilience, as identities constrain and enable social agents' attempts to respond to environmental imperatives and to enact the resilient behaviour.

Chapter 9 provides a historical analysis of the evolution of the opera organizational field in Italy, and fosters a discussion on the actual resilience of the sector in relation to the prominent changes that transformed both the society and the opera over time. It discusses the outcomes of the resilience of the operatic sector throughout its history. While challenged by deep societal, cultural and economic changes, the opera went through a transformative resilience that required scaling down its importance as a cultural expression, and this translated into the reduction of the number of opera houses and of their funding. The authors conclude that the operatic sector is still wandering between different target publics that can support its existence—ranging from tourists to citizens, from intellectuals to lay people, from young people to adults—and that for this reason, its resilience, as the ability to combine change with essence, is continuously threatened by the option of becoming the Disneyland of the opera, focusing on mere reproduction and business-drawn entertainment.

Chapter 10 examines regional higher education institutions (RHEIs) in peripheral regions of both Finland and Estonia. While most of the literature on resilience focuses on a single type of entity or system, this chapter addresses universities as nested subjects of two different societal systems, higher education and the region, which each create a distinct form of adversity. Resilience comprises the co-evolution of RHEIs with the region in which they are positioned, as well as with the higher education system in which they operate. It is analysed in terms of mechanisms concerning the governance that regulates interactions among institutions, such as resource allocation decisions and core competencies.

Chapter 11, via a historical analysis, presents how a vibrant and culturally-disctinctive economic region the Basque region, was able to navigate through economic and institutional changes. This case shows the link between resilience and governance systems, especially industrial and innovation policies. Building on the field of evolutionary economic geography, it explores both the unexpected and predictable threats to regions that can come from recessions, crises and structural changes to the broader national and global economy. The authors distinguish between situations in which regions maintain previous economic specialization and those in which they shift towards new paths; they call them 'adaptation' and 'adaptability'—citing Boschma (2015)—two forms of resilience that refer to the three abilities of the conceptual typology presented above: absorbability, adaptability and transformability.

Final Remarks

In this edited book, the chapters present cases that display a high degree of publicness (Bozeman, 2004), a dimension that pushes social entities to cultivate resilience.

The chapters are grounded in different disciplinary perspectives or research streams that address organizations and societies. The result is a multidisciplinary perspective on resilience that enhances best practices and cross-fertilization of findings, theories and methods throughout the social sciences.

According to Collin (2009, p. 103), *multidisciplinarity* refers to cases in which different disciplines work independently on different aspects of a project and within their boundaries. In contrast, *interdisciplinarity* refers to the reciprocal recognition of contributions and perspectives within different disciplines, while *transdisciplinarity* refers to the integration of such perspectives into a harmonized, coherent whole.

Our aim is to trigger future interdisciplinary and/or transdisciplinary research that produces a holistic understanding of resilience and to support policymakers, managers, regional/local planners and scholarly communities in pursuing resilience as important for our present and future organizations and societies. These imperatives have become ever more urgent as individuals, organizations and societies deal with the challenges posed by the COVID-19 pandemic alongside the grand challenges facing humankind, with climate change at the forefront.

We presented our perspective on resilience along two key phases. First, we reviewed the literature on resilience and identified change and stability, as well as the temporal dimension, as its most fundamental traits. Then, we elaborated the absorptive, adaptive and transformative resilience typology and the temporal sequence of foresight, mechanisms and outcomes. This novel theoretical and analytical framework allows us to map resilience consistently onto a variety of cases and to maintain a general 'umbrella-concept' that unifies them.

Second, our organizing principles act as a 'lens' through which the individual chapters can be interpreted and compared to generate a holistic perspective on resilience while respecting the specific conceptual and theoretical perspectives and postulates being followed by the individual authors in their respective contexts.

The final chapter of this edited volume reassesses and discusses the core conceptual and theoretical premises sketched out in this introductory chapter against the backdrop of the empirical contributions of the individual, case chapters and the volume as a whole. In so doing, we hope to provide a valuable platform for future studies and policy debates on this critically important societal phenomenon.

References

Bazerman, M., & Watkins, M. (2004). *Predictable surprises: The disasters you should have seen coming, and how to prevent them*. Harvard Business School Press.

Bhamra, R. (2016). *Organisational resilience: Concepts, integration, and practice*. CRC Press.

Bhamra, R., Dani, S., & Burnard, K. (2011). Resilience: The concept, a literature review and future directions. *International Journal of Production Research, 49*(18), 5375–5539.

Bodin, P., & Wiman, B. (2004). Resilience and other stability concepts in ecology: Notes on their origin, validity, and usefulness. *ESS Bulletin, 2*(2), 33–43.

Borhanuddin, B., & Iqbal, A. (2016). Nokia: An historical case study. *Electronic Journal of Computer Science and Information Technology: Ejcist, 6*(1), 1–14.

Boschma, R. (2015). Towards an evolutionary perspective on regional resilience. *Regional Studies, 49*(5), 733–751.

Bozeman, B. (1984). Dimensions of publicness: An approach to public organization theory. In Bozeman, B., Straussman, J. (Eds.), *New directions in public administration* (pp. 46–62). Belmont, CA: Crooks/Cole.

Bozeman, B. (2004). *All organizations are public: Comparing public and private organizations*. Beard Books.

Bozeman, B., & Bretschneider, S. (1994). The 'publicness puzzle' in organization theory: A test of alternative explanations of differences between public and private organizations. *Journal of Public Administration Research and Theory, 4*(2), 197–224.

Britt, T., Shen, W., Sinclair, R., Grossman, M., & Klieger, D. (2016). How much do We really know about employee resilience? *Industrial and Organizational Psychology, 9*(2), 378–404.

Bruneau, M., Chang, S. E., Eguchi, R. T., Lee, G. C., O'Rourke, T. D., Reinhorn, A. M., Shinozuka, M., Tierney, K., Wallace, W. A., & von Winterfeldt, D. (2003). A framework to quantitatively assess and enhance the seismic resilience of communities. *Earthquake Spectra, 19*(4), 733–752.

Burnard, K., & Bhamra, R. (2011). Organisational resilience: Development of a conceptual framework for organisational responses. *International Journal of Production Research, 49*(18), 5581–5599.

Carpenter, S., Walker, B., Anderies, J., & Abel, N. (2001). From metaphor to measurement: Resilience of what to what? *Ecosystems, 4*, 765–781.

Christensen, T., & Lægreid, P. (2011). *The Ashgate research companion to new public management*. Ashgate.

Christensen, T., Lægreid, P., Roness, P. G., & Røvik, K. A. (2007). *Organization theory and the public sector: Instrument*. Taylor & Francis.

Collin, A. (2009). Multidisciplinary, interdisciplinary, and transdisciplinary collaboration: Implications for vocational psychology. *International Journal for Educational and Vocational Guidance, 9*(2), 101–110.

Coutu, D. L. (2002). How resilience works. *Harvard Business Review, 80*(5), 46–56.

de Bruijne, M. L. C., Boin, A., & van Eeten, M. J. G. (2010). Resilience. Exploring the concept and its meaning. In L. K. Comfort, A. Boin, & C. C. Demchak (Eds.), *Designing resilience. Preparing for extreme events* (pp. 13–32). Pittsburg: University of Pittsburg Press.

Donaldson, L. (2001). *The contingency theory of organizations*. Sage Publications.

Duchek, S. (2020). Organizational resilience: A capability-based conceptualization. *Business Research, 13*, 215–246.

Farnham, D., & Horton, S. (1999). Managing public and private organisations. In S. Horton & D. Farnham (Eds.), *Public management in Britain* (pp. 26–45). Palgrave.

Feldman, M. S., & Orlikowski, W. J. (2011). Theorizing practice and practicing theory. *Organization Science, 22*(5), 1240–1253.

Fisher, D. M., Ragsdale, J. M., & Fisher, E. C. (2019). The importance of definitional and temporal issues in the study of resilience. *Applied Psychology, 68*, 583–620.

Folke, C., Carpenter, S. R., Walker, B., Scheffer, M., Chapin, T., & Rockström, J. (2010). Resilience thinking: integrating resilience, adaptability and transformability. *Ecology and Society, 15*(4), 20.

Frigotto, M. L. (2018). *Understanding novelty in organizations: A research path across agency and consequences*. Chem: Springer International Publishing.

Frigotto, M. L. (2020). Reframing resilience on novelty and change. In E. Powley, B. Caza, & A. Caza (Eds.), *Research handbook on organizational resilience* (pp. 53–69). Emerald Group Publishing Limited.

Gilboa, I., & Schmeidler, D. (1995). Case-based decision theory. *The Quarterly Journal of Economics, 110*, 605–639.

Giovannini, E., Benczur, P., Campolongo, F., Cariboni, J., & Manca, A. (2020). *Time for transformative resilience: The COVID-19 emergency* (EUR 30179 EN). Publications Office of the European Union. ISBN 978-92-76-18113-2 (online first).

Giustiniano, L., Clegg, S. R., Cunha, M. P., & Rego, A. (2018). *Elgar introduction to theories of organizational resilience.* Edward Elgar Publishing.

Gotham, K. F., & Campanella, R. (2010). Toward a research agenda on transformative resilience: Challenges and opportunities for post-trauma urban ecosystems. *Critical Planning, 17*(Summer), 9–23.

Gould, S. J., & Verba, E. S. (1982). Exaptation—a missing term in the science of form. *Paleobiology, 8*, 4–15.

Grove, K. (2018). *Resilience.* Routledge.

Hamel, G., & Välikangas, L. (2003). The quest for resilience. *Harvard Business Review, 81*(9), 52.

Head, B. W. (2008). Wicked problems in public policy. *Public Policy, 3*(2), 101–118.

Holling, C. S. (1973). Resilience and stability of ecological systems. *Annual Review of Ecology and Systematics, 4*(1), 1–23.

Hu, X., & Hassink, R. (2017). Exploring adaptation and adaptability in uneven economic resilience: A tale of two Chinese mining regions. *Cambridge Journal of Regions, Economy and Society, 10*(3), 527–541.

Kalpakjian, S., & Schmid, S. R. (2016). *Manufacturing processes for engineering materials*. Boston: Pearson.

Kayes, D. C. (2015). *Organizational resilience: How learning sustains organizations in crisis, disaster, and breakdown.* Oxford University Press.

Knight, F. H. (1921). *Risk, uncertainty, and profit.* Houghton Mifflin.

Kossek, E. E., & Perrigino, M. B. (2016). Resilience: A review using a grounded integrated occupational approach. *The Academy of Management Annals, 10*(1), 729–797.

Kurikka, H., Kolehmainen, J., & Sotarauta, M. (2018). Constructing regional resilience in a knowledge economy crisis: The case of the Nokia-led ICT industry in Tampere. In P. Benneworth (Ed.) *Universities and regional economic development* (pp. 163–179). Routledge.

Langley, A., & Abdallah, C. (2011). Templates and turns in qualitative studies of strategy and management. In D. D. Bergh & D. J. Ketchen (Eds.), *Building methodological bridges* (Research Methodology in Strategy and Management, Vol. 6, pp. 201–235). Emerald Group Publishing Limited.

Lengnick-Hall, C., Beck, T., & Lengnick-Hall, M. (2011). Developing a capacity for organizational resilience through strategic human resource management. *Human Resource Management Review, 21*(3), 243–255.

Levinthal, D. A. (2008). Explorations in the role of novelty in organizational adaptation: An introductory essay. In J. G. March (Ed.), *Explorations in organizations* (pp. 95–103). Stanford Business Books.

Lindeberg, R. (2020, June 15). Sweden's Prime Minister rejects criticism of coronavirus strategy. *Time*. https://time.com/5853595/sweden-coronavirus-lockdown-criticism/.

Linnenluecke, M. K. (2017). Resilience in business and management research: A review of influential publications and a research agenda. *International Journal of Management Reviews, 19*(1), 4–30.

Logan, D. C. (2009). Known knowns, known unknowns, unknown unknowns and the propagation of scientific enquiry. *Journal of Experimental Botany, 60*(3), 712–714.

Manca, B., Benczur, P., & Giovannini, E. (2017). *Building a scientific narrative towards a more resilient EU society, Part 1: A conceptual framework. JRC Science for Policy Report*. European Commission.

Manyena, S. B. (2006). The concept of resilience revisited. *Disasters, 30*(4), 434–450.

March, J. G. (1991). Exploration and exploitation in organizational learning. *Organization Science, 2*(1), 71–87.

McDonald, N. (2006). Organisational resilience and industrial risk. In Hollnagel, E., DD Woods, N. Leveson (Eds.), *Resilience engineering: Concepts and precepts* (pp. 155–179). Hampshire: Ashgate.

Meadows, D. H., Meadows, D. L., Randers, J., & Behrens, W. W. (1972). The limits to growth. *New York*, pp. 27, 102.

Nair, H. A., Sri Ramalu, S., & Kumar, M. (2014). Impact of innovation capacity and anticipatory competence on organizational health: A resource based study of Nokia, Motorola and Blackberry. *International Journal of Economic Research, 11*(2), 395–415.

North, D. C. (1990). *Institutions, institutional change, and economic performance*. Cambridge University Press.

Padgett, J. F., & Powell, W. W. (2012). *The emergence of organizations and markets*. Princeton University Press.

Peters, T. J., Waterman, R. H., & Jones, I. (1982). *In search of excellence: Lessons from America's best-run companies*. Harper Collins.

Pike, A., Dawley, S., & Tomaney, J. (2010). Resilience, adaptation and adaptability. *Cambridge Journal of Regions, Economy and Society, 3*(1), 59–70.

Pirotti, G., & Venzin, M. (2016). *Resilient organizations: Responsible leadership in times of uncertainty*. Cambridge University Press.

Powell, W. W. (1998). Learning from collaboration: Knowledge and networks in the biotechnology and pharmaceutical industries. *California Management Review, 40*(3), 228–240.

Ramanujam, R., & Roberts, K. H. (Eds.). (2018). *Organizing for reliability: A guide for research and practice*. Stanford University Press.

Rittel, H. W., & Webber, M. M. (1973). Dilemmas in a general theory of planning. *Policy Sciences, 4*(2), 155–169.

Roe, E., & Schulman, P. R. (2008). *High reliability management: Operating on the edge* (Vol. 19). Stanford University Press.

Ruiz-Martin, C., López-Paredes, A., & Wainer, G. (2018). What we know and do not know about organizational resilience. *International Journal of Production Management and Engineering*, *6*(1), 11–28.

Ruth, M., & Goessling-Reisemann, S. (2019). *Handbook on resilience of socio-technical systems*. Cheltenham, UK & Northampton, MA: Edward Elgar Publishing.

Satyal, P., Shrestha, K., Ojha, H., Vira, B., & Adhikari, J. (2017). A new Himalayan crisis? Exploring transformative resilience pathways. *Environmental Development, 23*, 47–56.

Schaffer, A., & Schneider, M. (2019). Towards a responsible resilience. In M. Ruth & S. Goessling-Reisemann (Eds.), *Handbook on resilience of socio-technical systems* (pp. 9–29). Edward Elgar Publishing.

Tsoukas, H., & Chia, R. (2002). An organizational becoming: Rethinking organizational change. *Organization Science, 13*(5), 567–582.

Vanhove, A. J., Herian, M. N., Perez, A. L. U., Harms, P. D., & Lester, P. B. (2016). Can resilience be developed at work? A meta-analytic review of resilience-building programme effectiveness. *Journal of Occupational and Organizational Psychology, 89*(2), 278–307.

Vogus, T. J., & Sutcliffe, K. M. (2007). Organizational resilience: Towards a theory and research agenda. *2007 IEEE International Conference on Systems, Man, and Cybernetics, SMC 2007* (pp. 3418–3422). [4414160] (Conference Proceedings: IEEE International Conference on Systems, Man and Cybernetics).

Walker, B., Holling, C. S., Carpenter, S. R., & Kinzig, A. (2004). Resilience, adaptability and transformability in social–ecological systems. *Ecology and Society*, *9*(2), 1–9.

Walker, B., & Salt, D. (2006). *Resilience thinking: Sustaining ecosystems and people in a changing world*. Island Press.

Weick, K. E., & Sutcliffe, K. M. (2001). *Managing the unexpected: Assuring high performance in an age of complexity*. Jossey-Bass.

Weick, K. E., Sutcliffe, K. M., & Obstfeld, D. (1999). Organizing for high reliability: Processes of collective mindfulness. In R. I. Sutton & B. M. Staw (Eds.), *Research in organizational behavior* (Vol. 21, pp. 81–123).

Westrum, R. (2006). A typology of resilience situations. In E. Hollnagel, D. D. Woods, & N. Leveson (Eds.), *Resilience engineering: Concepts and precepts* (pp. 55–66). Ashgate Publishing Company.

Williams, T. A., Gruber, D. A., Sutcliffe, K. M., Shepherd, D. A., & Zhao, E. Y. (2017). Organizational response to adversity: Fusing crisis management and resilience research streams. *Academy of Management Annals, 11*(2), 733–769.

Woods, D. D. (2019). Essentials of resilience, revisited. In M. Ruth & S. Goessling-Reisemann (Eds.), *Handbook on resilience of socio-technical systems* (pp. 52–65). Edward Elgar Publishing.

Yin, R. K. (2009 [1984]). *Case study research*. Sage Publications.

Zolli, A. (2012). *Resilience: Why things bounce back*. Simon & Schuster.

PART II

Resilience in Organisations

CHAPTER 2

Decision Premises, Learning and Organizational Resilience Addressing Novel Adversities

Maria Laura Frigotto, Loris Gaio, Alessandro Narduzzo, and Marco Zamarian

Introduction

Organizational resilience refers to the ability to bounce back, respond and recover when facing disturbances (Linnenluecke, 2017) or adverse

M. L. Frigotto · L. Gaio · M. Zamarian
Department of Economics and Management, University of Trento, Trento, Italy
e-mail: marialaura.frigotto@unitn.it

L. Gaio
e-mail: loris.gaio@unitn.it

M. Zamarian
e-mail: marco.zamarian@unitn.it

A. Narduzzo (✉)
Faculty of Economics and Management, Free University of Bozen-Bolzano, Bolzano, Italy
e-mail: anarduzzo@unibz.it

R. Pinheiro et al. (eds.), *Towards Resilient Organizations and Societies*, Public Sector Organizations,
https://doi.org/10.1007/978-3-030-82072-5_2

triggers (Fisher et al., 2018). Resilience addresses both exceptional and devastating events, as well as a larger set of disruptions and disturbances that in various ways do not match with those occurrences that 'the system is designed to handle' (Boin et al., 2010, p. 8). Wildavsky (1988) added a relevant distinction between adversities that can be foreseen (and that belong to the area of 'anticipation') and those that consist of unknown challenges that are unanticipated before they become manifest (that map into the area of resilience). As such, novelty is a grounding condition of disturbances or adverse triggers (Frigotto, 2020). Novelty can assume different degrees up to an extreme at which it consists of something that is not deemed possible. This range implies that organizations need to prepare themselves to face what is so unknown that it is not thought of (Frigotto, 2018).

From this perspective, resilience consists of the ability to detect the novelty that can be triggering adversities; as such, it is an ability that is essentially undetermined and ill-defined, as Perrow (1999) and Wildavsky (1988) revealed. Weick developed this conceptualization further by reframing adversities as 'the unexpected', namely, in terms of what is not expected and not thought, given the present approach to giving sense to the world known as 'sensemaking' (Weick, 1993; Weick & Roberts, 1993; Weick & Sutcliffe, 2001). Through this lens, resilience is also 'less deterministic' (Linnenluecke, 2017, p. 8) and highly dependent on the moment and the context in which resilience is enacted. The inclusion of novelty into resilience requires organizations to acquire a mindset that deems the unthinkable possible and to structure themselves into specific roles, procedures and units that support this mindset coherently with the posture of 'expecting the unexpected' postulated by Weick and Sutcliffe's contribution in 2001.

In addition, in the field of crisis management, the two prevailing approaches to increase the ability to deal with emergencies are the planning and analysis of contingencies (Boin & McConnell, 2007; Levac et al., 2012). Both approaches try to increase organizational resilience by preparing the management systems to deal with known and recurrent crises; nevertheless, they are substantially ineffective when organizational resilience depends on the ability to cope with novel and unexpected adversities and consists of learning capabilities (Lalonde, 2007).

In this chapter, we illustrate and theorize the difficulties that novel and unexpected emergencies pose to organizations and that make them actually struggle to be resilient. We build on the framework outlined by

Simon (1991) to explain how organizations learn to deal with novel problems; this framework dates back to Simon and Newell (1971). In this framework, decision premises affect the representation of the problem and, ultimately, the possibility to detect, interpret and respond to novel situations. From this perspective, the ability to revise the initial decision premises, i.e., to expand the perceptual limits of observation and to conceive a novel representation of the problem, provides the foundation of the ability to detect unknown situations and, ultimately, to be resilient in the face of novelty in adversities.

We theorize organizational resilience as pertaining to the ability to revise decision premises in the face of novel and unexpected adversities by combining the resilience literature with Simon's contribution. We develop this conceptualization into a set of structural elements that can be adopted by organizations to build resilience. First is a mindset that contemplates the unknown among the possible situations to be faced and stimulates the revision of decision premises. Second, the organizational role of the 'Challenger of Decision Premises' (CDP) is deliberately designed to challenge the existing decision premises to consider novelty that might not be apparent.

In the next section, we report the real case of a fire emergency that occurred in Italy in 1993.

We introduce this case in the front end of our chapter with an illustrative purpose (as in the tradition of, for instance, Weick, 1993) to display the specific issues that novel and unexpected emergencies pose to organizations and their attempts to be resilient. Third, we build on Herbert Simon's learning theory on the solution of new problems, adapting it to the context of emergency management to provide our theoretical framework of resilience in the face of novelty adversities. In the fourth section, we develop the role of the 'Challenger of Decision Premises'. Finally, after having outlined the theoretical perspective building our model, in the last section, the case of the fire illustrated in section two is recalled with explicit reference to the proposed theoretical framework.

The chapter concludes by arguing that organizations can prepare and be more resilient in dealing with new emergencies. In this case, preparedness means learning to revise the decision premises and develop a new appropriate representation of the situation while the novel emergency is being addressed.

Fighting an Everlasting Fire

This section presents the narrative of a firefighting intervention operated by a brigade in Northern Italy as an illustration of the issues that the unexpected raises in the ability of organizations to detect and respond to adversities. This incident was disclosed by the Fire Chief and the Deputy Chief of the Fire Department that operated the intervention, in the context of an open interview that occurred in 2015. The interview was contextualized in a larger research project aimed at grounding, in the empirical experience of nearly 40 years of firefighting activity, what novelty consists of in the context of emergency management. The following narrative reports a case in which novelty is presented in context, providing the background for our theoretical elaboration. In the last section, the case will be revisited and related to the theoretical contribution developed throughout the chapter.

One evening in November 1993, a fire broke out in an industrial plant producing frozen meals in Bolzano, Italy. It was a long and complicated intervention, lasting 11 hours. After 7 hours, the fire was still spreading; the high heat produced structural damage to the building, hampering firemen operating in the face of over 360 degrees Celsius for a long time. However, we are not retelling it in this context for the exceptional risk it produced but because this case illustrates the essence of the unexpected in the view of the professional firefighters involved, i.e., the difficulty in understanding and making sense of the situation.

In this intervention, a brigade of 10 firemen was sent out; the Fire Chief (FC) acted as incident commander,[1] and his Deputy as senior Officer (DC). Since the fire was large, other firemen were recalled from off-duty. It was already dark when they started to fight the fire, and a very dark and intensifying smoke hampered the detection of fire and the ability to tackle it directly. Therefore, they first started to fight the fire from outside; then, as is routine in these cases, the fire squad opened the windows and started fans to remove the smoke and identify the origin of the fire. They located the core of the fire and attacked it from both the inside and the outside. However, when they thought they had tamed the fire, the unexpected occurred:

[1] The "incident commander" is the person in charge of the solution of the emergency. The role is specifically important for large emergencies involving several organizations, as this person is in charge of coordinating the efforts.

FC: *"At one time, and I remember that perfectly well, this fire was more or less clear where it was; then suddenly another one started, in a different place. Later, a second outbreak and then a third, somewhere else. Then, while operations were in progress, a further outbreak was reported in the basement, where we had just passed."*

At this point, the officers started re-analysing the situation, but the understanding they had built up to that moment and that had led them to attack the fire showed several discrepancies:

FC: *"I must say that I was very confused, I remember, very confused, because the first outbreak could actually be there, I explained it to myself. The second one was already a bit anomalous, but it could be related in some way to the first. But the new outbreak, after three quarters of an hour of intervention, two floors below the first fire? that was really strange."*

In addition, a new outbreak has been reported in the basement, where the incident commander just passed by; that piece of evidence did not fit a logical explanation of how these new fires could have started:

FC: *"It was strange because we in the basement had seen three bags of potato starch used to prepare the gnocchi that were soaking wet because the water from the pipes had leaked from the second-floor walls to the basement. We had walked in the pulp of wet starch, doing: splosh-splosh. [...] In short, the situation was no longer correct.*

DC: *"At least at first analysis, there was no logical correlation between the first fire and the following ones."*

In this situation, they started exploring all the possible explanations:

FC: *"So, when you hear that down in the basement it burns again, you ask yourself, how is that possible? How can it be? [...] In short, one evaluates several hypotheses to give a reason to what is happening."*

DC: *"At first, I [...] had assumed that there was a channel connecting the second floor with the basement, and that something had fallen down that burned. For example, an elevator or a conduit."*

However, their assessment was made difficult due to the lack of information. For example, in this case, maps of the building were not provided.

A large part of this analysing activity was performed in teams, at the Incident Command Post, a temporary direction unit that is established near the site to coordinate operations. Information on operations converges to this post, where commanders reason on why each action is performed and thus update their picture of the situation.

> *FC:* *"The scene is put together one piece after the other. And then you start discussing; 'But what can it be?' You try to integrate the current understanding with additional information [...]. For example, it is possible that someone in the crew already knows the building for having made inspections for fire prevention. All this information is then shared."*

During this discussion, all the details were assessed, and the multiplicity of observers was exploited. In this case, while it is normal that workers and managers of the factory remain around the building or even inside in the areas that are not on fire, both FC and DC noticed that they had met a man several times during their inspections.

> *FC:* *"I may be confused, I may have been in the wrong direction, but there were two of us and we both noticed the presence of this person."*

They set a context to validate the hypothesis that that man could be an arsonist. They asked the police to hold him for an identity check; thus, had they not observed any new outbreaks in the meantime, this holding would have supported the arsonist hypothesis. The hypothesis was validated and, in fact, it later came out that the man was a former employee that had been fired shortly earlier. Therefore, it was understood that there was someone who was setting the fire in new places while their intervention was in progress.

The Challenge of New Emergencies

Organizations coping with novelty may increase their resilience in essentially two ways. First, they can react to novel emergencies as they happen by adapting their response to the needs imposed by the new situation (that is part of a processual resilience); second, they can work before the emergency occurs, trying to enlarge the solutions to all the plausible novel emergencies they can think of (that is part of the ex-ante elaborated resilience-promoting factors) (Fisher et al., 2018). Emergency management systems can apply both of these solutions, also in combination. However, the latter approach has been well developed by both scholars and practitioners, unfolding under the themes of 'anticipation' (Wildavsky, 1988) and 'preparedness' (Hémond & Robert, 2012; Perry et al., 2001). Likewise, the issue concerning how to support and to design an organization that is able to detect and respond to novel and unexpected emergencies is still an open question in both the literature and from practitioners' perspective. In particular, in the literature on resilience, there are studies that conceive of resilience as an ongoing activity that takes place together with the unfolding of events (Frigotto, 2020; also see first chapter of this book), some of them linking resilience to mindfulness, i.e., the ability to sustain awareness of the present moment (Frigotto & Zamarian, 2015). These studies underline that processes and structures in organizations devoted to building reflection and designed to diversify perspectives help enhance resilience. They explain how organizations can continuously support resilience while standard operations are being performed by means of maintaining structures that are focused on different domains or by supporting reflection on the existing procedures while supporting experimentation and tolerating error.

In other words, they recognize that organizations need to combine what March (1991, p. 71) defines as 'exploration' and 'exploitation', intended respectively as pointing at 'search, variation, risk taking, experimentation, play, flexibility, discovery, innovation' or at 'refinement, choice, production, efficiency, selection, implementation, execution'. The extant literature elaborates on how to combine exploration and exploitation within the same organization (e.g., O'Reilly & Tushman, 2013 on ambidexterity). However, it does not explain with sufficient depth, at a more micro level, how these activities are combined in the decision-making behaviour of the same individual and within the same organizational team.

Our idea of organizations learning from novel emergencies as they happen draws on Simon's (1991) theory of learning. Simon conceives of decision-making as an inferential process based on premises derived from norms and goals (Cohen, 2007). Problem solvers rely on norms, beliefs and goals that are taken for granted. However, solving new problems implies violating existing norms or reconsidering predefined goals.

This formulation seems particularly appropriate to analyse problem-solving in crisis management. In fact, Roberts and Wernstedt (2018) observe that emergency management systems consider how to choose between available alternatives without explicitly taking into account values and norms that constrain those decisions or to what extent the decision process consists of automatic actions. Similarly, Simon's framework on solving new problems acknowledges the importance of these premises (Simon, 1957, 1991).

In the field of emergency management, the concept of decision premises has been used to explain how stable structures, such as disaster management systems, can react in a flexible approach to facing unexpected events (Grothe-Hammer & Berthod, 2017), such as sudden and large inflows of refugees (Meyer & Simpsa, 2018). An account of failures in dealing with unexpected crises as reported by Page et al. (2006) while investigating the Hurricane Katrina incident notes that decision premises are often deformed by several factors: (a) former commitments to past choices, (b) negative information avoidance and defence of prior choices, (c) delusion of control over uncontrollable events and (d) wishful thinking.

To understand the challenges that new emergencies pose to emergency management organizations[2] and to analyse what specific issues they pose in terms of resilience, this chapter takes a problem-solving perspective (Dynes, 1994; Simon, 1957, 1991) and conceives new emergencies as new problems to solve. Unfortunately, problems setting is itself a problematic issue, and identification and definition may not necessarily result in a classification task. In real situations, the available information (i.e., contradictory, partial, and unreliable, etc.) and the evolving conditions make it more difficult for the decision-makers to understand whether the ambiguous and unclear situation is familiar or novel.

Therefore, decision-makers perceive unclear and ambiguous stimuli that make them confront three possible alternatives: inaction, routinized response, or original solution (Billings et al., 1980). Inaction means that the organization does not react, because nothing has been detected and

[2] In this chapter, we refer to emergency management organizations to indicate a class of high-reliability organizations (Weick & Sutcliffe, 2001), that is, organizations that operate in complex and high-risk environments and still perform effectively and make few mistakes.

therefore an emergency is not even perceived. Routinized response is the familiar response that the organization executes when the situation is perceived as familiar. Finally, an original solution is triggered when the organization detects that the situation is different from usual ones and that it requires a new problem formulation. Hence, solving new problems and learning from novel situations needs three major conditions to occur. First, the organization has to be able to perceive that the situation at hand is different from the usual ones. Second, the organization has to be able to react by adapting its response to the situation. Third, to be resilient, the organization needs to react and respond in a timeframe consistent with the survival of the system. To accomplish the first steps, problem solvers need to develop a problem representation, a process that is analysed in the next section.

Acquiring New Problem Representations

According to Simon and Newell (1971), problem solvers usually do not have full knowledge of the environment they operate in; therefore, they normally create a representation of the problem. To do so, problem solvers tend to use a base of knowledge they already retain in their various memories; they can rely on pre-acquired knowledge of the task environment they are operating in and on their own past experience with similar tasks and with components of the whole task they are facing. Additional sources of information are programmes (i.e., standard operating procedures) and more abstract pieces of knowledge that do not pertain to a specific situation but that are nevertheless considered relevant. For instance, when confronting a novel emergency that may affect an undefined number of people, an emergency management system that is still trying to identify the causes may adopt standard procedures to mitigate the negative effects of the hazard (Simon, 1991). A further source of knowledge that problem solvers can use is simulations, which can help generate hypothetical or counterfactual thinking.

If problem solvers are not able to gather any relevant information, they can try to construct a representation of the problem in a more abstract form. For instance, a city emergency management team may not have prepared a plan for dealing with blackouts, but in the event of a blackout, the team can reason in abstract terms about the main consequences produced by a prolonged lack of electrical power and plan the response, the priorities and the actions to undertake to mitigate the effects of the crisis.

To conceptualize novel situations, building on Simon (1991), we need to define the conditions that allow the actors to create cognitive representations of new problems. One of the most problematic situations is faced when actors fail to perceive the novelty and thus treat what is different and new as something familiar. To avoid this failure, decision-makers need to construct a representation of the problem that does not exclusively derive from an existing corpus of knowledge; this condition can be achieved in two complementary ways: by focusing on new information or by acquiring new sources of information (Simon, 1991).

Normally, problem solvers approach a situation that looks familiar by means of the usual representation of the problem. This approach should indicate an appropriate solution. Nevertheless, when the problem is novel and different, the decision-makers may notice anomalies in how the situation is characterized or evolves. If the anomalies persist, decision-makers start doubting the current representation of the problem. To define a novel problem representation, the decision-makers need to reconsider the decision premises, which are composed of the following: beliefs; organizational arrangements (such as roles); communication channels; and, more generally, pieces of knowledge that are taken for granted when decisions are made. Following Simon (1991), we contend that decision premises are a fundamental element in this respect, as decision-making consists of a process of inference.

According to Cohen (2007), decision premises should be studied as a unit of analysis to understand organizational behaviour at large. For instance, *authority* can be framed as the acceptance of premises set by hierarchical superiors. Similarly, *trust* can be defined as the acceptance of premises by others without further inquiry.

Given the importance of decision premises in building a new representation of the problem, it is necessary to understand how the decision premises are formed. In organizational settings, communication is extremely important with respect to the formation of decision premises in at least two ways. First, decision premises are shared within the organization through communication channels. Second, communication responsibility and communication channels are also elements forming the decision premises; what makes legitimate the communication and its content is also subject to decision premises. Therefore, any solution that organizations may consider to revise the decision premises should incorporate communication.

According to Simon (1991), to elaborate a problem representation that is useful to deal with novel problems, problem solvers have two complementary options. First, they can learn how to use an existing problem representation and to explore its limits. For instance, problem solvers may allocate some attention to assessing to what extent this representation is coherent with pieces of evidence of the current situation. This effort exposes the decision-makers to the usual two types of errors. A type 2 error (false negative) exists when our representation fails to acknowledge actual states of the problem; a type 1 error (false positive) exists when the representation considers states of the problem that do not exist. In other words, the first option consists of assessing to what extent the representation of the problem is still useful to understand the situation. The second option consists of creating a new representation for the novel problem. Nevertheless, creating a new problem representation is only the first step that organizations can undertake. The next is to enable organization members to learn how to use the new problem representation.

How Simon (1991) describes the process through which problem solvers approach a novel situation guided by decision premises can be reformulated in cognitive terms as a sensemaking effort (Weick, 1995), that is, an attempt to make sense of something that is not immediately and clearly understood. Weick (1995, p. 4) agrees that sensemaking involves 'placing stimuli into some kind of framework' that is provided, in Simonian terms, by the decision premises. In fact, decision premises define the boundaries and context for the processes of cue noticing, filtering and classifying that are essential elements of sensemaking. Trying to capture the complexity of sensemaking in a synthetic image, Weick (2001) links sensemaking to cartography and to the effort of orienting within a situation that seems to be underdefined, unclear or equivocal. Along with this image, we observe that Simon's decision premises provide the initial coordination system that problem solvers adopt to orient themselves when facing a novel situation.

An additional and convincing bridge connecting, problem-solving perspective and sensemaking is provided by Schön (1983, p. 40), who observes that 'problems do not present themselves to the practitioners as givens. They must be constructed from the materials of problematic situations which are puzzling, troubling, and uncertain. To convert a problematic situation to a problem, a practitioner must do a certain kind of work. He must make sense of an uncertain situation that initially makes no sense'. In Simon's (1991) language, decision premises serve as building blocks to do that kind of work.

What we have thus far outlined to explain how organizations approach novel problems by acquiring and developing appropriate problem representations is not limited to a cognitive dimension but rather involves precise and observable patterns of behaviour that Simon associates with the idea of organizational roles.

The Structure of Roles

According to Simon (1991), organizational roles depict the role embodied by single individuals in organizations or defined by a set of tasks. 'Roles tell organization members how to reason about the problems and decisions that face them: where to look for appropriate and legitimate informational premises and goal (evaluative) premises, and what techniques to use in processing these premises' (Simon, 1991, pp. 126–127). From this perspective, roles are not systems of 'prescribed behaviours', as they are typically considered but are rather systems of 'accepted decision premises'. Roles instruct people on how to reason about the representation of the problem and the decisions—where to look for appropriate and legitimate informational and goal premises and what techniques to use in legitimating these premises.

Roles imply responsibilities, division of labour and coordination mechanisms that regulate organizational behaviour. They can be general in nature and persistent across time and organization. For instance, in business firms, some roles, such as selling, production, and accounting, etc., historically tend to always be present and are defined in functional terms.

In the field of emergency management systems, crisis management has been traditionally conceptualized by decomposing the overall problem into four interrelated subproblems: preparedness, mitigation, response and recovery. This cognitive representation of the management of crises provides the scaffolding to create distinct roles and decision premises in each of these four elements.

In some cases, such as in military or military-like organizations, roles are formally and explicitly defined hierarchically. Alternatively, roles can emerge by imitation from other organizations that are taken as models. For instance, a well-known role system in emergency management, such as the Incident Command System (ICS) developed in the USA in the

1970s, has been subsequently adopted by other countries and eventually became an international standard (York & MacAlister, 2015).

As a further example, firms that build their competitive advantage on safety, efficiency and/or customer satisfaction underpin differentiated roles that eventually contribute to generate that distinctiveness (Simon, 1991). Roles are connected to specialization and to the development of domain-specific knowledge that is coherent with the goals of the firm. Consistent with this line of thought, we can also assume that organizations may create new roles to redefine their goals.

The Role of Challenger of Decision Premises

Among the new roles that existing organizations can adopt, we are interested in roles that increase the organizational ability to perceive, react and learn how to cope with novel problems deriving in particular from new and unexpected emergencies. From the perspective of Simon's (1991) decision premises, novelty requires emergency management organizations to redefine the decision premises they use to make sense of the world (Weick, 1995). This approach implies, first, acknowledging the idea that not all possible emergencies are already known, even though the organization has already acquired a considerable amount of knowledge through previous experience, and that the problem representation that was built by relying on that knowledge is not always useful. A second implication for emergency management organizations concerns how they can prepare for novel emergencies. In fact, a resilient response to novelty is not attained by preparing the organization response in advance, given that the emergency is not known in advance and cannot be anticipated. Instead, the response has to be elaborated *during* the setback. As decision premises are discussed and reconstructed in relation to novelty, the actions and the states of response and recovery are learned throughout the crisis. However, this learning does not imply that nothing can be done before the crisis. In contrast, the elaboration and exercise of a repertoire of standard responses provides the necessary ingredients for further combination and ex novo generation of responses when novelty is faced. In addition, preparation can consist of training the ability to challenge decision premises, as they are typically taken for granted (Frigotto, 2018).

Under such revised decision premises, emergency detection ceases to be a simple task of classification, where the decision-makers use contextual information to identify which type of crisis they are facing. In contrast, it becomes a task that concerns the acquisition of continuous awareness on the decision premises that underpin organizations' decisions and operations. Nevertheless, decision-makers may not be able to assess that novelty is implied in the current situation; they may perceive the situation as implausible or unthinkable and therefore out of the spectrum of possibilities. Alternatively, they eventually may not perceive it at all. In other words, once new and unexpected emergencies are deemed possible, then the emergency recognition cannot be simply reduced to technical rationality and requires the ability to scrutinize and make sense of weak, contradictory and evolving cues (Weick, 1995). Not only the situation itself may appear novel to the decision-makers but also their own actions may produce unintended consequences.

Because of these reasons, to increase resilience in facing novel and unexpected crises, organizations may introduce a dedicated role in charge of challenging decision premises that is responsible for continuously doubting the conventional representation of the situation while it unfolds.

We represent this role in Fig. 2.1. Consistent with Simon's (1991) perspective, we modelled this role within a role system that results from a division of labour aimed at letting individuals specialize in specific areas. Each role features a set of accepted decision premises coherent with the

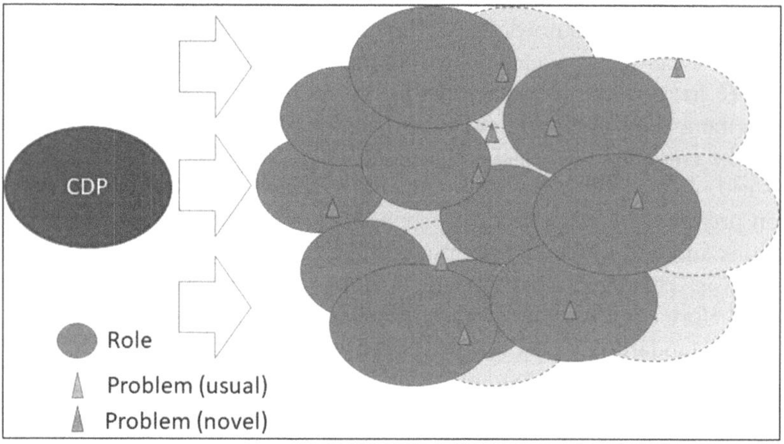

Fig. 2.1 The challenger of decision premises as a role (*Source* Authors own elaboration)

need to monitor and explore a specific subset of problems. Decision premises are 'sticky' and partly define each role and, consequently, the expectations that others have of the actions of the person occupying that role. Therefore, all else equal, we cannot expect roles to evolve significantly on their own. The process of challenging the decision premises, then, is paramount for the ability of the organization to face novel situations, as a novel situation, by definition, is a situation that falls outside the scope of the existing decision premises.

Coherently with this Simonian approach, decision premises are legitimized through a learning process. Each role, as we noted above, encompasses a set of decision premises that are considered legitimate as long as they allow the decision-maker to produce outcomes that are coherent with the design of the role he/she was assigned and, in turn, as long as the role thus played is coherent with organizational goals. The legitimacy of discrete, individual actions is thus mainly a matter of conformity. The ability to face novelty at the organizational level is clearly outside the scope of these actions. Suchman (1995), examining the strategies that organizations employ for maintaining legitimacy, underscores the need to exert bridging efforts that can encompass logics that are different from the ones currently prevailing within the organization/role. One significant example of bridging effort of this kind is the so-called 'doubting Thomases' that have the explicit mandate to question others' taken-for-granted assumptions (Ashforth & Gibbs, 1990). In Fig. 2.1, for the sake of clarity, we represent the process of challenging decision processes as pertaining to a new role (i.e., Challenger of the decision premises, or CDP).

An explicit mandate, however, does not translate automatically in the needed level of legitimacy to act in this fashion. March and Simon (1958) clarify that problem-solving activities can happen because of a process that they call 'recognition'. In this cognitive process, problem-solving actions and problem situations are matched. This process appears obvious for standard roles stemming from division of labour, however, understanding why it can be applied to a role characterized as being devoted to discussing accepted decision premises requires a further step. In fact, we are talking about a role that aims (as a rule) to apply the recognition process to situations that are (or could be) novel. In fact, we claim that the process of challenging decision premises can work under the logic of recognition in two distinct cases. The first such case is when an event, or a series of events, had dire consequences for the survival of the organization and the organization itself only admitted a standard problem-solving logic based on division of labour, roles with sticky decision premises and the ex-ante conviction that all relevant contingencies had been taken care of. In case of failure, it is reasonable to believe that the organization would not only revise the decision premises of each role, or even redesign its system of roles, but also integrate a different logic in decision-making. A second case is the case of organizations facing such an unforgiving environment that constantly discussing the decision premises regulating its problem-solving processes represents a basic strategy to face the risk of annihilation. Further, we should observe that only relying on the principle that a person embodying this role needs to be recognized as an authoritative source of knowledge and competence would entail an inherent element of frailty for the organization.

From this perspective, reasoning about a problem essentially means ascertaining a) where to look for appropriate and legitimate decision premises and b) how to process these premises; what other and apparently unrelated contexts may provide alternative decision premises that seem appropriate? Under different premises, what boundaries of the problems, previously unforeseen, become evident? What new states are unveiled? What future consequences can be inferred? What new domains of expertise gain a critical importance in identifying a solution? Filling this role implies a legitimate challenge to the explanations of the situation that seems to fit most of the evidence and thus urges consideration of new information premises that are otherwise underweighted or missing and the processing of these premises to construct novel representations. To reach this goal, we propose to introduce a new role, associated with the following specific duties: setting novel and different decision premises that provide the grounds of assumption upon which rest formulating and endorsing problem solutions that would otherwise be rejected, as they are not compatible with the conventional beliefs.

Whoever exerts this role has the responsibility to question the accepted decision and goal premises that provide the grounds for any decision-making. In addition, this role implies the ability to develop a new representation of the problem and to use it for the decision to be made. Consequently, problem-solving is not conceived of as a linear sequence of phases but rather as an iterative and circular process, where premises are constantly being questioned as well as the co-evolution of premises, problems and solutions.

In addition, the role also implies enabling organizational members to learn how to use the new representation of a novel problem. In terms of organizational learning, this role entails two complementary processes: connecting new information and knowledge first to the existing culture and second to the existing role system. This process can be hard to undertake when organizations assume that, because of their expertise, everything is already known, and further explorations of the problem may unveil some inconsistencies in the problem representation.

Emergency management organizations can quickly react to critical events by executing complex responses involving various organizations or subunits; nevertheless, this expertise requires relying on a shared and consistent problem representation that may be endangered by new representations.

A Theoretical Perspective on the Everlasting Fire

Conceptualizing organizational resilience as a process of learning to solve novel and unexpected problems led us to consider the combination of decision premises, problem representations and role systems, as proposed by Simon (1991), to explain the organizational capability of dynamically solving new problems. In many instances, resilience is portrayed as the ability of an existing structure of roles to be robust in the face of adversity (Linnenluecke, 2017). In our approach, in contrast, resilience consists of the ability to change by means of learning to scrutinize and challenge the current system of decision premises. To acquire this form of resilience, organizations may deliberately introduce and support the CDP role described above.

The case presented at the beginning of this chapter (second Section) concerned an emergency management organization facing a novel emergency that lies outside the realm of organizational decision premises. After having outlined the theoretical framework, the case is commented below, and further theoretical development is provided.

At first, the emergency resembled a normal fire; nothing was disconcerting or unexpected. Nevertheless, during the operations, firefighters began to notice some discrepancies between what they observed and what they expected. These discrepancies were initially explained according to the usual decision premises. Confronted with the first anomaly, actors thought that they had not seen the fire when they had gone through the basement because of the dense smoke. Confronted with the second anomaly, firefighters thought that fire does not spread from top to bottom. However, from previous experiences, they knew that such a spread could happen through conduits; often, these conduits are not visible. Confronted with the third oddity, that a person was repeatedly seen walking inside the building, firefighters guessed that this was perhaps an employee, as often happens in plants; they also considered the possibility that, because of the smoke, the person in question was not always the same. In terms of sensemaking, the discrepancies triggered a need for explanation (Weick, 1995), which is initially found within the space of the possibilities consistent with the assumed premises. In terms of a trade-off between exploration and exploitation (March, 1991), at the beginning, the problem solvers try to explain the situation by relying on the decision premises and, therefore, by exploiting a consolidated problem representation. Since the discrepancies persist, problem solvers also explore alternative possibilities not backed up by assumed premises. In other words, what we observe is an ambidextrous response, consisting of both exploitation and exploration, that enriches the organizational response and, ultimately, its resilience.

The fundamental discrepancy that forced firefighters to question their representation of the problem was *timing*; after many hours, the fire had not yet been tamed. The longer the fire lasted, the more relevant the discrepancy appeared. Eventually, all the discrepancies were account by, but to make sense of them and to formulate the hypothesis that the arsonist was still around to light additional fires, firefighters needed to reconsider their problem representation by including a possible state that was not initially conceived. In fact, arsons were certainly included into the problem representation conceived by an experienced fire brigade; nevertheless, the accepted decision premises considered the model of an arsonist that lights the fire and then flees the scene. In this case, the fire flared up in a way that was considered inconsistent until the firemen formulated an alternative (novel) hypothesis that contrasted with the accepted decision premises and acted to test the former.

In devising the hypothesis that the arsonist was still lighting fires, the Fire Chief and his Deputy played the role of the CDP. As a matter of fact, they tried to think beyond the consolidated problem representation and learned to solve the novel emergency while it was unfolding. Moreover, while they noticed the discrepancies, they also started challenging their own decision premises. They considered a novel representation of the problem and used that representation to conceive and execute an action (i.e., asking the police to stop the suspect with an excuse) that could allow them to learn whether their hypothesis was supported by additional evidence. The cycle of sensemaking is then complete (Weick, 1995); the surprise generated by the discrepancies moves beyond the need for explanation and, instead, triggers a sequence of actions that eventually produce a revision of the decision premises.

This case suggests further reflections on the role of the CDP that we outlined to increase organizational resilience in dealing with novel and unexpected emergencies.

First, thinking out of the box implies questioning the current system of knowledge, that is, decision premises and accepted representations of the problem. Legitimacy is a critical aspect of this process and of the CDP role. Not surprisingly, in this emergency, the role was filled by experienced officers at the top of the hierarchy. Nevertheless, we wish to emphasize that these conditions are not necessary requirements to fill the role, provided that the CDP role is legitimated by the hierarchy. Second, challenging the decision premises is not the only main task of the CDP; this role implies that organizations learn and use new problem representations constructed on revised decision premises and behave accordingly. To reach this collective achievement, the CDP may rely on organizational communication.

Conclusions

In this chapter, we conceived of organizational resilience as the ability to perform the exploration of a new set of alternatives to solve novel problems when the exploitative application of the current set seems unexpectedly ineffective (March, 1991); at that point, discrepancies are noticed, and they may trigger a revision of the decision premises. Building on Simon (1991) and his insightful remarks on the importance of decision premises to guide organizational behaviour, we can anticipate and explain why organizations may face fundamental difficulties in integrating two distinct perspectives, such as proactiveness and reactiveness, in the context of conflicting decision premises. On the one hand, resilience is intrinsically a processual property and is connected to the unfolding of the events; on the other hand, what the organizations learn to increase their resilience in dealing with a novel crisis is a capability that will be available 'ex-ante' and that we associate with the introduction of a CDP within the role system. The case being explored contributes to a richer understanding of resilience when organizations are dealing with novel or unexpected crises. We argue that preparedness can enhance resilience, when and if it includes learning on how to solve new crises while they unfold. We defined a particular profile within the organizational role structure, the CDP, that may be decisive to identify solutions that initially were not even considered as they were not part of the representation of the problem.

By designing behaviours and roles that support the challenge and reformulation of decision premises and that can be learnt before novel and unexpected adversities take place, but also by leaving their processual deployment and specific content to the time slot when adversities hit, our chapter contributes to the understanding of resilience as a phenomenon that occurs and can be designed both in foresight and while adversities take place.

Acknowledgements Funding for this chapter was provided by the second Research Grant awarded by the Autonomous Province of Bozen-Bolzano as part of the specific research project on Recognizing and reacting to new emergencies: an organizational perspective (funding agreement 2/40.3, 13.02.2014). We thank Guido Ferrari and Ernst Preyer for their help in reconstructing the case described in the chapter. Any mistake or inaccuracy is the sole responsibility of the authors.

References

Ashforth, B. E., & Gibbs, B. W. (1990). The double-edge of organizational legitimation. *Organization Science, 1*(2), 177–194.

Billings, R. S., Milburn, T. W., & Schaalman, M. L. (1980). A model of crisis perception: A theoretical and empirical analysis. *Administrative Science Quarterly, 25*, 300–316.

Boin, A., Comfort, L. K., & Demchak, C. C. (2010). The rise of resilience. In L. K. Comfort, A. Boin, & C. C. Demchak (Eds.), *Designing resilience: Preparing for extreme events* (pp. 1–12). University of Pittsburgh Press.

Boin, A., & McConnell, A. (2007). Preparing for critical infrastructure breakdowns: The limits of crisis management and the need for resilience. *Journal of Contingencies and Crisis Management, 15*(1), 50–59.

Cohen, M. D. (2007). Perspective—Administrative behavior: Laying the foundations for Cyert and March. *Organization Science, 18*(3), 503–506.

Dynes, R. R. (1994). *Community emergency planning: False assumptions and inappropriate analogies, 1994*. University of Delaware, Disaster Research Center Article, 275.

Fisher, D. M., Ragsdale, J. M., & Fisher, E. C. S. (2018). The importance of definitional and temporal issues in the study of resilience. *Applied Psychology*, advance online publication.

Frigotto, M. L. (2018). *Understanding novelty in organizations: A research path across agency and consequences*. Palgrave MacMillan.

Frigotto, M. L. (2020). Reframing resilience on novelty and change. In *Handbook of organizational resilience* (pp. 53–69). Edward Elgar Publishing.

Frigotto, M. L., & Zamarian, M. (2015). Mindful by routine: Evidence from the Italian Air Force Tornado crews flying practices. *Journal of Management & Organization, 21*(3), 321–335.

Grothe-Hammer, M., & Berthod, O. (2017). The programming of decisions for disaster and emergency response: A Luhmannian approach. *Current Sociology, 65*(5), 735–755.

Hémond, Y., & Robert, B. (2012). Preparedness: The state of the art and future prospects. *Disaster Prevention and Management: An International Journal, 21*(4), 404–417.

Lalonde, C. (2007). Crisis management and organizational development: Towards the conception of a learning model in crisis management. *Organization Development Journal, 25*(1), 17–26.

Levac, J., Toal-Sullivan, D., & O'Sullivan, T. L. (2012). Household emergency preparedness: A literature review. *Journal of Community Health, 37*, 725–733.

Linnenluecke, M. K. (2017). Resilience in business and management research: A review of influential publications and a research agenda. *International Journal of Management Reviews, 19*(1), 4–30.

March, J. G. (1991). Exploration and exploitation in organizational learning. *Organization Science, 2*(1), 71–87.

March, J. G., & Simon, H. A. (1958). *Organizations*. Wiley.

Meyer, M., & Simsa, R. (2018). Organizing the unexpected: How civil society organizations dealt with the refugee crisis. *VOLUNTAS: International Journal of Voluntary and Nonprofit Organizations, 29*(6), 1159–1175.

O'Reilly, C. A., III., & Tushman, M. L. (2013). Organizational ambidexterity: Past, present, and future. *Academy of Management Perspectives, 27*(4), 324–338.

Page, R. A., Jr., Tootoonchi, A., & Rahman, S. (2006). Rational decision stages: The breakdown of rationality in strategic planning and implementation. *Competition Forum, 4*(1), 205–212.

Perrow, C. (1999). Organizing to reduce the vulnerabilities of complexity. *Journal of Contingencies and Crisis Management, 7*(3), 150–155.

Perry, R. W., Lindell, M. K., & Tierney, K. J. (Eds.). (2001). *Facing the unexpected: Disaster preparedness and response in the United States*. Joseph Henry Press.

Roberts, P. S., & Wernstedt, K. (2018). Herbert Simon's forgotten legacy for improving decision processes. *International Public Management Journal, 22*(4), 591–616.
Schön, D. A. (1983). *The reflective practitioner*. Ashgate Publishing.
Simon, H. A. (1957). *Administrative behavior* (2nd ed.). Free Press.
Simon, H. A. (1991). Bounded rationality and organizational learning. *Organization Science, 2*(1), 125–134.
Simon, H. A., & Newell, A. (1971). Human problem solving: The state of the theory in 1970. *American Psychologist, 26*(2), 145.
Suchman, M. (1995). Managing legitimacy: strategic and institutional approaches. *Academy of Management Review, 20*(3), 571–610.
Weick, K. E. (1993). The collapse of sensemaking in organizations: The Mann Gulch disaster. *Administrative Science Quarterly, 38*(4), 628–652.
Weick, K. E. (1995). *Sensemaking in organizations* (Vol. 3). Sage.
Weick, K. E., & Roberts, K. H. (1993). Collective mind in organizations: Heedful interrelating on flight decks. *Administrative Science Quarterly, 38*(3), 357–381.
Weick, K. E., & Sutcliffe, K. M. (2001). *Managing the unexpected: Assuring high performance in an age of complexity*. Jossey-Bass.
Wildavsky, A. B. (1988). *Searching for safety*. Transaction Books.
York, T. W., & MacAlister, D. (2015). *Hospital and healthcare security*. Butterworth-Heinemann.

CHAPTER 3

Installing an Action Space for Resilience in Surprising Situations

Johannes M. Lehner, Eva Born, Peter Kelemen, and Rainer Born

Introduction

As soon as this so-called layer touched me, I was overthrown, because it was much bigger than I thought it was.

I didn't even think what to do, I just worked, like a robot. And whatever I did, I did automatically.

J. M. Lehner
Institute of Organization Science, Johannes Kepler University, Linz, Austria
e-mail: johannes.lehner@jku.at

E. Born (✉) · P. Kelemen · R. Born
Department of Corporate Economy, Faculty of Economics and Administration, Masaryk University, Brno, Czech Republic
e-mail: eva.born@econ.muni.cz

P. Kelemen
e-mail: peter.kelemen@mail.muni.cz

R. Pinheiro et al. (eds.), *Towards Resilient Organizations and Societies*, Public Sector Organizations,
https://doi.org/10.1007/978-3-030-82072-5_3

These quotes from a ski-hiker describing how he got hit by an avalanche exemplify the context focused upon in this chapter. Such a situation of surprise leaves no room for beforehand planning or preparation, evaluation and reflection of the event. To survive, the ski-hiker must be trained in certain rules, but he has to simultaneously expand his option space where rules are misleading.

In the current volatile, uncertain, complex, ambiguous environments (D'Aveni, 1995; Fiksel, 2015), under strong competitive pressures (Asano, 2012), organizations are required to cope with crises (Kahn et al., 2013), economic distress (Klehe et al., 2012) and surprises (Buchanan & Denyer, 2013; Sutcliffe & Vogus, 2008). The resulting interest in the value of resilience (Moenkemeyer et al., 2012; Välikangas & Romme, 2013), led to calls for additional research into the antecedents of successfully managing surprise (e.g., Meneghel et al., 2016). On the organizational level this also provides the motivation to explore the relationships and trade-offs between exploitation of existing knowledge and organizational codes and the exploration into new domains of knowledge through organizational learning (March, 1991).

In this chapter we focus on the role of rules in exploitation processes in surprising situations, and in processes of exploration in the sense of expanding the actor's option space where directly applicable rules are lacking or where the rigid following of rules may be detrimental. The goal of this chapter is to answer the following research question: *What is the relationship between types of skill development and resilient action in surprising situations?* For this, we explore the link between types of training and background knowledge and resilient action. We begin with an overview of current research on resilience, adopt a definition of resilience and resilient action. A summary of literature about rules and routines follows and we link these concepts by focusing on a specific mode of skill development, called drill. In the Empirical Study section, we describe the research setting and methods we used to collect and analyse data. Results of the analysis, summarized in the Findings section, are then used to create a model of relationships between modes of skill development and resilient action in situation and surprise. Finally, we discuss the implications of this research.

Theoretical Background

A diverse set of research deals with both the necessity and the rigidity of rules or routines of individual actors and organizations. This has been examined already from various perspectives, such as organizational learning (March, 1991), organizational routines (Feldman, 2000, 2003; Feldman & Pentland, 2003), and by studying the interplay between rule-following and rule-breaking (Ortmann, 2010). Literature on sense-making, such as by Weick (1995), provides further options for exploring the conditions and antecedents for dealing with unexpected situations, particularly by emphasizing the influence of the actor's identity. Somewhat contrasting the primary focus on the organizational level of these contributions, we focus on the individual and view the organization as the context for resilient action.

Resilience and Resilient Action

Resilience has been the subject of research for decades, with a large number of definitions being formulated in various research fields and from different perspectives (Linnenluecke, 2017), sparking the formation of multiple branches of resilience research. One of these branches describes resilience as the ability of a system to bounce back to its original state after encountering adversity (Sawalha, 2015), with some authors asserting that more resilient systems do not only return to their previous state, but come out of the adverse event more prosperous than before (Carvalho et al., 2012). Another branch views resilience as the ability of a system to remain within a certain threshold when faced with adversity. Gaillard (2007) claims that a system is resilient as long as it maintains its original function or identity despite adversity. This may be achieved through adjustments within the system which enable the system to adapt (McCarthy et al., 2017; Ortiz-de-Mandojana & Bansal, 2016). In this chapter, we adopt the view of *resilience* as the ability of a system or an individual to remain within a certain threshold following adverse events, this threshold being represented by the system's or individual's ability to continue operations and maintain its identity.

Means of achieving resilience are also being debated. One line of research suggests that resilience is a result of the implementation of certain structures, strategies (Somers, 2009) and culture (Daskon, 2010) within an organization. Others suggest that resilience results from behaviours at the individual level, which enhance the ability of the entire system to withstand adversity (Lengnick-Hall et al., 2011). We propose to reconcile these two views by adding to the above definition resilience to be potentially supported by specific organizational conditions. This definition of *resilient action* thus corresponds to the use of the term in, for example, Smith et al. (2014), who suggest that specific resilient practices maintain resilience, or Smith et al. (2013), who reserve the term resilient action for actions which address a specific safety barrier.

Antecedents of Resilient Action

The Role of Rules

Knowledge is the ability to draw distinctions between concepts within a certain domain of action based on context and theory (Tsoukas, 2005). According to Gatarik and Born (2012), knowledge is composed of four components: expert knowledge (including experience and expertise), procedural knowledge (including rules and routines), folk- and cultural knowledge and explanatory meta-knowledge. First, we focus on rules, which can be defined as repetitive, unchanging patterns of behaviour. Tsoukas (2005, p. 74) refers to rules as 'generalizations connecting types of behaviour by types of actors to types of outcomes'. In this sense, Tsoukas emphasized the role of a decision-maker's ability to distinguish such situations that fit the type of behaviour mandated by a rule. Based on this distinction, an individual would then decide whether to follow a rule.

Rules provide a means to coordinate and control processes, streamline decision-making by providing a pre-determined response and protect an organization from uncertainty by fixing certain parameters and providing the possibility of predictable behaviour in uncertain situations (Becker, 2004). Additionally, rules may act as shock absorbers at the organizational level by gradually aligning certain aspects of each rule to current demands of an organization's environment (Berente et al., 2016). Moreover, rules can be a resource when attempting to balance and manage conflicting goals in an organization, even allowing an organization to accomplish multiple conflicting goals at the same time by facilitating new connections between members of an organization (Salvato & Rerup, 2018). Certain routines can also lead to new outcomes and novel solutions in organizations (Deken et al., 2016).

Rules can be broken, which traditionally is negatively framed in the organizational literature as a form of deviance (Martin et al., 2013; Tyler & Blader, 2005). Ortmann (2010), however, claims that the possibility of rule-breaking is necessary for the effective functioning of organizations. This is due to what he refers to as *drift*, incremental changes in rules which result in rules no longer fulfilling their purpose. Thus, following rules without reflection may have disastrous results. Ortmann (2010) provides examples of such cases, such as friendly fire occurring in Iraq, with more in literature (e.g., Oliver et al., 2017, 2019; Schakel et al., 2016).

The idea that rules can change over time is supported by Feldman (2000), who argues that the changes result from agents following rules while reflecting on the outcomes. If following a rule has unintended outcomes or does not show the intended outcomes, or if agents perceive a potential of the rule to lead to greater outcomes, they change the rule. These changes occur gradually over repeated instances of rule-following, possibly benign and unnoticed (Feldman, 2003). However, as Ortmann's (2010) concept of drift emphasizes, these small changes may accumulate to the point of no return. A similar effect has been shown on the organizational level for the trade-off between exploration and exploitation already in March's (1991) seminal work. The short-term benefits of rule following, in March's terms following the organizational code, are offset by a lack of code development which is only possible through deviation from rules.

Kœnig et al. (2016) distinguish two types of rules: complex rules which cannot be expected to be followed strictly and absolutely, as they are too specific to fit a large number of situations; and basic rules, which can be expected to be followed strictly by every competent actor, because they are broad enough that they will fit essentially any situation in such a way that strictly following the rule will lead to the fulfillment of its original purpose. To illustrate this distinction Kœnig et al. (2016, p. 5 citing Reynaud, 1993, pp. 35-36) use the complex rule of speed limits and the simple rule of stop signs in traffic. The rule of speed limits in traffic cannot be expected to always be strictly followed, as such strict adherence would defeat the original purpose of the rule: to increase road safety. For example, when overtaking, adhering to the speed limit would make the manoeuvre take longer, thus reducing safety. Contrary to this, the basic rule of stop signs can be expected to always be strictly observed, *ceteris paribus*, as it is broad enough that following it never hurts its original purpose. As such, Kœnig et al. provide an interesting third perspective into the debate about adherence to rules by confirming that there are indeed rules that need to be broken when the situation demands it; but that there are also rules that should never be broken. However, the idea of basic rules works with the assumption of unchanging circumstances and competent actors. In volatile environments where circumstances change often, even basic rules may be required to change to adhere to new facts. Alternatively, a repertoire of basic rules may be created from which members of an organization can choose a basic rule to follow appropriate to the situation at hand.

The Power of Drill

Rules are also viewed as a container through which knowledge is shared (Kieser & Koch, 2008). A widely used technique for transferring rules is drill, used successfully in sports (Reade et al., 2008), in disaster response (Alim et al., 2015), in military training or when teaching mental procedures, such as mathematical operations (Hsiao et al., 2018). We use the term "drill" metaphorically to generalize it to all methods of repetitive training either at teaching settings or jobs, which require trainees to rehears methods, rules, tactics and behavioural patterns over and over again until these patterns can be exercised in an automated manner. By making lower level processes effortless and automatic, drill allows more cognitive capacity to be used for higher level thinking. Additionally, drill supplies actors with a repertoire of broad patterns of behaviour and rules, from which those actors can subsequently choose a response appropriate to their situation. This is in accordance with the notion of basic rules (Kœnig et al., 2016), which are broad enough to be strictly followed. However, drill has also been criticized in the sense that simple drill leads to rigid patterns of thinking and action, reducing flexibility and potential for novelty (Lehtinen et al., 2017). On the other hand, research in teaching mathematics has shown that if properly supplemented, drill can result in innovative solutions (Baroody, 2003). This resonates well with the notion that knowledge is comprised of multiple components (Gatarik & Born, 2012), as simple drill transfers only one of these components, rules. The other components then need to be transferred in some other way as a supplement to drill.

Training for resilience using drill has, so far, received little attention, with research focused instead on training using scenarios of escalating situations (e.g., Bergström et al., 2011), mental therapy and control of thought patterns (e.g., Reivich et al., 2011), or coaching (e.g., Grant et al., 2009). Robertson et al. (2015) offer a systematic review of resilience training interventions used in organizations. The connection between outcomes of drill and resilient action also received little attention. Furthermore, it remains unclear what kind of supplementary knowledge allows use of drilled procedures to create new solutions. This chapter fills this research gap by revealing the link between drill supplemented by background knowledge and resilient action in the field in a military organization. Although change of rules has received attention (e.g., Feldman, 2000; Feldman & Pentland, 2003), little has been revealed about how the purpose of a rule may change. For exploring into this we build on the concept of exaptation.

Exaptation

The term 'exaptation' is used to refer to the process of using old means to achieve new ends. As an example, Gould and Vrba (1982) tell the story of the exaptation of feathers. The original function of feathers was thermoregulation. Only later have feathers been exapted for flight (Gould & Vrba, p. 11). Exaptation as a concept has since made the leap into other areas of research, such as innovation management and entrepreneurship. In innovation management and entrepreneurship, exaptation has been demonstrated as an important process in the creation of new products and new market niches, with cases such as Viagra, a drug originally developed to counter heart disease, being exapted as a means to combat erectile dysfunction (Dew & Sarasvathy, 2016). Additionally, Ching (2016) found that exaptation has a positive effect on organizational performance by allowing organizations to make use of their old assets or perceived junk in new ways, thereby opening new possibilities.

New insights and ideas often emerge as a result of knowledge exchange between actors from different backgrounds (e.g., Andriani & Cattani, 2016). People come up with new theories and ideas as they perceive reality. These possibilities cannot be fully transferred onto them from other actors or rules, there are always potential new possibilities that emerge from actors' interactions with their environment, if those actors are given the freedom to make these interactions and the option of making use of new possibilities when they find them (Felin et al., 2016). Exaptation occurs when old assets are used for new purposes. These assets include such that were designed for some purpose, assets that were originally by-products, or assets that had an unknown purpose or no purpose at all (Garud et al., 2016). This may also apply to knowledge and talent, if organizational conditions allow it. In our case, exaptation is used in the context of learned procedures being used in novel ways to achieve previously unforeseen results. Thus, rules can be the source of not only exploitation, the use of already known solutions, but, through exaptation, also a source of exploration, the creation of new solutions (March, 1991).

Empirical Study

As the empirical context we chose the Austrian Military due to the nature of the environments in which it operates, such as the Golan Heights in Syria, Kosovo, or Chad; places where stakes are high and unexpected events occur frequently, providing a rich source of data about managing surprise. The history of the Austrian Military reaches back centuries, presently relying on professional soldiers, employees and conscripts to achieve its goals. It cooperates with numerous international organizations in peace-keeping missions around the world. The Commander-in-Chief is the Austrian Federal President, though the power of supreme command rests in the hands of the Minister of Defence. The military receives its resources from the federal budget, and its employees are state employees. The goals of the military are set by the interests of the Republic of Austria. From the point of view of publicness, defined as 'the degree to which organizations are affected by political authority' (Bozeman, 1987, p. xi; cf. Walker & Bozeman, 2011), this makes the Austrian Military public to a large degree, as a significant portion of its goals and means to achieve them are determined by political authority. However, through certain elements such as cooperation with private entities, for example, interpreters in missions and deployments, the military maintains a degree of privateness.

We rely on theoretical sampling (Eisenhardt & Graebner, 2007), selecting a setting that matches the described problem. Finding patterns that are outside the scope of ordinary management allows us to place into perspective data that would average out across large categories (Starbuck, 1992). By using an extreme setting, we may uncover what makes individuals, groups and organizations able to cope with surprise. Studies of high reliability focus on environments where high reliability is necessary (Achour & Price, 2010; Gittell et al., 2006).

Another reason for selecting the Austrian Military, as opposed to other military organizations, is their unique style of leadership and approach to training. This doctrine, referred to in this text as mission command tactics (*Auftragstaktik* in German), equips the Austrian Military with high flexibility by allowing autonomy in the decision-making of frontline members in their area of influence (Wittmann, 2012), contributing to the organization's ability to cope with surprise and requiring all members of the Austrian Military (further referred to as 'officers') to be highly trained and well informed. Thus, the setting should provide data concerning methods of employee development.

Research Setting

Respondents for semi-structured interviews were selected based on open-ended pilot interviews with the Editor in Chief of the Austrian Military Journal at the Austrian National Defence Academy, with representatives of the Department for Security Policy and the Department of Planning and Evaluation at the Federal Ministry of Defence and Sports. The pilot interviews resulted in contacts to respondents for semi-structured, narrative-based (Czarniawska, 2004) interviews which provided the core of our data, and in combination with documents also provided triangulation for the ideas that emerged from the qualitative analysis (Jick, 1979; Suddaby, 2006).

Ten respondents were included in semi-structured interviews. These were all men of diverse educational and professional backgrounds and military rank. Seven were commissioned officers (COs), three were non-commissioned officers (NCOs). The NCOs graduated from the Army Sergeant Academy (*Heeresunteroffiziersakademie*) in Enns, Austria. The COs were subject to six years of training and education, including one preparation year, a Bachelor program of three years, and a Master program of two years.

Data collection began after receiving a list of respondents and took place over a period of two months, between November and December 2017. Interviews lasted between 90 and 130 minutes. All interviews were recorded with prior acceptance of respondents, transcribed and sent to their respective respondents for confirmation of accuracy. Data-collection stopped after ten interviews, based on simultaneous data analyses of interviews and supplementary documents revealing category saturation (Strauss & Corbin, 1990).

Analysis

Analysis of interview data follows grounded theory (GT) (Glaser & Strauss, 1967) using techniques of constant comparison, theoretical sensitivity, theoretical sampling and theoretical saturation. First-order categories are generated from personal interpretations of events by people who experienced them (Van Maanen, 1979), utilizing MAXQDA software which facilitated the identification of nestings and overlaps among codes. Based on first-order interpretations, second-order concepts were formulated, which offer a deeper and more theoretical insight into the observed phenomena and their relationships. Two coders met regularly with other members of the research team to gain insight and to be challenged to find alternative explanations for findings. Inter-coder agreement checks were performed to ensure trustworthiness of the research (Lincoln & Guba, 1985).

Findings

We describe the results of our data analysis on the level of second-order concepts leading to a model which connects training practices and behavioural patterns that aid with resilient action in unexpected situations. Although officers train a wide range of routines to guide behaviour, they encounter contexts in which they cannot follow trained procedures. In such circumstances, officers must rely on reflection and evaluation to find new solutions. These include engaging in a set of routines in circumstances different from situations which those routines were created for, as well as completely new actions.

Background Knowledge

> *...they have been briefed thoroughly on the political situation, which parties exist, we had briefings on each and every minister. We had it before we deployed, and we had it within the mission. And whenever newcomers came, we briefed them again.* [R1—01:02:33]

The Austrian Military functions in contexts where it is difficult to predict consequences of actions. Background knowledge of rules stands at the centre of these predictions. It allows the existence of the specific organizational conditions of the Austrian Military and enables behavioural patterns of its members. Therefore, officers are armed with knowledge from various fields relevant to their deployment, such as local geography, politics and national culture. This additional background knowledge allows them to evaluate their situation with greater richness, as they can contextualize situations appropriately.

One respondent described how during his deployment, he intended to build positive relationships with locals, believing it would contribute to the mission. However, he ran into cultural differences, giving an example of men holding his hand when they walked together down the street. Thanks to his background knowledge of the area and local culture, he knew this was a sign of trust. Therefore, he tolerated the behaviour, as he didn't want to lose the trust of the locals and exhibit hostile behaviour.

Officers are briefed on the history of the conflict that they are trying to resolve. This contextual knowledge allows them to judge the relevance of information. Respondents described situations where context knowledge enabled them to decide correctly, such as whether a course of action which would lead to escalation is appropriate. Similarly, economic and social knowledge is also used to judge whether following guidelines benefit the objective of a mission. A respondent describes how he repeatedly had to make the decision whether to arrest certain types of criminals. He argued that while arresting criminals was generally the right thing to do, in this case, the criminal activity in question was the primary source of income for the majority of the country's citizens. Systematically arresting these criminals would thus result in an increase in overall poverty. The respondent therefore sought different solutions.

Officers obtain background knowledge through a combination of organizational systems of training, and of personally motivated engagement. Regular debriefing takes place following every mission. During debriefing sessions, assessments are made of what did or did not work during the mission, and why. Briefing sessions also happen at the start of a mission, which also repeat every time new officers arrive at the area of deployment, so that they all have the necessary background knowledge. The basis for these briefings, as well as ground rules of engagement and common practices, is regularly updated based on new knowledge. As for background knowledge obtained through personal engagement, this can take place in the form of talks with individuals from the area of deployment, such as expats or refugees. Officers understand that background knowledge is included in their training because wrong behaviour at the wrong time can lead to failure of a mission. Additionally, background knowledge also allows officers to reflect on their situation in greater detail. This combined with the knowledge of the limits of applicability of routines results in the ability to make good decisions even in volatile situations.

Training

> *You grip (parachute string) in your right hand, you pull first right, wait two seconds, then you pull left. It works automatically, you do not need to think about it.* [R7—00:27:51]

Officers undergo rigorous training to ensure that they are prepared for any challenge. Training takes years and covers a lot of ground. One might say that training in the Austrian Military never ends, as the respondents underwent multiple extra training courses over the duration of their military service. Even during deployment, they keep training and learning new things.

Outputs of training in the Austrian Military include automatized action and possession of background knowledge. Automatized action is the result of drill, a type of training which consists of repeating the same set of steps. Based on data, two interconnected types of drill were identified, pure drill and preaptative drill. Pure drill refers to the basic military training consisting of repeated sets of steps. These sets are repeated until they can be executed without thinking, thus making mental capacity available for other cognition. Pure drill has the goal of enabling ***automatized*** action, its result can be compared to a guitarist switching the positions of his fingers between chords. A guitarist thinks about which chord to play, not where his fingers need to go. Officers describe experiencing a similar feeling, acting out certain sets of procedures without thinking about the individual steps. Pure drill is also used to teach rules of behaviour in certain situations, what kind of information is necessary for certain decisions, or use of certain equipment. New drilled procedures can be developed during deployment. One respondent stated that they organized a competition with such a goal, which resulted in techniques discovered during the mission being incorporated into drilled procedures.

Learning only through drill may have unintended consequences. A respondent described a situation that almost escalated due to soldiers following drilled behaviour. Coming suddenly under fire from an unknown assailant, the soldiers prepared their guns and almost opened fire. However, in this case, returning fire would have been the wrong decision. The respondent told his soldiers not to fire and found out that the person firing at them was a panicking policeman. To prevent escalations in such situations, drill is supplemented with education of background knowledge, resulting in preaptative drill. Supplementing pure drill with background knowledge thus results in a readiness to adapt to new situations before these new situations occur.

The second possible supplement to pure drill is experience of new contexts. This gives officers opportunities to consider the application and limits of routines. Unexpected orders require a check of drilled procedures and routines for the possibility of their application and their limitations. Exposure to different contexts in training and experience enhances analogical capabilities which have been found also as part of exaptative innovation (Mastrogiorgio & Gilsing, 2016, p. 1422), where the ability to link different domains of knowledge and experience creates the possibility of 'creative synthesis'. By combining drill and context learning of background knowledge, officers receive experience of congruity by repeatedly applying routines, as well as experience of disruption of congruity by breaking routines in new contexts. This process has been labelled *punctuated incongruity* by Patil and Tetlock (2014).

Stabilizing the Action System

> *...I said to myself: wait a minute. What is really important for you now, that the space is narrow, that is not really important. I get enough air, I can move...you must just work through these structured procedures.* [R7—00:15:55]

Officers need to cope with situations that put them under high mental and emotional pressure, yet they rarely panic or become disorganized. Instead, respondents reported that even in situations of high stress, they were able to remain calm. They maintain their calm using specific techniques, such as situations assessment, which is trained through drill.

Aside from the drilled situation assessment technique, respondents developed a practice of short-term self-induced tunnel vision. The individual focuses his attention on one point, such as basic biological functions. After that, the individual expands his focus, thereby preventing himself from being overwhelmed by simultaneously occurring stimuli. Short-term tunnel vision may seem like it would prevent individuals from forming a complete picture of their surroundings. However, for example, Weick (1993) demonstrates that an unstable action system and lost sense of reality leads to a breakdown in operations. Without stabilizing via short-term tunnel vision, the individual would already be unable to take action. Additionally, once stability of the action system is lost, it is very difficult to gain it back again. This means that it may be more beneficial to lose a few seconds of awareness and stabilize the action system, than it is to lose a long time of awareness to lack of stability.

Automatized action contributes to stabilizing the action system in a completely unknown situation by allowing officers to cool down, reflect on the situation and stabilize *while* simultaneously taking steps to reduce the severity of the situation; such as when an officer was able to figure out the reason why his reserve parachute would not open after his primary parachute failed in freefall, while he was undertaking the drilled steps for opening the parachute. Because officers do not need to think about these first-reaction steps, they can instead focus on maintaining their stability, calming down and reflecting. Thus, automatized action may function as a shock absorber.

In addition to drilled procedures, horizontally expanded expertise, *i.e.* learning about things from outside one's primary domain of expertise, allows for successful coping with situations that are completely unpredictable and new. A respondent described how his horizontally expanded expertise allowed him to maintain focus in a new situation. He underwent a training course about landmine injuries, which falls outside his primary domain of expertise, by looking at pictures of such injuries. This course proved essential, as he encountered a landmine accident during a mission after passing the course. The respondent decided to treat victims until help arrived. Though the injuries were gruesome, the respondent was able to keep calm and work through the procedures.

Expanding Option Space

> *I just came up with that. I thought, how can I get rid of this as soon as possible, as simply as possible?* [R6—00:25:13]

Officers often find themselves in situations that can be characterized as existing in *Fog of war*, i.e. an environment where information necessary for timely decisions is not readily available. There is uncertainty, which may be reduced with routines and preparation. There are, however, situations where this isn't an option. One case is situations that have occurred unexpectedly and for the first time, so there are no specific routines to follow. Another case is when the routines are in place, but the situation differs sufficiently from the model situation upon which the rules were based, so the routines do not fit. After the action system is stabilized, it is decided based on sufficient background knowledge whether the routine should be followed, or whether new solutions need to be found. In such cases, officers conduct an analysis of the situation, which serves as basis for future behaviour and is part of automatized behaviour. During the analysis, multiple factors are considered, including the consequences of various options of future action. The result of the analysis is usually a new solution. Expanding the option space provides the opportunity for learning on the individual and organizational level. Once a new solution is found, the individual or group remembers it and may use it again in the future. As for organizational learning, debriefing sessions are one example of processes that allow it.

Coming up with the solution is made possible in part by horizontal expansion of expertise during training. In addition to finding new solutions, analyses enable individuals to choose the right sequence of automatized steps in the right situation. In this context, respondents likened drill to a toolbox from which the right tool is chosen for the right situation. This choice of tool is dependent on sufficient background knowledge about the tool and the situation. If there is enough time for evaluation and reflection, officers rely on a supporting staff composed of Non-Commissioned Officers (NCOs) who provide the analysis and a set of viable solutions. The officer then chooses an option from the set or rejects them all and comes up with his own solution. However, responsibility for the decision lies upon the deciding officer. This structured process generally leads to decisions of higher quality. If there is no time for this approach, the individual must decide alone while maintaining a structured approach, made possible by remaining mentally stable and by possessing knowledge of which factors are relevant in a specific situation. Officers of the Austrian Military are required to possess this knowledge.

A Relational Model Between Skill Development and Resilient Action in Surprising Situations

Our findings show that drill takes the form of teaching routines through repetition, as well as the form of education of background knowledge as a supplement to routines. Drill prepares actors for well-known, expected and recurring situations. Beyond that, drill has implications for dealing with the unexpected, providing officers with the knowledge of routines. This knowledge of drilled procedures enables automatized action, building on autonomous cognitive processes, referred to as Type 1 thinking (Kahneman, 2003; Laureiro-Martínez & Brusoni, 2018). In situations where pressure might lead to panic, automatized action absorbs shock, stabilizes the action system and provides a first response. Possession of routines increases the ability to stabilize the action system, a common behavioural pattern identified in successful dealing with unexpected events, and allows for greater control over one's cognitive processes (Kahneman, 2003).

Drill is supplemented with background knowledge through education to enable reflection during action, re-interpretation and exaptation of those routines. For example, one respondent used his knowledge of aerodynamics and trained practice of moving one's body in the air for the purpose of opening his reserve parachute when it initially failed to open. Supplementary background knowledge transforms pure drill into preaptative drill, by serving as a basis for reflection of potential consequences of actions, limits of rules and their applications in situations of low pressure. This allows for decision-making in situations of low pressure beyond simple rule following and exploitation of routines. The preaptation of drilled routines may facilitate innovation, expansion of option space and change of drilled procedures. Even in situations of high pressure, background knowledge allows for expansion of option space by providing context.

Exposure to new situations provides context to knowledge acquired in training. Obtained expertise allows more appropriate use of drilled routines, if expansion is vertical by repetition within the same type of situation. However, if expertise is expanded horizontally, across different situations, it allows exaptation of learned practices and innovation, as was the case with Respondent 7 who used a rope to send signals instead of a malfunctioning radio. The relationships between the forms of training, knowledge and behavioural patterns supporting dealing with unexpected

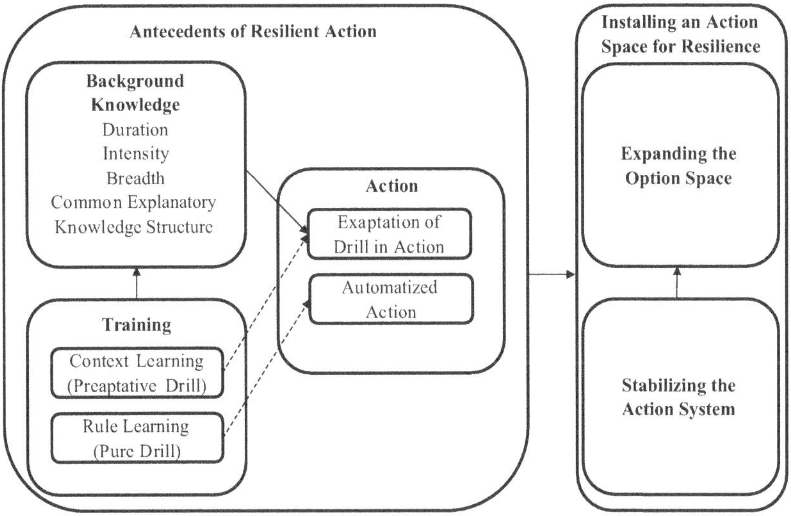

Fig. 3.1 Relationships between types of skill development and resilient action in situations of surprise (*Source* Authors' own work, based on research data)

events are visualized in Fig. 3.1. In surprising situations, pure drill supplemented by background knowledge allows automatized action and exaptation of previously learned procedures, thereby allowing actors to stabilize and reflect upon their situation. If this stability and reflection is maintained, appropriate and potentially new solutions may be found that enable actors to maintain operations and identity despite the mental and temporal pressures characteristic of surprising situations.

Discussion and Conclusion

Our research highlights the underappreciated role of drill in dealing with unexpected situations. We distinguish pure drill, capturing its traditional meaning, and preaptative drill, referring to findings in evolutionary biology (Gould & Vrba, 1982). We assume that there are certain forms of drill, analogical to repeating cycles of variation, selection and retention, which provide surplus skills, which eventually prove to be exaptative. Although the concept of exaptation has been explored in organizational literature before in studies of innovation (e.g., Dew & Sarasvathy, 2016), this study is, to the best of our knowledge, the first to demonstrate the impact of training on the ability to deal with unexpected situations. Our results show that drill, even the pure one, may function as a source or even means for exaptation by providing a pool of learning experiences. Seemingly redundant learning experiences obtained through drill might help to expose and to transfer these patterns or explanatory structures to different contexts. Thus, drill provides tests of the impact of implicit explanatory background knowledge and thus facilitates the adaptation of these patterns. Furthermore, our research results show that rules can act as a shock absorber, which is in line with previous findings (*e.g.* March & Shapira, 1987). However, we expand upon this notion by showing that rules help absorb shock not only by adjusting themselves at the organizational level over time, but also by providing the possibility to act on the individual level while thinking about the current situation and coming up with new ideas. We also shed light on the role of rules in exploration processes (March, 1991) as a facilitator of finding new solutions.

This chapter contributes to discussion of training and management development, presently mainly focused on cognitive learning and single events of experiential learning (e.g., Shotter & Tsoukas, 2014; Waddock & Lozano, 2013), by revealing possible links between different types of drill and the ability to manage surprise. The results show that both forms of drill contribute to managing surprise. Pure drill provides behavioural patterns and skills, which enable automatized action in situations where pressure is too high for reflection. Automatized action is a result of exaptation of behavioural patterns gained through pure drill. Pure drill can be enhanced by background knowledge of rules through education and experience, leading to preaptative drill. Education about explanatory background knowledge leads into the research of cognitive science (e.g., Born & Gatarik, 2013; Bruner, 1990) leading to an ability to understand when and why behaviour should follow a given stimulus. Preaptative drill therefore facilitates coping with unexpected situations in which individuals still have time and internal stability to reflect.

The study findings suggest that incorporating explanatory background knowledge of learned behaviours into training may contribute to coping with surprise. This topic deserves further exploration, including the presence and impact of preaptative drill in other fields, e.g. how education or background knowledge can be effectively integrated into organizations' training systems. The links between background knowledge in training and behaviours leading to successful coping with unexpected situations need to be reinforced with further research. This can be realized using investigations similar to the one described in this chapter, within new contexts, such as business organizations, and organizations in cultures different from the organizational setting investigated in this study. These investigations should focus on discovering cases that either support or refute the links suggested here.

The fact that our data are derived from the military contexts implies both limits and additional conclusions. Owing to its high degree of publicness (Bozeman, 1987), certain limitations are placed on the Austrian Military and its members, such as Rules of Engagement for certain missions, international law, or guidelines of international mission coordinators, such as NATO. Although these limitations certainly constrain decision-making, they may also guide it and serve as additional rules in the already wide toolset of military servicemen in surprising situations. Adherence to these kinds of rules does, however, contribute to the uniqueness of the Austrian Military as a subject of research, and their existence should be kept in mind when interpreting the results of the research. The public sector in general, including such heterogenous fields like the military or health care, is highly institutionalized and regulated through a plethora of rules. Thus, the discussion of rules in this chapter and the insights into drill as a source of exapted rules has special relevance for this sector. In addition, however, other sectors which are usually considered to be more dynamic and where both rules and drill are frequently dismissed as hindering adaptation to new developments might reconsider the necessity for drill.

Although our research focuses on the antecedents of individuals' ability to handle surprise, some broader conclusions at the organizational level can be made. So far, an organization's explorative capabilities have been proposed to be dependent primarily on structural conditions, such as its ambidexterity (Gibson & Birkinshaw, 2004) or environmental moderators (e.g., Jansen et al., 2006). Our results suggest that training and background knowledge for continuous development of organizational code may simultaneously enhance an organization's capability for exploitation and exploration. In these contexts, rule-breaking has obtained overly negative connotations in literature and in practice. We follow up on the idea of rule-breaking with the notion of preaptative drill, which points to the necessity of both rule-following and rule-breaking, the latter being contingent upon sufficient background knowledge. The findings of our research especially highlight the role of explanatory background knowledge as essential for resilient behaviour in critical situations. Together with drill to learn rules, for which we used the term exaptative drill, this could be also paraphrased as reflective and corrective use of rules. Such utilization of rules depends on knowledge of how those rules were created to understand the limits of the application of rules based on context. How the neglect of context-dependence may lead to disasters has been shown prominently in several reports (e.g., Weick, 1993).

Generalizing from individual behaviour, which was the focus of this chapter, we propose that enabling for reflective correction in the application of explanatory knowledge provides the basis for survival even in rigid organizations and can help stabilize the system and secure resilience in critical, unexpected situations. Our findings, summarized in Fig. 3.1, provide some guidance for designing training systems and policies. Drill should not only be established to train behaviours in single situations, but the context of training shall be changed to allow to test behaviours in different situations and to force reflection on the power of drilled procedures. This provides rules and trained procedures with a surplus as a first basis for exaptation of rules. This may be combined with courses and seminars which provide background knowledge on the coming about of rules, their history, and their ultimate goal.

Acknowledgements Funding for this chapter was provided by the Grant Agency of Masaryk University (GAMU) as part of the Specific research project MUNI/A/1223/2018 *Rozvoj dovedností a znalostí pro zvládání nečekaných situací* (Development of skills and knowledge for management of unexpected situations).

References

Achour, N., & Price, A. D. F. (2010). Resilience strategies of healthcare facilities: Present and future. *International Journal of Disaster Resilience in the Built Environment, 1*(3), 264–276.

Alim, S., Kawabata, M., & Nakazawa, M. (2015). Evaluation of disaster preparedness training and disaster drill for nursing students. *Nurse Education Today, 35*(1), 25–31.

Andriani, P., & Cattani, G. (2016). Exaptation as source of creativity, innovation, and diversity: Introduction to the special section. *Industrial and Corporate Change, 25*(1), 115–131.

Asano, K. (2012). *Rethinking a business continuity plan (BCP): What should companies learn from the Great East Japan Earthquake* (NRI Papers No. 173). Tokyo: Nomura Research Institute Ltd. Online at: https://www.nri.com/global/opinion/papers/2012/pdf/np2012173.pdf.

Baroody, A. J. (2003). The development of adaptive expertise and flexibility: The integration of conceptual and procedural knowledge. In A. J. Baroody & A. Dowker (Eds.), *The development of arithmetic concepts and skills: Constructive adaptive expertise* (pp. 1–33). Lawrence Erlbaum Associates.

Becker, M. C. (2004). Organizational routines: A review of the literature. *Industrial and Corporate Change, 13*(4), 643–678.

Berente, N., Lyytinen, K., Yoo, Y., & King, J. L. (2016). Routines as shock absorbers during organizational transformation: Integration, control, and NASA's enterprise information system. *Organization Science, 27*(3), 551–572.

Bergström, J., Dahlström, N., Dekker, S., & Petersen, K. (2011). Training organisational resilience in escalating situations. In E. Hollnagel, J. Pariès, D. Woods, & J. Wreathall (Eds.), *Resilience engineering in practice: A guidebook* (pp. 45–57). Ashgate.

Born, R., & Gatarik, E. (2013). Cognitive science and knowledge management: Reflecting the limits of decision making. In S. Kreitler (Ed.), *Cognition and motivation: Forging an interdisciplinary perspective* (pp. 321–351). Cambridge University Press.

Bozeman, B. (1987). *All organizations are public: Bridging public and private organizational theories*. Jossey-Bass Inc Publications.

Bruner, J. (1990). *Acts of meaning*. Harvard University Press.

Buchanan, D. A., & Denyer, D. (2013). Researching tomorrow's crisis: Methodological innovations and wider implications. *International Journal of Management Reviews, 15*(2), 205–224.

Carvalho, H., Cruz-Machado, V., & Tavares, J. G. (2012). A mapping framework for assessing supply chain resilience. *International Journal of Logistics Systems and Management, 12*(3), 354–373.

Ching, K. (2016). Exaptation dynamics and entrepreneurial performance: Evidence from the internet video industry. *Industrial and Corporate Change, 25*(1), 181–198.

Czarniawska, B. (2004). *Narratives in social science research*. Sage.

D'Aveni, R. A. (1995). Coping with hypercompetition: Utilizing the new 7-S's framework. *Academy of Management Perspectives, 9*(3), 45–57.

Daskon, C. D. (2010). Cultural resilience—The roles of cultural traditions in sustaining rural livelihoods: A case study from rural Kandyan villages in Central Sri Lanka. *Sustainability, 2*(4), 1080–1100.

Deken, F., Carlile, P. R., Berends, H., & Lauche, K. (2016). Generating novelty through interdependent routines: A process model of routine work. *Organization Science, 27*(3), 659–677.

Dew, N., & Sarasvathy, S. D. (2016). Exaptation and niche construction: Behavioral insights for an evolutionary theory. *Industrial and Corporate Change, 25*(1), 167–179.

Eisenhardt, K. M., & Graebner, M. E. (2007). Theory building from cases: Opportunities and challenges. *The Academy of Management Journal, 50*(1), 25–32.

Feldman, M. S. (2000). Organizational routines as a source of continuous change. *Organization Science, 11*(6), 611–629.

Feldman, M. S. (2003). A performative perspective on stability and change in organizational routines. *Industrial and Corporate Change, 12*(4), 727–752.

Feldman, M. S., & Pentland, B. T. (2003). Reconceptualizing organizational routines as a source of flexibility and change. *Administrative Science Quarterly, 48*(1), 94–118.

Felin, T., Kauffman, S., Mastrogiorgio, A., & Mastrogiorgio, M. (2016). Factor markets, actors, and affordances. *Industrial and Corporate Change, 25*(1), 133–147.

Fiksel, J. (2015). *Resilient by design: Creating businesses that adapt and flourish in a changing world* (2nd ed.). Island Press.

Gaillard, J. C. (2007). Resilience of traditional societies in facing natural hazards. *Disaster Prevention and Management: An International Journal, 16*(4), 522–544.

Garud, R., Gehman, J., & Giuliani, A. P. (2016). Technological exaptation: A narrative approach. *Industrial and Corporate Change, 25*(1), 149–166.

Gatarik, E., & Born, R. (2012). *Sharing expertise als Kern von Wissens management*. Springer-Verlag.

Gibson, C. B., & Birkinshaw, J. (2004). The antecedents, consequences, and mediating role of organizational ambidexterity. *Academy of Management Journal, 47*, 209–226.

Gittell, J. H., Cameron, K., Lim, S., & Rivas, V. (2006). Relationships, layoffs, and organizational resilience: Airline industry responses to September 11. *The Journal of Applied Behavioral Science, 42*(3), 300–329.

Glaser, B. G., & Strauss, A. L. (1967). *The discovery of grounded theory: Strategies for qualitative research*. Aldine.

Gould, S., & Vrba, E. (1982). Exaptation—A missing term in the science of form. *Paleobiology, 8*(1), 4–15.

Grant, A. M., Curtayne, L., & Burton, G. (2009). Executive coaching enhances goal attainment, resilience and workplace well-being: A randomised controlled study. *The Journal of Positive Psychology, 4*(5), 396–407.

Hsiao, H. S., Lin, C. Y., Chen, J. C., & Peng, Y. F. (2018). The influence of a mathematics problem-solving training system on first-year middle school students. *Eurasia Journal of Mathematics, Science and Technology Education, 14*(1), 77–93.

Jansen, J. J. P., Van Den Bosch, F. A. J., & Volberda, H. W. (2006). Exploratory innovation, exploitative innovation, and performance: Effects of organizational antecedents and environmental moderators. *Management Science, 52*(11), 1661.

Jick, T. D. (1979). Mixing qualitative and quantitative methods: Triangulation in action. *Administrative Science Quarterly, 24*(4), 602–611.

Kahn, W. A., Barton, M. A., & Fellows, S. (2013). Organizational crises and the disturbance of relational systems. *Academy of Management Review., 38*(3), 377–396.

Kahneman, D. (2003). A perspective on judgment and choice: Mapping bounded rationality. *American Psychologist, 58*(9), 697–720.

Kieser, A., & Koch, U. (2008). Bounded rationality and organizational learning based on rule changes. *Management Learning, 39*(3), 329–347.

Klehe, U. C., Van Vianen, A. E., & Zikic, J. (2012). Coping with economic stress: Introduction to the special issue. *Journal of Organizational Behavior, 33*(6), 745–751.

Kœnig, G., Vandangeon-Derumez, I., Marty, M. C., Auroy, Y., & Dumond, J. P. (2016). Compliance with basic rules: The challenge of dialogical, enabling and disciplinary management. *M@n@gement, 19*(1), 1–45.

Laureiro-martínez, D., & Brusoni, S. (2018). Cognitive flexibility and adaptive decision-making: Evidence from a laboratory study of expert decision makers. *Strategic Management Journal, 39*(4), 1031–1058.

Lehtinen, E., Hannula-Sormunen, M., McMullen, J., & Gruber, H. (2017). Cultivating mathematical skills: From drill-and-practice to deliberate practice. *ZDM, 49*(4), 625–636.

Lengnick-Hall, C. A., Beck, T. E., & Lengnick-Hall, M. L. (2011). Developing a capacity for organizational resilience through strategic human resource management. *Human Resource Management Review, 21*(3), 243–255.

Lincoln, Y. S., & Guba, E. G. (1985). *Naturalistic inquiry*. Sage.

Linnenluecke, M. K. (2017). Resilience in business and management research: A review of influential publications and a research agenda. *International Journal of Management Reviews, 19*(1), 4–30.

March, J. G. (1991). Exploration and exploitation in organizational learning. *Organization Science, 2*(1), 71–87.

March, J. G., & Shapira, Z. (1987). Managerial perspectives on risk and risk taking. *Management Science, 33*(11), 1404–1418.

Martin, A. W., Lopez, S. H., Roscigno, V. J., & Hodson, R. (2013). Against the rules: Synthesizing types and processes of bureaucratic rulebreaking. *Academy of Management Review, 38*(4), 550–574.

Mastrogiorgio, M., & Gilsing, V. (2016). Innovation through exaptation and its determinants: The role of technological complexity, analogy making & patent scope. *Research Policy, 45*(7), 1419–1435.

McCarthy, I. P., Collard, M., & Johnson, M. (2017). Adaptive organizational resilience: An evolutionary perspective. *Current Opinion in Environmental Sustainability, 28*, 33–40.

Meneghel, I., Borgogni, L., Miraglia, M., Salanova, M., & Martínez, I. M. (2016). From social context and resilience to performance through job satisfaction: A multilevel study over time. *Human Relations, 69*(11), 2047–2067.

Moenkemeyer, G., Hoegl, M., & Weiss, M. (2012). Innovator resilience potential: A process perspective of individual resilience as influenced by innovation project termination. *Human Relations, 65*(5), 627–655.

Oliver, N., Calvard, T., & Potočnik, K. (2017). Cognition, technology, and organizational limits: Lessons from the Air France 447 disaster. *Organization Science, 28*(4), 729–743.

Oliver, N., Calvard, T., & Potočnik, K. (2019). Safe limits, mindful organizing and loss of control in commercial aviation. *Safety Science, 120*, 772–780.

Ortiz-de-Mandojana, N., & Bansal, P. (2016). The long-term benefits of organizational resilience through sustainable business practices. *Strategic Management Journal, 37*(8), 1615–1631.

Ortmann, G. (2010). On drifting rules and standards. *Scandinavian Journal of Management, 26*(2), 204–214.

Patil, S. V., & Tetlock, P. E. (2014). Punctuated incongruity: A new approach to managing trade-offs between conformity and deviation. *Research in Organizational Behavior, 34*, 155–171.

Reade, I., Rodgers, W., & Spriggs, K. (2008). New ideas for high performance coaches: A case study of knowledge transfer in sport science. *International Journal of Sports Science & Coaching, 3*(3), 335–354.

Reivich, K. J., Seligman, M. E., & McBride, S. (2011). Master resilience training in the US Army. *American Psychologist, 66*(1), 25.

Reynaud, J. D. (1993). *Les règles du jeu*. Paris: ArmandColin.

Robertson, I. T., Cooper, C. L., Sarkar, M., & Curran, T. (2015). Resilience training in the workplace from 2003 to 2014: A systematic review. *Journal of Occupational and Organizational Psychology, 88*(3), 533–562.

Salvato, C., & Rerup, C. (2018). Routine regulation: Balancing conflicting goals in organizational routines. *Administrative Science Quarterly, 63*(1), 170–209.

Sawalha, I. H. S. (2015). Managing adversity: Understanding some dimensions of organizational resilience. *Management Research Review, 38*(4), 346–366.

Schakel, J. K., van Fenema, P. C., & Faraj, S. (2016). Shots fired! Switching between practices in police work. *Organization Science, 27*(2), 391–410.

Shotter, J., & Tsoukas, H. (2014). In search of phronesis: Leadership and the art of judgment. *Academy of Management Learning & Education, 13*(2), 224–243.

Smith, M. W., Ash, J. S., Sittig, D. F., & Singh, H. (2014). Resilient practices in maintaining safety of health information technologies. *Journal of Cognitive Engineering and Decision Making, 8*(3), 265–282.

Smith, M. W., Giardina, T. D., Murphy, D. R., Laxmisan, A., & Singh, H. (2013). Resilient actions in the diagnostic process and system performance. *BMJ Quality and Safety, 22*(12), 1006–1013.

Somers, S. (2009). Measuring resilience potential: An adaptive strategy for organizational crisis planning. *Journal of Contingencies and Crisis Management, 17*(1), 12–23.

Starbuck, W. H. (1992). Learning by knowledge-intensive firms. *Journal of Management Studies, 29*(6), 713–740.

Strauss, A. L., & Corbin, J. (1990). *Basics of qualitative research.* Sage.

Suddaby, R. (2006). From the editors: What grounded theory is not. *Academy of Management Journal, 49*(4), 633–642.

Sutcliffe, K., & Vogus, T. J. (2008). The pragmatics of resilience. In K. M. Sutcliffe & T. J. Vogus (Eds.), *The SAGE handbook of new approaches in management and organization* (pp. 498–500). SAGE Publications Inc.

Tsoukas, H. (2005). *Complex knowledge: Studies in organizational epistemology.* Oxford University Press.

Tyler, T. R., & Blader, S. L. (2005). Can businesses effectively regulate employee conduct? The antecedents of rule following in work settings. *Academy of Management Journal, 48*(6), 1143–1158.

Välikangas, L., & Romme, A. G. L. (2013). How to design for strategic resilience: A case study in retailing. *Journal of Organization Design, 2*, 44–53.

Van Maanen, J. (1979). The fact of fiction in organizational ethnography. *Administrative Science Quarterly, 24*(4), 539–550.

Waddock, S., & Lozano, J. M. (2013). Developing more holistic management education: Lessons learned from two programs. *Academy of Management Learning & Education, 12*(2), 265–284.

Walker, R. M., & Bozeman, B. (2011). Publicness and organizational performance. *Journal of Public Administration Research and Theory, 21*(Suppl 3), i279–i281.

Weick, K. E. (1993). The collapse of sensemaking in organizations: The Mann Gulch disaster. *Administrative Science Quarterly, 38*(4), 628–652.

Weick, K. E. (1995). *Sensemaking in organizations* (Vol. 3). Sage.

Wittmann, J. (2012). *Auftragstaktik—Just a command technique or the core pillar of mastering the military operational art?* Miles-Verlag.

CHAPTER 4

Building Resilience in Temporary Organizations: Lessons from a Shipyard

Anne Russel, Stéphanie Tillement, and Benoit Journé

Introduction

This chapter discusses the organizational and occupational dimensions of sustained reliable performance (Perrow, 2011) in temporary organizing contexts. Studying organizations through a temporary lens (Söderlund, 2000) has enabled the identification of clear differences between permanent organizations, mainly characterized by "*production processes and continual development*" (Lundin & Söderholm, 1995, p. 439), and temporary organizations, characterized by having a predetermined lifetime. Temporary organizations have been defined as new forms of organizations that adapt to deal with new "*problems concerning the complexity*

A. Russel (✉) · S. Tillement · B. Journé
Département SSG, IMT Atlantique, Nantes, France
e-mail: anne.russel@imt-atlantique.fr

S. Tillement
e-mail: stephanie.tillement@imt-atlantique.fr

B. Journé
e-mail: benoit.journe@univ-nantes.fr

R. Pinheiro et al. (eds.), *Towards Resilient Organizations and Societies*,
Public Sector Organizations,
https://doi.org/10.1007/978-3-030-82072-5_4

and the uncertainty of the task, the complexity among the interdependent activities, the task's uniqueness, the lack of standardized procedures and the temporary nature of the task" (Söderlund, 2000, p. 64). Thus, it seems that temporary organizations and temporary forms of organizing are an appropriate solution for dealing with organizational complexity.

The aforementioned authors also show that complexity presents a risk for organizational performance and can impact the organization's ability to adapt to a frequently changing environment or to a new industrial tempo. In our case, we suggest switching from a temporary organization perspective (often restricted to project-based organizations in the project management literature) to the more dynamic approach of temporary *organizing*. We define *organizing* as the emergent process of production of an organization by the organizational actors and through the reflectivity of actors (Weick, 1979).

Other authors emphasize the safety issues that stem from organizational complexity. Indeed, normal accident theory (NAT) (Perrow, 2011) and theory about high reliability organizations (HROs) (Weick & Roberts, 1993) show how major accidents can be caused by complexity. NAT demonstrates that complex and tightly coupled systems, such as in nuclear power plants, are exposed to a high level of risk and will inevitably have accidents. Perrow shows that, in the case of the Three Mile Island accident, it was the characteristics of the system itself that made the accident inevitable.

In contrast, the resilience engineering perspective (Furuta, 2015; Hollnagel et al., 2006) views resilience as part of a systemic process which aims to prevent major accidents from happening: "*From a systemic view, resilience is the intrinsic ability of a system to adjust its functioning prior to, during, or following changes and disturbances, so that it can sustain required operations under both expected and unexpected conditions*" (Furuta, 2015, p. 446). The different conceptions of resilience that are held by the resilience engineering theorists and the high reliability theorists emphasize the importance of its temporal dimension. High reliability theorists seek to understand the principles that organizations rely on to manage the unexpected: while developing a very dynamic approach, they oppose the anticipation of events to their containment. Resilience is one principle that can be used to contain unexpected events when they occur and is therefore associated with re-activeness. In their view, resilience is mainly an ex-post strategy. Hollnagel et al. (2006) and Furuta (2015) adopt a more holistic perspective of resilience which encompasses anticipation and therefore goes beyond the dichotomy between ex-ante and ex-post dimensions of resilience. In this chapter, we adopt the resilience engineering perspective, which encompasses what happens before, during and after unexpected events. More precisely, we adopt Hollnagel's vision of resilience as enabling safety by "*looking at what goes right*" rather than "*what goes wrong*" (Hollnagel, 2016, p. 189).

It therefore seems that, when dealing with issues related to high levels of safety in complex settings, it is longstanding organizations with strong organizational routines that offer the most appropriate forms of organizing. However, few researchers have looked at how actors in temporary organizing contexts, where routines and habits are not shared by all members of the organization, enhance and sustain resilience when facing uncertainty in safety–critical contexts (Saunders, 2015; Saunders et al., 2016). For instance, in complex projects, where work is always singular and is distributed between several companies and occupations, a common organizational safety culture or individual sensemaking appear insufficient to support reliable performance.

This chapter addresses this gap in the literature by demonstrating that temporary organizations can also use resilient mechanisms to deal with major safety issues, and that temporary forms of organizing can help complex projects to be efficiently and safely carried out. In this perspective, we define project resilience as the ability of a project to prevent major accidents from happening while maintaining its intended level of industrial performance. We examine this proposition by studying the case of an inter-organizational and safety–critical project: the construction by a shipyard of a series of ships. This project is managed by a public organization but involves many private contractors and a wide array of occupations. Thus, inter-organizational and inter-occupational coordination are crucial for reliable performance. As a temporary organization which must ensure a high level of safety while maintaining performance in an uncertain situation, under time pressure, this case is particularly relevant for enriching the literature on project resilience.

In such temporary settings, where permanent and more temporary forms of organizing must be coordinated, we argue that the occupational dimension is essential to enhancing resilience and sustaining reliable performance. Looking at the meso-level, i.e. the professional occupations involved in the project, we question how temporary forms of organizing and occupational groups together contribute to the resilience of the whole project. We show that the ability of the project to coordinate temporary organizing forms is key to achieving (safe) performance.

In HROs, safe performance is achieved by developing a strong organizational safety culture that is shared by all members of the organization. By contrast, we show that in complex and temporary projects, safe performance is achieved by articulating a wide variety of organizational actors who do not share the same occupational cultures and habits and who become involved for different periods of time. Building on the concept of communities of practice developed by Lave and Wenger (Lave, 1991; Lave & Wenger, 1991) and on the articulation work literature, we show that the articulation of work between various levels of participation helps the project to be more efficient and to ensure occupational and organizational safety, highlighting the link between high-quality activity and the safety of future users of the ships.

The chapter discusses the mechanisms and conditions that contribute to organizational resilience in temporary organizations. Through the study of a construction project that has to deal with complexity and safety issues, we demonstrate the key roles that temporary organizing and occupational communities play in the project's resilience. More precisely, this chapter addresses the following questions: How is resilience expressed in temporary organizations? Can temporary forms of organizing be compatible with sustainable occupational expertise? Under which conditions can temporary and more permanent forms of organizing be coordinated to ensure safe organizational performance?

By studying the case of a specific occupational group—the boilermakers—we show how they prevent major accidents by continually anticipating, adapting and reacting to normally disturbed situations. Taking an ethnographic approach (Garfinkel, 1967; Van Maanen, 1979) based on the observation of the routine daily activity of the field actors, we highlight that in complex projects resilience is first enhanced by the use of temporary organizing forms that provide greater flexibility and help the project to adapt to a discontinuous production flow. We then demonstrate that resilience is also built at an occupational level. Adopting an occupational lens (Brown & Duguid, 1991; Gherardi, 2018) shows the extent to which resilience, seen as the situated ability to anticipate and adapt to safety issues, is embedded in a long-term trajectory. The occupation thus appears to enable the existence of a common set of values and principles around which workers belonging to various companies and working under different contracts can come together. Finally, we demonstrate that the project's resilience is conditioned by the ability of the project's management to coordinate different expertise and levels of participation. The chapter concludes by discussing the implications of considering resilience in temporary organizing contexts.

Ensuring Resilience in Temporary Organizing Contexts

Unlike permanent organizations, which have stable processes and personnel that enable enduring work routines and knowledge to be developed, temporary organizations "*bring together a group of people that are unfamiliar with one another's skills, but must work interdependently on complex tasks*" (Bechky, 2006, p. 3). Söderlund (2000) proposes a typology of permanent and temporary forms of organizing which are categorized according to two main criteria: the structure (permanent or temporary) and the type of participation (permanent or temporary). This typology gives rise to four forms of organizing: temporary organizing (temporary structure and temporary participation); project organizing (temporary structure and permanent participation); temporary employment (permanent structure and temporary participation); and permanent organizing (permanent structure and permanent participation). So, in this first perspective, an organization that corresponds to one of these four organizational forms can be considered as temporary since either its participation or its structure has temporary aspects.

Another view of temporary organizations proposes taking a more processual perspective, which focuses on the role of the "*individual and collective agents*" (Bakker et al., 2016, p. 1708) and considers the structural dimension as an evolving rather than a stabilized component. Consequently, in adopting a processual lens, these authors use the term organiz*ing* instead of organizat*ion* to show the constantly evolving nature of the organizational forms studied. Therefore, for them, clear differentiation between permanent and temporary organizing may not be relevant. Rather, they consider that "*in temporary organizing, what is permanent and what is temporary are sometimes fuzzy and often intertwined*" (Bakker et al., 2016, p. 1708), and they contend that temporary organizing should be understood as a complex mix of temporary and permanent elements. This second definition of temporary organizing proposes a deeper understanding of the phenomenon and encourages further studies to analyse more accurately the dynamics involved (Bakker et al., 2016).

In this chapter, we adopt a processual view of forms of temporary organizing to study how the permanent and temporary dimensions are effectively intertwined and how this contributes to project resilience. Indeed, temporary organizing can be considered to be a mechanism for resilience that is employed by certain organizations when facing normally disturbed situations and evolving in more dynamic and changing contexts. This enables the mobilization of a more agile workforce (outsourcing, contracting, etc.) and of more adaptive structures (group projects), oriented towards shorter-term tasks. Temporary organizing is therefore a way of dealing with organizational complexity, such as that relating to the uniqueness of tasks or the interdependence of activities (Söderlund, 2000).

Interestingly, this stream of the literature seems to associate temporary organizing with support for resilience, whereas researchers who have studied HROs consider that it is the permanent nature of organizations that supports resilience. Indeed, according to high reliability theorists, the success of HROs in ensuring continuous high levels of safety while constantly experiencing high levels of technological risk and unpredictable events is partly explained by the fact that they have developed a strong organizational safety culture and strategy (Milch & Laumann, 2016). Weick and Roberts (1993) emphasize the roles of individual mindfulness and heedful interacting as pillars of resilience in highly disturbed contexts. More recently, Weick and Sutcliffe (2015) put forward a set of principles that support high reliability through anticipating the unexpected events and reacting to them once they have occurred.

In line with the situated and dynamic organization approaches, we therefore focus on the organizational, interactional and individual mechanisms that constitute pillars of resilience in temporary organizing contexts. We draw our inspiration from the five pillars of reliability defined by HRO researchers (Weick & Sutcliffe, 2015) while adhering to Hollnagel's concept of resilience, which includes strategies for anticipating and adapting to unexpected events (Hollnagel, 2016). Saunders (2015) is one of the few authors who has considered how to apply HRO principles to safety–critical projects and remarks that, in the case of temporary projects, "*these [high reliability] practices were often fragile, with much depending on the tenacity and strength of will of individual project managers rather than being embedded in the organization's culture and memory*" (p. 1262). In our view, this fragility is linked to the specific features of temporary organizations. Complex industrial projects, in particular, bring together different skills and specific working practices. Hence, in settings that are characterized by disorganization and organizational differences, it appears that organizational or individual sources of resilience are not fully applicable (Milch & Laumann, 2016). Furthermore, in the face of increased inter-organizational complexity and unstable work processes, Milch and Laumann (2016) show that it is more difficult to build, maintain and develop steady interrelations and knowledge. They highlight the phenomenon of dilution of competences, which arises from the fact that contract workers are unfamiliar with the local work environment and lack industry-specific knowledge and experience. The challenge is how to build and sustain these skills and expertise in the face of temporariness and fragmentation.

We argue that the resilient capability of complex projects relies not only on their use of forms of temporary organizing but also on the occupational groups who develop long-term and inter-organizational skills. Consequently, deepening our understanding of the role these groups play may improve our knowledge of how this particular organizational form is able to maintain a high level of safe performance.

Coordination Between Occupational Groups as a Source of Project Resilience

By focusing on the occupational dimension, our approach is in line with the practice-based view of safety and reliability (Gherardi, 2018; Gherardi & Nicolini, 2000; Tillement et al., 2009). Through the practice lens, safety and resilience are seen as a "*collective knowledgeable doing [that emerges] from the working practices of a community*" (Gherardi, 2018, p. 12). Following the concept of communities of practice (Brown & Duguid, 1991; Lave & Wenger, 1991; Wenger, 2010), these authors highlight the role of occupational identity in developing resilient capabilities to deal with unexpected situations. Bourrier (1996) identifies coordination processes between occupational groups as being one of the main success factors for dealing with complex and risky events such as outages in nuclear power plants. Her analysis also shows the importance of the coordination of scheduling and carrying out maintenance work. However, her approach to coordination is based more on a strategic analysis of power relationships between groups than on professional cultures, knowledge and expertise.

Taking the case of a modernization project by a rail company, Tillement et al. (2009) highlight the limitations of written procedures for reacting to incidents and insist on the importance of the situated and sophisticated skills developed by each occupational group, which are based on practical and relational knowledge mediated by discursive and material artefacts such as plans or installations. Observing two different teams, they show that the resilience of the project's organization is supported by occupational communities that are able to deal with unexpected events by developing flexibility through sharing a "*coherent vison of the work to be done and the methods to be used*" (p. 246) and by identifying the most competent member to solve the problem. However, in Tillement et al.'s (2009) case, if resilience is enhanced inside each team, different "*occupational groups have divergent representations concerning the nature of occupations and on the appropriate risk control practices*" (p. 250); indeed, sharing practices across boundaries is a key issue in inter-organizational projects.

Kellogg et al. (2006) note that coordination across occupational boundaries is difficult because "*expertise and interests [are] 'at stake' for community members*" (p. 26). They demonstrate how the company members they observed develop coordination practices, similar to Galison's (1999) concept of a 'trading zone'. In this perspective, '*enacting a trading zone does not require equivalence or similarity of interpretations or interests [...] Instead, members of different communities coordinate their actions temporarily and locally, navigating their differences in norms, meanings and interests only as needed*' (Kellogg et al., 2006, p. 39). In the same vein, Bechky (2006) shows that in temporary organizations, coordination between the various stakeholders is permitted through a role structuration, where individuals play a predetermined role and adapt their attitude to the particular situation they face. This coordination ability, based on dual behaviour which combines occupational belonging and the ability to adapt, appears to be a condition for ensuring resilience in temporary projects.

Methods

To understand how temporary organizing and occupational groups mutually support organizational resilience, we draw on an on-going longitudinal case study of a particular occupational group—the boilermakers—in a naval construction project, an activity which is carried out both by internal teams belonging to the principal company and by teams of contractors. The principal company is a shipyard. It is an old semi-public company whose activities and funding depend to a large extent on governmental decisions. We chose the boiler-making activity for two reasons. Firstly, the activity, which mainly consists of installing the pipes in the vessel, is key to the safety of the ship in the medium and long terms. The quality of the installation and the welding are critical to ensuring safety and avoiding the occurrence of major accidents. Secondly, as boiler-making work is fragmented into many operations and between various teams and companies, managing co-activity with other occupational groups (e.g. painters, mechanics or electricians) is essential but very complex. Since co-activity and complexity increase the possibility of unexpected events happening (LePlat & Faverge, 1967; Perrow, 2011), resilience is crucial for carrying out the activity efficiently and safely.

Data Collection

We draw on the data collected by one author who was involved from June 2018 to July 2019 in a major research programme, which was carried out in two main phases. In the first phase of the study, she met with several middle managers in the department in charge of installing all the pipes in the vessel and she observed coordination meetings. She also conducted interviews to better identify the safety and industrial issues they were dealing with. This first phase allowed her to obtain a global understanding of the construction project and to more clearly identify the type of complexity involved in the project. During the second phase, she successively followed three teams of boilermakers who were employed by three different companies. Two were subcontractors and the third was a team employed by the principal company which was responsible for the whole construction project. She spent five days with each team, following their shift schedules and shadowing them (Journé, 2005; McDonald, 2005) on the construction site. This enabled her to identify how they worked and organized themselves, which difficulties they were facing and which other occupational groups they interacted with. She completed her observation through individual semi-structured interviews with team members in order to collect more information about their professional background and experience. Interviewees were selected in such a way as to obtain a representative sample which would reflect the various profiles and the divergent views of the global organization. Finally, in order to validate

Table 4.1 Data collection summary

1st phase: understanding the global context		2nd phase: targeted observation of one specific occupation		
Over a 6-month period		Over a 6-month period		
10 days of multiple observations	Interviews with middle-management	15 days of team shadowing	Interviews with the boilermakers + confrontation / validation of the research assumptions	Confrontation / validation of the assumptions with the Middle-management
Participation in 5 daily coordination meetings and 2 weekly coordination meetings	1 Site manager	5 days with team 1	4 boilermakers + 1 welder from team 1	Discussions with installation managers during the team's break times
	1 Installation manager	5 days with team 2	5 boilermakers from team 2	
Following of 3 installation managers	2 Contract managers	5 days with team 3	3 boilermakers + 1 team manager from team 3	
	1 Occupation manager			

her research assumptions, she presented them to the workers during the interviews and subjected them to the workers' views. This allowed her to consolidate and adjust her findings. She also discussed her hypotheses with the company's middle management (Table 4.1).

Data Analysis

The researcher's observations were all documented in field notes and the interviews were fully transcribed. She categorized these data manually in order to evidence the role that the principal company and the boilermakers each played in project resilience. The field notes constitute the primary source of information, and they helped to clarify the organizational context in which the project took place and to identify the articulation issues between the organization's formal rules and the boilermakers' occupational practices. They were useful for describing how the various groups of actors worked, coordinated and communicated with each other. The field notes were complemented by the interviews, which provided more information about the actors' motives and preoccupations. They were essential for understanding why middle management and team workers behave differently and do not share values and habits across organizations. They also helped to correct certain assumptions that stemmed from the observation phase. Finally, discussing her assumptions with the boilermakers and the installation managers helped the researcher to refine her classification work and to distinguish between what was shared by members of the team and occupation and what was more specific to an individual or a restricted group.

Empirical Findings

This section shows the role of three main actors and their respective practices in enhancing resilience. The actors are the project organization, the occupational groups and the installation managers. Each actor contributes to resilience through specific processes. First, the project organization has designed an adapting structure in which the actors are prepared to permanently adapt to changes and evolutions in the shipyard's organization. Second, the occupational groups maintain a high level of expertise in a sustainable way. Finally, the installation managers articulate the project constraints with the occupational working practices. These results provide the answers to the three questions posed in the Introduction to this chapter.

Achieving Resilience by Adapting the Workforce to Carry Out a Technologically and Organizationally Complex Project

The naval construction project studied here presents a huge technological challenge for the principal company responsible for its completion. The project involves building a series of vessels whose technology is completely new and unique. The company last undertook such an ambitious project several decades earlier. At that time, building vessels with high levels of industrial and information technology was the company's core activity, and it recruited a large number of employees in professions and occupations required by the construction projects. Many employees were manual workers involved in building and assembling the various components of the vessels. They belonged to a variety of professional occupations: painting, boiler-making, electrical work, welding, etc. The different occupations required for the various construction steps are shown in Table 4.2.

Most of the workers were permanent employees of the principal company, which also relied on outsourcing for small parts of the project. However, decades later, when the new project began, the company had lost many manual competencies; as its core activity now relates more to new technological issues, the number of manual workers employed has reduced considerably. The company was therefore facing two major challenges. Firstly, as its internal workforce had progressively moved to ship repair and maintenance tasks, it had lost some of its occupational expertise and its ability to build entire ships. There was also a lack of competent

Table 4.2 Professional occupations and activities

	Fabrication Department	Installation Department	Logistics Department	Quality Department
PIPEWORK	Pipe workshop	Boilermakers Welders	Pipe warehouse	Pipe quality controllers
STRUCTURE	Structure workshop	Shipwrights Mechanics		
ELECTRICITY	Wire workshop	Electricians		
PAINTING		Painters		
		Safety Department		
CROSS-FUNCTIONAL ACTIVITIES		Firemen	Storekeepers	Supervisors

and experienced managers who were capable of leading large construction projects. Secondly, as the number of manual workers had considerably reduced, the company now had to rely on a large number of contractors and subcontractors to help it meet its deadlines. The contractors thus play a new role: they do not provide the lost expertise which was previously available inside the company; instead, they help the company to re-acquire the expertise that it has lost but that the contractors have maintained. The contractors are therefore also a source of training for the company, which is able to learn from the contractors' experience in different industrial settings. Outsourcing thus constitutes a form of temporary organizing (Söderlund, 2000) which directly contributes to a first component of project resilience: its ability to meet fixed objectives, i.e. building a series of vessels.

The complexity of the naval project lies in its volatility: the activities on the construction site are constantly changing in such a way that no two days are alike. This also means that as each vessel progresses through the construction process, some stages require the presence of certain occupational groups that were needed less in earlier stages or will be needed in subsequent stages. For instance, the role of the shipwrights is crucial for building the overall structure of the ship, but once the project reaches the assembling stage, the shipwrights are less present. As in many projects, the principal company thus has to adapt the workforce to the demands of the project. A solution was to engage contracting and subcontracting companies which could provide a temporary workforce when needed. This pool of adaptive resources thus directly contributes to the performance of the project, as they create a continually available and adequate workforce to do the necessary work without exceeding the estimated budget.

We also observed that the projects employed different types of outsourcing practices to meet its organizational needs, which we categorize into two types: long-term contractors and occasional contractors. The former are those who have worked on the ship construction project for a long time. They have developed a good knowledge of the organizational rules and of the way the project is structured and led. As they collaborate on a regular basis with the principal company, they tend to be responsible for project tasks that last for several months. The occasional contractors do not work for the project on a regular basis and constitute a more heterogeneous group of workers. Some of them only work on the project for a few days, while others come and go, spending a few weeks or months at the construction site each time. Their knowledge of the project is thus more limited and so the principal company cannot rely on them to the same extent. However, the occasional contractors are also a necessary workforce for the project because they help the principal company to cope with the many issues and unexpected events that are inherent in technically complex industrial projects: manufacturing errors, changes of schedule, plan modifications, on site installation problems, etc. Using temporary forms of organizing that complement the permanent organization appears to enhance project resilience, allowing it to adapt the required workforce to the production flow of the project.

Occupational Groups Contributing to Resilience by Maintaining Operational Expertise Throughout the Project

The teams of boilermakers we studied belong to one community which share common practices and values and have the same vision of how a good job should be carried out. In this section, we first show why the boilermakers constitute a community of practice in the sense developed by Lave and Wenger (1991), where they are united around a shared domain of interests, the same community and a common set of practices. We then highlight how these characteristics contribute to the project's performance and safety: by enhancing its flexibility and reactivity, the community contributes to the project's overall performance, and, by developing a deep sensitivity to practice, it acquires a situated understanding of occupational and industrial safety issues.

The three teams of boilermakers we studied belong to three different companies and work under different contracts: some of them are directly employed by the principal company (team C), others are contractors (teams A and B) and a few are subcontractors who are temporarily employed by a contractor (teams A and C). They also have different levels of knowledge of the project, different kinds of previous experience and different occupational backgrounds. Despite all these differences, the boilermakers are part of an occupational community in the sense that they share a set of common values and all agree about what constitutes good boiler-making and how it should be done. For them, boiler-making is first and foremost manual work, which they learn through observation and practice. They consider boiler-making to be precision work that has to follow an ordered process and requires time to be done correctly. In addition, they have formed a physical community which gets together during and outside of working hours and which has created an occupational network beyond the organizational and project boundaries.

The boilermakers also have a shared domain of interest—boiler-making—which, in this project and in the particular context of marine infrastructure, is the activity of assembling, installing and fixing the pipes in the vessel. Many of them chose to become boilermakers because they were good with their hands and enjoyed the material dimension of the job. They have developed a particular boiler-making vocabulary, sometimes using nicknames to refer to particular tools and materials, and they have developed certain procedures that are specific to the boiler-making activity.

Finally, the boilermakers share a common set of practices, which we observed in the three teams studied. A good example of this is the way each team is structured, following the same hierarchical organization. At the top, the team manager is responsible for the contractual link with the principal organization and for coordinating the team's work progress. Each team is divided into sub-groups, led by senior boilermakers who coordinate the work and are responsible for ensuring that the installation complies with the principal company's assembly plan; they take responsibility if any errors are detected. Also, in each team the boilermakers work in pairs, usually composed of a senior and a more junior worker.

They have also developed the same habits and routines: when installing a pipe, they generally follow the same steps, i.e. examining the installation plan, measuring the location where the pipes have to be installed, loading the pipes, making adjustments when needed, and finally installing the pipes with the help of the welder. To do their work efficiently, they also rely on the same tools, which they carry in one of the many pockets of their blue overalls or in their leather case. These include a pencil, a small notebook, a tape measure, different sizes of wrenches, etc., and their mobile phone calculator app. In the following paragraphs, we will see how this community functioning enables the boiler-making group to contribute to the project's efficiency and to meet the expected deadlines.

Firstly, the occupational teams are structured in a way that make them flexible and enable them to reorganize quickly when faced with unexpected changes. They are led by senior experts whose technical legitimacy is recognized and respected. This enables the teams to react more thoughtfully and quickly when a problem comes up. This formal organization, similar in the three teams, favours collective decision-making based on technical expertise. Indeed, if there is any doubt or disagreement, the decision will often be taken by the more experienced worker. Furthermore, their organization remains flexible and can be changed according to the situations that arise. For example, when a particularly technical task is to be carried out, the manager can decide to pair two senior workers so that he can be sure that the work will be done perfectly. So, the boilermaker teams have a top-down, but not rigid, organization: as the project progresses and new situations arise, they can redesign their organization and adapt in a flexible way that contributes to the project's resilience.

The teams' efficiency and ability to deal with unexpected situations also rely on strong leadership, embodied by the team manager or by the section managers, who generally have previous boiler-making experience and who are respected and trusted by the other members of the team. This leadership is essential for the team's resilience: when the team faces unexpected situations or great pressure, the team leaders play a key role in encouraging the other workers and in achieving their shared goal.

Their work follows organizational routines which structure their activity and give them the opportunity to share their respective knowledge and experience. For example, we observed that the teams have a daily routine of taking collective breaks. These breaks are convivial times when the workers talk about their personal lives, make jokes or complain about their work problems, depending on the mood of the day. These moments have a direct impact on their ability to work together efficiently. Because they are moments of sharing, they help to reinforce the team spirit and are opportunities for getting to know each other better. This reinforces the workers' ability to trust each other when they are working together in a risky context.

Finally, the boiler-making community shares common values, attitudes and concerns about their occupation and its risks which transcend the organizational boundaries while ensuring a high level of industrial safety. A first challenge for the workers when they arrive on site is therefore to learn to adapt to the constant changes without putting themselves in danger. To avoid accidents, the workers develop a sense of awareness and learn to always be careful to look out for any structural changes. For instance, when a boilermaker arrives in a particular section of the site, he looks at the area and checks if there have been any changes since he was last there. Likewise, he will be very careful about where he puts his feet; if a tool, a cable or an air duct is lying on the floor, he will systematically take it away and try to hang it on a scaffold.

Another major preoccupation of the practitioners is industrial safety, which ensures that their work is safe and under control. By establishing routinized checking procedures and by continually practising these, they develop a more situated and embedded understanding of the potential risks. As different occupations can be working on the same line of pipe at the same time, the workers have to deal with work fragmentation. In this context, checking procedures ensure global coherence, which has a direct impact on the industrial safety of the installation process. The boilermakers' technical expertise also lies in their ability to use the various tools they need in their daily activity. However, practice is essential to acquire some skills, and takes time. For instance, it takes at least six months for a beginner to be able to correctly chamfer a pipe, and the boilermakers believe it takes 10 years to become a senior boilermaker and 15 or 20 years to be an expert. It is also through practising that the workers learn which tools are more appropriate to ensure a better quality of installation, which directly contributes to industrial safety.

To conclude, the boilermakers constitute a community of practice which develops an in-depth understanding of the project's risks and constraints. This contributes to the project's resilience by ensuring a high level of performance while maintaining occupational and industrial safety.

Coordinating Working Practices in Temporary Organizing Contexts: Support for Project Resilience

We have seen that the boiler-making activity in this naval project is composed of different teams belonging to different companies, with boilermakers working under different work contracts. This diversity offers the project some flexibility because it enables the principal company to continually adapt the number of workers in the worksite according to its evolving workload. At the same time, to deal with the different rules and working practices between the various teams of boilermakers, the company has set up coordination mechanisms that bring together the different teams of workers around the same priority: avoiding co-activity constraints. These coordination mechanisms take the form of weekly and daily meetings attended by representatives of the various occupational groups co-operating on the shipyard, and we show how they help to prevent unexpected events and contribute to the workers' safety.

The purpose of the weekly coordination meeting, which gathers together representatives of all the occupations and teams working in a specific ship section, is to monitor the schedule. At this meeting, the participants review the work to be carried out each day in each sector by each occupational team. The manager of each team confirms whether the planned tasks can be done or should be rescheduled. The aim of the meeting is to avoid co-activity whenever possible and to articulate the work between the planned and the actual activity, which reduces loss of time and enhances the workers' efficiency. However, if an unexpected event happens, the team cannot wait until the next weekly meeting to solve the problem and a daily coordination meeting has therefore also been put in place.

The purpose of the daily coordination meeting is to adjust the planned work to the situation on site. The daily meeting thus enables greater situated management of the co-activity between the various occupational groups by creating space for informal work discussions that overlap with the formal meeting (box 1). They provide an important opportunity for the managers to make arrangements and find practical solutions for their teams.

Box 1: Informal talks during a coordination meeting

As the coordination meeting drags on, two managers in charge of two different teams of boilermakers start a discussion on co-activity issues in their sector:

Manager A: When will you finish the welding on pipeline B32? We really need to start the installation on B33.

Manager B: This afternoon, I hope, but it depends on the air ducts. I'm not sure that Logistics have activated them. Always the same problem…

M A: How many of you are there just now?

M B: Three with the welder.

M A: Ok. There can be six of us. So maybe my guys could start the measurements right now.

M B: Ok, my guys are cool so no problem if your guys work in the same sector.

M A: Great.

By setting up various coordination meetings, the principal company can better anticipate the frequent organizational changes that are inherent in complex industrial projects and find collective solutions when blocking points arise (box 2).

Box 2: Coordination meetings managing occupational issues

Tuesday:

8:30: The Installation Manager meets the Team Manager in the team workspace. The Team Manager informs the Installation Manager about a pipe-installation issue: a piece of pipe is too long and needs to be recut on site because it has already been welded. This problem has held up the team since the beginning of the morning.

8:45: The Installation Manager and the Team Manager go and see the pipe on board. They realize that this operation risks damaging the painting. Moreover, a scaffold is preventing the boilermakers from cutting the pipe. The Installation Manager needs the opinion and authorization of the Section Manager to take a decision.

9:00: The Installation Manager participates in the daily coordination meeting and shares the pipe issue with the other members. For the Section Manager, the priority is to reach the next milestone: he advocates for the quicker solution, which seems to be cutting the pipe on board. The Installation Manager in charge of the painting is worried about the potential damage. He suggests the boilermakers use a saw instead of a grinder to cut the pipe. Finally, the Installation Manager in charge of the scaffolder team plans an intervention in the morning.

9:30: End of the daily meeting. The Installation Manager calls the Team Manager and tells him they can cut the pipe with a saw once the scaffolds are removed.

10:30: The scaffolders go on board and rearrange the scaffolds.

11:00: The boilermaker in charge of cutting the pipe arrives on board and realizes he doesn't have a saw. It takes him almost an hour to find the right one.

13:00: End of the working day for the boiler-making team. The boilermaker hasn't finished the work.

Wednesday:

9:30: The boilermaker finishes cutting the pipe with the saw. He informs the Team Manager, who remarks that the event has caused a delay to the schedule.

10:00: The Team Manager shares the information with the Installation Manager who has just left the daily meeting. The Installation Manager informs the Coordination Manager, who makes a change to the schedule.

The second role of the weekly meeting is to ensure the occupational safety of the workers by defining the organizational conditions that enable safe co-activity. For example, when the boilermakers and the welders are working together, the painters may be prevented from working because the welding sparks will damage the painting. In this case, the solution may be to install a temporary separating wall so that both occupations can work at the same time without any risks. These coordination practices thus contribute to the progress of work on the construction site; they allow the project to be more resilient by improving its overall performance and by anticipating potential accidents.

Discussion and Conclusion

Resilience in the Tension Between Permanent and Temporary Forms of Organizing

Researchers have emphasized that new forms of organizing tend to be more fragmented and temporary (Kellogg et al., 2006) in order to enhance flexibility and performance. However, most works have studied resilience in long-standing organizations from a systemic perspective. They have shown that both anticipation and adaptation are supported by strong organizational routines (Hollnagel et al., 2006). Even if the literature on temporary organizing and the literature on resilience are rarely articulated, they emphasize near-opposite views of the foundations of resilience: flexibility on the one hand, stability on the other hand.

Based on this observation, we seek to combine these two research areas by studying how resilience can be expressed and enhanced in contexts where temporary forms of organizing articulate with the sustainable structure of occupations. We study the construction of a new series of ships by a shipyard, where occupational groups, notably the boilermakers, are temporarily involved and gathered together in a project-based organization. Taking a dynamic approach, we define temporary organizing as a complex and always evolving mix of temporary and permanent elements. This perspective enables us to make three theoretical and methodological contributions.

First, unlike the cases studied by Bourrier (1996) and Tillement et al. (2009), the project under study is fundamentally a temporary structure and does not juxtapose with a larger routinized or bureaucratic organization. Moreover, every worker is a temporary worker in this project-based organization. Thus, the challenge for resilience is not to articulate the permanent and temporary organizational structures, but to articulate a temporary project organization with more permanent occupations. In the cases studied by Bourrier (1996) and Tillement et al. (2009), organizational resilience is threatened by the rivalries between historical occupational groups that are representatives of the permanent structure and the emerging ones that are representatives of the project-based organization. Our case differs from theirs and highlights another configuration: since all the workers are involved temporarily in a transient ship construction project, there are no major conflicts or rivalries between the various occupational groups. All the workers are gathered around the same object, the ship, which plays the role of a boundary object (Bechky, 2006; Leigh Star, 2010). In our case, the tensions do not lie at the inter-occupational level but, rather, at the inter-organizational level. We observe tensions which are associated with power relationships between the boilermakers of the principal company and the contractors, and symbolic dimensions: the former consider themselves as more legitimate, with the latter being seen as a secondary workforce. In this particular organizational configuration, the relations between occupational groups, which favour robust coordination mechanisms, support resilience rather than constituting vulnerability.

Second, we show that resilience is also grounded within each community of practice, which transcends organizational boundaries and thus contributes to the project's overall coordination ability. The community of boilermakers we observed is similar to the communities described by Brown and Duguid (1991), who define them as "*more fluid and interpenetrative than bounded, often crossing the restrictive boundaries of the organization to incorporate people from outside*" (p. 49). Similarly, the boilermakers' occupational groups are constantly evolving. The arrival of newcomers and the discussions and sharing of various experiences help to enrich their knowledge and expertise. This learning process (similar to *apprenticeship*) is embedded in the legitimate participation of the members of the community of practice (Lave & Wenger, 1991) and thus is conditioned by the possibility of the actors being fully integrated into the community's social life and sharing its occupational values.

Finally, from a methodological point of view, our study highlights the value of adopting a meso-level of analysis to study the practices and processes that enhance resilience. Surprisingly, this level of analysis is rarely used either in the temporary organizing literature (Bakker et al., 2016) or in the resilience engineering's perspective, which has mainly focused on the organizational or individual dimensions. Our group-level analysis enables us to show in greater detail how the various communities of practice manage to coordinate their activity, and to highlight the role of discussions and inter-group communication in dealing efficiently with unexpected situations. This demonstrates in a more situated and deeper way the organizational mechanisms of resilience by describing the concrete adaptation and reaction practices developed to deal with unexpected situations. From a longer term perspective, this practice-based view of resilience emphasizes the role of occupations in supporting long-lasting learning dynamics, which are able to go beyond the temporary forms of organizing that lie both in the project structure and in workers' participation.

Managerial Contributions

In safety–critical projects such as the one under study, resilience partly relies on the involvement of key individuals who perform an interfacing role between project managers and occupational groups. However, frequent turnover hinders the ability of the workers to build sustainable resilient practices. Moreover, the frequently changing structure of the project organization tends to result in disengagement from the long-term goals. It is thus crucial to reflect upon the organization's ability to build long-lasting learning dynamics that can ensure enduring organizational resilience. We propose two conditions for the organization to maintain its resilient capacity in the long term: keeping key individuals in lasting positions and retaining key competences throughout the project.

First, coordination between the occupational groups and project management mainly relies on the key role of the installation manager and on his ability to interact efficiently with the team manager. As the installation manager needs time to acquire his coordination ability and to become familiar with the technicalities of the boilermakers' work, staying longer in his position could contribute to enhancing resilience in the longer term. This observation reveals a major discrepancy between the perspective of the project managers, whose goal is to use this position to educate the newcomers about the site constraints before they join the field offices, and the perspective of the workers, who need a single and reliable interlocutor to respond efficiently to the project managers' requests.

Secondly, as contract workers possess rare competences, they can easily negotiate a better salary or a better position with the highest bidder. In this context characterized by high levels of competition, the principal company must develop a competence retention strategy to avoid 'losing' the more competent workers. Workers give two main reasons for leaving a project: the feeling of not being involved in the whole project and the lack of technicity and diversity of the tasks. Thus, involving contract workers in the global project and informing them about the overall contribution of their work is making to the project are essential for project resilience. This entails building partnership relations with contractors, based on long-term contracts and on shared training programmes. The ability of the project to retain competences also relies on the workers sharing their knowledge and training in order to become multi-skilled experts. In a time-pressured context of occupational distribution, the experts lack the time to train the beginners. As a consequence, we recommend that the work of the occupational groups should be considered as a global process of legitimate peripheral participation in communities of practice (Lave, 1991).

Limitations and Avenues for Further Research

In our study, we focused on one specific occupational group, i.e. the boilermakers, which enabled us to highlight foundations of resilience linked to learning dynamics (similar to apprenticeship) that enable the development and maintenance of shared and situated practices. For future research, it would be interesting to study another occupational group, such as electricians, in order to test the generalization of our results on a larger scale. In addition, studying the practices of different occupational groups in parallel might enable a better understanding of the basis of inter-occupational coordination. Finally, as we paid little attention in this study to contractual agreements and their effects on coordination, this could merit further study. Finally, our case focused on a complex project that was led by a semi-public nature organization, which contracted out activities to private companies. To better qualify the effects of the degree of publicness (Bozeman & Bretschneider, 1994) on project resilience, it could be interesting to compare this particular case with other cases where projects are led by private companies.

References

Bakker, R. M., DeFillippi, R. J., Schwab, A., & Sydow, J. (2016). Temporary organizing: Promises, processes, problems. *Organization Studies, 37*(12), 1703–1719.

Bechky, B. A. (2006). Gaffers, gofers, and grips: Role-based coordination in temporary organizations. *Organization Science, 17*(1), 3–21.

Bourrier, M. (1996). Organizing maintenance work at two American nuclear power plants. *Journal of Contingencies and Crisis Management, 4*(2), 104–112.

Bozeman, B., & Bretschneider, S. (1994). The "publicness puzzle" in organization theory: A test of alternative explanations of differences between public and private organizations. *Journal of Public Administration Research and Theory, 4*(2), 197–223.

Brown, J. S., & Duguid, P. (1991). Organizational learning and communities-of-practice: Toward a unified view of working, learning, and innovation. *Organization Science, 2*(1), 40–57.

Furuta, K. (2015). Resilience engineering. In J. Ahn, C. Carson, M. Jensen, K. Juraku, S. Nagasaki, & S. Tanaka (Eds.), *Reflections on the Fukushima Daiichi nuclear accident: Toward social-scientific literacy and engineering resilience* (pp. 435–454). Springer.

Galison, P. (1999). Trading zone: Coordinating action and belief. *The Science Studies Reader, 13*, 137–160.

Garfinkel, H. (1967). What is ethnomethodology? In H. Garfinkel (Ed.), *Studies in ethnomethodology* (pp. 1–34). Prentice-Hall.

Gherardi, S. (2018). A practice-based approach to safety as an emergent competence. In C. Bieder, C. Gilber, B. Journé, & H. Laroche (Eds.), *Beyond safety training: Embedding safety in professional skills* (pp. 11–21). Springer.

Gherardi, S., & Nicolini, D. (2000). The organizational learning of safety in communities of practice. *Journal of Management Inquiry, 9*(1), 7–18.

Hollnagel, E. (2016). Resilience engineering: A new understanding of safety. *Journal of the Ergonomics Society of Korea, 35*(3), 185–191.

Hollnagel, E., Woods, D., & Leveson, N. (2006). *Resilience engineering: Concepts and precepts*. CRC Press.

Journé, B. (2005). Etudier filemanagement de l'imprévu: Méthode dynamique d'observation in situ. *Finance Contrôle Stratégie, 8*(4), 63–91.

Kellogg, K. C., Orlikowski, W. J., & Yates, J. (2006). Life in the trading zone: Structuring coordination across boundaries in postbureaucratic organizations. *Organization Science, 17*(1), 22–44.

Lave, J. (1991). Acquisition des savoirs et pratiques de groupe. *Sociologie Et Sociétés, 23*(1), 145–162.

Lave, J., & Wenger, E. (1991). *Situated learning: Legitimate peripheral participation*. Cambridge University Press.

Leigh Star, S. (2010). This is not a boundary object: Reflections on the origin of a concept. *Science, Technology, & Human Values, 35*(5), 601–617.

LePlat, J., & Faverge, J. M. (1967). *Recherche communautaire sur la sécurité dans les mines et la sidérurgie: Étude no. 3/6, recherche dans les mines de fer français* (Community research on safety in mines and the steel industry: Study No. 3/6, Research in French iron mines). Doc. No. 8085/65 f, 1967.

Lundin, R. A., & Söderholm, A. (1995). A theory of the temporary organization. *Scandinavian Journal of Management, 11*(4), 437–455.

McDonald, S. (2005). Studying actions in context: A qualitative shadowing method for organizational research. *Qualitative Research*, *5*(4), 455–473.

Milch, V., & Laumann, K. (2016). Interorganizational complexity and organizational accident risk: A literature review. *Safety Science*, *82*, 9–17 (2016).

Perrow, C. (2011). *Normal accidents: Living with high risk technologies* (Updated). Princeton University Press.

Saunders, F. C. (2015). Toward high reliability project organizing in safety-critical projects. *Project Management Journal*, *46*(3), 25–35.

Saunders, F. C., Gale, A. W., & Sherry, A. H. (2016). Responding to project uncertainty: Evidence for high reliability practices in large-scale safety–critical projects. *International Journal of Project Management, 34*(7), 1252–1265.

Söderlund, J. (2000). Temporary organizing-characteristics and control forms. In R. A. Lundin & F. Hartman (Eds.), *Projects as business constituents and guiding motives* (pp. 61–74). Springer.

Tillement, S., Cholez, C., & Reverdy, T. (2009). Assessing organizational resilience: An interactionist approach. *M@n@gement*, *12*(4), 230–264.

Van Maanen, J. (1979). The fact of fiction in organizational ethnography. *Administrative Science Quarterly, 24*(4), 539–550.

Weick, K. E. (1979). *The social psychology of organizing* (second edn.). McGraw-Hill. Reviewed by K. E. Weick in *M@n@gement*, 2015, *18*(2), 189–193.

Weick, K. E., & Roberts, K. H. (1993). Collective mind in organizations: Heedful interrelating on flight decks. *Administrative Science Quarterly*, *38*(3), 357–381.

Weick, K. E., & Sutcliffe, K. M. (2015). *Managing the unexpected: Sustained performance in a complex world (3rd Edition).* John Wiley & Sons.

Wenger, E. (2010). Communities of practice and social learning systems: The career of a concept. In C. Blackmore (Ed.), *Social learning systems and communities of practice* (pp. 179–198). Springer.

CHAPTER 5

A Practical Perspective on Resilience in Organizations: The Interplay Between Structure and Action

Anouck Adrot, Oriane Sitte de Longueval, and Alexandre Largier

Introduction

In many sectors, organizational resilience represents a useful way to bounce back from incidents and promote activity continuity (Lovins & Lovins, 1982, cited by Wildavsky, 1988). Accordingly, a large spectrum of tools, norms and standards—what we label here as 'frameworks'—has been produced and internationally appraised. However, frameworks do

A. Adrot (✉)
Paris-Dauphine University PSL, Paris, France
e-mail: anouck.adrot@dauphine.psl.eu

O. S. de Longueval
Université de Genève, Genève, Switzerland

A. Largier
Institut de radioprotection et de sûreté nucléaire (IRSN), Paris, France
e-mail: alexandre.largier@irsn.fr

R. Pinheiro et al. (eds.), *Towards Resilient Organizations and Societies*, Public Sector Organizations,
https://doi.org/10.1007/978-3-030-82072-5_5

not always fit into organizational settings, and gaps can emerge between resilience frameworks on the one hand and resilience in action on the other. Moving away from strict rules does not necessarily result into a negative outcomes (Walls & Hoffman, 2013). However, discrepancies between resilience frameworks and action can generate uncertainty. For instance, they can undermine overall confidence in an organization's ability to prepare for, detect and address events (Shrivastava, 1987).

As those insights suggest, there is a need to better understand how resilience frameworks and action relate to each other in practice. Previous research has highlighted their interplay through a literature review (Hale & Borys, 2013) but has fallen short of providing details on the conditions under which such interplay shapes practice. In this chapter, we approach organizational resilience through the practice-based lens offered by Schatzki (1996). Approaching resilience as a practice allows us to focus on the interplay between action and structure. By doing so, we distinguish on the one hand structural aspects of resilience and, on the other, enacted resilience (that we approach as action). Based on such conceptualization, this chapter addresses the knowledge gap identified by with the following question: *What is the nature of the interplay between structure and action that both comprise resilience as practice?*

To properly investigate this question, our analysis is based on two empirical cases from two French organizations: a public administration in charge of coordinating resilience at a regional level (Fed), and a service in charge of Crisis Management Teams (CMTs) in a public transportation company (Ral). These two organizations developed knowledge intensive capabilities in order to frame, experiment and develop resilience. While they adopted radically different practical modalities in settling resilience capabilities, they experienced similar difficulties that we analyse in this chapter.

Our findings detail the interplay between structure and action that both comprise resilience as practice. More specifically, our findings outline how, at the initial steps of an organization's framing of resilience, general and practical understanding can shape action while coming at odds with the organization's teleo-affective structure. By drawing on practice theory, the chapter opens the black box of resilience as a practice. Our findings inform discussion on three major points: (i) resilience, as a practice is evolutionary and complex; (ii) organizations need to fully consider resilience's teleo-affective structures before designing organizational resilience; and (iii) proponents of resilience and their agency are essential.

Organizational Resilience and Practice

For two decades, the notion of resilience has gained momentum (Manyena, 2006). Increasing attention from authorities, the public and organizations towards the concept stems from growing likelihood of unexpected but highly destructive events. Resilience can be defined as '*the ability of an entity, individuals, community, or system to return to normal condition or functioning after the occurrence of an event that disturbs its state*' (Wiig & Fahlbruch, 2019, p. 1).

Organizations are particularly vulnerable because a large spectrum of events can disrupt their activities and significantly impact their functioning without notice. Organizational environments have also grown complex: threats of a diverse nature now impact each other and organizations have progressively become vulnerable (Perrow, 2006). This has strong implications for organizations' awareness of their inner vulnerabilities, threats and the need to develop organizational capabilities to handle them.

In this context, organizational resilience was defined as '*a deliberate effort to become better able to cope with surprise*' (Lovins & Lovins, 1982, cited by Wildavsky, 1988). This effort corresponds '*to the maintenance of positive adjustments under challenging conditions such that the organization emerges from these conditions strengthened and more resourceful*' (Vogus & Sutcliffe, 2007, p. 3418). Because the characteristics of disasters are changing and bringing unforeseen events (Djalante & Lassa, 2019), a practical adaptation of resilience frameworks by organizations is of paramount importance. While the absence of any framework can be a major impediment to the implementation of resilient practices, an overly tight normative framework can prevent the emergence of resilience.

In line with this view, the two definitions provided here both uncover the practical dimension of resilience. Practices correspond to '*an organized, open-ended, spatial–temporal manifold of actions*' (Lindberg & Rantatalo, 2015, p. 564). Practices are not easy to conceptualize, even though they contribute to the fabric of organizations as well as their transformation (Schatzki et al., 2001).

In line with this view, the definition of organizational resilience provided above highlights how resilience involves 'efforts', indicating continuous intentional, behavioural and emotional involvement of individuals and groups of individuals who work for the organization (we refer to them in this chapter through the term 'agent'). Resilience is therefore not understood as the mechanistic implementation of formal rules but, rather, as a manifold of actions undertaken by agents. These actions might remain untracked or uncontrolled and correspond to some sort of organizational slack necessary for organizational reliability (Schulman, 1993). The latter definition outlines the transformative dimension of resilience and suggests that, in order to become resilient, organizations shape their own activities. This transformation targets the development of both proactive and reactive capabilities, respectively, designed to bounce forward or bounce back events (Pettersen & Schulman, 2019). Hence organizational resilience as practice fully participates in the development of crucial capabilities, yet still remains challenging to grapple with empirically.

In our view, considering the practical dimension of resilience helps address the challenge of how best to approach the situatedness of resilience. But what is resilience as practice? Both scholars and practitioners lack knowledge of the practical achievement of organizational resilience (Boin & Van Eeten, 2013; Duit, 2016). Addressing this need, we detail in the coming section our rationale for drawing on Schatzki's view of practice. We then detail this perspective as applied to the question of resilience, and outline the remaining question regarding the nature of the interplay between resilience structure, on the one side, and resilience action on the other side.

Schatzki's Approach to Practices

This chapter argues for Schatzki's conceptualization of practices as a valuable lens to better understand the dynamics underlying resilience. The practice view of organizations, as offered by Schatzki (2006), posits that organizational essence lies in its activities. Practice results from the interplay between its two major components, namely action and structure, which are both essential to any organizational activity. Figure 5.1 represents the mutual ties between action and structure. On the one hand, action, which describes what people concretely achieve (for instance running, filling a form or using equipment), represents the most straightforward expression of practice. On the other hand, the structure of practice corresponds to collective understanding and meaning of what

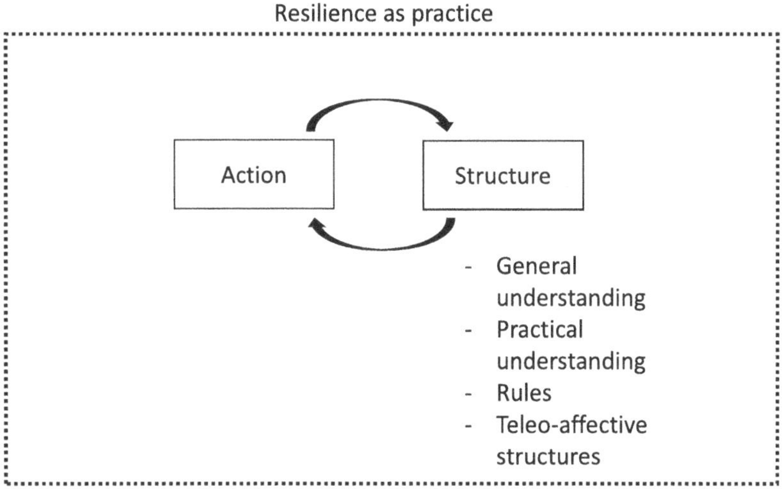

Fig. 5.1 Resilience as a practice: social arrangements between actions and structure, inspired from Schatzki (2002)

is correct or acceptable (Lindberg & Rantatalo, 2015). Practice intelligibility stems from structures, which organise and regulate action. Reciprocally, action contributes to the delineation of practice structure. In other words, practices emerge from the influence of structures on action, and vice versa.

We now consider more thoroughly the major elements that comprise the structure of resilience as practice. In Schatzki's terms, practices are made of four major components: (1) Practical understanding corresponds to the practical knowing of what to do in a specific situation. For instance, practical understanding could be knowing which forms to use in a bureaucratic process or even how to send an email. According to Schatzki, the practical understanding corresponds to the knowledge of how '*to carry out desired actions through basic doings and sayings*' (2012, p.16). This type of knowledge relies on practical rather than dialogical intelligibility. From this perspective, practical understanding embeds in action rather than being driven by formal rules or reasoning. (2) Rules correspond to the '*explicit directives, admonishments or instructions that participants in the practice observe or disregard*' (Schatzki, 1996, p. 1864). Rules play an essential role in the continuity and intelligibility of practices. However, actors can also bypass rules, which means that social action can diverge from explicit norms and standards. (3) Teleo-affective structures include a large spectrum of emotions, beliefs and rituals that direct action and belong to the practice rather than the actors. Actors are not totally aware of the emotional, affective and teleological dimension of practice. (4) General understanding corresponds to the shared belief between actors involved in a practice.

The adoption of a practice-based view of resilience leads to an important point: resilience evolves through an interplay between structure on the one hand, and action on the other. Social and material arrangements bridge (Schatzki, 2002; Suchman, 2007) concrete actions undertaken by practitioners and the structures that govern these actions (including norms, rules, protocols, directions from hierarchy, strategic objectives and methodologies). Approaching organizational resilience through Schatzki's lens provides two major sources of insights on resilience. First, it suggests resilience is part of the social fabric of the organization rather than a spontaneous reaction to events. Second, it draws attention to the numerous and invisible ties between structure and action.

Resilience Structure and Action Interplay

Apparent examples of the gap between resilience structure and action abound in the literature. For instance, in the case of the Bhopal disaster, Union Carbide hardly considered experts' recommendations regarding its daily routine, thereby undermining its capability to deal with the explosion of its factory in December 1984 (Shrivastava, 1987). As another example, the 2012 Concordia accident resulted from a clear departure of the ship's captain from formal frameworks. These two examples echo Schatzki's view on the importance of the interplay between resilience structure and action. This interplay, stemming from social arrangements, is not always contradictory and might be more complex.

In organizations, informal social arrangements—those primarily concerning humans, artefacts and things (Schatzki, 2002)—can occur in relation to a spectrum of topics (Benson, 1977). In situations requiring resilience capabilities, social arrangements may concern the distribution of tasks or the nature of emergency practices (Adrot & Garreau, 2010). So far, social arrangements related to resilience have mostly been observed in situations where organizations need to address specific incidents.

They have been less frequently considered in relation to the development of resilience capabilities. From existing research on this topic, we learnt that social arrangements between structure and action related to resilience play an important role in organizational functioning and represent an important source of human agency (Reynaud, 1989). In line with this view, agents need to articulate highly structured frameworks to emerging patterns of action (Moynihan, 2012). This means that, well before incidents, organizations ought to overcome a seemingly dichotomous relation between resilience structure and action (Boin & Van Eeten, 2013). To do so, they need to know more about the nature of the interplay between structure and action, which has remained partially unexplored so far, In order to address this gap, this chapter proposes examining two empirical case studies.

Case Studies

This chapter takes a comparative approach to two distinct cases. Because of constraints around anonymity, we label these two organizational entities Ral and Fed. Both Ral and Fed are part of larger organizations that faced unexpected events. In addition, they were both involved in the development of resilience capabilities. However, Ral and Fed abided by divergent resilience frameworks. Ral developed an expert-oriented view of resilience by creating a service dedicated to the management of crisis management teams (CMTs). By contrast, Fed made the choice of approaching as transverse matter by developing collaborative and transverse capabilities. We provide in the remainder of this section additional detail on each case under investigation.

Ral manages crisis management teams (CMTs) and was created by a formerly public organization specialized in railway transportation. In recent years, the growing density of urban spaces and cities has resulted in the French population increasingly relying on railway transportation for daily needs. In addition to that, the railway infrastructure has benefited from major technological advances. This has made trains one of the safest modes of transport in Europe. In the busiest regions, even minor traffic events—such as an electricity blackout, heavy rains or even high temperatures—can lead to the cancellation of one or several trains, leaving sometimes hundreds of people waiting in the station. In such conditions, stations located in the busiest regions of France can be overwhelmed with users. In the wake of a dramatic blackout that resulted in physical violence in a rail station, the organization decided to formulate a strategy for resilience. A project was launched to build internal expertise. In line with this vision, Ral was created, comprising teams of experts in charge of managing critical situations. Thanks to these experts, the organization increased its capability to manage a safer and also more efficient system of mass evacuation in case of incidents. When our investigation was taking place, Ral was composed of 88 employees, half of them coming from safety professions and the other half from sales professions. They could be mobilized 365 days a year and 24 h a day. Their deployment was ordered by a national Operating Manager during the occurrence of an unexpected incident. When Ral is triggered, its members physically go to the incident site. There, their mission is double: sales agents provide guidance to travellers and, if necessary, water and food. Safety agents provide security through their armed presence and respond to any disruptive behaviour.

Fed is a public organization in charge of resilience and crisis coordination in one of the busiest regions in France. Its mission is legally defined at a regional level and targets civil safety, continuity of economic activity and social well-being in the case of disrupting events such as terrorist attacks, extreme weather and even flooding. According to French legal frameworks, management of local events falls under the responsibility of a mayor (in cases where a municipality is involved) or a prefect (in cases where the event involves multiple municipalities). However, some events could require additional equipment to those locally available and involve regional decision-making. This is where Fed intervenes. In such cases, its mission is to orchestrate the supply of necessary equipment to alleviate the economic and social costs associated with an incident. Fed is also in charge of gathering and transmitting information to regional decision-makers in a timely fashion, as well as liaison between organizations involved in the response to an incident. When our investigation was taking place, Fed was comprised of approximately 80 employees who had each developed through the years strong but specific expertise on resilience. For many decades, Fed had favoured siloed expertise, mostly based on specific hazards, such as floods, chemical risks, etc. Some years ago, though, Fed initiated an organizational transformation project, taking the opportunity to renew its own vision of resilience. Fed's new vision consisted of approaching incidents from a holistic and transversal stance, which had two implications: (i) implementation of transversal management of resilience across Fed services (which meant that not only one but all Fed services were in charge of handling a specific incident); and (ii) development of situational awareness within the organization. Situational awareness allows the anticipation of the cascading effects of one specific event. It can be illustrated by this short example: a flood can block deliveries and access to commercial activities, thereby significantly endangering economic activity at a regional level. While Fed was in charge of handling the cascading effects of events such as floods, it still lacked situational awareness and collaboration across services before its transformation. This resulted in Fed's decision to develop dialogue between its various but complementary sources of expertise. This combined with Fed's willingness to diffuse its new vision of resilience and reorganize its processes, based on the idea that resilience is an important matter for everyone and requires all services' expertise and contribution. For this reason, Fed aimed at overcoming existing expertise silos. Table 5.1 summarizes the specifics of functioning emerging from Ral and Fed's organizational contexts.[1]

Multiple reasons accounted for our decision to compare Ral and Fed. First, both organizations shared contextual and structural commonalities, which allowed us to focus on the differences between their practice of resilience. In addition to similar size and public nature, they both represent organizations whose resilience can significantly impact the economic activity of a European region. Moreover, they both elaborated innovative visions of resilience in the aftermath of a disruptive event. By innovative, we mean that they investigated resilience standards and best practices, in particular by exploring state of the art. Both organizations framed their own strategy based on shared representation of what resilience should be. Fully aware of the need to adapt organizational structures in order to implement a resilience strategy, both Ral and Fed were involved in projects that resulted in new organizational settings. They both undertook the implementation of an innovative vision of resilience, thereby designing new processes, activities and task distribution. For instance, Ral initiated reflection on the impact of a transportation blackout on well-being in dense urban areas (as well as the economic impact of people's inability to attend their workplace). In a similar way, Fed thoroughly examined its responsibility in emergency coordination and collaborated

[1] Please note that the dimensions of the case studies depicted here correspond to the main characteristics of organizations investigated in this volume. Additional detail relating to the transformative dimension of resilience, and public nature of organizations in the introduction and other chapters of this volume.

Table 5.1 Commonalities and differences between Ral and Fed

	Ral	*Fed*
Sector	Transportation	Civil safety
Publicness	The state is one of Ral's major stakeholders. Ral is in charge of managing transportation activities and infrastructures as a common good	Public organization. In charge of economic resilience and coordination between public and private organizations to support regional response to events
Response to incident	Consists of supporting the continuity of transportation activities and managing passengers' flow and evacuation through the transportation network	Support to overall regional activity continuity and civil safety
Trigger for search for resilience	Major incident in a station that impacted both users, personnel and transportation flows	Organizational diagnosis and search for productivity and relevance
Resilience framework	Siloed Expert-oriented	Transverse Every member of Fed contributes to its resilience, in particular through situational awareness and occupational agility
Resilience drivers	Creation of Ral and Crisis Management Teams—CMTs—dedicated to resilience and developing the capabilities needed to be resilient	Redefinition of organigrams, task distribution, diffusion of a crisis-prone culture in a transversal fashion

with researchers to reflect on its need to better perform its mission. Another similarity lies in their enthusiasm with respect to their chosen path for resilience.

Data Collection and Analysis

The authors collected data at Ral and Fed from 2015 to 2018. Observing Ral and Fed in routine, emergency and critical situations helped triangulate data, including interviewees' claims about their emotions as compared with their actual experience on the field. For instance, an interviewee once claimed '*craving for opening one's heart to the team*' when meeting one of

Table 5.2 Data collection

Data source	*Ral*	*Fed*
Interviews	10	10
Observation	Team observation > 30 h. The CMTs' activities as well as their interactions were observed in the train stations through 6 h observation sessions	Crisis cells > 40 h (in routine, exercises, large-scale emergencies and critical settings)
Archives	Internal and external archive related to Ral's history. Existing research on Ral and railway management	Internal archive including returns on experience and transformation project

the authors for the first time. The observation of the interviewee's actual practices and interactions with their subordinates (including the team) helped refine the meaning of such a claim. Finally, archives have played an important role in us better understanding the cultural legacy, events (particularly past critical situations) and past interactions that shaped the teleo-affective structure of Ral and Fed. Table 5.2 represents data collection.

The analysis was completed in an iterative and dialogical fashion. By iterative, we mean that the authors met on a regular basis from the start of the project. By dialogical we mean that the findings were regularly discussed between the authors, which supported the refinement of the initial analysis.

Findings

Based on Schatzki's thinking, the findings uncover the nature of the interplay between the structure and action that composes resilience as a practice. To ensure the clarity of our findings, this section is divided into four parts that examine the interplay between resilience action and structures, namely: (i) practical understanding; (ii) general understanding; (iii) rules; and (iv) teleo-affective structures. In each subsection, we focus our analysis on the ties between the ongoing flow of resilience action and one of the components of the structure of resilience practice. Figure 5.2 represents how resilience practice structure and resilience practice action were connected in Ral and Fed.

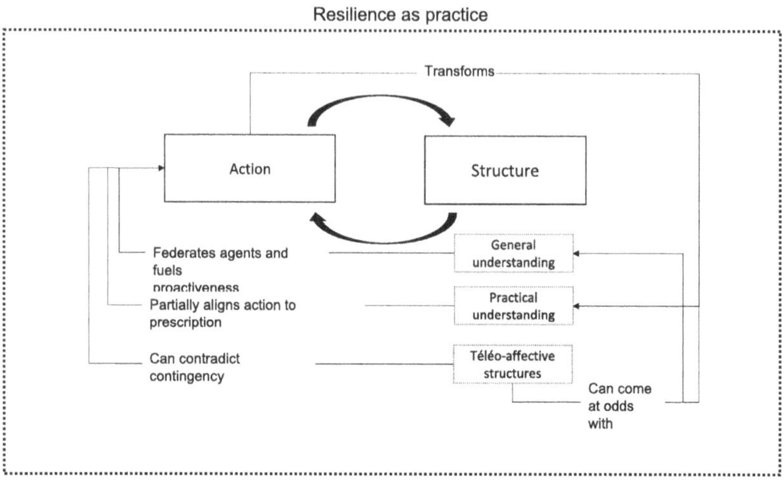

Fig. 5.2 Resilience as practice in Ral and Fed: interplay between structure and actions (inspired from Schatzki, 2002)

General Understanding

As a reminder, general understanding corresponds to the shared belief between actors involved in a practice. Both Ral and Fed presented a general understanding of the ideal of resilience as framed by its proponents. We demonstrate in the following paragraphs how that general understanding united actors, bolstering motivation and fueling initiatives to develop resilience capabilities. Consequently, resilience action was significantly inspired by general understanding.

Rather than developing its general understanding of resilience from scratch, Ral based it on existing examples and knowledge. Drawing on well-known cases of resilience and high reliability organizations (HROs), Ral framed resilience as a specific source of expertise and collaborative skills. From this perspective, the founders of the CMTs promoted expert leadership and encouraged CMTs to act as experts, and rely on self-evaluation and collegial agreement on objectives. At the same time, the creation of the CMTs provided to their members a sense of empowerment consistent with a general understanding of resilience in HROs. The CMT members also developed strong affective ties among each other. These ties, in addition to fostering a strong sense of belonging within the service, contributed to uniting the CMT members in a shared view of resilience as essentially collaborative. This supported CMT innovation and improvement of their processes.

Based on organizational diagnosis, Fed developed a general understanding that resilience was a collective capacity, resulting from decentralized distribution of responsibilities and agile coordination. According to this view, proponents of resilience in Fed argued that it had to develop its ability to orchestrate expertise, share information and collaborate, not only within Fed but also with Fed's partners. Fed's proponents had a strong motivation for diffusing this general understanding of resilience among its stakeholders and partners. From this perspective, Fed's general understanding was a strong driver to resilience action. For instance, Fed applied successfully for a grant to fund a large-scale crisis simulation exercise that would involve more than one hundred organizations, as well as the majority of its internal services. Fed invited hundreds of practitioners to participate and massively communicated on its general understanding of resilience. This action contributed to strengthening a shared understanding of resilience as a transverse matter and had a powerful effect on action. In particular, multiple unexpected and exogenous events in the same year (including terrorist attacks, critical resources shortages and floods) compelled Fed's members to cope with major stress and encouraged collective reflexivity about their practices in Fed. Fed's members hoped to act in accordance with Fed's general understanding of resilience. When they could not do so, they experienced significant frustration. This illustrates how the newly generated general understanding of resilience influenced action.

Practical Understanding

Practical understanding corresponds to the practical knowledge of what to do in a specific situation. At the initial stages of organizational transformation towards resilience, Ral and Fed managed to promote a practical understanding of resilience that aligned with the general understanding framed and supported by the resilience proponents. The practical understanding developed and supported consistency between general understanding on the one hand and action on the other. However, the alignment between actions and practical understanding eventually faded because of two major factors. First, the contingency of actions in certain events prevented agents' abiding by the practical understanding. Second, ongoing action reframed practical understanding. These factors resulted in progressive questioning of Ral and Fed's general understanding of resilience.

Consistent with the general understanding of resilience, the Ral's CMTs increased their ability to handle specific missions related to resilience, which very few other agents could achieve. For instance, they developed processes and know-how for mass evacuation and management of large numbers stuck on a platform (such as when a train is cancelled). They became knowledgeable of train stations to the point where they always kept in mind which train they could rely on to evacuate a specific place at a specific time. They elaborated several techniques to deal with stressed clients and cool down tense situations involving frustrated customers. Finally, the CMTs developed their own skills in order to avoid any member of the team being assaulted or hurt by a customer (which had happened to train station managers in critical situations). This practical understanding of resilience shaped action as the CMT members began to use them intuitively. The CMTs designed such techniques and know-how across the occupational profiles of their team. For instance, the CMT members in charge of customer relationship management learnt basic elements of safety. They were aware that safety is not their source of expertise and frequently made sure that they were not alone when interacting with a customer. By doing so, they enacted and reinforced an expert-oriented vision of resilience. However, the diffusion of resilience practical understanding across services eventually contradicted Ral's initial vision of resilience as strictly driven by experts. Ral acknowledged the importance of train station managers inspiring and learning from the source of expertise as constituted by the CMTs. The image of the CMTs as highly reliable and robust teams also encouraged Ral's members with respect to resilience. While Ral's vision of resilience focused on experts, it tended to become more transversal as other teams were inspired by CMT practices.

In Fed, general understanding promoted the development of practical understanding. Practical understanding concerned good practices to anticipate economic, social and ethical dilemmas that an incident such as a hydrocarbon shortage could bring about for the authorities in an economically productive region. By making the effort to draw a systemic overview of the effect of a hydrocarbon shortage on the economy, Fed's agents managed to identify and alert partners that they needed to involve in a response in a timely manner. This practical understanding aligned with the general understanding of resilience as a shared responsibility. Accordingly, Fed developed experience and a certain level of mastery in the management of information transmission as well as the command chain that would result if the region was impacted. It developed information platforms and technologies that aimed at easing information transmission within Fed and between Fed and its partners. The implementation of these technologies resulted in the adoption of new protocols among Fed's partners that were tested in large-scale exercises and used during incidents.

From this perspective, the development of Fed's practical understanding of resilience significantly shaped resilience action. Fed's practical understanding was not only formal but also had an informal dimension. Consistent with the general understanding that resilience relies on coordination between proactive organizations and individuals, Fed's agents spent part of their worktime in crisis cells, clarifying incorrect information that was transmitted through the command chain. This supported transverse coordination. In addition, they developed informal social networks and collaborative ties with other organizations to promote effective transmission of information. By doing so, Fed developed informal social bonds and connectiveness (as defined by Putnam, 2000) as a source of reliance for resilience. This aspect was hardly formally stated by interviewees, but frequently observed in crisis cells. Finally, the practical understanding of resilience also involved curiosity, in particular towards alternate modes of information transmission such as social media. Hence, practical understanding had a framing effect (as approached by Wong-Parodi et al., 2015) on resilience action. However, in extreme situations (such as terrorist attacks), Fed also confronted information retention from partners, which meant that Fed had to deal with partners who radically departed from its practical and general understanding of resilience. In addition, emerging resilience action could contradict Fed's practical understanding. For instance, during some incidents, some Fed partners were not able to implement the protocols associated with the use of the platforms devoted to transversal coordination, and they failed to provide information. Because of the lack of information, Fed agents could not support clarification and orchestration of resilience. This reduced the ability of Fed agents to abide by their practical understanding of resilience. In the mid-term, this impeded Fed agents' confidence in resilience practical understanding and led them to feel less concerned by the need for transverse coordination or indirectly to promote siloed coordination.

Rules

In both organizations, the framing and application of the rules related to resilience relied on support from proponents of resilience. However, they were at odds with the contingency of actions (including ad hoc action and others' action), which generated frustration among agents.

In Ral, rules related to resilience were initially designed by the team itself, in a collegial fashion. This mindset (as well as the framing of rules that resulted from it) was in line with Ral's general understanding of resilience as a matter of experts. These rules were institutionalized in the CMTs and had a strong impact on cohesion within and between the CMTs. These rules also fostered motivation and a sense of empowerment within the teams. However, it faded when the founders and initial leaders of the CMTs were replaced by managers who came from other services and had not experienced the creation of the CMTs as an embodiment of Ral's vision of resilience. This eventually generated tensions between Ral and other services. For instance, Ral had defined the conditions under which the CMTs were triggered and would take an active role in an incident. However, these rules did not align with the protocols released and implemented in railway national crisis centres.

Fed's general understanding of resilience as a transversal concern implied that the rules dictating resilience action were predefined at a minimum level. According to this view, each partner had to determine its own internal rules and would refer to the framework proposed by Fed for coordination. This vision was based on the metaphor of an orchestra, where every agent masters its own course of action so well that the hierarchy only gives a hint of what needs to be achieved so as to support coordination. As a result, the rules regarding resilience were defined at their minimum in order to give room to each coordinating organization to develop its own additional rules. However, some partners' rules were not precisely defined enough to make Fed's rules applicable. For instance, in the aftermath of the flooding of an urban area, Fed's agents were asked by health care partners to determine which entity was responsible for evaluating whether hospitals could be reused or not. While Fed's rules stated that each partner was in charge of handling its own assets, hospitals, at that time, did not benefit from rules to cover this peculiar circumstance. Facing such divergence between Fed and its partners' rules engendered frustration among agents.

Teleo-Affective Structure

Teleo-affectivity represents a particular component of practice structure. While a teleo-affective structure has a strong experiential dimension (driven by emotions and intentions that can emerge on the spur of the moment), it is also grounded in culture, history and the legacy of organizations. This section explains how the newly created general and practical understandings of resilience came to be at odds with teleo-affective structures inherited from the organization's past.

Ral's teleo-affective structure was not brand new but rather made from its organization's cultural legacy. Ral's teleo-affective structure can be characterized by strong delineation of professions and a strict hierarchy between operational staff and decision-makers. Practical and general understandings of resilience drew on an ideal of collegiality and empowerment of the CMTs. However, the overall teleo-affective structure of the organization from which Ral was created played an ambivalent role in the emergence and establishment of resilience as a practice within Ral. According to the CMTs' general understanding of resilience, work was collegial, iterative and involved trial-and-error. However, CMT members eventually aligned with Ral's formal and strict hierarchy, as suggested in both interviews and observations. In a nutshell, the CMT members had past experience either in safety or commercial activity. While CMTs' own understanding drew on a spirit of fraternity within teams, the teleo-affective structure of Ral implied a strong legacy of hierarchy. These two sets of beliefs and values contradicted each other, generating frustration within the teams regarding the right place for collegiality in resilience practice, as well as the correct basis for their identity. At certain points—especially when the legitimacy of CMTs within Ral was questioned—some members of CMTs struggled to figure out their professional identity as either CMTs members or as safety or CRM specialist. These struggles impeded—and sometimes endangered—CMT cohesion.

In Fed, practical understanding, general understanding and action all contributed to generating positive emotions between practitioners with respect to collaboration. However, the teleo-affective structure of Fed hardly supported such practice because of Fed's legacy in terms of identity, culture and professional background. Fed's teleo-affective structure was even called into question by the evolution of the legal framework of emergency management at the national level in France. Legal guidelines released in 1996 and 2004 were consistent with Fed's general understanding of resilience and outlined the necessity for organizations to develop transverse capabilities, risk policy and procedures to handle rare but disrupting events. In spite of national and local incentives for transformation, Fed's agents' mindset remained strongly influenced by its teleo-affective structure that comprised values such as hierarchy and a siloed approach to resilience. For instance, Fed's firefighters tended towards a firefighting approach to an incident, while Fed's members who had a background as police officers tended to see events from their own professional perspective. Such teleo-affective structures had a strong impact on action. In critical situations, Fed's members still tended to reflect these siloes and lacked the training and preparation to shift to a transversal approach to resilience. Fed agents led their counterparts from other organizations to adopt a systemic, transversal view on events. But in failing to share this conception, they became frustrated when they realized that their counterparts (or even some colleagues in Fed) were remaining stuck in a silo mentality.

The findings of this chapter open the black box of the interplay between action and structure that lies at the core of resilience practice. They first reveal the complexity of this interplay, which can be both synergic and contradictory. More specifically, they outline that the general understanding of resilience, to some extent, shapes resilience action. Moreover, practical understanding plays an important role in resilience practice consistency by interlinking action to general understanding. However, action can also shape practical understanding, thereby inducing inconsistencies within the structure of resilience practice. Action and its contingency can also come to be at odds with rules. Finally, structure is not always consistent. The components of structure can contradict each other with the teleo-affective on one side and understanding on the other. The following tables sum up the findings. Table 5.3 provides a summary of the common evolution of the interplay between resilience action and resilience structures. Figure 5.2 (at the beginning of the chapter) shows the interplay between resilience practice, structure and action. Finally, Table 5.4 provides a comparative view on the evolution of the structures of resilience practice for Ral and Fed.

As shown in Table 5.4, while Ral and Fed promoted seemingly opposite approaches to resilience, but both faced contradictions between teleo-affective structures and resilience understanding.

Table 5.3 Overview of the interplay between resilience structure and resilience action

Structure of resilience as a practice	*Definition*	*Interplay with action*
General understanding	Broad understanding of resilience, covers frameworks, overall vision and rationale	Shaped action and federated agents
Practical understanding	Knowing of what to do in a specific setting	Shaped action but was also modified by action, at the expense of general understanding/practical understanding/action alignment
Rules	Normative definition of action	Went in contradiction with the flow of resilience action
Teleo-affective structure	Set of emotions, intentions and cultural grounds that predefine what is acceptable or not	Contradicted resilience general understanding

Discussion

Ral and Fed represent two different organizations, both characterized by the emergence of divergences between resilience action and an ex-ante organizational framework. Rad had elaborated an expert-oriented vision of resilience, embodied by newly created CMTs. But progressively, the capabilities developed by the CMTs diffused throughout the organization. Conversely, Fed had planned the transversal management of resilience, which confronted the persistence of the siloed distribution of tasks. From this perspective, Ral and Fed failed to impose their initial vision of resilience in the long run. The findings of this chapter outline how arrangements within resilience practice (specifically between action and structure) eventually led these organizations to deviate from their resilience vision and frameworks. No matter how compliant or innovative their vision of resilience was, in the end, the organizations both experienced some contradictions between framed and enacted resilience. This resulted in conflicts, discomfort, motivation collapse, and productivity loss. To nuance our view, resilience in practice was not strictly contradictory. Rather, structure and action mutually influenced each other,

Table 5.4 Synthesis of findings

Case	*General understanding*	*Practical understanding*	*Rules*	*Teleo-affective structures*
Ral	Specific skills and know-how within the CMTs. Diffusion of skills across professional types within the teams	Specific know-hows of mass evacuation and management of stressed passengers. Implied the need for exemplarity, which eventually promoted the leaking of the CMT's practical understanding	The rules initially internally and collegially designed within the service. However, the actors progressively lost the prerogative of self-defining resilience rules in the course of action. Growing inconsistencies between action and rules	Affective ties to the CMTs' belonging and identity. Promoted values and rituals towards collegiality. Contradicted Ral's teleo-affective structure that included a strong sense of hierarchy
Fed	Resilience is an important matter for everyone and requires orchestration of distributed skills and information	How to share common knowledge on incidents and incident response, how to collaborate, transmit information, distribute responsibilities and rely on partners' capacity to develop and implement their inner protocols in case of need	Rules were defined in a top-down fashion. Parcimonious definition of rules in order to leave room for actors' autonomy in the development of resilience capacities and processes. Rules could not be implemented in the course of action	New and positive emotions associated to collaboration. Importance of one's expertise as a source of legitimacy

which led to practice evolution. The comparative design of this study outlines how such contradiction is not inherent to one approach specifically (either expert-oriented or transverse) but rather stems from the articulation between the organizational framing of resilience and resilience in action.

Looking more deeply at the two cases under investigation, this chapter outlines three major points. First, the articulation between resilience structure and action is evolutionary. Second, the nature of this articulation is complex. Third, the articulation between the structure and action underlying resilience practice depends on the role played by resilience proponents. We detail each of these points here, and, based on this discussion, conclude the chapter by providing practical recommendations for organizations.

First, the results highlight that the relationship between resilience structure (including rules, beliefs, visions and frameworks) and resilience action is not static but rather evolutionary. In both Ral and Fed, the initial framework of resilience manifested through evolving practice. Resilience action initially aligned with practical understanding. The spur to action (such as projects and concrete initiatives) also aligned with resilience understanding. As highlighted by our findings, general understanding and practical understanding both represent important drivers for the translation of a vision of resilience into practice. That said, contradictions eventually emerged between practical understanding and action or between rules and action. Both Ral and Fed eventually confronted patterns of action that were dissonant with their practical understanding of resilience. From this stance, the chapter echoes existing research that has highlighted the dynamic dimension of resilience (Limnios et al., 2014). Future avenues to improve our work would consist of drawing a process view of the interplay between action and structure that composes resilience in practice. By doing so, we could more precisely chart the evolution of resilience as practice.

Second, this chapter allows a nuanced understanding of the seeming contradiction between resilience as framed and resilience as operated. Previous literature has documented the emergence of gaps between conception and practices (Wong-Parodi et al., 2015). At first glance, the contradictions that seemingly characterize Ral and Fed could lead to the inaccurate conclusion that however resilience is conceived, organizations shape actual resilience through action primarily. In line with other chapters in this volume, this chapter suggests that the management of ex-ante resilience is more complex. Examining more deeply the cases, we learnt that organizations can initiate innovative avenues for organizational resilience based on both action and structure. This means that resilience practice simultaneously bears synergies and contradictions that, in our view, have to be managed to grant a return on investment. For instance, the evolution of Ral and Fed reveals how the relative inertia of the teleo-affective structure—at least in relation to resilience—in an organization can be at odds with resilience understanding. Such findings are not surprising and echo previous depictions of teleo-affective structures as invisible but powerful (Iedema et al., 2006). The teleo-affective structure does not only bear the values, ideals, emotions and myths associated with resilience. It also comprises organizational memory, past structures, values, emotions and interaction patterns. Despite the innovation and relevance of a plan for resilience, organizational legacy and structures participate in the framing of practical understanding, general understanding and rules. For instance, Fed was previously designed in a siloed fashion to manage incidents and crises. Despite its intention to approach resilience as a transversal matter, it remained strongly influenced by the existing structures that it had previously developed that matched with the silo-oriented view. More than that, siloed expertise proved to be particularly helpful to Fed, confronting tensions resulting from the gap between the formal definition of roles and the actual sources of knowledge.

Third, both in Ral and Fed, resilience was initiated by proponents of resilience who not only found practical opportunities to promote general and practical understanding of resilience; as well, these persons translated a specific vision into concrete action. Their presence and interactions contributed to the fueling of positive emotions and affective ties, which could contribute to an evolution of the teleo-affective structure (Schatzki, 2006). By contrast, the turnover of people who initiated resilience vision significantly impeded its implementation, in particular as organizations could not deal with contradictions between rules and action or teleo-affective structure. From this perspective, the agency of proponents of resilience seems to represent either a strong inhibitor or a strong driver to resilience implementation and is therefore worth examining. To that extent, the findings of this chapter converge with previous literature on the importance of human agency, as well as the importance of institutional work in relation to resilience (Barin Cruz et al., 2016), and the influence of institutional entrepreneurs in organizational contexts characterized by strong institutional pressure (Battilana, 2006). Putting the cases of Ral and Fed into perspective through this literature, one can infer that resilience proponents correspond to crucial drivers for the promotion of resilience practice (in particular when teleo-affective structure impedes the shaping of action from resilience understanding and rules). From the findings of this chapter, one could assume that resilience proponents, through their contribution to institutional work on resilience, promote resilience practice consistency overtime. Additional research is necessary to infer, refine and nuance such assumption. From this perspective, we need to better understand the role of proponents' agency in addressing contradictions between understanding and teleo-affective structure. Data analysed for this chapter does not provide enough detail on this specific point and, to that extent, we recommend additional investigation of the role of proponents in resilience practice.

How can organizations address inconsistencies between resilience structure and action? We identify two practical avenues for organizations to handle these inconsistencies. We first propose that organizations develop awareness of their teleo-affective structure—comprising organizational legacy and past experience—when desiging resilience. Through organizational diagnosis, organizations can scan their own teleo-affective structures before initiating transformation (reorganization, creation of processes, teams, structures, etc.). In addition, organizations can reflect on ways to transform their teleo-affective structure to reduce resilience practice inconsistencies. The findings of the chapter suggest that time is important: by the time organizations had framed resilience understanding, they had developed scant awareness of their teleo-affective structure. As a sequential organizational diagnosis seems tricky to implement, we propose that the 'reflection in action' perspective on resilience (Yanow & Tsoukas, 2009) could help raise awareness of the inherent inconsistencies of resilience practice. Second, we recommend that organizations fully consider the possibility of supporting resilience proponents from an institutional perspective. In terms of policy and frameworks, the findings of this chapter suggest that dedicated recommendations regarding resilience proponents could be enriched and refined. By doing so, organizations would support institutional work on resilience, in particular by empowering resilience proponents in their narratives. They would also support the production of general and practical understanding, which represents the second avenue to maintaining consistency between action and structure of resilience practice over time. Going further, we suggest that frameworks and policies provide enough room for human agency to avoid the rise of inconsistencies between resilience structure and action.

References

Adrot, A., & Garreau, L. (2010). Interagir pour improviser en situation de crise. Le cas de la canicule de 2003. *Revue Française de Gestion*, *36*(203), 119–131.

Barin Cruz, L., Aguilar Delgado, N., Leca, B., & Gond, J.-P. (2016). Institutional resilience in extreme operating environments: The role of institutional work. *Business & Society, 55*(7), 970–1016.

Battilana, J. (2006). Agency and institutions: The enabling role of individuals' social position. *Organization, 13*(5), 653–676.

Benson, J. K. (1977). Organizations: A dialectical view. *Administrative Science Quarterly, 22*(1), 1.

Boin, A., & Van Eeten, M. J. (2013). The resilient organization. *Public Management Review, 15*(3), 429–445.

Djalante, R., & Lassa, S. (2019). Governing complexities and its implication on the Sendai framework for disaster risk reduction priority 2 on governance. *Progress in Disaster Science, 2*, 100010.

Duit, A. (2016). Resilience thinking: Lessons for public administration. *Public Administration, 94*(2), 364–380.

Hale, A., & Borys, D. (2013). Working to rule or working safely? Part 2: The management of safety rules and procedures. *Safety Science, 55*, 222–231.

Iedema, R., Rhodes, C., & Scheeres, H. (2006). Surveillance, resistance, observance: Exploring the teleo-affective volatility of workplace interaction. *Organization Studies, 27*(8), 1111–1130.

Limnios, E. A. M., Mazzarol, T., Ghadouani, A., & Schilizzi, S. G. (2014). The resilience architecture framework: Four organizational archetypes. *European Management Journal, 32*(1), 104–116.

Lindberg, O., & Rantatalo, O. (2015). Competence in professional practice: A practice theory analysis of police and doctors. *Human Relations, 68*(4), 561–582.

Lovins, A. B., & Lovins, L. H. (1982). *Brittle power: Energy strategy for national security*. Brick House Publishing Company.

Manyena, S. B. (2006). The concept of resilience revisited. *Disasters, 30*(4), 434–450.

Moynihan, D. P. (2012). A theory of culture-switching: Leadership and red-tape during hurricane Katrina. *Public Administration, 90*(4), 851–868.

Perrow, C. (2006). Disasters ever more? Reducing U.S. vulnerabilities. In H. Rodriguez, E. L. Quarantelli, & R. Dynes (Eds.), *Handbook of disaster research* (pp. 42–54). Springer.

Pettersen, K. A., & Schulman, P. R. (2019). Drift, adaptation, resilience and reliability: Toward an empirical clarification. *Safety Science, 117*, 460–468.

Putnam, R. D. (2000). Bowling alone: America's declining social capital. In L. Crothers & C. Lockhart (Eds.), *Culture and politics* (pp. 223–234). Springer.

Reynaud, J.-D. (1989). Les règles du jeu. *L'action collective et la régulation sociale, 2*, 270. Armand Colin.

Schatzki, T. (1996). *Social practices: A Wittgensteinian approach to human activity and the social*. Cambridge University Press.

Schatzki, T. (2002). *The site of the social: A philosophical account of the constitution of social life and change*. Penn State Press.
Schatzki, T. (2006). On organizations as they happen. *Organization Studies, 27*(12), 1863–1873.
Schatzki, T., Knorr-Cetina, K., & Von Savigny, E. (2001). *The practice turn in contemporary theory* (Vol. 44). Routledge.
Schatzki, T. R. (2012). A primer on practices: Theory and research. In J. Higgs, R. Barnett, S. Billett, M. Hutchings & F. Trede (Eds.), *Practice-based education: Perspectives and strategies* (pp. 13–26). Brill Sense.
Schulman, P. R. (1993). The negotiated order of organizational reliability. *Administration & Society, 25*(3), 353–372.
Shrivastava, P. (1987). *Bhopal: Anatomy of a crisis*. Paul Chapman Publishing.
Suchman, L. (2007). *Human-machine reconfigurations: Plans and situated action*. Cambridge University Press.
Vogus, T. J., & Sutcliffe, K. M. Organizational resilience: Towards a theory and research agenda. *2007 IEEE International Conference on Systems, Man and Cybernetics, 2007* (pp. 3418–3422). IEEE.
Walls, J. L., & Hoffman, A. J. (2013). Exceptional boards: Environmental experience and positive deviance from institutional norms. *Journal of Organizational Behavior, 34*(2), 253–271.
Wiig, S., & Fahlbruch, B. (2019). *Exploring resilience: A scientific journey from practice to theory*. Springer.
Wildavsky, A. B. (1988). *Searching for safety, 10*. Transaction publishers.
Wong-Parodi, G., Fischhoff, B., & Strauss, B. (2015). Resilience vs. adaptation: Framing and action. *Climate Risk Management*, *10*, 1–7.
Yanow, D., & Tsoukas, H. (2009). What is reflection-in-action? A phenomenological account. *The Journal of Management Studies, 46*(8), 1339–1364.

CHAPTER 6

Growing and Adapting During Continuous Change: Building Employee Resilience in the Public Sector

Esme Franken, Geoff Plimmer, Sanna Malinen, and Jane Bryson

Resilience in the Public Sector

Employee resilience is essential in public sector organizations, particularly when demands are high and difficult to meet, and when the environment is uncertain and continually evolving. Also, many public sector jobs can be characterized by high, ambiguous, and often competing demands and ever-changing circumstances; a context where continuous learning, collaboration and adaptability are essential. Employee resilience,

E. Franken (✉)
School of Business and Law, Edith Cowan University, Joondalup, Australia
e-mail: e.franken@ecu.edu.au

G. Plimmer · J. Bryson
Wellington School of Business & Government, Victoria University of Wellington, Wellington, New Zealand
e-mail: geoff.plimmer@vuw.ac.nz

R. Pinheiro et al. (eds.), *Towards Resilient Organizations and Societies*, Public Sector Organizations,
https://doi.org/10.1007/978-3-030-82072-5_6

and its development, are therefore particularly salient in this context (Lengnick-Hall et al., 2011).

In viewing resilience as developable, it is not a fixed trait but instead is a dynamic capability at the individual level, in which employees 'innovate, adapt to change', and, arguably, 'create change' (Teece et al., 2016, p. 18). This focus on reciprocal interactions with the environment during both day-to-day challenges, as well as crises, blurs the distinction between ex-ante and ex-post resilience. This is because it assumes the requirement to be resilient to change is continuous in many KIOs, and that in order to adapt in crisis, a culture where employees can develop their resilience in more routine circumstances, is required.

Earlier views of individual resilience considered it as a personality trait, similar to constructs like grit, hardiness, and the ability to bounce back from hardship (Bonanno, 2004; Credé, et al., 2017; Richardson, 2002). The more modern view of resilience concerns 'a key capability enabling employees to manage and adapt to continually changing circumstances' (Näswall et al., 2019, p. 353). This contemporary understanding concerns the individual's capacity to engage with work-related personal, social and contextual resources, and therefore acknowledges the person–environment interaction in resilience development (Näswall et al., 2019; Pangallo et al., 2015). It sees resilience as involving particular capabilities that allow individuals 'to adapt to challenges and seek out opportunities for continuous improvement' (Näswall et al., 2019, p. 354).

The broader interpersonal system of workplaces shapes resilience. Resilience development involves a constant interaction between an individual and their work context (Mansfield et al., 2014). Leadership, social support and workplace climate and culture, for instance, play important enabling and motivating roles (Cooper et al., 2019; Khan et al., 2019; Kuntz et al., 2016; Nguyen et al., 2016). In turn, the development and enactment of resilience reciprocally contributes to the collective capacity of a workforce's overall resilience.

J. Bryson
e-mail: jane.bryson@vuw.ac.nz

S. Malinen
UC Business School, University of Canterbury, Christchurch, New Zealand
e-mail: sanna.malinen@canterbury.ac.nz

We adopt a definition of employee resilience as 'the capacity of employees to utilise resources to continually adapt and flourish at work, even when faced with challenging circumstances' (Kuntz et al., 2016, p. 460). It consists of employee behaviours associated with learning, adaptability and collaboration. This definition aligns well to the framework adopted in this volume. Resilience here can be both an independent and dependent variable, and likely works in both linear and non-linear ways. It can be influenced by workplace contextual factors, such as leadership (Nguyen et al., 2016), and is related to outcomes, such as job satisfaction, engagement (Näswall et al., 2019) and wellbeing (Tonkin et al., 2018).

Resilient behaviours can lead to, or include, making both radical and small incremental changes. The behaviours can also be either proactive (ex-ante) or reactive (ex-post). Logically, these behaviours also provide a way of dealing with ambiguity and uncertainty. With resilience, smaller day-to-day challenges build capacity to deal with larger crises. In resilience enabling workplaces, people are aware of what is happening, are managing vulnerabilities, and adapt and respond accordingly (Lee et al., 2013; Mallak, 1998). Consequently, they achieve desirable outcomes, despite 'adversity, strain, and significant barriers to adaptation or development' (Sutcliffe & Vogus, 2003, p. 94). When a workplace is healthy and resilient, its people can effectively prepare for, survive and thrive in challenging environments (Lee et al., 2013; Vogus & Sutcliffe, 2007). Notably, our conceptualization of resilience does not necessitate a severe disruption or a crisis for resilience to be enacted; rather, resilient responses can be developed and used during routine times (Kuntz et al., 2016).

Public sector managers play a pivotal role in enabling employee resilience. Managers can support employee resilience through mechanisms such as modelling, social exchange, task allocation, process determination and the setting of rewards (Nguyen et al., 2016; Franken, 2019). More specifically, leadership behaviours influence daily interactions between the employee and manager, and these constant interactions shape resilience development, both in good and in bad ways. For example, when managers back staff, foster their growth and build the whole team, employee resilience grows (Franken, 2019). In contrast, micromanagement and poor support for learning and development undermine resilience (Franken & Plimmer, 2019).

This chapter begins with a brief description of the research method, followed by an overview of public sector context and the need for resilience. We then move to a discussion on the behaviours associated with employee resilience capability, followed by recommendations for developing growth-oriented leadership to enable this capability. This chapter concludes with a discussion on resilience-enabling leadership, its relation to the public sector and its values, and its significance in preparing for the future of work.

Method

In this chapter we draw on our series of studies in the New Zealand public sector to describe and explain how employee resilience can be enabled by public sector managers. Specifically we draw on 26 interviews and two focus groups undertaken in 2017 and 2018 with New Zealand public servants and line managers ($n = 33$). Participants came from the areas of commerce, auditing, policy and operations, reflecting the occupational diversity of New Zealand's wider public service (State Services Commission, 2019). Initial interview information ($n = 20$) was collected using the critical incident technique, and subsequently analysed using Saldaña's (2015) causation coding technique—to pinpoint the mechanisms through which certain leadership behaviours can impact resilience. These interviews were completed once saturation was reached (Guest et al., 2006). The final six interviews and the focus groups were used for validating the preliminary results.

Public Sector Environments and Need for Resilience

Public services are increasingly both expanded and dispersed, and public organizations are consequently forced to take a more networked approach to organizational structures and decision-making (Stoker, 2006). These new networked approaches often consist of collaborative processes both within and between organizations, that can include private organizations and stakeholders. The challenge is for public organizations to stay aligned and accountable to democratic laws and public values, while also exercising more discretion to allow for effective collaboration and innovation (Bryson et al., 2014; Plimmer et al., 2017a).

The networked approaches mean that stakeholder relationships are more frequent, deeper and dynamic. They are also often situated in turbulent and trying conditions. Although governments and societies understandably expect workforces to meet these challenging demands, unfortunately employee capability is often missing in these discussions (Plimmer et al., 2017a). Instead, public administration reforms have often focussed on organizational and institutional structure, performance management, the use of market structures, and appropriate incentives (Bach & Bordogna, 2011; Christensen et al., 2007; Hood, 2006). Human resource capability has not really featured, despite its potential (Plimmer et al., 2017b). Individual level, workplace relevant behaviours that concern interactions with the environment have not been sufficiently studied, despite them being the fractals from which group and organizational level capabilities might grow (Hall et al., 2016).

One response to rising demands on public agencies has been to shift from centralized, bureaucratic forms of public administration to more decentralized, market-driven methods of organizing (Bryson et al., 2014). These trends have intensified work, with not just longer hours, but also the proportion of effective labour performed for each hour (Cameron, 1998; Green, 2004). Increased pressure and controls, cultures that expect compliance and negative behaviours such as bullying now also seem too common (Omari & Paull, 2015; Plimmer et al., 2017c). These changes put pressure on workers (Christensen & Lægreid, 2011a): 'many large-scale reforms that have occurred in the public sector have involved a loss of resources, especially in terms of people, time, and budgetary support' (Noblet et al., 2006, p. 338). Clearly public sector organizations are faced with a need for both tight and innovative resource use to cope with increasingly complex demands. This ever-changing context demands a resilient workforce:

> *We have the constant challenge that there's always churn and change so that does push us to, "Either you're resilient or you're not," and there's an element of that that comes through so some people find policy is not for them pretty quickly, but those who can survive ...well if you survive the first 12 months, you'll be fine!* [Interview—Manager]

Public sector organizations are both hierarchical bureaucracies and paradoxically, often decentralized and networked, increasingly resembling hybrid organizations (Fossestøl et al., 2015). Leadership can occur at any level of an organization, and many positional leaders lead in ways that support resilience (Zeier et al., 2018). Some, however, do not (Franken, 2019).

Resilient Employee Behaviours

There are many conceptualisations of resilience, but the one adopted for this research is that employee resilience is centred on three core behaviours: network leveraging, learning and adaptability (Kuntz et al., 2017). These behaviours are not discrete, rather they relate to and build on each other, and also interact with the work environment to protect and acquire job and personal resources, such as connections, feelings of competence, and control.

For example, working well with others (network leveraging) supports learning through the flourishing of new, and diverse, ideas. Being adaptable can also help learning, as new repertoires are practiced. Adaptable people often work better with others (O'Connell et al., 2008). These three behaviours can also help in the acquisition of other resources, such as skills and connections (Hobfoll, 2011). Resilient behaviours thus bolster one's ability to deal with challenges and crises effectively.

Combined, these behaviours represent 'the capacity of employees to utilise resources to continually adapt and flourish at work, even when faced with challenging circumstances' (Kuntz et al., 2016, p. 460). Resilient behaviours are separate from, but precede, attitudes such as job satisfaction, engagement, commitment and wellbeing (Brennan, 2017; Näswall et al., 2019; Tonkin et al., 2018; Youssef & Luthans, 2007).

The core behaviour of network-leveraging consists of effective collaboration between colleagues, sharing knowledge and information and cooperating across teams, networks and functions (Lengnick-Hall et al., 2011; Uzzi, 1997). These behaviours help people access and exchange resources, which in turn makes dealing with challenge and crises easier (Mitchell et al., 2015). Teams collaborate to use collective competencies to resolve shared issues and challenges (Hardy et al., 2005):

> *When I talk about things with other people I get good ideas or like things become more clear to me so I find that really helpful. You can really get so much groundwork done working with other people's [work] that they did before.* [Interview—Employee]

Learning, the second behavioural component of employee resilience, supports innovation, and helps develop the competencies that are necessary in overcoming, and learning during challenges and crises (Kuntz et al., 2017; Walker et al., 2020). This ex-ante skill enables individuals to be resilient during routine challenges, build resilience capacity before severe crises and be adaptive in the midst of crises. Like network leveraging, this skill is particularly salient in the public sector, where under-resourcing and complex demands are common (Cameron, 1998; Christensen & Lægreid, 2011b). Goals that are learning-centred, rather than rigid and performance-oriented, foster wellbeing and growth as well as performance. They support deep and sustained learning that ultimately build capacities such as adaptive resilience (Winters & Latham, 1996).

The third key behavioural component of resilience is adaptability. It occurs when employees use their resources (both personal and job-related) to respond swiftly (ex-post) to changes and uncertainties. Adaptability helps individuals use experiences involving change or challenge in order to grow and develop personally and professionally (Kuntz et al., 2017). It also means that employees can effectively adapt to changing demands and stressors that arise and develop in a particular context. In doing so, they use learning to improve and modify their adaptive responses over time.

Table 6.1 exemplifies the behavioural components of employee resilience, with examples from interviews with public employees and managers.

These behaviours are all closely interwoven and reinforce each other. For instance, network leveraging supports adaptability, which in turn helps learning (Folke et al., 2010). A resilient employee with appropriate support would collaborate well with others, adapt accordingly and also contribute to individual and organizational learning. Resilient employees adapt to changing job circumstances, and acquire and use personal, work, and social resources well. In contrast, a person who lacks resilience-enabling support may find collaboration difficult; and not learn easily. They may also struggle with change.

Resilience is often thought of as an outcome (Zautra & Reich, 2011), but the capacity itself has strong and significant downstream consequences for employees and workplaces. Job satisfaction, wellbeing and engagement are three known outcomes of employee resilience (Malik & Garg, 2020; Näswall et al., 2019). A resilient workplace is defined as one that achieves 'desirable outcomes amid adversity, strain, and significant barriers to adaptation or development' (Sutcliffe & Vogus, 2003, p. 94). It is an essential capacity in modern organizations, constantly facing change and challenge.

Table 6.1 Resilient behaviours and examples

Resilient behaviour	*Behavioural examples*	*Exemplifying quotes*
Network leveraging	Collaborating internally with peers, managers and teams Collaborating with people and teams in other organizations Seeking support from managers when required Exchanging resources with peers and managers Seeking resources from peers	*I thrive off being able to bounce ideas off other people just more to make sure that what you're thinking and doing is the right thing* *It is kind of a team approach in going 'right, what do we need to do, what bits of information do we need to get, who's going to do what, how are we gonna pull this all together?'*
Learning	Using mistakes as learning opportunities Re-evaluating performance on a continuous basis to improve own work Using feedback, including negative feedback, for learning and improvement of own work	*Not just learning from mistakes but learning from changes or other ways of doing things* *You can't function effectively within the team without being open to learning on a semi constant basis*
Adaptability	Managing resources effectively in order to cope with high workloads when needed Engaging in crisis management effectively Using change as an opportunity for growth	*You have to be adaptive all the time because you know that the government changes quite a lot and that's not really how the public sector should work...but it does ...* *We need to adjust to... be able to do really in-depth thinking about issues [and then] jump to doing discussions with stakeholders to then completely changing the direction we were going to take because it wasn't going to be acceptable. So constant change in that sense*

Note Adapted from Näswall et al. (2019) and Kuntz et al. (2017); own data sources

Leadership for Resilience and Growth

Although resilience likely depends to some extent on relatively stable individual characteristics (Donnellan & Robins, 2010), it is also shaped by the environment and specifically, leadership (Franken, 2019; Nguyen et al., 2016). The next section discusses and relates our findings to recommendations for public organizations and their leaders, specifically on how managers can engage in growth-oriented leadership (Franken, 2019) to build resilience in their workforce. Such leadership is relational and reflects a willingness to attend to the development needs of employees. It reflects calls for leadership models which facilitate employees' personal and vocational development (Zhang & Chen, 2013), rather than focusing on task and goal performance (Hargis et al., 2011; Howell & Avolio, 1993).

Resilience-enabling leadership is associated with the provision of resources. An employee with a resilience-enabling manager is provided with clear pathways for personal and professional growth, individualized feedback, trust and autonomy, as well as a functional norms for teamwork. These resources are likely to help develop resilient behaviours, maintain resilience capacity in the face of challenges, and further grow resilience as a result. This mirrors conservation of resources theory (Hobfoll, 1989), that when individuals gain resources, they protect and invest in them, and then become better placed to gain more resources (Demerouti et al., 2004; Ng & Feldman, 2012). In contrast, a resilience-harming manager may contribute to a reduction in resources. For example, poor or unclear feedback might mean that employees 'are more likely to engage in feedback avoidance in order to avoid further resource losses from interacting with the abusive supervisor' (Halbesleben et al., 2014, p. 1336). They may also be reluctant to show vulnerability, i.e. through problem solving or experimenting, in attempts to protect any remaining resources (Halbesleben, 2010). Resource provision, or loss, is relevant to the resilience development process, and needs to be considered when understanding how resilience can be both enabled and harmed by managers in organizations.

Resilience-enabling leadership is also capability, competence and confidence-enhancing. Such managers use their authority to develop adaptive, independent and autonomous employees, rather than relying on it to perpetuate traditional worker-manager dependencies and maintain command and control power structures (Heifetz, 1994; Wilson et al., 2017). The latter does not help employee growth and development and is increasingly ill-suited to today's dynamic environments. Instead, a set of beliefs and behaviours by managers are needed to foster employee resilience in subordinates.

Our analysis resulted in four core dimensions of leadership behaviours that foster resilience: *Seeing people as 'developable', not as broken or fixed*, *Supporting personal goals*, *Providing both challenging tasks and safe failures* and *Managing the whole team* (Table 6.2).

Table 6.2 Leadership beliefs and behaviours that foster resilience

Core dimension	*Representative quote*	*Process*
Seeing people as 'developable', not as broken or fixed	*I know the people I've grown and nurtured—and I think it is my responsibility to grow and nurture them. I look on attrition as success... we've got people who don't want to leave and are having to grow them to the point that they do*	Manager sees people as capable of change and development, relies less on hierarchy. Led to more confidence, lower stress and adaptive behaviours
Supporting personal goals	*If [employees] can see this is what I'm doing, this is the purpose, but these other things are out there and I could go there or do this, it gives them a sense of what the future could hold*	Managers develop staff by encouraging reflection and encourage a learning (rather than performance) goal orientation (Winters & Latham, 1996). Non growth supporting managers harmed morale, and were often focussed on managing up, but not down
Providing both challenging tasks and safe failures	*They need to know and understand that they have full support of their manager and their colleagues and to know that by making an error, the world isn't going to crumble down around you*	Requires reciprocal trust in manager and employee competence, which then enables autonomy and self-management. Motivates and encourages discretionary effort (Burke et al., 2007). The inverse of this is micromanagement which harms exchange processes, autonomy and work ownership (Hackman & Oldham, 1980)

(continued)

Seeing People as 'Developable', Not as Broken or Fixed

If a manager views resilience as developable, they are more likely to try and foster it. However, we found that managers with a formal hierarchical approach to their role typically saw employee resilience (and general capability) in traditional terms: they saw it as fixed and trait-based, i.e. having natural self-confidence and a proactive personality.

Table 6.2 (continued)

Core dimension	*Representative quote*	*Process*
Managing the whole team	*I always ask for a collaborative approach. And you know, bring them in as part of the situation. And work together on the result or an outcome, however we need to get there*	Builds norms for network leveraging, allows individuals to benefit from sharing knowledge and learning from each other (Malik & Garg, 2020). Managers build collaboration through fostering norms for collaboration, collaborating themselves with the team, and setting collective tasks

These managers, perhaps conveniently, could not see the pivotal role they could play in developing resilience.

> *It might be just that they have a degree of maturity, or that they will keep things in perspective or kind of, have their own personal ways of managing stuff. And other people can't, some people are just total stress bunnies and react to everything that happens in a negative way.* [Interview—Manager]

Although some managers saw resilience as a fixed trait, employees often saw their psychological state as dependent on how their managers treated them. They saw their resilience as both developable and damageable by managers. A quote about the impact of micromanagement illuminates this:

> *It takes away self-esteem because they don't believe in your ability to do a job. Well when you feel like you're constantly being checked up on and you're not allowed to just go up and meet with people or do things without them being there, you know...You can't learn in that respect.* [Interview—Employee]

In a more positive light, managers' behaviours could have healthy impacts on employees (such as through developing their resilience):

> *Oh it [my manager's behaviour] makes me want to turn up. Just want to get stuck in which is what it's about.* [Interview—Employee]

Our interviews found that growth-oriented leadership reduced demands on employees and stress, and promoted employee commitment, confidence, job motivation and feelings of being valued. These psychological states in turn helped employees be resilient. Employees engaged in adaptive behaviours, sought development opportunities and elicited continuous learning processes.

> *...he's [manager] always open to anything you want to suggest like if you bring a development opportunity and its relevant then you can be confident that you'll be able to do it within reason... to even have that brought to me as an opportunities kind of made me feel quite good because I wouldn't have thought I'd even be considered for this.* [Interview—Employee]

Supporting Personal Goals

Growth-oriented managers supported employees' subjective career successes, defined as the 'person's own preferences for development in an occupation, that is his/her individual perception of career experience' (Gattiker & Larwood, 1986, p. 80). Subjective success is important because objective success, such as promotion and pay increases, are sometimes limited in public sectors (Frank & Lewis, 2004; Lyons et al., 2006). A public manager who values employee growth and potential is subsequently developing committed and effective public servants (Ng et al., 2005). It likely also partly compensates for the low pay that characterizes some public sector jobs:

> *I've been told 'I can offer you at least 10,000 more than what you're on now'—it's not a more complicated job ... but the money isn't enough to make me want to change.* [Interview—Manager]

Growth-oriented leadership is relational. Consistent with other leadership constructs such as transformational, servant, organizing and paradoxical, resilience enhancing leaders respond to, care, and are seen to care, about those they are responsible for (Dong et al., 2017; Franken, 2019; Miao et al., 2014; Plimmer & Blumenfeld, 2012).

> *The best managers are people managers, they care about their staff, they put them into training, they develop them to become the best people they can. And then they know how to manage up. They're the best managers. Quite often you'll get managers that just manage up. So all they care about is looking*

> *good to the person above them and they don't care about the people below them.* [Interview—Employee]

Some research has found that these 'developmental' managers are not easy to come by in the public sector (Plimmer et al., 2017a), where layers of mixed ideologies such as new public management, market models and bureaucracies have led to strong management control, but weak management development and accountability. Our findings supported the idea that some managers are better at managing up than down, and are motivated to advance their own career but not that of their staff (Feldman & Weitz, 1991).

> *You've still got a lot of the same people in those leadership positions that have been there for 10 or 15 years and they got there through hanging around and being quite senior and knowledgeable about their jobs rather than being leaders per-se. So in that situation you don't have people who necessarily have the right sort of set of skills to lead or manage people.* [Interview—Manager]

Growth-oriented leadership is also about encouraging employees to make mistakes and then grow as a result. An employee explains this below:

> *If you let people make a few mistakes in a really low…you know, like there's a…the potential negative is really quite minor, but you let them kind of fail, or also encourage them to deal with difficult situations that as a fresh new person, they're pretty stressful, but they're actually not, you know what I mean, in hindsight you go 'yeah that wasn't really that bad'. I think that helps you to then develop up and be able to deal with more and more difficult situations.* [Interview—Employee]

Related to growth and development is learning (Hameed & Waheed, 2011), and managers can foster this through a learning orientation:

> *I say 'so, what have you learnt from this?' I'd say there's always some learning. So 'what DID you learn and what do you think you could do better next time?' So you just went ahead and did it off the back of your hand? And just made a decision? Or did you go and check that perhaps you should have done this, you know?* [Interview—Manager]

As can be expected, managers who do not foster growth in employees were found to have a negative impact on employee morale and motivation

(Moynihan, 2009; Pandey, 2010) limiting the possibilities for resilience development:

> *[Having a manager who is not growth oriented] is like doing a degree that never ends and it's like you can't get to a certain level and then you know, you get promoted, or you know, you just keep going forever trying to get a degree.* [Interview—Employee]

Managers may also lack the time (and prioritization skills) to work with employees to discuss and plan their growth and development opportunities:

> *I'm an investment advisor, so my next career step would be a senior investment advisor and for me in the last year I've struggled to understand what that progression looks like and I have asked a lot of questions about it but [my manager] doesn't have the time to really sit down and explain that.* [Interview—Employee]

Without growth-oriented managers, employees are left to navigate their opportunities. This is good for certain employees, mainly as it represents some capacity for resilience and self-management. However, not being supported in this way can place unnecessary stress and burden on employees:

> *And previously any kind of secondments or movements I've done I've made those myself, I've made those enquiries on my own, I haven't had anyone or a manager come to me and say you know, this would be a good idea for you or anything like that.* [Interview—Employee]

Providing Both Challenging Tasks and Safe Failures

A trusting relationship between employees and managers is important for resilience (Franken, 2019; Walker et al., 2020). With this trust comes the managers' belief in employee competence, which enables autonomy and self-management. Such independence is an essential part of employee resilience (Näswall et al., 2019).

> *I guess that's why I try to do, just assume that they are capable of doing their job and let them get on with it. Um, expect them to hold up their hand if*

they need help. And if need be, kind of get alongside them to help them with what they need. [Interview—Manager]

The quotes above and below establish that a balance of support is required for trust—a certain degree of autonomy with adequate help and guidance when required:

[My manager] has a lot of faith in me to manage myself to some extent. So he's, in saying that, he's very supportive and you know that if something happens and you need help, he'll be there and he'll do whatever needs to be done to make that happen. But yeah, doesn't micromanage, which is appealing. [Interview—Employee]

Trust, belief in competence and allowance of autonomy are often interwoven with learning. A resilience-enabling manager balances growth (and learning), trust and collaboration in the approach to leadership:

So what I say is 'you're a manager in your own right' When I see you're not managing yourself or you can't manage, that's where I step in. So that gives them some autonomy to make decisions for themselves. They can be right or wrong, I don't care. As long as there's that learning if it comes back to me. [Interview—Manager]

The balance between providing support and allowing autonomy can also come down to the different stages of trust development between managers and employees (Whitener et al., 1998):

What happens is you grow a trust with the individual you're working with and it might start off with direction but it ends up with suggestion. And that suggestion, once the trust is grown delivers what it was you want. Because you don't need somebody telling you to do it your way, you just need to make sure that the aim is achieved and you can't achieve the aim until you've built the trust. [Interview—Manager]

Trusting behaviours by managers are often reciprocated by employees, through a process of social exchange. There is a reciprocal trust that can emerge from the employee, whereby they feel that they trust their manager to value them and support them in their extra efforts. This is good for employee resilience (learning, development, extension of capabilities) and organizations:

> *[When] they've given me that respect...it's my responsibility to make sure that I get my work done.* [Interview—Employee]

Another employee experienced a sense of motivation to work and freedom when he feels trusted.

> *...I actually enjoy coming to work because you have the freedom to do stuff.* [Interview—Employee]

Extra discretionary effort can also result from a trusting employee–manager relationship (Burke et al., 2007):

> *If there is a big drama, all hands to the pump, I'll work extra or I'll call into meetings from home and all that kind of stuff and I think that's kind of a key to having a good, having a workforce that's kind of prepared to go that extra mile when there is a big issue on.* [Interview—Employee]

Positive leader–follower exchanges, underpinned by trust, matter in public contexts, and predict motivation among public sector employees (Gould-Williams & Davies, 2005). This is especially so when employees lack confidence in political leaders and ministers (Miao et al., 2014). Managers trusting their employees' capabilities and giving them autonomy likely provides employees confidence to address, experiment with and learn from the challenges of governance. Positive interactions with leaders promote trust in the leader–follower dynamic, even if trust is lacking elsewhere. This makes sense since 'direct leaders (e.g. supervisors) appear to be a particularly important referent of trust' (Dirks & Ferrin, 2002, p. 611). Trust-based experiences with a leader may also foster organizational commitment among public servants (Miao et al., 2014).

Both employees and (some) managers emphasized the importance of not micromanaging employees, but also providing support:

> *If they're given a task and a time to be completed by, one follow up three-quarters of the way through saying, "How you going? Need any help?" And then wait for them to come back with it. Not be on their back every couple of hours saying, "How you going?" [It] can give people confidence that they are trusted. [I help them] out when they need [it] but don't micromanage.* [Interview—Manager]

Micromanagement was thus identified as harmful for employee resilience. This likely stems from the pressure on managers to achieve short term political deliverables at the expense of working proactively towards long-term goals (Pandey, 2010).

Micromanaging behaviour sometimes caused a lack of trust. When managers do not believe in the competence and growth potential of employees, they tend to control processes in ways that damage the dyadic relationship and resilience itself (Weibel & Six, 2013). While in some cases lack of belief in employee competence might be warranted (for example, with new employees), at times it seemed more a matter of managerial style than employee competence. This is harmful for resilience development.

> *It's the micromanagement that is a disguise for performance management… And it's just like setting impossible goals, saying OK, well there's a problem with your performance.* [Interview—Employee]

Excessive control or micromanagement led one employee to feel as though she was being treated like a child.

Micromanaging is therefore damaging and can turn the exchange process negative, thwarting individual autonomy and leaving employees unfulfilled and lacking ownership of their work (Hackman & Oldham, 1980). Social exchange can work in a negative and harmful way, whereby 'employees will respond negatively to unfair treatment' (Boddy, 2014, p. 116). In our research, we found that some employees who experienced micromanagement, for instance, would reciprocate with more counter-productive behaviours. One employee spoke on behalf of his team when he said:

> *We really didn't want to do anything else, we didn't want to do any more than our job.* [Interview—Employee]

Another employee noted that:

> *[Micromanagement] can allow people to get a bit complacent. Because you think if no one is going to talk to me about this or if everything I'm doing is just going to be acceptable … you sort of get a bit complacent and think I'll just keep doing it the way I'm doing it because no one's telling me otherwise and you don't learn to evolve or change.* [Interview—Employee]

All in all, the ability to balance support with autonomy and lack of micromanagement characterize growth-oriented leaders, creating trusting, positive interactions between leaders and team members, enabling employee resilience. Importantly, employee-centric culture, including trusting relationships, has been suggested to be the foundation of an adaptive, resilient, organization, a base on which a culture of collaboration and learning can be built (Walker et al., 2020).

Managing the Whole Team

Managers who foster collaboration are important for resilience because they help to build behavioural norms for network leveraging and allow individuals to experience the benefits that come from sharing knowledge and learning from each other (Malik & Garg, 2020). When employees recognize and utilize others' skills and resources they are better equipped to face challenges and perform resiliently. Managers can create a culture of collaboration in various ways, through fostering norms for collaboration, involving themselves in collaboration with the team and setting collective tasks for employees:

> *I always ask for a collaborative approach. And you know, bring them in as part of the situation. And work together on the result or an outcome, however we need to get there.* [interview—Manager]
>
> *[My manager will] put me on a project and tell me the people who need to be brought in on that project and he's also open to me bringing in more people if I think it's suitable.* [Interview—Employee]

Such a collaborative' approach helps employees build valuable networks between each other.

Leadership that encourages employees to work 'with groups inside and outside of the organisation' (Hsieh & Liou, 2016, p. 84) builds resilience, and meets the demands for effective public service operations inclusive of intra- and inter-agency collaboration and networked governance (Campbell, 2016; Silvia & McGuire, 2010; Stoker, 2006). Effective collaboration is not just a product of network leveraging ability. It also relates to increased learning, problem solving and adaptability in employees, all of which tie directly into employee resilience (Getha-Taylor, 2008; Kuntz et al., 2017; Lengnick-Hall et al., 2011).

Some managers understand the importance of collaboration, and have the intention to promote it, but may struggle with executing it in reality. This may be a product of the layering of various reform models, where public servants and their managers must work within multiple, contradictory logics (Fossestøl et al., 2015):

> *You get mixed messages, like I say, do it at whatever cost, and then you did that and the cost was too high. So it's the same with collaboration it's like, you know, you all have to work together as a team, there's too much talking. You know, you guys are wasting too much time because you're working together, I'm gonna get you to work on stuff individually. But make sure you ask the senior people before you do anything, but don't talk to each other. Um so I guess that's the best way I can answer that is, you always think you're doing the wrong thing, you spend the whole day worried that you're gonna get told you did something wrong.* [Interview—Employee]

The impact of this can be that employees learn to accept that not speaking up, or withholding ideas from each other, is actually safer than showing vulnerabilities through experimenting and sharing ideas with others:

> *I've probably switched off and I think that's fair to say with a lot of public servants who have been there for 10 years, you get taught that doing nothing and wasting time and keeping your head down and keeping out of the way, is better than actually working with anyone.* [Interview—Employee]

Concluding Remarks

This chapter extends conceptual and empirical understandings of resilience in public sector workplaces, with specific regard to the nature of employee resilience and how managers can facilitate it. Four key takeaways are: resilient responses are core to continual adaptation and flourishing at work; employee resilience is developable; resilience enabling leadership focuses on supporting growth and development and micromanaging behaviours can be harmful to employee resilience.

The public sector context increasingly requires resilient employees, organizations and institutions. This is exemplified by the collaboration and learning required for addressing 'wicked problems' (Stoker, 2006), and the adaptiveness demanded by uncertain environments (Karp & Helg, 2008). This research shows more specifically how factors in the public sector context can influence resilience. Employee-level resilience possibly works at organizational levels too, as the behaviours likely help the integration of both exploration and exploitation (March, 1991). Learning, network leveraging and adaptability have clear correspondences to exploration, but also probably provide a foundation for efficiency and use of existing resources too. Other research has found that aggregated individual-level employee experiences help integrate exploitation and exploration (Plimmer et al., 2017a). Reciprocally, environments that integrate exploration and exploitation likely support employee resilience.

We expect employee resilience may also help public organizations in their ongoing struggle to live up to the values the public hold them to. Organizations vary in the degree to which they are public, but most are public in some way. Participants in this study worked for organizations that were high in publicness, and so characterized by complex tasks, professional orientation, diverse stakeholders, 'conflicting environmental demands, and low managerial autonomy' (Antonsen & Jørgensen, 1997, p. 1467). Employee resilience, and accompanying supportive management behaviours, are likely needed to deal with this context, but the same context may not always encourage these right behaviours. For instance, low managerial autonomy likely limits the scope of support that can be offered. Complex tasks, diverse stakeholders and conflicting demands would make micromanagement tempting as a way to 'get things right'.

Despite these pressures both managers and employees in public organizations are expected to demonstrate 'public values', which concern the values (and expectations) attached to public organizations and delivery of public services particularly those value sets concerning intra-organizational life. Such relevant and identified public values include robustness (which includes adaptability, reliability etc.), innovation (which includes enthusiasm, risk readiness, etc.), productivity (which includes effectiveness, business-like approach, etc.) and self-development of employees (which includes good working environment) (Jørgensen & Bozeman, 2007). Employee resilience matches several of these public values. Adaptability likely supports robustness; network leveraging and learning would support self-development of employees and learning would enable innovation.

Employee resilience may also support the accountability of public sector employees (another set of public values that include professionalism and integrity). Its capability development would encourage professionalism, and the associated self- and other-awareness would work to enhance integrity.

Resilient behaviours—network-leveraging, learning and adaptability—help employees deal with complex public sector realities. Such behaviours are pertinent at the individual and team level, but they also model effective behaviours at higher levels in the public system. Implications for organizations are to develop, select, support and hold accountable managers capable of enabling growth and resilience in their teams.

When addressing the potential solutions for coping with the future of work, leadership matters. Resilient employees are well equipped to confront the increasingly uncertain and dynamic nature of workplaces, but they need to be supported and developed. The managerial behaviours identified here represent useful competencies for growth-oriented leaders. Additionally, this will require a view of the workplace as a learning environment, supportive of adaptability and those who facilitate it. Such an orientation may require not only investment in managerial and employee development opportunities, but also review of reward and signaling practices in organizations which may discount resilience-enabling behaviours and/or prioritize behaviours inimical to resilience.

For organizations, our findings provide an alternative to the top down command and control management that sometimes characterize government organizations (Plimmer et al., 2017a). Executive actions can facilitate line leadership behaviours that develop employee resilience, and build over time organizational capability to better deal with ambiguity, tension and the competing demand of public service life (Jørgensen & Bozeman, 2007). The resilience conceptualized in this paper was at the employee level, but we expect it would aggregate to organizational levels. It would be hard to imagine an organization as resilient if its employees were not. However, this is an empirical question for future research.

We hope the ideas in this chapter will inform more positive and adaptive behavioural norms at individual, group and organizational levels, contributing to the resilience of the wider public sector system.

References

Antonsen, M., & Jørgensen, T. B. (1997). The 'publicness' of public organizations. *Public Administration, 75*(2), 337–357.

Bach, S., & Bordogna, L. (2011). Varieties of new public management or alternative models? The reform of public service employment relations in industrialized democracies. *The International Journal of Human Resource Management, 22*(11), 2281–2294.

Boddy, C. R. (2014). Corporate psychopaths, conflict, employee affective well-being and counterproductive work behaviour. *Journal of Business Ethics, 121*(1), 107–121.

Bonanno, G. A. (2004). Loss, trauma, and human resilience: Have we underestimated the human capacity to thrive after extremely aversive events? *American Psychologist, 59*(1), 20–28.

Brennan, E. J. (2017). Towards resilience and wellbeing in nurses. *British Journal of Nursing, 26*(1), 43–47.

Bryson, J. M., Crosby, B. C., & Bloomberg, L. (2014). Public value governance: Moving beyond traditional public administration and the new public management. *Public Administration Review, 74*(4), 445–456.

Burke, C. S., Sims, D. E., Lazzara, E. H., & Salas, E. (2007). Trust in leadership: A multi-level review and integration. *The Leadership Quarterly, 18*(6), 606–632.

Cameron, A. (1998). The elasticity of endurance: Work intensification and workplace flexibility in the Queensland public hospital system. *New Zealand Journal of Employment Relations, 23*(3), 133–151.

Campbell, J. W. (2016). A collaboration-based model of work motivation and role ambiguity in public organizations. *Public Performance & Management Review, 39*(3), 655–675.

Christensen, T., & Lægreid, P. (2011a). Democracy and administrative policy: Contrasting elements of New Public Management (NPM) and post-NPM. *European Political Science Review, 3*(01), 125–146.

Christensen, T., & Lægreid, P. (2011b). Complexity and hybrid public administration—Theoretical and empirical challenges. *Public Organization Review, 11*(4), 407–423.

Christensen, T., Lie, A., & Lægreid, P. (Eds.). (2007). *Transcending new public management*. Ashgate.

Cooper, B., Wang, J., Bartram, T., & Cooke, F. L. (2019). Well-being-oriented human resource management practices and employee performance in the Chinese banking sector: The role of social climate and resilience. *Human Resource Management, 58*(1), 85–97.

Credé, M., Tynan, M. C., & Harms, P. D. (2017). Much ado about grit: A meta-analytic synthesis of the grit literature. *Journal of Personality and Social Psychology, 113*(3), 492–511.

Demerouti, E., Bakker, A. B., & Bulters, A. J. (2004). The loss spiral of work pressure, work–home interference and exhaustion: Reciprocal relations in a three-wave study. *Journal of Vocational Behavior, 64*(1), 131–149.

Dirks, K. T., & Ferrin, D. L. (2002). Trust in leadership: Meta-analytic findings and implications for research and practice. *Journal of Applied Psychology, 87*(4), 611–628.
Dong, Y., Bartol, K. M., Zhang, Z. X., & Li, C. (2017). Enhancing employee creativity via individual skill development and team knowledge sharing: Influences of dual-focused transformational leadership. *Journal of Organizational Behavior, 38*(3), 439–458.
Donnellan, M. B., & Robins, R. W. (2010). Resilient, overcontrolled, and undercontrolled personality types: Issues and controversies. *Social and Personality Psychology Compass, 4*(11), 1070–1083.
Feldman, D. C., & Weitz, B. A. J. (1991). From the invisible hand to the gladhand: Understanding a careerist orientation to work. *Human Resource Management, 30*(2), 237–257.
Folke, C., Carpenter, S., Walker, B., Scheffer, M., Chapin, T., & Rockström, J. (2010). Resilience thinking: Integrating resilience, adaptability and transformability. *Ecology & Society, 15*(4), 20–28.
Fossestøl, K., Breit, E., Andreassen, T. A., & Klemsdal, L. (2015). Managing institutional complexity in public sector reform: Hybridization in front-line service organizations. *Public Administration, 93*(2), 290–306.
Frank, S. A., & Lewis, G. B. (2004). Government employees: Working hard or hardly working? *The American Review of Public Administration, 34*(1), 36–51.
Franken, E. (2019). *Building people up: Leadership and employee resilience*. Thesis submitted to Victoria University of Wellington in fulfilment of the requirements for the degree of Doctor of Philosophy, Victoria University of Wellington.
Franken, E., & Plimmer, G. (2019). Mediocre and harmful public sector leadership. *International Journal of Public Leadership, 15*(4), 274–286.
Gattiker, U. E., & Larwood, L. (1986). Subjective career success: A study of managers and support personnel. *Journal of Business and Psychology, 1*(2), 78–94.
Getha-Taylor, H. (2008). Identifying collaborative competencies. *Review of Public Personnel Administration,28*(2), 103–119.
Gould-Williams, J., & Davies, F. (2005). Using social exchange theory to predict the effects of HRM practice on employee outcomes. *Public Management Review, 7*(1), 1–24.
Green, F. (2004). Work intensification, discretion, and the decline in well-being at work. *Eastern Economic Journal, 30*(4), 615–625.
Guest, G., Bunce, A., & Johnson, L. (2006). How many interviews are enough? An experiment with data saturation and variability. *Field Methods, 18*(1), 59–82.

Halbesleben, J. R. B. (2010). A meta-analysis of work engagement: Relationships with burnout, demands, resources, and consequences. In A. B. Bakker & M. P. Leiter (Eds.), *Work engagement: A handbook of essential theory and research* (pp. 102–117). Psychology Press.

Halbesleben, J. R., Neveu, J.-P., Paustian-Underdahl, S. C., & Westman, M. (2014). Getting to the "COR" understanding the role of resources in conservation of resources theory. *Journal of Management, 40*(5), 1334–1364.

Hall, C. M., Malinen, S., Vosslamber, R., & Wordsworth, R. (Eds.). (2016). *Business and post-disaster management: Business, organisational and consumer resilience and the Christchurch earthquakes*. Routledge.

Hackman, J. R., & Oldham, G. R. (1980). *Work redesign*. Addison-Wesley.

Hameed, A., & Waheed, A. (2011). Employee development and its affect on employee performance a conceptual framework. *International Journal of Business and Social Science, 2*(13), 224–229.

Hargis, M. B., Watt, J. D., & Piotrowski, C. (2011). Developing leaders: Examining the role of transactional and transformational leadership across business contexts. *Organization Development Journal, 29*(3), 51–66.

Hardy, C., Lawrence, T. B., & Grant, D. (2005). Discourse and collaboration: The role of conversations and collective identity. *Academy of Management Review, 30*(1), 58–77.

Heifetz, R. A. (1994). *Leadership without easy answers* (Vol. 465). Harvard University Press.

Hobfoll, S. E. (1989). Conservation of resources: A new attempt at conceptualizing stress. *American Psychologist, 44*(3), 513.

Hobfoll, S. E. (2011). Conservation of resources theory: Its implication for stress, health, and resilience. In S. Folkman (Ed.), *The Oxford handbook of stress, health, and coping* (pp. 127–147). Oxford University Press.

Hood, C. (2006). Gaming in targetworld: The targets approach to managing British public services. *Public Administration Review, 66*(4), 515–521.

Howell, J. M., & Avolio, B. J. (1993). Transformational leadership, transactional leadership, locus of control, and support for innovation: Key predictors of consolidated-business-unit performance. *Journal of Applied Psychology, 78*(6), 891.

Hsieh, J. Y., & Liou, K. T. (2016). Collaborative leadership and organizational performance: Assessing the structural relation in a public service agency. *Review of Public Personnel Administration, 38*(1), 83–109.

Jørgensen, T. B., & Bozeman, B. (2007). Public values: An inventory. *Administration & Society, 39*(3), 354–381.

Karp, T., & Helg, T. I. (2008). From change management to change leadership: Embracing chaotic change in public service organizations. *Journal of Change Management, 8*(1), 85–96.

Khan, Z., Rao-Nicholson, R., Akhtar, P., Tarba, S. Y., Ahammad, M. F., & Vorley, T. (2019). The role of HR practices in developing employee resilience: A case study from the Pakistani telecommunications sector. *The International Journal of Human Resource Management, 30*(8), 1342–1369.

Kuntz, J., Malinen, S., & Näswall, K. (2017). Employee resilience: Directions for resilience development. *Consulting Psychology Journal: Practice and Research, 69*(3), 223–242.

Kuntz, J. R., Näswall, K., & Malinen, S. (2016). Resilient employees in resilient organizations: Flourishing beyond adversity. *Industrial and Organizational Psychology, 9*(2), 456–462.

Lee, A. V., Vargo, J., & Seville, E. (2013). Developing a tool to measure and compare organizations' resilience. *Natural Hazards Review, 14*(1), 29–41.

Lengnick-Hall, C. A., Beck, T. E., Lengnick-Hall, & M. L. (2011). Developing a capacity for organizational resilience through strategic human resource management. *Human Resource Management Review, 21*(3), 243–255.

Lyons, S. T., Duxbury, L. E., & Higgins, C. A. (2006). A comparison of the values and commitment of private sector, public sector, and parapublic sector employees. *Public Administration Review, 66*(4), 605–618.

Malik, P., & Garg, P. (2020). Learning organization and work engagement: The mediating role of employee resilience. *The International Journal of Human Resource Management, 31*(8), 1071–1094.

Mallak, L. (1998, December). Putting organizational resilience to work. *Industrial Management*, 8–13.

Mansfield, C., Beltman, S., & Price, A. (2014). 'I'm coming back again!': The resilience process of early career teachers. *Teachers and Teaching, 20*(5), 547–567.

March, J. G. (1991). Exploration and exploitation in organizational learning. *Organization Science, 2*(1), 71–87.

Miao, Q., Newman, A., Schwarz, G., & Xu, L. (2014). Servant leadership, trust, and the organizational commitment of public sector employees in China. *Public Administration, 92*(3), 727–743.

Mitchell, G. E., O'Leary, R., & Gerard, C. (2015). Collaboration and performance: Perspectives from public managers and NGO leaders. *Public Performance & Management Review, 38*(4), 684–716.

Moynihan, D. P. (2009). Through a glass, darkly: Understanding the effects of performance regimes. *Public Performance & Management Review, 32*(4), 592–603.

Näswall, K., Malinen, S., Kuntz, J., & Hodliffe, M. (2019). Employee resilience: Development and validation of a measure. *Journal of Managerial Psychology., 34*(5), 353–367.

Ng, T. W., Eby, L. T., Sorensen, K. L., & Feldman, D. C. (2005). Predictors of objective and subjective career success: A meta-analysis. *Personnel Psychology, 58*(2), 367–408.

Ng, T. W., & Feldman, D. C. (2012). Evaluating six common stereotypes about older workers with meta-analytical data. *Personnel Psychology, 65*(4), 821–858.

Nguyen, Q., Kuntz, J. R., Näswall, K., & Malinen, S. (2016). Employee resilience and leadership styles: The moderating role of proactive personality and optimism. *New Zealand Journal of Psychology, 45*(2), 13–21.

Noblet, A., Rodwell, J., & McWilliams, J. (2006). Organizational change in the public sector: Augmenting the demand control model to predict employee outcomes under New Public Management. *Work & Stress, 20*(4), 335–352.

O'Connell, D. J., McNeely, E., & Hall, D. T. (2008). Unpacking personal adaptability at work. *Journal of Leadership & Organizational Studies, 14*(3), 248–259.

Omari, M., & Paull, M. (2015). Public sector work intensification and negative behaviors. *Journal of Organizational Change Management, 28*(4), 603–613.

Pandey, S. K. (2010). Cutback management and the paradox of publicness. *Public Administration Review, 70*(4), 564–571.

Pangallo, A., Zibarras, L., Lewis, R., & Flaxman, P. (2015). Resilience through the lens of interactionism: A systematic review. *Psychological Assessment, 27*(1), 1–20.

Plimmer, G., Bryson, J., Donnelly, N., Wilson, J., Ryan, B., & Blumenfeld, S. (2017a). The legacy of New Public Management (NPM) on workers, management capabilities, and organisations. *New Zealand Journal of Employment Relations, 42*(1), 19–34.

Plimmer, G., & Blumenfeld, S. (2012). Trade union delegate leadership and membership commitment: A cross-sectional analysis. *Leadership & Organization Development Journal, 33*(8), 750–762.

Plimmer, G., Bryson, J., & Teo, S. T. (2017b). Opening the black box: The mediating roles of organisational systems and ambidexterity in the HRM-performance link in public sector organisations. *Personnel Review, 46*(7), 1434–1451.

Plimmer, G., Proctor-Thomson, S., Donnelly, N., & Sim, D. (2017c). The mistreatment of public service workers: Identifying key risk and protective factors. *Public Money & Management, 37*(5), 333–340.

Plimmer, G., Wilson, J., Bryson, J., Blumenfeld, S., Donnelly, N., & Ryan, B. (2013). *Workplace dynamics in New Zealand public services* (pp. 56–60). Industrial Relations Centre, Victoria University of Wellington.

Richardson, G. E. (2002). The metatheory of resilience and resiliency. *Journal of Clinical Psychology, 58*(3), 307–321.

Saldaña, J. (2015). *The coding manual for qualitative researchers* (3rd ed.). Sage.

Silvia, C., & McGuire, M. (2010). Leading public sector networks: An empirical examination of integrative leadership behaviors. *The Leadership Quarterly, 21*(2), 264–277.

State Services Commission. (2019). *Workforce data*. https://ssc.govt.nz/our-work/workforce-data/. Accessed 15 December 2019.

Stoker, G. (2006). Public value management: A new narrative for networked governance? *The American Review of Public Administration, 36*(1), 41–57.

Sutcliffe, K. M., & Vogus, T. J. (2003). Organizing for resilience. *Positive Organizational Scholarship: Foundations of a New Discipline, 94*, 110.

Teece, D., Peteraf, M., & Leih, S. (2016). Dynamic capabilities and organizational agility: Risk, uncertainty, and strategy in the innovation economy. *California Management Review, 58*(4), 13–35.

Tonkin, K., Malinen, S., Näswall, K., & Kuntz, J. C. (2018). Building employee resilience through wellbeing in organizations. *Human Resource Development Quarterly, 29*(2), 107–124.

Uzzi, B. (1997). Social structure and competition in interfirm networks: The paradox of embeddedness. *Administrative Science Quarterly, 42*(1), 35–67.

Vogus, T. J., & Sutcliffe, K. M. (2007, October 7–10). *Organizational resilience: Towards a theory and research agenda*. Paper presented at the 2007 IEEE International Conference on Systems, Man and Cybernetics, Montreal.

Walker, B., Malinen, S., Naswall, K., Nilakant, V., Kuntz, & J. (2020). Organisational resilience in action: A study of a large scale extended-disaster setting. In E. H. Powley, B. Caza, & A. Caza (Eds.), *Handbook of organisational resilience*. Edward Elgar Publishing.

Weibel, A., & Six, F. (2013). Trust and control: The role of intrinsic motivation. In R. Bachman & A. Zaheer (Eds.), *Handbook of advances in trust research* (pp. 57–81). Edward Elgar Publishing.

Whitener, E. M., Brodt, S. E., Korsgaard, M. A., & Werner, J. M. (1998). Managers as intiaitors of trust: An exchange relationship framework for understanding managerial trustworthy behavior. *Academy of Management Review, 23*(3), 513–530.

Wilson, S., Cummings, S., Jackson, B., & Proctor-Thomson, S. (2017). *Revitalising leadership: Putting theory and practice into context*. Routledge.

Winters, D., & Latham, G. (1996). The effect of learning versus outcome goals on a simple versus a complex task. *Group and Organization Management, 21*(2), 236–250.

Youssef, C. M., & Luthans, F. (2007). Positive organizational behavior in the workplace the impact of hope, optimism, and resilience. *Journal of Management, 33*(5), 774–800.

Zautra, A. J., & Reich, J. W. (2011). Resilience: The meanings, methods, and measures of a fundamental characteristic of human adaptation. In S. Folkman

(Ed.), *Oxford library of psychology. The Oxford handbook of stress, health, and coping* (pp. 127–147). Oxford University Press.

Zeier, K., Plimmer, G., & Franken, E. (2018). Developing shared leadership in a public organisation: Processes, paradoxes and consequences. *Journal of Management & Organization, 27*(3), 564–581.

Zhang, Y., & Chen, C. C. (2013). Developmental leadership and organizational citizenship behavior: Mediating effects of self-determination, supervisor identification, and organizational identification. *The Leadership Quarterly, 24*(4), 534–543.

PART III

Resilience in Organizational Fields and Societies

CHAPTER 7

The Post-entrepreneurial University: The Case for Resilience in Higher Education

Mitchell Young and Rómulo Pinheiro

Introduction

Historically speaking, universities have been found to be highly resilient organizational forms. Since their inception in Europe in the middle ages, they have been able to adopt new functions, structures and values while retaining their essence and identity (Scott, 2006). The most important transformative turn occurred in the mid-nineteenth century, with the so-called Humboldtian revolutions, when research emerged as a core mission alongside academic autonomy as a cherished value (Nybom, 2003). In many European countries, the post-WWII period assisted in the rise of different types of higher education institutions (HEIs) with an explicit mandate to promote national and regional economic development, which

M. Young (✉)
Department of European Studies, Institute of International Studies, FSV, Charles University, Prague, Czech Republic

R. Pinheiro
Department of Political Science and Management, University of Agder (UiA), Kristiansand, Norway
e-mail: romulo.m.pinheiro@uia.no

R. Pinheiro et al. (eds.), *Towards Resilient Organizations and Societies*, Public Sector Organizations,
https://doi.org/10.1007/978-3-030-82072-5_7

provide the backbone for the establishment of binary higher education (HE) systems. More recently (last two decades or so), and as a result of an increasingly competitive environment (for students, staff, funding and prestige), both domestic and global, entrepreneurialism, and its emphasis on the 'market', has emerged as a feature of modern HEIs and systems alike (Alajoutsijärvi et al., 2021). As a means of responding to these (and other) external imperatives, universities and other types of HEIs are nowadays characterized by a multitude of missions, some of which are at odds or in tension with one another (Castells, 2001), leading some to suggest that such tasks are impossible to accomplish (Enders & Boer, 2009).

Few studies to date have taken stock of the distinct and incompatible ways in which the notion of the entrepreneurial university has developed, and how that affects its ability to incorporate other concepts into its model. Specifically, we are interested in the way the concept of resilience, broadly defined as the ability to adapt to changing circumstances while retaining its core attributes or essence (Walker & Salt, 2006), can be articulated to that of the entrepreneurial university. We ask in this chapter: to what extent are entrepreneurial universities likely to be resilient? In order to address this question, we first provide conceptual clarity by revisiting the seminal works of two scholars who have underpinned scholarly and policy debates in the last two decades, resulting in what we argue are two distinct schools of thought on the entrepreneurial university as an organizational archetype. In doing so, we investigate how the rise of New Public Management (NPM) in Europe in the late 1990s and early 2000s co-opted and reframed the concept of the entrepreneurial university in ways that make it incompatible with resilience thinking. We do this by, in the second part, laying out three tensions (or paradoxes) that emerge from this NPM-inflected version of the entrepreneurial university. We show how these are rooted in an ideational interpretation of the concepts of efficiency, competition, and diversity. Finally, by tying back into 'lost' elements of sociological conceptions of entrepreneurialism in HE, we demonstrate how resilience can potentially resolve the tensions identified in what we term a post-entrepreneurial model of the university.

The Entrepreneurial University: Tracing the Origins of a (Misunderstood) Idea

The existing literature on the topic points to two relatively distinct conceptions of entrepreneurialism in HE. These conceptions are aligned with two diverging schools of thought with disciplinary and normative undertones, one *sociological* stressing the importance of adaptation and change for the public good and the unique features of universities as fiduciary institutions, and the other *economic*, centred on the idea that competition and markets are the most efficient and sustainable ways to organize activities and the notion of universities as quasi-firms. Having presented the two schools, we go on to show how the entrepreneurial university concept has been extrinsically aligned with a NPM policy regime that emphasizes efficiency and competition and has been used to underpin a bold reform agenda aimed at the modernization of European HE systems and institutions.

The Sociological School

Since its inception in the 1970s, the sociological perspective's point of departure has been a recognition of the importance of HE as a public good and the effects accrued from the massification of HE systems after WWII. Inspired by the work of Israeli sociologist Joseph Ben David, it paid attention to comparative issues pertaining to structural differences among national HE systems, with an emphasis on flexibility, innovation and change (Clark, 1973, p. 6). Following the seminal work of Jencks and Riesman (1968), the sociological perspective interpreted broader system-wide developments in the 1970s as reflecting the rising power and influence of (North American) scholars and scientists as the fundamental 'academic revolution' of the time (Clark, 1973, p. 5). Further, the sociological perspective identified the meso level of the HE organizations (themselves rooted in national systems of HE) as the primary unit of analysis (p. 7). Burton Clark, as a principle voice in this tradition, was immensely concerned with the risk of co-optation by non-educational interests and agendas, particularly managerial and public policy ones.

Clark's (1983) seminal work *The higher education system: academic organization in cross-national perspective* sheds light on the building blocks that characterize HE as organizations by pointing to three key elements: (a) the fragmented nature ('loose web') of academic organizations substantiated around loose coupling among their various units and knowledge domains [what might also be termed the 'ambiguity of structure' (Pinheiro, 2012)]; (b) the role of academic and disciplinary norms and values ('beliefs') as mediating systems between societal demands and university responses; and (c) the balkanized system of authority from the lowest level of the departmental unit up to the national government with the 'middle-structure' of the central administration caught in between. Finally, Clark's work pointed to the process of adaptation and change within HE systems by referring to natural systems' evolution:

> [T]he fundamental adaptive mechanism of universities and larger academic systems is the capacity to add and subtract fields of knowledge and related units without disturbing all the others [...] Adaptability, in short, lies first in the internal variety of amalgamated, conglomerated organization. (Clark, 1983, pp. 186–187)

In the 1990s, the emergence of the first studies focusing on university crisis and change in Europe and the importance attributed to strategic planning (Maassen & Potman, 1990) propelled Clark to pay close attention to the processes of change and adaptation within the context of an entrepreneurial framework (Clark, 1998, 2004). Underpinning Clark's notion of entrepreneurialism in HE are three critical elements: *autonomy*, *differentiation* and the active role played by the *academic heartland.*

> A growing number of entrepreneurial universities now embody a new option for institutional self-reliance. In their more active autonomy, they marry collegiality to change as well as to the status quo... They know the difference between a university and a business firm. They also know that a complex university has many 'souls', some righteous others unrighteous. (Clark, 2004, p. 7)

For Clark, the quest for self-reliance starts with the search for opportunities to foster institutional differentiation (niche seeking) in the larger HE ecosystem. 'Greater differentiation, rather than simple imitation, becomes a virtual requirement. And standing still becomes a means of falling behind' (p. 161). Finally, Clark's case studies revealed the importance of the change processes initiated by or supported across departmental units while acknowledging different postures across disciplinary fields when it comes to embracing 'the market' and/or change more generally: 'Science and technology departments commonly become entrepreneurial first. Social sciences departments, aside from economics and business, find the shift more difficult and lag behind... Uneven adoption of new ways should be expected' (p. 88). In short, the sociological perspective on entrepreneurialism in HE stresses the importance of the public good, approaches HE institutions as complex systems, and focuses on evolutionary processes of renewal and change with the aim of fostering adaptation and differentiation.

The Innovation School

The second dominant perspective in the literature on the entrepreneurial university emerged in the early 1980s through the work of Henry Etzkowitz, a sociologist by training, but a scholar of innovation studies then based at a UK business school. Etzkowitz's focus was centred on the rise of 'entrepreneurial science' and its direct contribution to economic growth and innovation, which he termed the 'second academic revolution,' following the institutionalization of research as a core university activity in the late nineteenth and early twentieth centuries (Etzkowitz & Webster, 1998, 2001). According to this perspective, change is initiated not from the inside of the organization but from the outside, with inner dynamics centred on the protection of the status quo:

> Change in academia has always been notoriously slow when driven from within. As a conservative institution of medieval origins the university is always fearful of change, especially of revisions of academic norms that appear to be initiated by forces outside of the academy. (Etzkowitz & Webster, 1998, p. 21)

For Etzkowitz, this external pressure is an opportunity for change, and the author portrayed a more instrumentalist view of the university that pays almost exclusive attention to the research function and its interface with the outside world, most notably firms in the context of innovation and technology transfers. It conceives of research groups as 'quasi-firms' (Etzkowitz, 1983, 2003) that seek and secure funding that enables them to be globally competitive and thus thrive in a market economy. In short, the innovation perspective on entrepreneurialism in HE stresses the importance of external dynamics and events and the need to foster competitiveness through the infusion or institutionalization of a market-like ethos across the inner fabric of universities.

> The entrepreneurial university thus has interface capabilities such as liaison and transfer offices and incubator facilities to manage and market knowledge produced in the university at several levels, from specific pieces of

> protected intellectual property to technology embodied in a firm and propelled by an entrepreneur. (Etzkowitz, 2003, p. 113)

As far as governmental policy is concerned, the innovation perspective has been rather salient in providing a template for science and innovation policy throughout the world, most notably in Europe in light of the Lisbon Agenda (Pinheiro, 2015), but also elsewhere (Slaughter & Cantwell, 2012). It has done so through the concept of the 'triple helix', where university, industry and government articulate strategic actions for promoting innovation and economic growth at the national, regional and local levels (Etzkowitz, 2008; Etzkowitz & Leydesdorff, 2000). It has also melded with NPM ideas and discourses which began gaining prominence in the mid-1990.

Reframing the Entrepreneurial University Through the Prism of NPM

In this section, we show how the ideas of NPM align with those of the entrepreneurial university. Given that both concepts (NPM and the entrepreneurial university) were developing hegemonic positions in their relative fields at roughly the same time in the mid- to late 1990s and that influential international actors, such as the OECD, were engaged in championing both, some degree of mutual influence can be expected. OECD became the key player in popularizing NPM through its Public Management Committee (PUMA), and the 1995 report *Governance in Transition* (OECD, 1995), which was followed by several policy briefs and another report in 2005, *Modernizing Governance: The way forward* (Pal, 2012). The OECD likewise was quick to pick up on the entrepreneurial university concept and in the fall of 2000, through its Programme on Institutional Management in Higher Education, organized a major conference (Clark, 2004) followed by a journal volume on the topic (OECD, 2005). The OECD's interest is thus not merely coincidental but based on many overlapping and intersecting ideas in the discourses that surround those two concepts.

NPM is a notoriously difficult concept to precisely pin down (Barzelay, 2001; Gruening, 2001); however, there are some agreed upon ideational underpinnings that are common to most understandings. These trace back to Christopher Hood's (1991) seminal paper that identifies the freedom to independently manage and the use of markets as core principles for allowing public administration to become more 'business-like'. Further research specifies more concretely three concepts: disaggregation (distinct actors with a capacity to act), competition (a market-based landscape) and incentivization (a reason to act or change) (Dunleavy et al., 2006, see also Diefenbach, 2009; Pollitt & Bouckaert, 2011). In short, NPM entails a distinction between actors (with autonomy) and landscapes (with market-based competition) that is critical for further discussion.

Across Europe, there are many ways in which NPM has entered national and supranational policymaking that vary by intensity (Seeber et al., 2015) and aspect (Pollitt & Bouckaert, 2011). In HE policy, we have seen a move towards NPM-dominated policies in ways that often maintain the strong historical path dependencies of the national context (Bleiklie et al., 2011; de Boer et al., 2007; Paradeise et al., 2009; Young, 2015). Our argument here is more general, while the concept of an entrepreneurial university and the idea of HE systems as quasi-markets (Teixeira et al., 2004) appears to mesh well with the emphasis on business-like, market-oriented public management, upon closer inspection, we find that it embodies several inherent problems and contradictions when attempting to unite management and markets.

If the ideal NPM actor is a business competing on a free market, then to apply it to public administration requires the replication of two key elements: a) an entity that behaves like a business and b) a landscape that functions like a market. Attempts to apply these characteristics in the realm of HE raises two critical issues. First, while universities may be characterized as institutions (Meyer et al., 2006) and organizations (Krücken & Meier, 2006; Seeber et al., 2015), they have traditionally not been characterized as unified ones (Maassen & Olsen, 2007; Musselin, 2007); rather, the university has been seen as loosely coupled or an organized anarchy (March & Olsen, 1979; Weick, 1976). To compete in the way that NPM envisions, the university needs to become a unified actor; specifically, it should be a 'complete organization' (Brunsson & Sahlin-Andersson, 2000). Hence, disaggregation in the university sector involves aggrandizing the authority of the units which already have distinct identities. Disaggregation can be understood as the process of creating complete organizations and providing them the autonomy with which to make strategic decisions. This paradigm contrasts with the view that loosely coupled structures (individual academics and research groups) can behave in entrepreneurial ways (i.e. swiftly adapting to emerging situations), as defended by proponents of systems thinking (Pinheiro & Young, 2017).

The environment, in Europe specifically and across much of the world, in which universities operate is not the free market per se—though universities may enter that arena with some of their activities, particularly ones that are often associated with the entrepreneurial university (i.e. spinoffs, technology transfer, etc.). In an attempt to bring market forces (and their presumed benefits) to teaching and research activities in the university sector, there has been an expansion of quasi-markets, which are commonly depicted as a tool of NPM reforms (Pollitt & Bouckaert, 2011; Salamon, 2002). Quasi-markets are socially constructed by the government to foster competition but have several distinctive differences from regular markets in terms of both supply and demand: while suppliers in quasi-markets compete as independent entities, they don't necessarily aim to maximize profits; on the demand side, money is not necessarily the only mechanism of purchasing power (others include prestige, reputation, or bibliometric counts), finally, the user is not necessarily the consumer, i.e. councils that fund research are not the users of that research (LeGrand & Bartlett, 1993) (Table 7.1).

The entrepreneurial model follows the inspiration of Newtonian physics, which is based on reductionist and rationalistic principles and linear causality. It has much in common with what we have termed the innovation model of the entrepreneurial university (see also Pinheiro, 2016). This model hopes to reduce or at least make manageable the complexity of the university system and the context in which it is embedded. The post-entrepreneurial or resilient university model, on the other hand, embraces that complexity. It is rooted in complex systems

Table 7.1 Alternative university models

	Entrepreneurial	*Post-entrepreneurial*
Dominant logic	Efficiency	Resilience
Modus operandi	Reduce/manage complexity (plan, steer/control, compete)	Cherish complexity (foster emergence, self-organize, co-evolve)
Internal governance	Unified, top-down control	Loosely coupled
Positional objective	Through global competition/winning	Through requisite variety/thriving

Source Authors' own, following Pinheiro and Young (2017)

thinking, in which causality is often non-linear; i.e. emergent entities co-evolve with each other and their landscape and show the capacity to self-organize (Meadows, 2008). The inspiration for this model comes from evolutionary biology rather than Newtonian physics, and the overall positional objective for an organization is to thrive within a niche rather than to win a global competition.

Tensions and Their Resolution in a Resilience Model

As we have seen, the concept of the entrepreneurial university grew out of the idea of adaptivity and the perceived need for flexibility to adapt to changing societal demands and circumstances. Clark (1998) intended to showcase universities that were dynamic and changing. The word 'entrepreneurial' struck a chord, as it fits well with several discourses of that time, particularly those of economic competitiveness, regional development, globalization and NPM. In his own words, 'The use of "entrepreneurial" as the key term in the organizing framework, in place of the softer "proactive" and "innovative", was also provocative' (Clark, 2004, p. 3). The relative ambiguity of the concept allowed it to become imbued with unintended meanings that at times ran counter to Clark's aims of adaptability, diversity and dynamicism. There are three important areas of tension that occur with the NPM inspired push towards unified actorness, efficiency and isomorphism. In this section, we discuss those tensions and demonstrate how the post-entrepreneurial university model centred on a resilience paradigm (see Pinheiro & Young, 2017 for a more detailed description) addresses them in a way that cleaves to the sociological understanding of the entrepreneurial university.

The first tension, a push towards unified actorhood, assumes that the university can be treated as a single unit, specifically that the uppermost level of the university has authority similar to that of the uppermost level of a business. This reinforces the idea that inter-institutional university competition is the most important type of competition in the sector, thus legitimizing the importance of global rankings (Ramirez et al., 2016). However, as we have seen earlier, this was not part of Clark's vision for a balance of authority at all levels of the university:

> Balancing influence across multiple levels is an almost constant problem in entrepreneurial universities [...] Effective entrepreneurial universities are

> neither extremely centralized nor decentralized; they are administratively strong at the top, the middle and the bottom. (Clark, 2004, p. 175)

The post-entrepreneurial university is not a unified actor but rather a loosely coupled one. The term 'loose coupling' was coined to deal with inherent contradictions that could not be captured in the language of organizational scholars, particularly the demand for simultaneous connectedness and autonomy (Orton & Weick, 1990). For Orton and Weick, and similarly to modern conceptions on resilience systems (see Frigotto et al., 2022), to be loosely coupled, an organization needed to simultaneously exhibit both distinctiveness (being stable and closed to outside forces) and responsiveness (being flexible and open to outside forces). Loose coupling addressed both of these dimensions; however, in their review article, Orton and Weick (1990) found that much of the scholarship following Weick's seminal 1976 article simplified this dialectical dynamic and treated loose coupling as one end of a continuum in which it was opposed to tight coupling. Treating loose coupling as the authors originally intended allows us to avoid the binary sort of thinking that leads to overvaluing complete organizations and accepting that organizations have both connected and independent elements that are not reducible or rationalizable. In other words, a university can have the strengthened steering core that Clark (1998) called for without being a complete organization. The key is reaching a balance as described in the quote above.

Orton and Weick (1990, p. 219) also raised an issue with how binary rather than dialectical thinking is problematic: 'The last way in which researchers drift away from the dialectical interpretation of loose coupling is to describe it as managerial failure [...] These forms [universities, hospitals, etc.] are not failed bureaucracies, but distinct organizational forms'. However, it is precisely the sentiment, or even accusation, of managerial failure that lies behind the NPM reforms and buttresses their aim of enabling stronger management within public institutions. It is argued that fixing these management failures should allow the university to better respond to external pressures for efficiency, effectiveness and accountability (Pinheiro & Stensaker, 2014a).

Loose coupling treats strategy as an emergent pattern rather than a centrally planned activity. The network of units and actors that comprise the university system create a unique constellation of responses to their environment (societal, disciplinary and organizational). The identity of the university is formed not only by its culture but also by the ongoing decisions of the actors at the heartland level as well as the departments, faculties and central administration. This supports the idea of 'structure as something that organizations do, rather than merely as something they have' (Orton & Weick, 1990, p. 218). Structure in this way becomes a dynamic emergent property, not a planned or pre-determined reification.

The second tension, the push towards efficiency, assumes that streamlining processes and reducing waste will result in a more effective organization and thus a better use of public funds. Again, this is not essentially part of Clark's intention:

> The legitimacy of the portfolio [of income sources] depends on educational values guiding monetary decisions. There must be things that the university will not do no matter how much money is offered. Conversely, there must be 'useless' things it insists upon doing. (Clark, 2004, p. 174)

The post-entrepreneurial university maintains an appropriate level of slack. We conceive of slack as pertaining to repositories of redundant resources, human or otherwise, at the disposal of organizational actors. Organizational scholars have depicted slack as a buffer (Selznick, 1966) that protects the organization from external influences (Thompson, 2008). Taking this a step further, Sharfman et al. (1988) argued that slack can even be linked to efficiency; in other words, there is an optimal level of slack which, if absent, reduces organizational performance. Within the university sector, slack can be understood in a variety of ways: as having multiple research projects seeking the same knowledge, maintaining different disciplines and departments that cover the same topics, allowing researchers ample time to explore and take risks, maintaining a full array of disciplines to allow for the possibility of interactions between them and the creation of interdisciplinary knowledge, etc. Slack allows 'productive waste,' whose tolerance is a prime virtue that is necessary for creative destruction in the broader terms of the innovation economy (Janeway, 2012). Resilience scholars have identified 'redundancies' (another term for slack) as a critical antecedent of adaptive resilient systems, including their key role in fostering organizational learning (Giustiniano et al., 2018, pp. 91–92).

The third tension arises from the assumption that competition will lead to diversity. In this case, Clark's hope was to see universities diversify, and he envisioned that this could happen in his version of the entrepreneurial university:

> The mantra for reform becomes: complex universities operating in complex environments require complex differentiated solutions. One hundred universities require 100 solutions. (Clark, 2004, p. 183)

However, the idea of global competition that has found favour in many policy interpretations of the entrepreneurial university is more likely to produce homogenization than differentiation. To understand why, we turn to recent research on evolutionary competition. Kenneth Stanley and Joel Lehman asked why, if evolution is correct, we don't 'converge on a single optimal creature?' (2015, p. 115). Evolution, they argue, when understood as a universal theory of competition, does not logically include a mechanism to promote and sustain diversity, but rather 'drives towards everything converging to the best. And the best is only one thing' (p. 108). This quest to be the 'best' is one of the driving forces in both university ranking systems and policy initiatives (Young, 2015). The emergence of global university rankings (Hazelkorn, 2015) and discourses on the global organizational archetypes (Pinheiro & Stensaker, 2014b), such as world-class universities (Ramirez et al., 2016), demonstrate how the global context has taken a central role in shaping the context of the modern university. This has resulted in a convergence—a so-called 'emerging global model' for the university (Mohrman et al., 2008)—to which an ever-greater number of universities aspire.

A resilient approach to diversity would try to model itself more on natural evolution, which as Stanley and Lehman explain: 'But natural evolution isn't like these kinds of competitions because it drives towards divergence, towards a multitude of varying solutions to life's problems' (p. 109). It does this by creating *local* rather than global competition:

> Unlike global competition, local competition encourages the founding of new niches to escape competition. In discovering a new way to live that's free from previous competitors, competition is reduced—by running away from it. But in global competition there is no escape: No matter what an organism does it will always be judged against all others. That's why global competition naturally leads to convergence while local competition naturally enhances diversity and creativity. (Stanley & Lehman, 2015, p. 115)

There is a distinct lack of an alternative model or niche to which universities can escape and thrive, and thus under the current conditions, we would expect more homogenization than differentiation. This is not to say that some differentiation does not occur in the context of global competititon, but that the convergence forces are stronger in the context of hegemonic templates or archetypes like the research-intensive university (for a discussion see Hüther & Krücken, 2016).

The concept of requisite variety helps us reframe this dilemma in a way that allows resilience to be used to foster diversity. The concept comes from cybernetics (Ashby & Goldstein, 2011) and is based on the idea that 'the diversity of potential responses must be sufficient to handle the diversity of disturbances' (Page, 2011, p. 211). Applied to organizational studies, this means the internal variety in an organization—be it structures, skills, people or knowledge—must match the variety of the external environment if the organization is to thrive. That external environment is both local and global. In the case of universities, this is particularly challenging, as the number of missions that have been assigned to it has grown dramatically over the past few decades, making it 'a rather vulnerable institution that tends to be overloaded with multiple expectations and growing demands. The mission impossible of the modern university is that it means too many things to too many and too diversified stakeholders' (Enders & Boer, 2009, p. 166). Fulfilling the demands of requisite variety under these conditions is nearly impossible from a centralized perspective. The central steering core cannot understand, much less strategize about, all the disturbances and responses faced by the hundreds or thousands of people in the academic heartland. This is a classic situation of bounded rationality (Simon, 1991). Requisite variety thus requires autonomy at the lower levels of the organization and a strategy that emerges from them rather than being produced from the top. It also requires the establishment of new units that correspond to the new pressures and initiatives, as Clark described:

> Just as each new source of funding requires a university office, so do the new units of the developmental periphery require specialized offices to develop and process their activities, the office of continuing education, for example. Numerous administrative units paralleling the many research and teaching units of outreach are part of what makes the entrepreneurial university a proactive place [...] New assemblies of subjects – cognitive territories varying in content, time and place – require supporting

> tribes in both operating units and the administration, resulting in greater organizational density. (Clark, 2004, p. 176)

Diversity is in this view not only about finding unique things to do but about finding different ways of doing them. This aligns with university missions on their broadest level: seeking knowledge through different disciplines and methodologies and interacting with society and business in a plethora of ways. However, the global archetypes described above challenge diversity by standardizing the measurement of university achievement or excellence in a set of key indicators (Sørensen et al., 2016). Through standardized archetypes and indicators, the complexity of both the organization and the environment is simplified as a result of our attempt to rationalize it, as discussed by Ramirez et al. (2016).

Conclusion

Our core argument, rooted in concepts from complex systems literature, is that the successful fulfillment of the multiple missions of the modern university requires characteristics of loose coupling, slack and requisite variety which can be found in the idea of a post-entrepreneurial or resilience university based on some of the original elements in Clark's sociological model of the entrepreneurial university. Universities and political and economic systems are both related and nested (Pekkola et al., 2021), and while exerting pressures on one another, they also retain the ability to shield themselves from pressures (Young et al., 2017) that could take them over thresholds. Based on this perspective, it is a mistake to consider resilience as essentially just resistance to change. Resilient entities and systems are dynamic in the sense that they can and do change and adapt but also retain their identities by not crossing essential thresholds or identity boundaries. The university's continued existence is evidence of its remarkable resilience and adaptability since its origins in the Middle Ages.

While NPM has remained an important concept in understanding public policy changes since the 1990s, there have recently been calls in both public policy and HE studies to move beyond discussions of NPM (Broucker et al., 2017; Christensen & Laegreid, 2007). We argue that, correspondingly, university discourses need a concept less infused with NPM values and ideas than the entrepreneurial university archetype (as an ideal model), whose meaning, as we have shown, has shifted away from its sociological origins and whose hegemonic use leans towards the innovation perspective. Thus, the concept of a post-'entrepreneurial': or resilience university builds on the sociological foundations of the entrepreneurial university and the idea of complex and co-evolutionary systems that change in accordance to external stimulus yet retain their essential function and identity, i.e. it is resilient.

In fact, what we show in the section on tensions is maybe better described as a paradox. Policy initiatives that aim for diversity and effectiveness are in fact likely to do the opposite. The incentives for organizational behaviour promoted within these policies, push towards increasing homogeneity, despite policymakers' interest in a diversified system in which universities 'smartly' specialize and find niches. An overemphasis on efficiency drains away the slack which would have allowed for more exploration (March, 1991) and an ability to react to and address emerging scientific puzzles. And consolidation of centralized governance moves the locus of resource allocation further away from those with the expertise to effectively allocate it.

The resilient post-entrepreneurial university is entrepreneurial in that it captures many advantages of the entrepreneurial model, though not as a unified actor but intrinsically through and within the academic heartland. It is not static but dynamic, diversifying, looking for niches, and doing new things while retaining the core values and norms of what makes it a unique institutional type. Most importantly, the post-entrepreneurial university model respects the complexity inherent to both the university itself and the landscape in which it operates. Further research is needed, both empirical to flesh out the model and theoretical to build these connections more substantially, to demonstrate how complex systems theories can solve some of the many puzzles of university organization and action that are not properly conceivable within the rationalized entrepreneurial model that has gripped public policy debates in recent decades. It is by turning away from the efficiency/innovation unified model and refocusing on those post-entrepreneurial aspects that make it resilient, that the university will position itself to drive economic growth and social change while simultaneously remaining truthful to its cherished values and traditions, including an insurmountable commitment to safeguarding the public good.

References

Alajoutsijärvi, K., Alon, I., & Pinheiro, R. (2021). The marketisation of higher education: Antecedents, processes, and outcomes. In J. D. Branch & B. Christiansen (Eds.), *The marketisation of higher education: Concepts, cases, and criticisms* (pp. 17–45). Springer.

Ashby, R. W., & Goldstein, J. (2011). Variety, constraint, and the law of requisite variety. *Emergence: Complexity and Organization, 13*(1/2), 190.

Barzelay, M. (2001). *The new public management: Improving research and policy dialogue*. University of California Press.

Bleiklie, I., Enders, J., Lepori, B., & Musselin, C. (2011). New public management, network governance and the university as a changing professional organization. In P. Lægreid & T. Christensen (Eds.), *Ashgate research companion to new public management* (pp. 161–176). Ashgate.

de Boer, H., Enders, J., & Schimank, U. (2007). On the way towards new public management? The governance of university systems in England, the Netherlands, Austria, and Germany. In D. Jansen (Ed.), *New Forms of governance in research organizations: disciplinary approaches, interfaces and integration* (pp. 137–152). Springer.

Broucker, B., De Wit, K., & Verhoeven, J. (2017). Higher education research: Looking beyond new public management. In J. Huisman & M. Tight (Eds.), *Theory and method in higher education research* (pp. 21–38). Emerald Publishing.

Brunsson, N., & Sahlin-Andersson, K. (2000). Constructing organizations: The example of public sector reform. *Organization Studies, 21*(4), 721–746.

Castells, M. (2001). Universities as dynamic systems of contradictory functions. In J. Muller, N. Cloete, & S. Badat (Eds.), *Challenges of globalisation. South African debates with Manuel Castells*, (pp. 206–233). Maskew Miller Longman.

Christensen, T., & Laegreid, P. (2007). *Transcending new public management*. Ashgate.

Clark, B. (1973). Development of the sociology of higher education. *Sociology of Education, 46*(1), 2–14.

Clark, B. R. (1983). *The higher education system: Academic organization in cross-national perspective*. University of California Press.

Clark, B. R. (1998). *Creating entrepreneurial universities: Organizational pathways of transformation*. Pergamon.

Clark, B. R. (2004). *Sustaining change in universities: Continuities in case studies and concepts*. Society for Research into Higher Education & Open University Press.

Diefenbach, T. (2009). New public management in public sector organizations: The dark sides of managerialistic 'Enlightenment.' *Public Administration, 87*(4), 892–909.

Dunleavy, P., Margetts, H., Bastow, S., & Tinkler, J. (2006). New public management is dead—Long live digital-era governance. *Journal of Public Administration Research and Theory, 16*(3), 467–494.
Enders, J., & Boer, H. (2009). The mission impossible of the European university: Institutional confusion and institutional diversity. In A. Amaral, G. Neave, C. Musselin & P. Maassen (Eds.), *European integration and the governance of higher education and research* (pp. 159–178). Higher Education Dynamics Series. Springer.
Etzkowitz, H. (1983). Entrepreneurial scientists and entrepreneurial universities in American academic science. *Minerva, 21*(2), 198–233.
Etzkowitz, H. (2001). The second academic revolution and the rise of entrepreneurial science. *Technology and Society Magazine, 20*(2), 18–29.
Etzkowitz, H. (2003). Research groups as 'quasi-firms': The invention of the entrepreneurial university. *Research Policy, 32*(1), 109–121.
Etzkowitz, H. (2008). *The triple helix: University-industry-government innovation in action*. Taylor & Francis.
Etzkowitz, H., & Leydesdorff, L. (2000). The dynamics of innovation: From National Systems and "Mode 2" to a Triple Helix of university-industry-government relations. *Research Policy, 29*(2), 109–123.
Etzkowitz, H., & Webster, A. (1998). Entrepreneurial science: The second academic revolution. In H. Etzkowitz, A. Webster, & P. Healey (Eds.), *Capitalizing knowledge: New intersections of industry and academia* (pp. 21–46). SUNY Press.
Frigotto, L., Young, M., & Pinheiro, R. (2022). Resilience in organizations and societies: The state of the art and three organizing principles for moving forward. In R. Pinheiro, L. Frigotto & M. Young (Eds.), *Towards resilient organizations and societies: A cross-sectoral and multi-disciplinary perspective*. Palgrave.
Giustiniano, L., Clegg, S. R., Cunha, M., & Rego, A. (2018). *Elgar introduction to theories of organizational resilience*. Edward Elgar Publishing.
Gruening, G. (2001). Origin and theoretical basis of new public management. *International Public Management Journal, 4*(1), 1–25.
Hazelkorn, E. (2015). *Rankings and the reshaping of higher education: The battle for world-class excellence*. Springer.
Hood, C. (1991). A public management for all seasons? *Public Administration, 69*(1), 3–19.
Hüther, O., & Krücken, G. (2016). Nested organizational fields: Isomorphism and differentiation among European universities. In E. Berman & C. Paradeise (Eds.), *The university under pressure* (pp. 53–83). Emerald Group Publishing Limited.
Janeway, W. H. (2012). *Doing capitalism in the innovation economy: Markets, speculation and the state*. Cambridge: Cambridge University Press.

Jencks, C., & Riesman, D. (2002). *The academic revolution*. Transaction Publishers.

Krücken, G., & Meier, F. (2006). Turning the university into an organizational actor. In G. Drori, J. W. Meyer, & H. Hwang (Eds.), *Globalization and organization: World society and organizational change* (pp. 241–257). Oxford University Press.

LeGrand, J., & Bartlett, W. (1993). *Quasi-markets and public policy*. MacMillan.

Maassen, P., & Olsen, J. (2007). *University dynamics and European integration*. Springer.

Maassen, P., & Potman, H. (1990). Strategic decision making in higher education. *Higher Education, 20*(4), 393–410.

March, J. G. (1991). Exploration and exploitation in organizational learning. *Organization science, 2*(1), 71–87.

March, J., & Olsen, J. (1979). *Ambiguity and choice in organizations*. Universitetsforlaget.

Meadows, D. H. (2008). *Thinking in systems: A primer*. Chelsea green publishing.

Meyer, J. W., Ramirez, F. O., Frank, D. J., & Schofer, E. (2006). *Higher education as an institution* (CDDRL Working Papers, 57). Stanford University.

Mohrman, K., Ma, W., & Baker, D. (2008). The research university in transition: The emerging global model. *Higher Education Policy, 21*(1), 5–27.

Musselin, C. (2007). Are universities specific organisations? In G. Krücken, A. Kosmützky, & M. Torka (Eds.), *Towards a multiversity? Universities between global trends and national traditions* (pp. 63–84). Transaction Publishers.

Nybom, T. (2003). The humboldt legacy: Reflections on the past, present, and future of the European University. *Higher Education Policy, 16*(2), 141–159.

OECD. (1995). *Governance in transition*. Organization for Economic Cooperation and Development.

OECD. (2005). Higher education management and policy. *Special Issue: Entrepreneurship, 17*(3), 1–147.

Orton, D. J., & Weick, K. (1990). Loosely coupled systems: A reconceptualization. *Academy of Management Review, 15*(2), 203–223.

Page, S. (2011). *Diversity and complexity*. Princeton University Press.

Pal, L. (2012). *Frontiers of governance: The OECD and global public management reform*. Palgrave MacMillan.

Paradeise, C., Bleiklie, I., Enders, J., Goastellec, G., Michelsen, S., Reale, E., & Westerheijden, D. F. (2009). Reform policies and change processes in Europe. In J. Huisman (Ed.), *International perspectives on the governance of higher education: Alternative frameworks for coordination* (pp. 88–106). Routledge.

Pekkola, E., Pinheiro, R., Geschwind, L., Siekkinen, T., Carvalho, T., & Pulkkinen, K. (2021). Nested hybridity and value definition in public higher education. In J. Vakkuri & J.-E. Johanson (Eds.), *Hybrid governance, organisations and society: Value creation perspectives* (pp. 59–80). Routledge.

Pinheiro, R. (2012). University ambiguity and institutionalization: A tale of three regions. In R. Pinheiro, P. Benneworth, & G. A. Jones (Eds.), *Universities and regional development: A critical assessment of tensions and contradictions* (pp. 35–55). Routledge.

Pinheiro, R. (2015). Citius, Altius, Fortius: Mobilising the university for the 'Europe of Knowledge'. In B. Culum, F. Ribeiro, & Y. Politis (Eds.), *New voices in higher education research and scholarship* (pp. 1–17). IGI-Global.

Pinheiro, R. (2016). Humboldt meets Schumpeter? Interpreting the 'Entrepreneurial Turn' in European higher education. In S. Slaughter & B. J. Taylor (Eds.), *Competitive advantage: Stratification, privatization and vocationalization of Higher Education in the US, EU, and Canada* (pp. 291–310). Springer.

Pinheiro, R., & Stensaker, B. (2014a). Designing the entrepreneurial university: The Interpretation of a global idea. *Public Organization Review, 14*(4), 497–516.

Pinheiro, R., & Stensaker, B. (2014b). Strategic actor-hood and internal transformation: The rise of the quadruple-helix university? In J. Brankovik, M. Klemencik, P. Lazetic, & P. Zgaga (Eds.), *Global challenges, local responses in higher education. The contemporary issues in national and comparative perspective* (pp. 171–189). Sense.

Pinheiro, R., & Young, M. (2017). The university as an adaptive resilient organization: A complex systems perspective. In J. Huisman & M. Tight (Eds.), *Theory and method in higher education research* (Vol. 3, pp. 119–136). Emerald Publishing.

Pollitt, C., & Bouckaert, G. (2011). *Public management reform.* Oxford University Press.

Ramirez, F., Byrkjeflot, H., & Pinheiro, R. (2016). Higher education and health organizational fields in the age of "world class" and "best practices". In R. Pinheiro, L. Geschwind, F. Ramirez, & K. Vrangbæk (Eds.), *Towards a comparative institutionalism: Forms, dynamics and logics across health care and higher education fields* (pp. 35–57). Emerald.

Salamon, L. (2002). The new governance and the tools of public action. In L. Salamon, (Ed.). *The tools of government: A guide to the new governance* (pp. 1–47). Oxford University Press.

Scott, J. (2006). The mission of the university: Medieval to postmodern transformations. *The Journal of Higher Education, 77*(1), 1–39.

Seeber, M., Lepori, B., Montauti, M., Enders, J., De Boer, H., Weyer, E., Bleiklie, I., et al. (2015). European universities as complete organizations? Understanding identity, hierarchy and rationality in public organizations. *Public Management Review, 17*(10), 1444–1474.

Selznick, P. (1966). *TVA and the grass roots: A study in the sociology of formal organization*. Harper & Row.

Sharfman, M. P., Wolf, G., Chase, R., & Tansik, D. A. (1988). Antecedents of organizational slack. *Academy of Management Review, 13*(4), 601–614.

Simon, H. (1991). Bounded rationality and organizational learning. *Organization Science, 2*(1), 125–134.

Slaughter, S., & Cantwell, B. (2012). Chapter Three: Academic Capitalism: Reflections on Higher Education in the united States and European Union. In R. Barnett & M. Peters (Eds.), *The Idea of the University: Contemporary Perspectives* (pp.55-77). Peter Lang,

Sørensen, M., Bloch, C., & Young, M. (2016). Excellence in the knowledge-based economy: From scientific to research excellence. *European Journal of Higher Education, 6*(3), 217–236.

Stanley, K., & Lehman, J. (2015). *Why greatness cannot be planned: The myth of the objective*. Springer.

Teixeira, P., Jongbloed, B. B., Dill, D. D., & Amaral, A. (Eds.). (2004). *Markets in higher education: Rhetoric or reality?* Springer.

Thompson, J. D. (2008). *Organizations in action: Social science bases of administrative theory*. Transaction Publishers.

Walker, B., & Salt, D. (2006). *Resilience thinking: Sustaining ecosystems and people in a changing world*. Island Press.

Weick, K. E. (1976). Educational organizations as loosely coupled systems. *Administrative Science Quarterly, 21*(1), 1–19.

Young, M. (2015). Shifting policy narratives in Horizon 2020. *Journal of Contemporary European Research, 11*(1), 16–30.

Young, M., Sørensen, M., Bloch, C., & Degn, L. (2017). Systemic rejection: Political pressures seen from the science system. *Higher Education, 74*(3), 491–505.

CHAPTER 8

Organizational Persistence in Highly Institutionalized Environments: Unpacking the Relation Between Identity and Resilience

Lars Geschwind, Rómulo Pinheiro, and Bjørn Stensaker

Introduction

Universities rank among the most enduring organizational forms. Over time, they have adapted to changing circumstances while retaining a sense of stability in their inner core, i.e. the values, norms and traditions guiding

L. Geschwind (✉)
Department of Learning in Engineering Sciences, KTH Royal Institute of Technology, Stockholm, Sweden
e-mail: larsges@kth.se

R. Pinheiro
Department of Political Science and Management, University of Agder, Kristiansand, Norway
e-mail: romulo.m.pinheiro@uia.no

B. Stensaker
Department of Education, University of Oslo, Oslo, Norway
e-mail: bjorn.stensaker@iped.uio.no

R. Pinheiro et al. (eds.), *Towards Resilient Organizations and Societies*, Public Sector Organizations,
https://doi.org/10.1007/978-3-030-82072-5_8

academic behaviour. At their essence, universities are value-laden institutions, and thus highly cultural in nature (Dill, 1982). Resilient systems and organizations are characterized by their ability to adapt to changing circumstances while remaining within thresholds, i.e. while retaining their core function and identity (Walker & Salt, 2006; see also Chapter 1 of this volume). Despite growing academic interest in understanding the conditions under which resilient organizations adapt to challenging circumstances (Bhamra, 2015; Pirotti & Venzin, 2016), little attention to date has been paid to culture as a meditating factor, i.e. as an enabler or property of resilient behaviour. This is particularly salient when it comes to organizational fields or sectors characterized by a multiplicity of formal and informal rules emanating from a variety of carriers or sources; what organizational scholars term as 'highly institutionalized' environments (Scott, 2014). Such rules both constrain and enable social agents' attempts to respond to environmental imperatives, thus being of interest to students of resilient behaviour within complex organizational forms.

Given this backdrop, the chapter investigates how organizational identities are formed within the organizational field of higher education (HE) in the context of conflicting and even hostile environments. Moreover, taking a resilience prism, we shed empirical light on how identities evolve over time, in the light of specific configurations of the external environment, and how this process affects (either enables or constrains) key resilient attributes. Hence, the chapter bridges separate streams of the organizational literature to unpack change and adaptation processes in the context of resilient behaviour in a specific field. The research question being addressed is:

> *What is the relationship between organizational identity and resilience, and does it manifest itself empirically in the organizational field of higher education?*

We test our framework by undertaking an investigation of a case higher education institution (HEI) located in the Nordic region. The case in point—Örebro University—has undergone considerable identity changes during the last four decades, driven by both regulatory and cultural factors. Empirically, the paper investigates identity evolution, formation and legitimation by illuminating critical events associated with historical turning points or 'critical junctures', especially those affecting key external legitimacy issues.

In the next sections, we review the existing literature and outline our analytical framework, focusing, first, on the relationship between identity formation and adaptation or change, and second, on the antecedents associated with key attributes of organizational resilience within the context of HEIs. Our research quest is, thus, associated with empirically demonstrating the extent to which the aforementioned resilience attributes are affected by shifts in organizational identity over time. The closing part of the chapter discusses the main findings and reflects on their implications for future research.

Organizational Identity—An Elusive Construct

Seminal studies on organizational identity have identified several factors driving identity formation and change, including the circumstances surrounding the birth of the organization (Stinchcombe, 1965), strategic leadership (Gioia & Thomas, 1996), organizational recruitment and demographics (Selznick, 1957). Despite the continuing interest in the concept of organizational identity, it nonetheless remains an elusive construct, not least insofar how organizational identities are formed and evolve (Gioia et al., 2013). As is often the case with complex social phenomena, there is no universal definition of identity ('who we are as an organization'), but there is a consensus that organizational identity provides a guide for what an organization's members should do (Gioia et al., 2013). Recent studies have shed light on organizational identity as a mechanism for responding to institutional complexity (Kodeih & Greenwood, 2014), including adapting to shifting and/or multiple institutional logics (Raynard & Greenwood, 2014; Thornton et al., 2012), living with hybridity (Boers & Nordqvist, 2012), and while handling cross-level dynamics (Ashforth et al., 2011). As part of this interest, there is also a noticeable shift towards investigating process-related dimensions, i.e. the notion of identity 'as becoming' and as a more dynamic concept (Elsbach, 2013). Attention has also been paid to the gamut of methodologies used for measuring or assessing identity (Foreman & Whetten, 2014). Despite considerable progress, the field is still characterized by somewhat idiosyncratic descriptions of how identity formation takes place and the factors that are salient in this process.

Much research on organizational identity can be classified as belonging to either an essentialist or a strategic perspective (Glynn, 2008). The essentialist perspective is concentrated around the key properties of organizational identity as suggested by Albert and Whetten (1985)—the central character, the enduring nature and the distinctiveness of a given organization—and, as such, points back to the notion that identity and culture are intimately linked, as postulated in the old institutionalism tradition (Selznick, 1957). The strategic perspective is more associated with the link between identity and image, with identity seen as an asset for profiling and positioning the organization in more competitive environments (Gioia et al., 2010). That said, the weight given to the historical legacies and the path-dependencies of organizations as well as environmental adaptability suggests that both the essentialist and the strategic perspective may have several links with central institutional assumptions about organizational persistence and change (Glynn, 2008; Stensaker, 2004), aspects intrinsically linked to resilience both as a system's property as well as outcome (Ruth & Goessling-Reisemann, 2019).

The split between the various camps within research on organizational identity is unfortunate in several ways, not least with respect to the lack of cross-fertilization (He & Brown, 2013, p. 11). In line with Glynn (2008), we take the position that institutions (i.e. formal and informal rules) may both enable and constrain organizational identities and that the relationship between the focal organization and its environment is vital for understanding both change and continuity, affecting resilience—while also questioning its stability. Foreman and Whetten (2012) touch upon this issue while referring to the 'identity paradox'—the fact that identities are constructed through comparisons with others to find a balance between being distinctive and similar within a larger population.

From an institutional perspective, organizational identity is framed and embedded within the larger organizational field (DiMaggio & Powell, 1983) providing the focal organization with the material used in the identity formation process. Dominate institutional templates (derived from the field) help set the limits for the forming and acceptance of possible identities (Kraatz & Zajak, 1996). In other words, an institutional perspective builds a bridge between essentialist and strategic perspectives on identity by opening up for the possibilities that identities may stem from both micro- and macro-level factors, thus turning critical attention towards identity formation as an ongoing process (Glynn, 2008; Gioia et al., 2013; Stensaker, 2004).

However, this way of interpreting organizational identity—as an ongoing process—also makes it possible to link identity closer to resilience. If resilient organizations are characterized by their ability to adapt to changing circumstances while maintaining their core function (Walker & Salt, 2006)—identity and resilience become two concepts that are highly intertwined—and perhaps sharing key properties—as explained in the next section.

Identity and Resilience

The key elements of organizational identity—centrality, endurance and distinctiveness (Albert & Whetten, 1985)—which normally are perceived as stable elements of a coherent identity change character when assessed in a process perspective. The notion of resilience allows for a more flexible and adaptable identity to occur where the internal and external ingredients of the identity enable but also constrain possible actions.

For example, by adding resilience to existing research on organizational identity, we may provide answers to fundamental questions within organizational identity research—for example which element of a given identity that is central (Corley et al., 2006, p. 90)? Here, resilient organizations would most likely opt for what some label as 'optimal distinctiveness' (Brewer, 1991; see also Phillips et al., 2016)—suggesting that centrality is actually shaped by what is perceived as distinctive features of the organization. Of course, when facing expectations from their environments which are difficult to ignore or reject, resilient organizations might be forced to develop multiple (Pratt & Kraatz, 2009) or even hybrid identities (Battilana & Lee, 2014). The latter options could, of course, be imagined as an interesting alternative for younger and more recently established organizations having weak or at least less distinct identities where possibilities and boundaries are tested and pushed. As such, resilience could be argued to be something that is installed quite early in the organizational life-span, and not necessarily developed with increasing age. This is consistent with key findings from organizational theory (Drori & Honig, 2013; Stinchcombe, 1965).

However, opting for multiple or even hybrid identities might also suggest that resilience is not as enduring as one might imagine. However, allowing for some fluidity in the organizational identity is consistent with more recent claims that identity formation processes have no end-points (Alvesson & Robertson, 2016). The enduring character of the identity concept is then perhaps more related to the 'identity struggle' itself than to specific features of the identity. The consequence for resilience is that it is not necessarily linked to a 'real' identity but to perceptions of an identity suggesting that the idea of resilience is embedded in processes of translation, interest negotiation and social construction (Gioia & Chittipeddi, 1991; Gioia et al., 2000; Stensaker, 2015; Washington & Ventresca, 2004).

Based on the above discussion, we can outline some expectations as to how organizational identities develop from a process perspective.

> Our first expectation is that organizational identity—and resilience—is installed quite early in the organizational life-span.
> Our second expectation is that organizational identity—and resilience—is more dynamic and less enduring than imagined.

The Dynamics of Legitimacy in Forming Organizational Identities

While centrality, the enduring character, and distinctiveness originally were seen as key characteristics of organizational identity (Albert & Whetten, 1985), later contributions have suggested that, in addition to these dimensions, one should also add *legitimacy* and *adaptability* as central elements (Foreman & Whetten, 2012). The latter dimensions are more associated with an institutionalist perspective on organizational identity i.e. the relationship between a given organization and its external environment, and how this might lead to changes in the identity over time (Phillips et al., 2016). The adaptability element brings to the fore the notion that organizational identity formation can be embedded in more deliberate design attempts (Parent & Foreman, 2007), while the underlining of legitimacy suggests that identities are highly dependent on some sort of external support and acceptance (Elsbach & Kramer, 1996; Deephouse & Suchman, 2008), a central assumption within institutional theory (Phillips et al., 2016). By adding legitimacy and adaptability to the original elements constituting organizational identity, a better balance between the intrinsic and the extrinsic dimensions of identity formation is achieved. Furthermore, although it also opens for new questions regarding the specific conditions affecting the development of organizational identity and how intrinsic and extrinsic dimensions are balanced in the process.

Deephouse and Suchman (2008, p. 60) have suggested that legitimacy is a dichotomous construct—you either have it, or you do not. This is in line with earlier research defining legitimacy as a generalized perception that the 'actions of an entity is desirable, proper, or appropriate within some socially constructed system of norms, values, beliefs, and definitions' (Suchman, 1995, p. 574). This definition of legitimacy suggests that fields are characterized by coherence and a collective understanding with respect to what the dominant norms, values and standards are. However, this definition may be questioned in fields that are more heterogeneous, and where different actors are carriers of contrasting assumptions about the key criteria determining legitimation. The institutional assumption that organizations need to conform to the environment for legitimacy (Scott, 2014) may thus be a challenge given the existence of different 'moral', 'cognitive' and 'pragmatic' forms of legitimacy (Suchman, 1995), especially if these are held by different actors and groups in the environment (Bitektine & Haack, 2015). However, as demonstrated by resource-dependency theorists, organizational survival may not need to be conferred by a large segment of the society for a given organization to prosper (Pfeffer & Salancik, 1978, p. 194).

Conflicting and contended forms of legitimacy add an important dimension to both institutional theory and organizational identity studies, allowing researchers to investigate how identify formation processes are embedded in power struggles and interest articulation within a given field (Alvesson & Robertson, 2016), between insiders and outsiders alike (Drori & Honig, 2013; Gioia et al., 2010), and more specifically among different external stakeholders (Bitektine & Haack, 2015). While we agree that legitimacy is an important dimension in the forming of organizational identities, we see legitimacy as an intimate part of the centrality, the endurance and the distinctiveness of the organizational identity, and hence as the key mediator conditioning identity change or adaptability.

Identity Formation and Resilience in Contested Fields—Key Assumptions

If legitimacy is important when organizational identities and resilience are formed, the question arises as to how focal organizations obtain (and maintain) such legitimacy in highly contested or even hostile fields in the first place (Greenwood et al., 2011). The existence of specific configurations of identities can be expected to be dependent on the characteristics and the dynamics of the organizational field (Weerts et al., 2014). We suggest that the different elements of organizational identity—centrality, endurance and distinctiveness—which normally are perceived as unified and inseparable elements of a coherent identity emerging from within the organization (Albert & Whetten, 1985), may be affected in different ways in contested fields thus, conditioning the degree of resilience.

Hence, our take is that external legitimacy, first and foremost, conditions and shapes the *central* element of an organization's identity in contested fields. As different external stakeholders may be linked to and advocating for specific forms of legitimacy—being moral/normative, cognitive/cultural or pragmatic/regulative—(Scott, 2014; Suchman, 1995), emerging organizations will have to adapt to, and emphasize those forms of, legitimacy that are linked to supportive stakeholders, being constrained from adapting to others. Hence, our answer to one of the fundamental questions within organizational identity research—which element of the identity is central? (Corley et al., 2006, p. 90)—is that this is conditioned through the process of obtaining external legitimacy.

The question which arises is, of course, what happens when an organization has few or even none powerful external supporters and where it is not obvious how external legitimacy can be translated into a central element of the identity. On this issue, institutional theory may have different answers. Our hypothesis is that, when exposed to more hostile external stakeholders while still striving for legitimacy, organizations may downplay their *distinctiveness* as a way to position themselves as attractive and relevant for the highest possible number of external stakeholders. While the notion of 'optimal distinctiveness' (Brewer, 1991) is important in understanding how established and legitimate organizations may want to position themselves in a larger and more unified field, we argue that a search for 'optimal legitimacy' may be a viable option for new organizations entering conflicting fields. This may result in the forming of multiple (Pratt & Kraatz, 2009) and hybrid identities (Battilana & Lee, 2014).

However, in such contested fields, another option may also be to search for what might be labelled as *'non-threatening distinctiveness'*—identities that may push and explore existing perceptions of what possible identities might look like (Czarniawska, 1997) while still forced to search for distinctiveness within the broader acceptable boundaries of the field (Phillips et al., 2016). Here, we suggest that the identity formation process may be more or less innovative partly dependent on whether the focal organization may be said to already carry a less distinct or a more distinct identity. While one could imagine that organizations with a less distinct identity may be more likely to explore such possibilities, research has actually found that it is organizations having more distinctive perceptions of their identity that engage in such processes (Stensaker, 2004, p. 210; Tapper & Palfreyman, 2011). It is possible that this might be explained by the strong internal legitimacy of the organizational identity established in the emergent stage (Drori & Honig, 2013).

Organizational identity formation processes can be seen as ongoing with no formal start- and end-points (Alvesson & Robertson, 2016). This argument can be said to be somewhat in conflict with a key assumption within the organizational identity literature—the enduring character of organizational identity (Albert & Whetten, 1985). We suggest that the degree of *endurance* in organizational identity is highly dependent on the dynamic configuration of legitimating stakeholders in the environment over time. If contestation about key legitimacy issues among stakeholders is reduced over time, we assume that this will allow for an expansion of the central element of the focal organizations to build a broader base for its legitimacy. This may, at the same time, increase the need to develop its distinctive element in line with the optimal distinctiveness argument by Brewer (1991). In this case, endurance implies an adding-on of central elements very much in line with the assumed isomorphic processes as suggested in institutional theory (Scott, 2014), through processes of translation, interest negotiation and social construction (Gioia & Chittipeddi, 1991; Gioia et al., 2000; Stensaker, 2015; Washington & Ventresca, 2004).

However, if, over time, external stakeholders continue to be engaged in contestations over what valid legitimacy might imply in the field, and where the focal organization has a central character linked to specific legitimacy forms, we contend that the room for manoeuvre is reduced. This is in line with earlier evidence on how powerful external stakeholders might narrow down the options of available central elements of organizational identities (Elsbach & Kramer, 1996; Stensaker et al., 2016). In this case, the environment constrains available options and the central element of the organizational identity persists. In line with our earlier assumptions, we suggest that this will also reduce the possibilities for developing the distinctiveness of the organization as it might endanger the support from supportive external stakeholders.

Empirical Context: Scandinavian Higher Education

As a field, HE is relevant for testing out the role of external legitimacy in identity formation processes. First, it has been found rather suitable for studying both organizational identity (Clark, 1992; Stensaker, 2015; Weerts et al., 2014) and for testing central tenants from institutional theory (Maassen & Olsen, 2007; Ramirez & Christensen, 2013; Scott, 2014). Second, the field is characterized by conflicting expectations and values (Pinheiro et al., 2016a, 2016b), thus being highly relevant for analysing the role of complex and conflicting environments (Clark, 2004; Maassen & Olsen, 2007). Third, while the field has been criticized by some as an empirical testing ground for institutional theory due to its 'strong institutional/weak technical' character (Kraatz & Zajak, 1996), the Scandinavian countries are an exception to this rule due to the quite powerful role played by public authorities affecting the funding, the regulation of, and personnel policies in the sector (Huisman et al., 2002; Kyvik, 2009). Hence, in Scandinavia both the institutional and the technical environment can be characterized as strong, creating a field containing contested legitimacy forms. To illustrate this, we base our presentation of the empirical context on the three forms of legitimacy outlined by Suchman (1995) and Scott (2014), i.e. the *pragmatic/regulative*, *moral/normative* and *cultural-cognitive* forms of legitimacy.

Governmental influence (*regulative/pragmatic legitimacy*) in Scandinavian HE has always been strong (Kyvik, 2009), not least with respect to the role the field is intended to play in the economy (Pinheiro et al., 2012). The dominant role of the state is substantiated through its key influence as a funder and regulator, e.g. in the form of accreditation and evaluation (Hansen et al., 2019; Pinheiro et al., 2014). Hence, the political steering of the sector should, in a comparative perspective, be characterized as quite strong (Gornitzka & Maassen, 2007), although one can witness several changes in the role of the state in the region over the latter decades, moving towards providing HEIs with greater autonomy (Maassen & Stensaker, 2003). Still, the responsibility for deciding upon the domestic HE landscape is a task that has continued to be central to national governments in the region (Meek et al., 1996; Maassen & Stensaker, 2011), as illustrated by the many merger processes that the state has initiated during the last decade (Geschwind et al., 2016). As such, issues addressing diversity and differentiation rank high on the policy agenda in the region.

However, the Scandinavian region can also be said to be embedded in and an integrated part of the broader and more global field of HE, being exposed to various signals and expectations linked to *cultural-cognitive forms of legitimacy*. Of particular relevance here is the increasing prevalence of global organizational archetypes (Greenwood & Hinings, 1993), such as the 'entrepreneurial university' (Pinheiro & Stensaker, 2014) or the 'research university' (Kyvik, 2009), aimed at making HEIs more responsive and resilient to increasingly volatile technical and institutional environments (Karlsen & Pritchard, 2013). These ideals and ways to accomplish legitimacy have been supported by a range of stakeholders within the region that see adaptation to the market as vital (Kyvik, 2009; Salerno, 2007), pushing HEIs to become more professional and adaptive in their functioning (Christensen et al., 2019; Ramirez & Christensen, 2013).

Finally, in the Scandinavian countries, it is also possible to identify strong demands, aspirations and ideals that are linked to *normative/moral forms of legitimacy*. The region hosts several universities that were established in pre-modern times and that have acted both as producers and gatekeepers of the values, norms and ideals that dominate the field (Maassen & Olsen, 2007). These values and norms have often been linked to more global ideas related to the Humboldtian university and the more critical role HE should play in society in developing and stimulating truth and democracy (de Boer & Stensaker, 2007). For new institutions entering the field, established and powerful older universities may thus create an important frame of reference, both enabling but potentially also restricting the identity formation of the 'newcomers'. Studies have shown that established universities in the region both protested and were quite hostile towards the establishment of new HEIs, a critique that has continued although in different forms and through different arguments over the decades (Huisman et al., 2002; Kyvik, 2009).

The 'legitimacy landscape' identified above has two important implications for empirical studies. First, the Scandinavian region creates a complex environment for the ways in which identity construction as a process takes place. The regulative, cultural-cognitive and the normative forms of legitimacy can, in essence, be said to represent competing and conflicting arguments for the forming of an organizational identity, and mapping the different positions key stakeholders have had over time is therefore essential to understand their potential influence on the focal organizations. Second, the different forms of legitimacy may also represent important building blocks for understanding how identity is shaped in that they include both more abstract (desired images from the environment) and more concrete (past experiences about how the organization functions) dimensions. By tracing arguments, discourses and beliefs over time, the three forms of legitimacy assist us in unpacking the institutional processes involved since their relative impact in the identity formation process can be studied more analytically. Thus, by theoretically exploring the significance of regulative, normative and cultural-cognitive legitimacy on how the central and distinctive elements of the organizational identities develop over time (endurance), we build a bridge between studies on organizational identity, institutional theory and resilience on the one hand, and studies on organizations and historical reasoning within the social sciences on the other.

Identity formation is a complex process requiring the analysis of multiple data sources and levels of analysis over an extended time period. This is challenging due to the traditional nature of undertaking scientific inquiries, where longitudinal perspectives are rare and more in-depth analyses are both time and resource consuming, and hence often avoided. Our analysis relies on the officially communicated and/or 'narrated' (Czarniawska, 1997) organizational identity and we have limited our study to the official identity as expressed in sources from top managers and literature during three critical junctures (Capoccia & Kelemen, 2007). Hence, we do not claim that this represents a shared identity by all or even a majority. Furthermore, due to space limitations, rather than an extensive case study, the empirical section of this chapter should rather be considered an empirical 'vignette' based on a few written sources and literature with the aim to illustrate and test the theoretical framework. As such, it is far from comprehensive, but sufficient for our purposes (Benneworth, 2019). Quotations have been translated by the authors from Swedish.

Empirical Vignette: Örebro University

Critical Juncture 1: Aspirations to Become a New Kind of University

The history of higher education in Örebro can be traced back to the 1960s when professional education was established in the city (Sports, Engineering and Social Work, respectively). A new institution started out as a university college in 1977 (Högskolan I Örebro), as a standalone seat of learning but with close relations to one of the country's older, research universities as a 'satellite'. The decision to develop towards full university status was made early. Although education was first priority for the university college, research increasingly became part of the core business, e.g. through staff mobility and joint professorships with the neighbouring research university (Andrén, 2013). Already in the late 1980s, plans to become a university were developed and when a new Vice-chancellor was appointed in 1990; this future goal was even specified in the job advertisement: 'target university status, increased internationalization, educational development' (Lind, 2009, p. 30).

In his inaugural speech, the newly appointed Vice-chancellor also identified a number of features of the existing organization that he found beneficial for the aspiration to become a full university: 'At our disposal we also have the comparative advantages of the new university college: simplicity, transparency, affinity. Could it be any better? We can do whatever we want. If we want to' (Lind, 2004, p. 31). Being a new seat of learning, the Vice-chancellor argued, was also a possibility to develop a distinct identity, different from the existing flagship universities in the country. However, the Vice-chancellor also made specific reference to the hostile national environment when he compared the new university colleges' academic journey with the beginning of an Odyssey, navigating between Scylla and Charybdis, illustrating the open resistance from the older universities and a, so far, reluctant state (Lind, 2004, p. 33).

Increasingly during the 1990s, the university college developed its international profile, described as the 'educational center of the region with an international outlook' (Lind, 2004, p. 49). It was still considered important to stress the regional embeddedness, but the internationalization activities were considered a key feature of becoming a stronger, more recognized institution. However, the national HE and research policy in the early 90s stipulated a strict division of labour between research-oriented universities and teaching-oriented university colleges and there was no national scheme in place for university colleges to become full universities. This created a dead end for university colleges with aspirations. As the then, frustrated, vice-chancellor described it: 'We bang our heads in the research policy Berlin wall' (Lind, 2004, p. 63).

Critical Juncture 2: Vision 2005

Another critical juncture for the HEI was the initiation of a new forward-looking project titled 'Vision 2005', which included and engaged many people and took almost a year to complete (1995–1996). The task to develop a shared long-term vision was described as pioneer work, new to universities in the country, but in line with the new 'Freedom reform' then recently launched by the Government in 1993 following the logics of New Public Management. The main goal of the strategy was to become 'a respected university of good European standard' with researching teachers, learning students, a rich collaboration with society and an environment for encounters. The difference between being a university college focusing on undergraduate education and being a university with a more even balance between teaching and research was described by the Vice-chancellor in a 1997 speech: 'It will be noticed in the daily work, I assure you! One will discuss, inform and question at all levels' (Lind, 2004, p. 151). Not only was the internal life of the university expected to change, but also the relations to the surrounding society were expected to reach higher levels.

> The formation of the institution is also a changed relation to our environment. And by this, I mean not only the regional but also the national and the international. To avoid all misunderstandings, I want to strongly emphasize that this, or rather these, relations have always been there, at times very rich. What is now happening is a forceful development also in new fields. (Lind, 2004, p. 152)

The new Vice-chancellor decided that the university should be driven 'not by tradition but rather by vision' (Gidlund, 2009, p. 91). The new vision would cover the coming 10 years and was developed during one and half years. The key concept 'European research university' indicated two things as far as organizational identity was concerned: European rather than national ambitions and, in addition, that operations should be research-led. Another key identity marker was the task to renew the academic landscape and our society. The Ministry of Education encouraged Örebro to find its own profiled way: 'Don't copy, create your own profile' as referred to by the Board chairman at the time (Larsson, 2009, p. 48). Again, the ambition is to acquire a distinct identity in relation to the 'traditional' universities. The focus was also on the future and not on the past, neither the legacy of older Swedish universities nor its own historical path.

Critical Juncture 3: University Status Awarded

The goal of achieving university status was reached in 1999 due to a major shift in HE policy during the late 1990s, making it possible to transition from university college to university. Örebro University College was one of the institutions that in 1997 applied for and subsequently was assessed by a peer review panel commissioned by the national accreditation body. The panel was chaired by former Gothenburg University Vice-chancellor Jan S. Nilsson and in addition membered by five prominent scholars from the Nordic countries. In doing so, the university needed to comply with the assessment criteria established by the accreditation agency Högskoleverket, which were general for all HEIs (Andrén, 2013).

Based on the peer review report the national accreditation agency declined the application, which was also the case for two of the other applying university colleges. Only the university college in Karlstad was considered qualified to become a full university. However, the Government overruled its agency and approved the application anyway which spurred a debate on the relation between the government and Högskoleverket (Sjölund, 2002) but also earlier showed the fierce resistance from the existing universities (Andrén, 2013). Against this background, the first years were characterized by the hard work to gain legitimacy in the sector in the eyes of multiple and influential stakeholders (Lind, 2009). The promotion of three new universities had to be defended until the end. (Lind, 2004, p. 176) This created on the one hand a sense of 'underdog' mentality, cultivating the image of the brave innovative newcomer fighting against the old, established universities and the national accreditation agency (Larsson, 2009). However, the identity as being innovative and new was, during this early university period also complemented with links to the past and the university traditions. As an illustration, the new university decided to unveil a plaque with inscriptions in Latin with explicit references to the history of universities and Latin as the former *lingua franca*. Also in the inauguration speech, the Vice-chancellor made use of Latin phrases which had not been done before (Lind, 2004, pp. 199–202).

Hence, both continuity and change can be identified in the sources from this time. The then chairman of the board reflected a decade later upon the transition from university college to university:

> When *the university* college was transformed into a university, it meant an important change for the future but in many senses things remained as they were. [...] Obviously, it was symbolically important – not least for the self-esteem among management and staff – that [the university] was considered meeting the requirements that could be imposed on a university: it was no longer a species difference with respect to [two established universities] but rather a difference of degree. (Larsson, 2009, p. 59)

The then vice-chancellor illustrated the new situation: 'at the time of the foundation, the new university made a number of strategically important decisions. Perhaps the most important was what role the university should have in the academic field and in the surrounding society' (Gidlund, 2009, p. 90). Both internally and from external stakeholders, various expectations were expressed. Several new academic staff had been recruited to meet the new demands. Since 1999, the university has grown, both in terms of size but also regarding scope (faculties, programmes) and services (doctoral education, research). The scientific portfolio now also comprises a medical faculty and engineering education, to which the right to award degrees had to be applied for several times before the Swedish accreditation agency Högskoleverket finally awarded the examination rights. In the case of the medical doctor programme, the role of the other universities as well as the medicine professional association (Läkarförbundet) were important. In the words of the Vice-chancellor at the time: 'A complicating factor was the negative attitude among the six universities already providing medical doctor programmes, who were unwilling to welcome another player on the pitch' (Gidlund, 2009, p. 65).

As of the time of writing (Summer, 2020), Örebro University hosts about 17,000 students, almost doubled compared to when university status was reached, and close to 1300 total staff. It has become a full-fledged, comprehensive university with a growing research proportion. It is now a multi-faculty university with one of the broadest missions in the country, ranked among the best 400 universities in the world (THE, 2020).

Discussion

Identity Formation Over Time: Centrality, Endurance and Distinctiveness

Our empirical vignette shows an interesting trajectory over time. Higher education in Örebro was established as a teaching-only university college providing vocational programmes, e.g. social work. It was closely linked to one of the older universities in the country, serving as 'satellite' institution during the wave of HE expansion in the 1960s. Early on, plans to become a university emerged internally at the university. It appears that becoming a full-fledged university was important, not like the other 'traditional' universities but rather in a new, modern, novel way, in order to create a *distinct* identity. This vision met a hostile environment where the state was reluctant for a long time to enable university colleges to develop into universities, and the other, existing universities put up open resistance to newcomers like Örebro. The crucial policy change during the late 1990s opened the opportunity for university colleges to apply for university status. This process affected the institution's *central* identity formation fundamentally, and made it less distinct but rather more streamlined with other comprehensive European research universities. Örebro's identity has thus changed rather than been *enduring* through an expansion both in scientific scope and missions (more research) underlining the transformative potential of organizational identities (Parent & Foreman, 2007).

Identity, Legitimacy and the Regulative Pillar: The State

The vignette also shows that identity formation and change are strongly linked to external legitimacy. In order to gain legitimacy from the authorities and the organizational field, HEIs need to adjust and adapt to external shifts and dynamics which in turn sets in motion the need for identity reformation, challenging the notion of an *enduring* identity character (Gioia et al., 2013). One way of shedding light on this process is to investigate the role played by Scott's (2014) institutional pillars. Starting with the *regulative pillar*, the data shows that the state has played a vital role, both as enabler and constrainer. Shifting HE policies have either created major obstacles for the institutions in their quest for university status and permanent research funding or, instead, acted as an enabler and promoter by pushing universities to develop a distinct institutional profile. In the case of Örebro, the state in the 1980s and early 1990s upheld a division of labour among HEIs across the country, but in the late 1990s, HE policy changed. Not only was research funding allocated to university colleges, more importantly, but it also became possible to apply for university status (Andrén, 2013). However, the evaluation process meant that Örebro was becoming less distinct and more similar to already existing research universities, following the template provided both by the state agency's evaluation criteria and by the interpretation of them by the peer review panel. After the decision to 'promote' the university college to full-fledged university in 1999, increased financial support for research followed, which again decreased after only a couple of years due to yet another policy change focusing more on the older, well-established universities rather than the newcomers (Geschwind & Pinheiro, 2017).

Identity, Legitimacy and the Normative Pillar: The Organizational Field

The empirical vignette also attests to the importance of approaching identity construction from a broader perspective encompassing dynamics within a given organizational field (c.f. Pinheiro et al., 2016a, 2016b). Universities are not only affected by the actions of other universities, but they also use these to re-inforce their unique identities. Yet, at the same time, they also copy features of those they are trying to avoid becoming, largely as a result of the role attributed to socialization (e.g. hiring from other organizations), resource-dependencies (copying successful features from leading universities) and the strategic management of legitimacy imperatives emanating both inside and outside organizational boundaries (e.g. the quest to become world class, globally oriented, etc.). Stated differently, they have adopted a hybrid (Boers & Nordqvist, 2012) profile and identity, for example being locally engaged and globally oriented (Marginson & Rhoades, 2002). The case of Örebro is compelling in this sense, balancing regional embeddedness with internationalization ambitions. The early emphasis on not being 'traditional' was gradually replaced by many traditional features of universities, as shown here by the ceremonial use of Latin when becoming a full university.

Identity, Legitimacy, and the Cultural-Cognitive Pillar: The Role of Institutionalization

As HEIs grow and develop, their organizational identities become increasingly diverse, complex and hybrid in nature, reflecting not only internal dynamics but also, as this case has shed light on, external pressures within the organizational field and changing policy agendas over time. This hybridity, in turn, creates challenges both for the central administration and for the different units, as the academic heartland pulls and pushes in different directions challenging the strategic orientation set out by those at the top of the hierarchy, including leadership efforts to use identity as a strategic asset (Fumasoli et al., 2015). For the case HEI in this study, launching identity projects embedded in long-term visions and strategies has functioned as an important institutionalization process (Cooper et al., 2008), recognizing the past and present while finding out about the future for education, research and other academic tasks regionally, nationally and globally.

Identity and Resilience

As hypothesized at the onset, it turns out that as far as the case university is concerned, identity and resilience are rather dynamic attributes, taking into account critical shifts and legitimacy claims emanating from the environment, as postulated by institutional theorists (Greenwood et al., 2011). From the point of view of the notion of 'remaining within a threshold', the empirical case demonstrates that in spite of the adoption of new structural features and outlooks associated with dominant (hegemonic) archetypes in the field, domestic and internationally, the case university was, nonetheless, able to establish meaningful links with its past and cherished traditions. The result was increasing hybridity as a strategic means of bridging the multiple, and sometimes contradictory demands from the environment, with its enduring character or past identity. This dynamic process suggests that, as indicated in the existing literature (Pirotti & Venzin, 2016, Pinheiro & Young, 2017 see also Chapter 7 in this volume), resilient organizations operating in dynamic environments are capable of adapting to new environmental demands while ensuring that their core essence remains relatively stable over time. Contrary to earlier accounts suggesting that vulnerable organizations, characterized by weak legitimacy claims and restricted room for manoeuvre, are more constrained in their adaptive responses to environmental shifts (Clark, 1956) and/or subject to co-optation by external actors (Selznick, 1957), our empirical case suggests that less central organizations are also capable of mobilizing resources to ensure that environmental (legitimacy) demands are met without jeopardizing enduring features seemed to be central to their modus operandi, such as key identity-related attributes. In this way, resilient organizations, universities included, are characterized by the co-existence of enduring ('old') and emerging ('new') attributes, being able to bridge past trajectories with future aspirations.

Conclusion

In this chapter, we have discussed how an organizational identity can evolve in a resilient way over time in hostile environments where external legitimacy plays a key role. The aim has mainly been conceptual, with the ambition to combine theories and concepts to be further empirically tested in future studies. However, as a first test of our approach, we have in this chapter employed the Scandinavian HE sector as our empirical case. Our analysis, based on primary and secondary sources shows how the organizational identity at a Swedish university over a period spanning 40 years has evolved, becoming more complex and hybrid (Kodeih & Greenwood, 2014).

However, the uniqueness of our study is rooted in the fact that this development has taken place in environments that have been quite conflicting and even at times hostile. As such, our approach to resilience is somewhat different: while many studies of resilience focus on how organizations resist change, our case has illustrated resilience *towards* change, aligned with what the editors of this volume term as pertaining to 'adaptive resilience' (see chapter 1). We have shown—in line with Foreman and Whetten's (2012) arguments—that external legitimacy provides the boundaries for how identity and resilience can play out over time, but we have extended this idea by demonstrating how different forms of legitimacy can be used deliberately as tools to construct new identities also in situations where conflicting and hostile environments exist. We have identified three critical junctures in the recent history of the HEI that have enabled this outcome. These include necessary policy change at the state level (regulative pillar), changing dynamics in the organizational field (normative pillar) and institutionalization processes within the universities (cultural-cognitive pillar). Albeit recognizing the past and the institutional legacy, reflected in a layered, hybrid identity, the HEI is primarily forward looking rather than building on tradition. Furthermore, well-anchored visions and strategies have been important identity formation tools (Ramirez & Christensen, 2013). Conflicting and hostile environments have been tackled by emphasizing that the identity is 'special', 'novel', 'innovative' and even 'underdog' in the organizational field (cf. Huisman et al., 2002). In other words, our study rejects the idea of legitimacy as fundamentally dichotomous (either you have it, or not) (Deephouse & Suchman, 2008, p. 60), although our findings are very supportive of the notion of legitimacy as something fundamentally political (Deephouse & Suchman, 2008, p. 61). We would argue that it is exactly the latter characteristics that enable the quest for a distinct organizational character and identity—allowing for resilience to develop. As such, by establishing a clear empirical link between identity and adaptation or degrees of change, the chapter provides critical insights to scholars interested in unpacking the complex dynamics underpinning the emergence and evolution of resilient organizations operating in highly dynamic and complex organizational fields.

References

Albert, S., & Whetten, D. A. (1985). Organizational identity. In L. L. Cummings & B. M. Staw (Eds.), *Research in organizational behavior* (Vol. 14, pp. 263–295). JAI.

Alvesson, M., & Robertson, M. (2016). Organizational identity—a critique. In M. G. Pratt, M. Schultz, B. E. Ashforth, & D. Ravasi (Eds.), *The Oxford handbook of organizational identity* (pp. 160–180). Oxford University Press.

Andrén, C. G. (2013). *Visioner, vägval och verkligheter: Svenska universitetens utveckling efter 1940*. Nordic Academic Press.

Ashforth, B. E., Rogers, K. M., & Corley, K. G. (2011). Identity in organizations: Exploring cross-level dynamics. *Organization Science, 22*(5), 1144–1156.

Battilana, J., & Lee, M. (2014). Advancing research on hybrid organizing–insights from the study of social enterprises. *Academy of Management Annals, 8*(1), 397–441.

Benneworth P. (2019). The modernisation agenda and university irresponsibility repertoires. In M. Sørensen, L. Geschwind, J. Kekäle & R. Pinheiro (Eds.), *The Responsible University. Exploring the Nordic Context and Beyond* (pp. 61–86). Palgrave Macmillan.

Bhamra, R. (2015). *Organisational resilience: Concepts, integration, and practice*. CRC Press.

Bitektine, A., & Haack, P. (2015). The 'Macro' and the 'Micro' of legitimacy: Toward a multilevel theory of the legitimacy process. *Academy of Management Review, 40*(1), 49–75.

Boers, B., & Nordqvist, M. (2012). Understanding hybrid-identity organizations: the case of publicly listed family businesses. In A. Carsrud & M. Brännback (Eds.), *Understanding Family Businesses* (Vol. 15, pp. 251–269). International Studies in Entrepreneurship. Springer.

Brewer, M. B. (1991). The social self: On being the same and different at the same time. *Personality and Social Psychology Bulletin, 17*(5), 475–482.

Capoccia, G., & Kelemen, R. D. (2007). The study of critical junctures: Theory, narrative, and counterfactuals in historical institutionalism. *World Politics, 59*(03), 341–369.

Christensen, T., Gornitzka, Å., & Ramirez, F. O. (Eds.). (2019). *Universities as agencies: Reputation and professionalization*. Springer.

Clark, B. R. (1956). Organizational adaptation and precarious values: A case study. *American Sociological Review, 21*(3), 327–336.

Clark, B. R. (1992). *The distinctive college*. Transaction Publishers.

Clark, B. R. (2004). *Sustaining change in universites: Continuities in case studies and concepts*. Society for Research into Higher Education & Open University Press.

Cooper, D., Ezzamel, M., & Willlmott, H. (2008). Examining "institutionalization": A critical theoretic perspective. In R. Greenwood, C. Oliver, K. Sahlin, & R. Suddaby (Eds.), *The Sage handbook of organizational institutionalism* (pp. 673–701). Sage.

Corley, K. G., Harquail, C. V., Pratt, M. G., Glynn, M. A., Fiol, C. M., & Hatch, M. J. (2006). Guiding organizational identity through aged adolescence. *Journal of Management Inquiry, 15*(2), 85–99.

Czarniawska, B. (1997). *Narrating the organization: Dramas of institutional identity*. University of Chicago Press.

de Boer, H., & Stensaker, B. (2007). An internal representative system: The democratic vision. In P. Maassen & J. P. Olsen (Eds.), *University Dynamics and European Integration* (pp. 99–118). Springer Netherlands.

Deephouse, D., & Suchman, M. (2008). Legitimacy in Organizational Institutionalism. In R. Greenwood, C. Oliver, K. Sahlin, & R. Suddaby (Eds.), *The SAGE handbook of organizational institutionalism* (pp. 49–77). Sage.

Dill, D. D. (1982). The management of academic culture: Notes on the management of meaning and social integration. *Higher Education, 11*(3), 303–320.

DiMaggio, P. J., & Powell, W. W. (1983). The iron cage revisited: Institutional isomorphism and collective rationality in organizational fields. *American Sociological Review, 48*(2), 147–160.

Drori, I., & Honig, B. (2013). A process model of internal and external legitimacy. *Organization Studies, 34*(3), 345–376.

Elsbach, K. D. (2013). In M. Schultz, S. Maguire, A. Langley & H. Tsoukas (Eds.), Constructing Identity in and around Organizations. *Administrative Science Quarterly, 59*(3), NP1–NP3.

Elsbach, K. D., & Kramer, R. M. (1996). Members' responses to organizational identity threats: Encountering and countering the business week rankings. *Administrative Science Quarterly*, 442–476.

Foreman, P., & Whetten, D. A. (2012, September). *The identity paradox and an expanded framework of organizational identity*, 6–7. Presented at Proceedings of the New Frontiers in Management and Organizational Cognition Conference. National University of Ireland Maynooth.

Foreman, P. O., & Whetten, D. A. (2014). *Operationalizing and measuring organizational identity: A comprehensive review of past research.* Presented at Academy of Management Proceedings.

Fumasoli, T., Pinheiro, R., & Stensaker, B. (2015). Handling uncertainty of strategic ambitions: The use of organizational identity as a risk-reducing device. *International Journal of Public Administration, 38*(13–14), 1030–1040.

Geschwind, L., Melin, G., & Wedlin, L. (2016). Mergers as opportunities for branding: The Making of the Linnaeus University. In R. Pinheiro, L. Geschwind, & T. Aarrevaara (Eds.), *Mergers in higher education—The experience from Northern Europe* (pp. 129–143). Springer.

Geschwind, L., & Pinheiro, R. M. (2017). Raising the summit or flattening the agora? The elitist turn in science policy in Northern Europe. *Journal of Baltic Studies, 48*(4), 513–528.

Gidlund, J.-E. (2009). Utvecklingen av Örebro universitet. In T. Nybom & T Strömberg (Eds.), *Örebro universitet inför sitt andra decennium: en tänkebok om universitetets gårdag, nutid och morgondag*. Örebro universitet.

Gioia, D. A., & Chittipeddi, K. (1991). Sensemaking and sensegiving in strategic change initiation. *Strategic Management Journal, 12*(6), 433–448.

Gioia, D. A., Patvardhan, S. D., Hamilton, A. L., & Corley, K. G. (2013). Organizational identity formation and change. *The Academy of Management Annals, 7*(1), 123–193.

Gioia, D. A., Price, K. N., Hamilton, A. L., & Thomas, J. B. (2010). Forging an identity: An insider-outsider study of processes involved in the formation of organizational identity. *Administrative Science Quarterly, 55*(1), 1–46.

Gioia, D. A., Schultz, M., & Corley, K. G. (2000). Organizational identity, image, and adaptive instability. *Academy of Management Review, 25*(1), 63–81.

Gioia, D. A., & Thomas, J. B. (1996). Identity, image, and issue interpretation: Sensemaking during strategic change in academia. *Administrative Science Quarterly, 41*(3), 370–403.

Glynn, M. A. (2008). Beyond constraint: How institutions enable identities. In R. Greenwood, C. Oliver, K. Sahlin, & R. Suddaby (Eds.), *The Sage handbook of organizational institutionalism* (pp. 413–430). Sage.

Gornitzka, Å., & Maassen, P. (2007). An instrument for national political agendas: The hierarchical vision. In P. Maassen & J. P. Olsen (Eds.), *University dynamics and european integration* (pp. 81–98). Springer.

Greenwood, R., & Hinings, C. (1993). Understanding strategic change: The contribution of archetypes. *Academy of Management Journal, 36*(5), 1052–1081.

Greenwood, R., Raynard, M., Kodeih, F., Micelotta, E. R., & Lounsbury, M. (2011). Institutional complexity and organizational responses. *The Academy of Management Annals, 5*(1), 317–371.

Hansen, H. F., Aarrevaara, T., Geschwind, L., & Stensaker, B. (2019). Evaluation practices and impact: Overload? In R. Pinheiro, L. Geschwind, H. F. Hansen, & K. Pulkkinen (Eds.), *Reforms, organizational change and performance in higher education* (pp. 235–266). Palgrave Macmillan.

Huisman, J., Norgård, J. D., Rasmussen, J., & Stensaker, B. (2002). Alternative universities revisited: A study of the distinctiveness of universities established in the spirit of 1968. *Tertiary Education and Management, 8*(4), 316–332.

Karlsen, J. E., & Pritchard, R. (2013). *Resilient universities: Confronting changes in a challenging world*. Peter Lang.

Kodeih, F., & Greenwood, R. (2014). Responding to institutional complexity: The role of identity. *Organization Studies, 35*(1), 7–39.

Kraatz, M., & Zajak, E. J. (1996). Exploring the limits of New Institutionalism: The causes and the consequences of illegitimate organizational change. *American Sociological Review, 61*(5), 812–836.

Kyvik, S. (2009). *The dynamics of change in higher education: Expansion and contraction in an organisational field*. Springer.

Larsson, U. (2009). All den början bliver svår. In T. Nybom & T. Strömberg (Eds.), *Örebro universitet inför sitt andra decennium: en tänkebok om universitetets gårdag, nutid och morgondag*. Örebro universitet.

Lind, I. (2004). *Resan från högskola till universitet speglad i ett urval artiklar och tal 1990–1999*. Örebro universitetsbibliotek.

Lind, I. (2009). Resan hem. In T. Nybom & T. Strömberg (Eds.), *Örebro universitet inför sitt andra decennium: en tänkebok om universitetets gårdag, nutid och morgondag*. Örebro universitet.

Maassen, P., & Olsen, J. P. (Eds.). (2007). *University dynamics and European integration (Vol. 4)*. Dordrecht: Springer.

Maassen, P., & Stensaker, B. (2003). Interpretations of self-regulation: the changing state-higher education relationship in Europe. In R. Begg (Ed.), *The Dialogue between Higher Education Research and Practice* (pp. 85–95). Springer Netherlands.

Maassen, P., & Stensaker, B. (2011). The knowledge triangle, European higher education policy logics and policy implications. *Higher Education, 61*(6), 757–769.

Marginson, S., & Rhoades, G. (2002). Beyond national states, markets, and systems of higher education: A glonacal agency heuristic. *Higher Education, 43*(3), 281–309.

Meek, V. L., Goedegebuure, L., Kivinen, O., & Rinne, R. (1996). *The mockers and mocked: Comparative perspectives on differentiation, convergence and diversity in higher education*. London: Pergamon.

Parent, M. M., & Foreman, P. O. (2007). Organizational image and identity management in large-scale sporting events. *Journal of Sport Management, 21*(1), 15–40.

Pfeffer, J., & Salancik, G. R. (1978). *The external control of organizations: A resource dependence perspective*. Stanford University Press.

Phillips, N., Tracey, P., & Kraatz, M. (2016). Organizational identity and institutional theory: Taking stock and moving forward. In M. G. Pratt, M. Schultz, B. E. Ashforth, & D. Ravasi (Eds.), *The Oxford handbook of organizational identity* (pp. 353–349). Oxford University Press.

Pinheiro, R., Benneworth, P., & Jones, G. A. (2012). *Universities and regional development: A critical assessment of tensions and contradictions*. Routledge.

Pinheiro, R., Geschwind, L., & Aarrevaara, T. (2014). Nested tensions and interwoven dilemmas in higher education: The view from the Nordic countries. *Cambridge Journal of Regions, Economy and Society, 7*(2), 233–250.

Pinheiro, R., Geschwind, L., & Aarrevaara, T. (Eds.). (2016a). *Mergers in higher education: The experiences from Northern Europe*. Springer.

Pinheiro, R., Geschwind, L., Ramirez, F., & Vrangbæk, K. (Eds.). (2016b). *Towards a comparative institutionalism: Forms, dynamics and logics across the organizational fields of health care and higher education*. Research in the Sociology of Organizations, Vol. 45. Emerald.

Pinheiro, R., & Stensaker, B. (2014). Designing the entrepreneurial university: The interpretation of a global idea. *Public Organization Review, 14*(4), 497–516.

Pinheiro, R., & Young, M. (2017). The university as an adaptive resilient organization: A complex systems perspective. In J. Huisman & M. Tight (Eds.), *Theory and method in higher education research* (pp. 119–136). Emerald.

Pirotti, G. B., & Venzin, M. (2016). *Resilient organizations: Responsible leadership in times of uncertainty*. Cambridge University Press.

Pratt, M. G., & Kraatz, M. S. (2009). E pluribus unum: Multiple identities and the organizational self. In L. M. Roberts & J. E. Dutton (Eds.), *Exploring positive identities and organizations* (pp. 409–434). Routledge.

Ramirez, F. O., & Christensen, T. (2013). The formalization of the university: Rules, roots, and routes. *Higher Education, 65*(6), 695–708.

Raynard, M., & Greenwood, R. (2014). Deconstructing complexity: How organizations cope with multiple institutional logics. *Academy of Management Proceedings, 2014*(1), 12907.

Ruth, M., & Goessling-Reisemann, S. (Eds.). (2019). *Handbook on resilience of socio-technical systems*. Edward Elgar Publishing.

Salerno, C. (2007). A service enterprise: The market vision. In P. Maassen & J. P. Olsen (Eds.), *University dynamics and European integration* (pp. 119–132). Springer.

Scott, W. R. (2014). *Institutions and organizations: Ideas, interests, and identities*. SAGE Publications.

Selznick, P. (1957). *Leadership in administration a sociological interpretation*. Harper and Row.

Sjölund, M. (2002). Politics versus evaluation: The establishment of three new universities in Sweden. *Quality in Higher Education, 8*(2), 173–181.

Stensaker, B. (2004). The transformation of organisational identities. *Interpretations of policies concerning the quality of teaching and learning in Norwegian higher education*. University of Twente.

Stensaker, B. (2015). Organizational identity as a concept for understanding university dynamics. *Higher Education, 69*(1), 103–115.

Stensaker, B., Persson, M., & Pinheiro, R. (2016). When mergers fail: A case study on the critical role of external stakeholders in merger initiatives. *European Journal of Higher Education, 16*, 56–70.

Stinchcombe, A. L. (1965). Social structure and organizations. In J. G. March (Ed.), *Handbook of organizations* (pp. 142–193). Rand McNally.

Suchman, M. C. (1995). Managing legitimacy: Strategic and institutional approaches. *Academy of Management Review, 20*(3), 571–610.

Tapper, T., & Palfreyman, D. (2011). *Oxford, the collegiate university: Conflict, consensus and continuity*. Springer.

THE. (2020). Times higher education world university rankings. https://www.timeshighereducation.com/world-university-rankings.

Thornton, P. H., Ocasio, W., & Lounsbury, M. (2012). *The institutional logics perspective: A new approach to culture, structure, and process*. Oxford University Press.

Walker, B., & Salt, D. (2006). *Resilience thinking: Sustaining ecosystems and people in a changing world*. Island press.

Washington, M., & Ventresca, M. J. (2004). How organizations change: The role of institutional support mechanisms in the incorporation of higher education visibility strategies, 1874–1995. *Organization Science, 15*(1), 82–97.

Weerts, D., Freed, G., & Morphew, C. (2014). Organizational identity in higher education: Conceptual and empirical perspectives. In M. B. Paulsen (Ed.), *Higher education: Handbook of theory and research* (pp. 229–278). Springer.

CHAPTER 9

Resilience and Change in Opera Theatres: Travelling the Edge of Tradition and Contemporaneity

Maria Laura Frigotto and Francesca Frigotto

Introduction

Resilience has recently become of great interest in various areas of social science (Fisher et al., 2018; Linnenluecke, 2017; Williams et al., 2017). Resilience refers to the ability of an individual, an organization or a system to bounce back, respond and recover when facing disturbances (Linnenluecke, 2017). According to Bartezzaghi (2013), the popularity of resilience across academic disciplines and domains of life relates to the historical moment we are facing that is characterized by the perception of a general crisis, such as psychological resilience against increasing stress,

M. L. Frigotto (✉)
Department of Economics and Management, University of Trento, Trento, Italy
e-mail: marialaura.frigotto@unitn.it

F. Frigotto
Harp Department, Conservatory of Music G.B. Martini, Bologna, Italy
e-mail: francesca.frigotto@consbo.it

R. Pinheiro et al. (eds.), *Towards Resilient Organizations and Societies*, Public Sector Organizations,
https://doi.org/10.1007/978-3-030-82072-5_9

business resilience against the financial crisis, social resilience against waves of migration.

Given the ambiguity and ignorance of the state of the environment in many realms (Frigotto & Rossi, 2015), the hook offered by the concept of resilience is that it moves the focus from the ability to interpret the environment to the ability to resist it, ideally, independent of the source, form and manifestation of the disturbances. Resilience also reflects a trust in human abilities that is typical of contemporary, narcissistic society (Sennett, 1998). At the individual and organizational level of analysis, resilience lies in the so-called 'agency' of actors (Ruef & Aldrich, 2006). Nevertheless, at the system level of analysis (e.g. regional systems, industries, societies, etc.), the issue of 'the agency of resilience' (i.e. who has the ability to be resilience and how much effect and intention does that actor have on the outcome) is not easily addressed (Frigotto, 2018). Thus, this chapter performs a system-level analysis of resilience to add to the debate on the agency of resilience.

The other open issue in the resilience literature concerns the role of stability and change. Resilience both enhances and emphasizes the ability of systems to resist adversities: in other words, to survive. This skill has been represented by the stability of a system's outcome (Fisher et al., 2018) or, in some cases, with the achievement of a higher level of outcome that reflects 'the ability to thrive'. However, little attention has been given to the actual change that systems experience in order to achieve stability or an increased outcome level. Resilience is related to stability as much as it is related to the change (Frigotto et al., 2022, in Chapter 1, this volume). A closer look at the relationship between stability and change provides theoretical elaboration on the resilience concept that several scholars call for (Britt et al., 2016; Duchek, 2019; Fisher et al., 2018; Kossek & Perrigino, 2016; Linnenluecke, 2017; Vanhove et al., 2016). It also raises an important question: to what extent can an entity change in order to be considered a persisting entity and not a different entity? This is called the 'continuity of essence' in Chapter 1 and relates to the philosophical debate on essence and change originally referred to by the Greek Heraclitus (535–475 B.C.) who claimed that stability is an apparent and artificial state: given that everything is becoming, change is the only natural state.

The analysis in this chapter considers the opera as an organizational archetype (Greenwood & Hinings, 1993, p. 1052), defined as the holistic system of meaning (ideas, values and beliefs) that build an interpretive scheme and the organizations that adopt and embody it. Thus, an organization archetype includes i) a system of meaning,[1] ii) organisational structures (Opera Theatres or Houses (OHs)[2]) and iii) artistic and working systems and practices that mirror professions and their practical knowledge (Muzio et al., 2013). We depict the evolution of the system in regard to the three dimensions mentioned above from origin to now and explore their interconnections in line with studies on the emergence, change and evolution of organizations provided by Padgett and Powell (2012) and those on organizational archetypes (Cooper et al., 1996; Greenwood & Hinings, 1996).

This longitudinal perspective across centuries in the birth country of opera, Italy, provides the ideal empirical environment to study resilience at the system level over time. This perspective shows the connection between the agency of individuals and institutions to shed light on lower-level action and its nestedness into higher levels (and vice versa) for the production of the general outcome. This is relevant given that resilience can appear different according to the time, space and social scale considered (Carpenter et al., 2001; Walker et al., 2004; see also Frigotto et al., 2022, in Chapter 1, this volume), and it is necessary to assume a holistic perspective across levels to account for resilience as a whole. This case also allows discussion on how resilience looks over a long time span. The longitudinal view allows consideration of how much continuity is necessary to recognize resilience in the same entity. This issue links to the 'continuity of essence' as a core principle of resilience identified in Chapter 1 of this volume. The chapter is organized as follows: The next section briefly describes the debate growing in the literature around the concept of resilience and introduces the distinction between three different resilience types: absorptive, adaptive and transformative. Section three gives an overview of the literature on institutional change and organizational archetypes, providing categories and concepts that inform the understanding of the continuity of essence in resilience. Section four pertains to the research design. Section five illustrates the evolution of the opera in Italy as an organizational archetype with structure and artistic

[1] In this sense we will also refer to the opera as a genre of classical music consisting of a dramatic work in one or more acts set to music for singers and instrumentalists.

[2] The organizations that set on stage and promote operas that typically have their headquarters in theatres designed for the performance of opera.

professions. The last section discusses this evolution in terms of resilience outcomes.

Resilience: Between Absorption, Adaptation and Transformation

Resilience can be divided into three types that imply different changing dynamics and that vary across stability and change: absorptive resilience, adaptive resilience and transformative resilience (Frigotto, 2020; Frigotto et al., 2022, in Chapter 1, this volume).

Absorptive resilience is a form of stability of the system where change is controlled by limiting it. Here, the resilient outcome is such that change has nearly zero impact on the system (Linnenluecke, 2017). Absorptive resilience is measured in terms of return time and efficiency, where the possibility to return to the initial state is taken for granted. In this perspective, disturbances are temporary and involve 'a rather narrow range of predictable external conditions' (Holling, 1973, p. 1).

Adaptive resilience responds to unanticipated triggers that can be understood using the available knowledge. The resilience outcome reflects the achievement of a new, typically higher, performance level.

Transformative resilience responds to triggers that challenge 'sharp shifts', 'regime shifts' or 'critical transitions' and concern a variety of adversities that are typically unpredictable, unexpected or novel (Folke et al., 2010; Frigotto, 2018). Thus, resilience is measured by the effective 'persistence or probability of extinction' (Holling, 1973, p. 17) rather than the return to the former equilibrium. Transformative resilience requires a deep change of the present state while a continuity of essence is still recognizable. Despite being uncertain, it is typically associated with a higher level of performance, although it has also been linked to lower levels of performance and to high-risk survival.

As Carpenter et al. (2001) contend, resilience depends on the temporal, spatial and social scale of the observation. The latter is further divided into micro, meso and macro levels concerning, respectively, individual actors, organizations and systems. They also stress that these levels do not imply consistency with one another, and, if considered one-by-one, they might render a contrasting picture of resilience at some levels. An analysis of resilience concerning these levels can only assume a holistic approach that accounts for the nestedness of smaller elements into larger ones and for the complexity of the micro–macro interaction (Walker et al., 2004).

Archetype Change

Organizations belonging to an archetype are subject to the same environmental demands, i.e. 'distinctive prescriptions [...] (Greenwood & Hinings, 1996) – of the way that collective purposes should be defined and of how those collective purposes should be organized and accomplished' (Greenwood et al., 2014, p. 1214). Powell and DiMaggio (1991) outlined three pressures that induce organizations towards change: coercive (often conveyed through laws, regulations and accreditation processes), normative (grounded in the pressure to adopt shared and accepted values, standards and techniques) and mimetic (related to the need to imitate role models). These pressures refer to disturbances or adversities emerging at the level of laws, norms and behaviours, respectively. In the literature on resilience, disturbances are the triggers that require the social entity to change and show resilience (Linnenluecke, 2017).

The institutional literature has widely addressed how change occurs in institutions when pressures operate and, conversely, how change does not occur despite them. Through decoupling (Meyer & Rowan, 1977), organizations separate the source of their legitimacy from the source of their survival, showing conformity in their windows that is not in their operations (Boxenbaum & Johnsson, 2008, p. 80). Oliver (1991) elaborated on strategies of resistance that organizations put in place to respond to institutional processes of change, and that range from passive conformity to proactive manipulation. While the initial debate was framed in terms of transformational and incremental change (e.g. Powell & DiMaggio, 1991; Oliver, 1991), according to Cooper et al. (1996), later, more attention was given to the variety of possibilities, between total change and total stability or inertia, by accounting for intermediate modes of change as well as for their 'evolutionary or revolutionary pacing' (Greenwood & Hinings, 1996, p. 1023).

Cooper et al. (1996) use 'archetype transformation' and 'sedimentation' to track how organizations change from one archetype to another. Transformation refers to the case 'in which one archetype sweeps away the residues of the other' (Cooper et al., 1996, p. 625) as a reaction to dramatic change; sedimentation is when the new archetype is piled on the old one, and both are competing. While the first case stresses complete change, the second stresses persistence that occurs 'even when the formal structures and processes seem to change, and even when there may be incoherence' (Cooper et al., 1996, p. 624). In some sense, sedimentation describes change through the 'extension' of the archetype (Cooper et al., 1996, p. 644), meaning that change is important, but also 'unresolved' and not stabilized into a new state (Cooper et al., 1996, p. 625).

This discourse found new interest with institutional logics identifying patterns of material practices, assumptions, values, beliefs and rules that organizations take as reference for their action and cognition (e.g. the market logic or the religion logic) (Thornton & Ocasio, 1999, p. 804; Thornton, 2004). Building on the latter, scholars considered how organizations change by adhering to more than one logic, making 'hybrid organizations' (e.g. Pache & Santos, 2010) or by combining logics into 'hybridised logics' (Greenwood et al., 2014, p. 1217). McNulty and Ferlie (2002, p. 362) showed that even when conflicting logics trigger change, when they are too different, change does not reach completion: 'there were some pockets of change, but no organizational transformation'.

Intending to define change across the individual, organizational and system levels through networks, Padgett and Powell (2012) identified several mechanisms by which new organizational archetypes emerge as a result of 'genuine novelty' (p. 1) that, as a new ingredient at the beginning of the process, ignite new archetypes as new sprouts, as a result of adoption and diffusion or as a result of renovation. They stress the role of individual agents that, intentionally or otherwise, assume positions in networks that were previously non-connected or that benefit from their multiple roles, producing a convergence with the literature on institutional entrepreneurs (Hardy & Maguire, 2008) and the role of agency in change. Groups of individuals with their own professional institutions also play a role in spreading change (Muzio et al., 2013).

This literature provides the language and concepts describing how change occurs and needed to discuss if that change displays resilience and of what kind.

Research Design

This paper builds on a case study analysis used for exploratory purposes (Yin, 2009) for further development of the theory on resilience in relation to change (Siggelkow, 2007).

The case selected is the change in the opera since its foundation. Our study is longitudinal and depicts the evolution of opera as a cultural archetype, as an organizational form and as the professions of music workers, over time. For the historical evolution of opera as a cultural archetype, we relied on specialized literature in musicology. In terms of organizational form, our data include economic and financial reports, legislative debate, and the laws that were passed, as well as specific managerial literature and media reports discussing the changes in OHs. For information on artistic professions in the opera and the opera as an employer, the collection of the 30 years' experience by one of the authors, interviews with experts in the field and the contracts of musicians in opera houses over the last 50 years serve as a rich source of data. The latter reflects the need for more grounded approaches to organizational understanding (Reason & Bradbury, 2008).

The evolution of the opera provides a good case for studying resilience at the system level because OHs' survival has been challenged several times. By the middle of the nineteenth century, there were about 200 OHs in Italy, and today there are 13 OHs that belong to Lyric-Symphonic Foundations (LSFs) with national recognition and continuous in-house production and 29 that have local relevance as Theatres of Tradition (ToT) with very few of their own productions, mainly acting as seasonal outlets or peripheral halls for LSFs. Over the 400 years during which this drop took place, several initiatives have failed that had been previously successful. Society has changed greatly in political, economic and cultural terms, and the opera has become less interesting and less relevant to the resulting society. Since their legislative recognition, the 29 ToT have often lacked the resources for activity, while the 13 LSFs granted 'some' national funding have all gone through default procedures several times. In 2020 (time of writing), 9 of the 13 LSFs are operating under remediation procedures following an assessed default situation, paired with burning debates on the opportunity and necessity of public interventions to save them. Some of the 13 LSFs were forced to close temporarily, and their workforce were laid off and redirected to other professions. Eventually, the government, encouraged by public opinion, chose to intervene, saving some of the Italian OHs.

This chapter does not concern itself with resilience displayed by one or by a set of OHs, like when resilience is analysed in companies that have survived several crises over the years (such as Nokia; Duchek, 2018). In those cases, the level of analysis is the organization; in this chapter, it is the system, or 'organisational field' from an institutionalist perspective (Powell & DiMaggio, 1991). On this matter, an analysis focusing on one organization would be limited. In fact, both legitimacy and the funding necessary to survival comes from outside the ability of an OH to produce income. While each OH is funded dependent on its choice of titles and marketing, and each OH will have a higher or lower level of box-office success, these elements of competition are too limited to lead to an actual differentiation or to a survival, à la Schumpeter (1934), that implies the death of some and the continuity of others because of their decisions and actions. For these reasons, we also do not draw attention to the many OHs that closed along the way. The question remains whether the system has changed too much to display a continuity over resilience, or, in other terms, whether it has denatured its essence such that today it has nothing to do with the Italian tradition of opera.

In terms of archetype, the opera provides a good case for studying resilience. An archetype within the neo-institutional literature is 'a set of structures and systems that reflects a single interpretive scheme and mirrors a holistic perspective that reconciles 'narrowly drawn organizational properties' under overall patterns towards which all organizations tend to converge (Greenwood & Hinings, 1993, p. 1052). Following Cooper et al. (1996, p. 625), the opera allows the study of archetypes that are 'institutionally specific'. We stress the cultural grounds of the archetype by drawing attention to the fact that the opera is a system derived from a cultural type of communication and expression that is also a form of art or entertainment, with stylistic, aesthetic, rhetorical and communicative rules. The communicative rules are also codified and studied within musicology, and their change over time contributes to the analysis of the resilience of the system.

The Opera as an Archetype

Operatic Essence and Meaning

The opera has survived 400 years, enduring transformations of society, taste, mores, government systems, laws and economies. In this first subsection, we address the evolution of systems of meanings that contribute to organizational archetypes in the periods of emergence and diffusion, of struggling, and of renovation and renewal.

Sprouting and Spreading

The opera was born in royal theatres as a combination of words and music called *recitar cantando* in the form of the *serious melodrama* and on minor stages in the form of comic operas and burlesque. The first public theatre was opened in Venice in 1637 for the merchant bourgeoisie, and the business model spread across the Italian peninsula. These theatres mainly performed operas during carnival time and for about one month within a series of festivals (Della Seta, 1993). Towards the end of the eighteenth century, there were about 100 theatres, which expanded to 200 by the mid-nineteenth century; basically, each city had one or more theatres that represented, even through the buildings' architecture, the social relevance of the *melodrama*.

The opera became the expression of the romantic period in Italy. During the Independence Wars (1848–1866), it was used to communicate and spread nationalist sentiment against the foreign sovereigns ruling the Italian territory. In particular, composer Giuseppe Verdi wrote operas such as 'The Battle of Legnano' and 'Nabucco' that represented a similar struggle and fighting attitude. As it was forbidden to propagandize nationalist thoughts, nationalists used the opera like a secret code to communicate: singing 'Va pensiero' from Nabucco became like hailing insurrection, and writing 'VIVA VERDI' on the walls of the streets was often changed into 'VIVA V.E.R.D.I', meaning long life to the king of Piedmont that should be King of Italy (Vittorio Emanuele Re D'Italia).

Towards the end of the nineteenth century, opera composers found inspiration in the novels of their contemporaries that described everyday life in the countryside (e.g. the Novels by Giovanni Verga and the Rustical Chivalry by Pietro Mascagni), real facts that occurred in the chronicles in Italy (e.g. Pagliacci by Ruggiero Leoncavallo) or fascinating new texts that were appearing in other countries, such as the discovery of West America or the colonialist relationship between the USA and Japan that were turned into operas by Puccini (respectively, The Girl of the Golden West and Madame Butterfly).

Operas were popular performances as they were able to speak to different levels of society, namely the new aristocrats, the bourgeois and the masses, meeting their tastes and expectations. OHs were initially funded by aristocrats and royals, then impresarios turned them into a business, renting theatres from the municipality, commissioning new operas and organising production. Such business was rarely profitable; many went bankrupt. Often the economic success of theatres was due to bundling strategies, for example, with gambling (Ernani & Iovino, 1993).

Struggling

The opera started having trouble when it stopped being a popular expression of culture and entertainment. Two elements grounded the debate then and still ground it today: the need for financial support beyond the box-office flow and the societal value of operas. This might be independent or might progressively rely less and less on the choice of opera as entertainment.

In 1867, the Italian Parliament cancelled all support to the opera theatres and transferred the responsibility of any intervention from the state to the municipality level because of the lack of resources (Balestra & Malaguti, 2003, p. 38). The operation of OHs depended on 'the mood of the councilmen' when the issue was discussed in the House (Ruggieri, 2004).

In 1885, the music publisher Ricordi, who had commissioned many operas from famous composers, gave a speech in front of the Milan city council on the critical economic situation of the Theatre La Scala, asking for public support and arguing that the opera, as 'an Italian excellence of glorious tradition', should be publicly funded (Ernani & Iovino, 1993, p. 7). Nevertheless, the OH in Genoa was closed from 1879 to 1883, as was Bologna in 1891 and La Scala in 1897–1898 because of lack of funds. The opera was considered 'a good for an elite', especially if compared to the need to publicly fund the construction of streets, aqueducts, hospitals and schools (Balestra & Malaguti, 2003, p. 39). In Italy, and in Milan in particular, socialist ideas spread, such as those concerning the social role of the theatre, the public utility of the arts and the public support of opera. In 1901, a referendum took place asking whether the municipality should support the costs of the La Scala. The turnout was low among the very few voters of the time, and the result was 'no' (Barigazzi, 2014).

In terms of cultural production systems, according to musicologists, starting from the mid-1800s, OHs began evolving from 'laboratories of novelty' to museums of 'magnificent performances' of previously released operas (Rosselli, 1985). In the early days of opera, novel productions were funded by the wealthy nobles or bourgeois first, and then by the *mecenate*; in the last century, new operas were rare, and the opera transformed into great and magnificent reproductions, or sometimes reinterpretations, of operas, where the excellence of the performance comes from the quality of the artists and producers involved.

The framework on performance defined by Toscanini at La Scala (1920s) represents a milestone in the operatic management system and represented a model for other theatres at that time. The performance was becoming an 'event', not because of a novel opera, but because great interpreters were involved. Toscanini brought this concept to completion by adding the perfection of performance. La Scala became the apotheosis of a repertoire system where preparation was well-structured and performers were linked to the theatre, so that the previous year's productions could be reassembled with very few rehearsals. For example, over one week in 1927, the first performances of three repertoire productions and of one new production, on top of rehearsals, were staged with no lapses in the extremely high artistic standards (Sachs, 1987). Toscanini is well-known for his 'new way of working' and his 'tyrannical method' that produced a holistic performance that encompassed the aesthetic and even the moral facets of the opera. Toscanini's method incorporated the trend towards educating the public to 'consider the theatre not as something for amusement, but as something with a moral and aesthetic function that becomes part of the life of a society, part of the life of a culture' (Sachs, 1987, p. 9, quoting the words of conductor and musicologist Gianandrea Gavazzeni).

The opera is no longer the status symbol it was until probably the 1990s when, for instance, the première at La Scala was in the news for several days and fed magazines with in-depth reports on dames' expensive and excessive outfits. Opera also stopped being related to the élites, and, consequently, stopped being interesting to those who wanted to enter their circle. The amateurs also thinned out, given that the new cultural archetypes had become the popular expression in music (e.g. rock, pop, etc.). The public attended OHs less frequently also because new technologies allowed them to reproduce music at home. In general, knowledge of the opera became less widespread, in contrast with the beginning of the twentieth century in which every radio station broadcasted operas and everybody still knew the repertoire and the interprets.

In the last few decades, the musical critique has also changed dramatically. By writing in the newspapers about operas and new productions being performed in OHs, music critics informed non-experts about forthcoming productions providing context, background and the meaning of operas and production choices. For instance, during the direction of the conductor Riccardo Muti at La Scala (1986–2005), very remote operas from the past by composers such as Spontini or Cherubini were newly performed. However, they were under-appreciated by the general public, who were less and less knowledgeable on the opera and had fewer good critics to guide them. This repertoire also brought the public further in feeling the opera as something elitist and ancient that challenged the resistance even of those that had bought an expensive dress to go to the prima (in fact, in several cases, the media reported disheartened people that left the theatre after 3 or even 5 or 6 hours of opera).

Re-novelling

More recently, the opera has tried to reposition itself towards a new target, in particular, young people and tourists. The OH in Florence engages schools in the production of the performances, building a strong link with the local territory, or through joint-production with pop stars. A different way was explored by Fenice in Venice that addresses the tourist market with a repertoire of classics such as Traviata. This performance is repeated many times all over during the year and critics claim this endless repetition has transformed the OH into an 'operatic Disneyland' (The Economist, 2015) and transformed the opera production system (Trevisan, 2015). As a result, all 13 OHs doubled, or even more, the number of performances per year and kept the budget nearly stable.

OHs are also attempting to renew themselves within the reproduction of the tradition. Since operas can also be enjoyed by watching a performance on a screen, some OHs have pushed the renovation of the classics and on the 'feeling of the opera' that can only be appreciated live (as a representation of this feeling, think of the Julia Roberts in the movie 'Pretty woman', that is moved by compassion for Traviata and cries at her first-time performance at the opera). A recent production of Carmen in Florence in 2018, surprised the public with a totally different ending of this traditional opera. In the original libretto, Carmen is killed by her partner when she wants to break up with him but, in this new version,

Carmen kills him for self-defence instead. The intent was to contribute to the modern discussion of violence against women. Though this new ending, the OH revived its previous role as a reflection on hot topics, combining the need to perform traditional, well-known operas and the need to remain relevant for society.

An interesting example of this occurred at the Arena in Verona in 2019. The American soprano, interpreting the Ethiopian princess in Verdi's Aida, refused to put on the theatrical blackface to 'appear Ethiopian', as tradition says, claiming 'I will not have my face made up in black, and it will be the first time in 106 years. It is institutionalized racism' (Manca, 2019). While this is not a debate triggered by the OH, as in the case of Carmen, it shows that the opera is dialoguing with the present times and its debates. Finally, the opera is also picking up new themes in newly written operas. For instance, the new 'Noi due, quattro' by Elisa Fuksas shows the alienation of people that communicate mainly through mediating technologies such as mobiles and social networks and is unable to build real and face to face relationships.

Operatic Organizational Structures

The second building block of the archetype is the organizational structure. On this topic, in 1921, the La Scala Opera House was re-founded as an organization called an Autonomous Entity (AE), a legal personality under public law that owned the theatre (the building) and was in charge of organizing the activity. Resources were guaranteed by public funding, including grants from the city and the central government, as well as private funding, including individual and corporate contributions (Sachs, 1987). The attribution of regular subsidies was related to the recognition of special public interest in the opera as a form of culture and national heritage (Sicca, 1997).

Between 1929 and 1938, 11 other OHs formed AEs and were supported by municipalities and taxes on other forms of entertainment, such as radio and television subscription fees (Trezzini, 1994). In the later years, the situation of OHs became critical several times when what they did were not in public taste and they spent more than the funding covered; the government struggled to finance OHs that were increasingly draining resources and displaying a 'persistent emergency state' (Ruggieri, 2004).

In 1967, the Corona Act reformed the system by recognizing 11 OHs and two concert institutions for a total of 13 (this set was increased in 2003 with the Opera House in Bari). This law changed the performing arts sector from 'ad hoc funding' to the regular subsidies (Sicca, 1997, p. 205) justified by the recognition of the 'relevant general interest' of the State in the OHs as 'they enable the musical, cultural and social education of the national collectivity' (Law 800/67).

In 1985, law #163 introduced a new *ad hoc* fund for the performing arts granted within the Yearly Budget Act of the State; this fund was called the 'Unified Fund for Performing Arts' and was meant to give stability to the performing arts organizations by securing yearly resources (Trezzini, 1994; 2006). However, funds were distributed every year among the various organizations that produced arts; given that the plethora of applicants was variable and the resources available were unstable, the goal of this reform was limited.

A further important element defined through the AE form and the Corona Act concerned the governance of OHs. The mayor of the city in which an OH was located nominated the president of the OH while the superintendent was nominated by the Ministry of Tourism and of the Performing Arts. The superintendent was in charge of the OH activities, supported by the Artistic Director on the matter of artistic programming and performance responsibility. The duality in the leading roles produced ambiguity (Cori, 2004) on i) the distinctive competencies they had to have, as both sat in the board of directors, and were responsible for the artistic productions and other activities of the OH and ii) the responsibility and merit (or blame) that could be claimed for the OH performance. The result was, respectively, that i) both figures were recruited more for their political networks than their competencies and ii) each claimed for himself or attributed responsibility to the other according to the context and the advantage that could be derived with the result that no clear responsibility was identifiable (Sicca, 1997).

In 1996, the Veltroni Act 'Privatization and Managerialization' of AEs was passed after a period in which politicians contended that the state could not afford to keep funding the increasing economic and financial 'urgencies' of OHs given strong budgetary constraints deriving from the 'Maastricht parameters' to join the Euro.

This act ruled the mandatory transformation of AEs into organizations of private law defined as LSFs. This transformation implied two main changes. First, it allowed private funders to benefit from a tax deduction of 30% if they committed to give funds for at least six years. Private funders were also entitled to sit on the Board of Directors with the State, the Region and the Municipality if they contributed with a fund that was no less than 12% of the total funds for at least six years. Second, it introduced an accounting and reporting system akin to that of private organizations that was more oriented to result and performance.

The act took until 2000 to become operational because the Constitutional Court had to rule on its constitutionality, putting OHs in three years of limbo. The Bassanini Act (2001) overcame this impasse by transforming by law the OHs into LSFs and by stating the public nature of OH despite the private legal form.

The objectives of the Veltroni Act were, essentially, not achieved, and OHs faced increasing continuous crises. Between 2005 and 2010, five of the 14 LSFs almost defaulted, and the Ministry took charge through 'special commissioners' (Ferri, 2016). Private contributions never reached the hoped-for percentages, and later amendments to the Act reduced the private participation quota to 5% of state funding for at least 2 years (instead of 3).

Towards the end of 2013, the Bray Act was passed. It was meant to respond to the needs of the many LSFs facing deep financial and economic crises and to the reducing resources and the OHs' inability to manage them. It established a strict minimum performance standard, identified in both the economic and financial structural equilibrium, to be reached within three years and to be met by all OHs in default conditions that wanted to access the 'special fund' that represented the only way to avoid closure. The standard was intended to delineate between survival and closure. The request to benefit from the 'special fund' implied the willingness of the LSF to revise scheduled artistic programmes and implement downsizing and salary reduction if necessary. LSFs that did not meet the standards were at first said to be destined to compulsory administrative winding up and later (Act # 175/2017) to lose the status of LSF and exit its public funding and control system to become Lyric Symphonic Theatres with a lower level of public support. Lay-offs and salary decreases occurred, and later laws moved the deadline from December 2016 to December 2018 (Act # 160/2016) and then to December 2019 (Act # 205/2017) and reduced the requirements, asking for a yearly economic equilibrium and a tangential rather than structural equilibrium of assets and liabilities. The actual implementation of the Bray Act by the established deadlines would have required implementing decrees that should have occurred at least six months before the deadline, but this never came to fruition. This communicated to LSFs that the cut-off promised by law was not going to be pursued as it was written.

During these changes, the opera as an organization experienced adversities from different sides that challenged the idea that they should receive public funding. The ambiguity in the public nature of the opera and the uncertainty in the actual provision of yearly funding were at the heart of these continuous adversities. Respectively, the 13 OHs risked default. They faced complete shut down a few times, the last in 2014, but remain to this day.

The objectives behind the transformation into LSFs were not achieved, and the LSFs found themselves facing a growing crisis; between 2005 and 2010, five foundations defaulted, though they did not close. After the reform, which led to overcoming the old lyrical institution based on public interest, private contributions should have been the norm, but they rarely reached the percentage necessary for achieving balance. The numerous changes to the legislative decree n. 367/1996 that occurred between 1998 and 2010, such as a further lowering of the participation rate of private individuals to 8% of state funding for at least 2 years (instead of 3), are only 'buffering measures' to solve specific and contingent problems, and did not substantially and incisively affect the institutional set-up, the production structure or the financing mechanisms. They did, however, change the OHs dramatically, as they oriented more to their sustainability than to their excellence, making a musician more akin to an assembly line worker than an artist.

Operatic Professionalism: From Amateurs to Professional Artists

The third building block of the archetype analysed here concerns rules, practices and behaviours. These often converge into professions that are involved in archetypes (Muzio et al., 2013). The generation of AE stabilized the production of operas over the years. While the laws addressed all the institutions that organized an operatic season of more than one month, in those theatres that were more active for longer periods, the operatic season was extended throughout the year. Moreover, artistic work was pushed from dilettantism to professionalism, as it could be performed during the whole year, producing a significant increase in quality. In the AE, the superintendent had authority over hiring artists or workers and the president had the power to refuse. The president, as already said, was also the mayor and the main contributor to the OH. In this legislative framework, the OHs in Rome, Florence and Milan worked for the financial stabilization of their artists.

Between 1934 and 1938, two kinds of institutions related to OHs were founded: governmental institutions that controlled the decisions and operations of OH under the Ministry of Popular Culture and governmental institutions that protected workers in theatres through unions (Balestra & Malaguti, 2003, p. 42). The union of performing arts workers provided general improvement of the working conditions and salary, but it also transformed the approach of performing arts workers towards the public, government and the OH itself. According to Pestalozza (1981) during fascism, musicians developed a strong parasitic and patronizing approach towards the state, exploiting the fact that the state wanted to secure their intellectual support and offered corporate-union assistance and an organization that allowed them to benefit from the welfare state. The influence of this framework continued after this period. For example, Nicola De Pirro played a primary role in the definition and leadership of the OHs, remaining in the governmental General Management of Performing Arts until 1963 (Balestra & Malaguti, 2003).

In the 1920s, Toscanini was the first to conceive of the orchestra musician as a professional as we understand it today. As mentioned earlier, his pursuit of performance excellence implied the professionalism of artists as natural (Sachs, 1987). However, the fact that many OHs worked through 'seasons' of half a year or shorter, with interruptions between them (Della Seta, 1993), led to the need for many artists to have jobs for the 'quieter periods'. Well-known anecdotes are shared by artists and musicologists on the matter. In the 1920s, Maestro Gui, hunting for orchestra musicians, was told that in a nearby city there was a good trombone player in the café by the sea in Viareggio (interview with Music Critic and Artistic Director, Daniele Spini, Firenze, 26/09/2019). Similarly, in the choir in the Arena di Verona in 1950, one of the tenors was the local barber that used to sing arias out loud while doing his 'other job', and altos were school teachers and hairdressers (interviews with experts in Verona, 2015–2016).

When the artist of the opera was allowed to focus on a single profession, the quality of performances greatly increased. The technical level required to qualify for a short-list today was not even considered possible 30 years ago. For the trumpet, for instance, the mastery of the 'double staccato' is a basic technical element for a professional player today, but was considered nearly impossible in 1960. Higher education for artists was done in conservatories for musicians, singers and composers and, since 1971, in universities for other aspects of the performing arts (DAMS at Bologna University). Until the Mascagni Act in the mid-1980s, instructors in the conservatories also worked in OHs, so competencies for performing in OHs were acquired in regular education. After the Mascagni Act, instructors had to opt for either the conservator or the OH, leading to a lack of orchestral competencies and practical knowledge of new artists. The effect was fewer young artists qualifying for operatic jobs. Instead, they were given temporary positions with little pay that did not include rest days over a production and began a few days after the start of the rehearsals scheduled for a production. Indeed, this also impacted the quality of the performance.

In social terms, the profession of the artist in the OH was respected, at least until the 1990s. It provided prestige, recognition and paid well. Later, a growing discussion on the budget for performing arts and culture puts OHs in a bad light, framing OH workers as parasitic, living on others' ability to produce wealth. In addition, especially in technical professions, OHs, like other fields in the cultural sector, were often used politically as a social buffer to unemployment, with positions in excess of what was required. For the same political reason, OH workers have typically shown a rigid attitude towards change and negotiation and have always claimed their contractual rights. For instance, they obtained some integrative 'allowances for humidity' or 'for black tie', acknowledging the special conditions of their work. In addition, strikes in OHs were not unusual. Since 2014, with the Bray Act, salaries have dropped and many allowances have been cancelled. Altogether, the social perception of the OH profession has changed dramatically (interviews with Orchestra professionals, 2016–2018).

Discussion

In this chapter, the literature on resilience was related to the literature on change in institutions, and, more precisely, in organizational archetypes. This provides the first contribution to both streams of literature, as it establishes a link that supports cross-fertilization. Resilience was analysed through the evolution of the opera and, as a further contribution to resilience analysis, presented a picture of resilience that accounts for the main components of an archetype: symbolic meanings, organizational structures, professional knowledge and behaviours building a social system that includes aesthetic, economic, legislative and sociological aspects (Greenwood & Hinings, 1993).

From a longitudinal perspective, we showed that the opera experienced coercive, normative and mimetic pressures in relation to disturbances that triggered change. Laws during the nineteenth century that directed the opera towards educational or cultural aims, and later to managerialization, introduced coercive disturbances. The role of first-in-class played by La Scala functioned both as a source of normative and mimetic pressure. Over time, the opera evolved from being a popular expression, to elitist, to entertaining and to an educational form of culture, and from a public system to a managerialized one where efficiency is the target. This evolution shows the contours of a plurality of institutional logics (Kraatz & Block, 2008; Thornton, 2004) pertaining to the opera. In the early days, the opera reflected the logic of amusement and entertainment that supported a market or business logic when it was a popular form of divertissement. Then, it responded to a logic of exhibitionism related to the need for nobles to show off their status and power when it became the main expression of nobles and their courts. Recently, it has included the logic of business that assumes there is a market for opera, especially for opera reproductions of ancient cultural expressions; the logic of culture, conceiving opera as a system of meaning that can still speak to contemporary society and the logic of opera professions, supporting the idea that the opera contains artistic excellence and performance can be cultivated by artists.

This chapter also addresses the extent to which we can talk of resilience when deep change occurs (Frigotto et al., 2022, in Chapter 1, this volume) and when a long time scale is considered (Carpenter et al., 2001). Our analysis showed that the opera went through transformative resilience, as it was challenged in its survival and identity several times since its birth. The opera has changed dramatically since its early days, so much that we hardly understand the operatic works of the early days when they are performed (e.g. Muti's choices of openings at La Scala). Several directions of transformation are visible, ranging from the disneyfication (fitting with a box-office/business logic) to the componentization of opera's pieces, including the change of ending and of performing traditions (fitting with a logic of contemporary cultural relevance). Moreover, intense transformation was introduced by legislation towards determined managerialization and strict attention to costs and revenues in line with the broader introduction of new public management in all areas of public organizations since the 1990s and that triggered the opera to lean towards the private organization model. To the resilience discourse, the most important question concerns the continuity of essence in this evolution, or, in other terms, if these pressures and conflicting institutional logics have transformed the nature and identity of opera or if it is possible to recognize a red thread across these changes.

Political assessments of the need for change in the opera have typically resulted in new laws and new nominations to the top roles in OHs. However, our analysis showed that, despite the intent of the legislation, and compared to the intent and determination of specific actors (e.g. impresarios or Toscanini) that acted as institutional entrepreneurs producing and spreading change (Battilana et al., 2009; Hardy & Maguire, 2008) or organizations within the system (e.g. La Scala) or other institutions (e.g. fascism and its political propaganda), agency played a limited role in the evolution of the opera and, therefore, on resilience. For example, the objective pursued with the transformation to LSFs was not achieved, nor was the 2013 Bray Act able to push OHs towards efficiency and business logic. This is witnessed by the fact that the deadlines in the Bray Act that foresaw the closing down of OHs had to be postponed several times. Similarly, the traditional operatic repertoire was not abandoned nor exclusively and slavishly reproduced for box-office logic.

In our interpretation, this means two things. First, that a holistic perspective on change is necessary, one that considers the various actors and logics involved and puts them in perspective for an integrated understanding of the overall outcome that might not reflect the actors' intentions nor their design. This requires rich data and different competencies for a multifaceted understanding of actors and logics. In this case, organization studies, musicology and music practice were necessary, which are the areas of expertise of the authors. This also implies that change derives from the interplay between the micro, meso and macro levels and that one level considered in isolation cannot account for change, similar to the relevance of the social scale in the observation of resilience (Carpenter et al., 2001).

Second, the opera as an archetype has gone through a transformative kind of resilience and is still transforming but has not abandoned its original nature of cultural and entertaining artistic expression that combines reflection with amusement. The latter has been 'reproduced as in chemistry' (Padgett & Powell, 2012) through the staging of traditional operas with renewed interpretations, endings and social reflections. In the eyes of some, the latter is the essence of opera that should be treated as the line of continuity that is preserved and along which resilience is observed. Others instead think that the opera can only survive through new cultural tastes and little funding by becoming keener to adapt to contemporary entertainment. Several music critics have envisioned the denaturing of opera in the future, given that, in several aspects, it has been heading towards a business-driven factory rather than a cultural organization. The co-existence of these different logics may make the opera a hybrid organization (Pache & Santos, 2010). Further, the opera maps onto different organizational archetypes that also co-occur and whose competition has not been solved; this situation configures archetype sedimentation (Cooper et al., 1996). The transformation itself, described as 'sweeping away' the residues of previous archetypes (Cooper et al., 1996, p. 625), has not taken place, given that the tension between logics and the decoupling of OHs and the various pressures are still taking place. change is still ongoing and only future studies will be able to analyse the whole evolution when opera reaches its final destination.

Acknowledgements The Authors wish to thank Giuseppe Bargiacchi, Giorgio Brunetti, Cristiano Chiarot, Pierangelo Conte, Maria di Freda, Luigi Maria Sicca, Daniele Spini, Enrico Sciarra, Alberto Triola, Giovanni Verona, Luca Zan, and all the Artists we interviewed, for sharing and discussing with us their views on the evolution of the opera and of its meaning, structure and professions. All the mistakes and omissions remain our own.

References

Balestra, C., & Malaguti, A. (2003). *Organizzare musica. Legislazione, produzione, distribuzione, gestione nel sistema italiano*. Franco Angeli.

Barigazzi, G. (2014). *La Scala racconta*. Hoepli.

Bartezzaghi, S. (2013, January 23). L'età della resilienza. *La Repubblica*. Retrieved October 2, 2021 from https://ricerca.repubblica.it/repubblica/archivio/repubblica/2013/01/23/leta-della-resilienza.html

Battilana, J., Leca, B., & Boxenbaum, E. (2009). How Actors change institutions: Towards a theory of institutional entrepreneurship. *The Academy of Management Annals, 3*(1), 65–107.

Boxenbaum, E., & Jonsson, S. (2008). Isomorphism, diffusion and decoupling. In R. Greenwood, C. Oliver, K. Sahlin, & R. Suddaby (Eds.), *The SAGE handbook of organizational institutionalism* (pp. 78–98). SAGE Publications.

Britt, T. W., Shen, W., Sinclair, R. R., Grossman, M. R., & Klieger, D. M. (2016). How much do we really know about employee resilience? *Industrial and Organizational Psychology, 9*(2), 378–404.

Carpenter, S., Walker, B., Anderies, J. M., & Abel, N. (2001). From metaphor to measurement: resilience of what to what? *Ecosystems, 4*(8), 765–781.

Cooper, D. J., Hinings, B., Greenwood, R., Brown, J. L., Cooper, D. J., Hinings, B., ... Brown, J. L. (1996). Sedimentation and transformation in organizational change: The case of canadian law firms. *Organization Studies*, 17(4), 623–647.

Cori, E. (2004). *Aspetti istituzionali e dinamiche organizzative nel teatro d'opera in Italia*. FrancoAngeli.

Della Seta, F. (1993). *L'organizzazione dei teatri e le condizioni del musicista, in Italia e Francia nell'Ottocento*. EDT.

Duchek, S. (2018). Entrepreneurial resilience: A biographical analysis of successful entrepreneurs. *International Entrepreneurship and Management Journal, 14*(2), 429–455.

Duchek, S. (2019). Organizational resilience: A capability-based conceptualization. *Business Research, 13*(1), 215–246.

The Economist. (2015). Give the tourists what they want (March 24). Online at: https://www.economist.com/prospero/2015/03/24/giving-the-tourists-what-they-want

Ernani, F., & Iovino, R. (1993). *La Repubblica degli enti lirici-sinfonici. Problemi e prospettive del teatro d'opera in Italia (1967–1992)*. EDT.

Ferri, P. (2016). *I commissariamenti nel settore culturale italiano: obiettivi, azioni, risultati*. Editoriale scientifica.

Fisher, D. M., Ragsdale, J. M., & Fisher, E. C. S. (2018). The importance of definitional and temporal issues in the study of resilience. *Applied Psychology, 68*(4), 583–620.

Folke, C., Carpenter, S. R., Walker, B., Scheffer, M., Chapin, T., & Rockström, J. (2010). Resilience thinking: integrating resilience, adaptability and transformability. *Ecology and Society, 15*(4), 20.

Frigotto, M. L. (2018). *Understanding novelty in organizations: A research path across agency and consequences*. Palgrave Macmillan.

Frigotto, M. L. (2020). Reframing resilience on novelty and change. In E. Powley, B. Caza & A. Caza (Eds.), *Research handbook on organizational resilience*, (pp. 53–69). Emerald Group Publishing Limited.

Frigotto, M. L., & Rossi, A. (2015). An explanatory coherence model of decision making in ill-structured problems. *Mind & Society, 14*(1), 35–55.

Frigotto, M. L., Young, M., & Pinheiro, R. (2022). Resilience in organizations and societies: The state of the art and three organizing principles for moving forward. In R. Pinheiro, L. Frigotto, & M. Young (Eds.), Towards resilient organizations and societies: A cross-sectoral and multi-disciplinary perspective (pp. 3–45). Palgrave.

Greenwood, R., & Hinings, C. (1993). Understanding strategic change: The contribution of archetypes. *Academy of Management Journal, 36*(5), 1052–1081.

Greenwood, R., & Hinings, C. R. (1996). Understanding radical organizational change: Bringing together the old and the new institutionalism. *Academy of Management Review, 21*(4), 1022–1054.

Greenwood, R., Hinings, C. R., & Whetten, D. (2014). Rethinking institutions and organizations. *Journal of Management Studies, 51*, 1206–1220.

Hardy, C., & Maguire, S. (2008). Institutional entrepreneurship. *The Sage handbook of organizational institutionalism, 1*, 198–217. London: Sage.

Holling, C. S. (1973). Resilience and stability of ecological systems. *Annual Review of Ecology and Systematics, 4*(1), 1–23.

Kossek, E. E., & Perrigino, M. B. (2016). Resilience: A review using a grounded integrated occupational approach. *The Academy of Management Annals, 10*(1), 729–797.

Kraatz, M. S., & Block, E. S. (2008). *Organizational implications of institutional pluralism. The Sage handbook of organizational institutionalism* (Vol. 840, pp. 243–275). Sage.

Linnenluecke, M. K. (2017). Resilience in business and management research: A review of influential publications and a research agenda. *International Journal of Management Reviews, 19*(1), 4–30.

Manca, B. (2019). Tamara Wilson, il soprano protesta contro l'Aida all'Arena di Verona: "Non mi farò truccare il volto di nero, è razzismo istituzionalizzato" *Il Fatto Quotidiano*. 27 Luglio. Retrieved October 2, 2021 from https://www.ilfattoquotidiano.it/2019/07/27/tamara-wilson-il-soprano-protesta-contro-laida-allarena-di-verona-non-mi-faro-truccare-il-volto-di-nero-e-razzismo-istituzionalizzato/5352769/

McNulty, T., & Ferlie, E. (2002). *Process transformation?: A case of reengineering in health care*. Oxford University Press.

Meyer, J. W., & Rowan, B. (1977). Institutionalized organizations: Formal structure as myth and ceremony. *American Journal of Sociology, 83*(2), 340–363.

Muzio, D., Brock, D. M., & Suddaby, R. (2013). Professions and institutional change: Towards an institutionalist sociology of the professions. *Journal of Management Studies, 50*(5), 699–721.

Oliver, C. (1991). Strategic responses to institutional processes. *Academy of Management Review, 16*(1), 145–179.

Pache, A.-C., & Santos, F. (2010). When worlds collide: The internal dynamics of organizational responses to conflicting institutional demands. *Academy of Management Review, 35*, 455–476.

Padgett, J. F., & Powell, W. W. (2012). *The emergence of organizations and markets*. Princeton University Press.

Pestalozza, L. (1981). Lo Stato dell'organizzazione Musicale: La Svolta Del Fascismo e La Sua Lunga Durata. *Musica-Realtà, II/5* (Agosto 1991), 143–160.

Powell, W. W., & DiMaggio, P. J. (1991). *The new institutionalism in organizational analysis*. University of Chicago Press.

Reason, P., & Bradbury, H. (2008). *The Sage handbook of action research: Participative inquiry and practice*. Sage.

Rosselli, J. (1985). *L'impresario d'opera*. EDT.

Ruef, M., & Aldrich, H. (2006). *Organizations evolving*. Sage.

Ruggieri, M. (2004). Il teatro lirico tra pubblico e privato (1898–2001). *Economia Della Cultura, Numero Speciale, 1*, 39–98.

Sachs, H. (1987). *Arturo Toscanini dal 1915 al 1946*. EDT.

Schumpeter, J. A. (1934). *The theory of economic development; an inquiry into profits, capital, credit, interest, and the business cycle*. Harvard University Press.

Sennett, R. (1998). *The corrosion of character: The personal consequences of work in the new capitalism*. WW Norton & Company.

Sicca, L. M. (1997). The management of opera houses: The Italian experience of the Enti Autonomi. *International Journal of Cultural Policy, 4*(1), 201–224.

Siggelkow, N. (2007). Persuasion with case studies. *Academy of Management Journal, 50*(1), 20–24.

Thornton, P. H. (2004). *Markets from culture: Institutional logics and organizational decisions in higher education publishing*. Stanford University Press.

Thornton, P. H., & Ocasio, W. (1999). Institutional logics and the historical contingency of power in organizations: Executive succession in the higher education publishing industry, 1958–1990. *American Journal of Sociology, 105*(3), 801–843.

Trevisan, P. (2015). *Reshaping Opera. A Critical Reflection on Arts Management*. Ph.D. Dissertation, Ph.D. Program in Management, Ca' Foscari University in Venice.

Trezzini, L. (1994). Il quadro di riferimento dello spettacolo dal vivo in Bodo C. (a cura di), *Rapporto sull'economia della cultura in Italia*, 1980–1990, Presidenza del Consiglio dei Ministri, Dipartimento per l'informazione e l'editoria, Roma.

Trezzini, L. (2006). Dalle prime normative al Fondo unico per lo spettacolo. *Economia Della Cultura, 16*(1), 7–14.

Vanhove, A. J., Herian, M. N., Perez, A. L. U., Harms, P. D., & Lester, P. B. (2016). Can resilience be developed at work? A meta-analytic review of resilience-building programme effectiveness. *Journal of Occupational and Organizational Psychology, 89*(2), 278–307.

Walker, B., Holling, C. S., Carpenter, S. R., & Kinzig, A. (2004). Resilience, adaptability and transformability in social–ecological systems. *Ecology and Society*, *9*(2), 1–9.

Williams, T. A., Gruber, D. A., Sutcliffe, K. M., Shepherd, D. A., & Zhao, E. Y. (2017). Organizational response to adversity: Fusing crisis management and resilience research streams. *Academy of Management Annals, 11*(2), 733–769.

Yin, R. (2009). *Case study research design and methods*. Sage.

CHAPTER 10

Being Resilient Between the Region and the Higher Education System? Views on Regional Higher Education Institutions in Estonia and Finland

Jari Kolehmainen, Heli Kurikka, Anne Keerberg, and Garri Raagmaa

Introduction

The chapter explores the resilience of regional higher education institutions (RHEIs), which must be resilient because they are exposed to changes in the higher education system (HES), such as with policies of

J. Kolehmainen (✉) · H. Kurikka
Tampere University, Seinäjoki, Finland
e-mail: jari.kolehmainen@tuni.fi

H. Kurikka
e-mail: heli.kurikka@tuni.fi

A. Keerberg
Tallinn University of Technology, Tallinn, Estonia
e-mail: anne.keerberg@nooruse.edu

R. Pinheiro et al. (eds.), *Towards Resilient Organizations and Societies*, Public Sector Organizations,
https://doi.org/10.1007/978-3-030-82072-5_10

'picking winners' that emphasize excellence, efficiency and centralizing resources (Pinheiro & Young, 2017; Sørensen et al., 2016). RHEIs are also impacted by the development trajectories of their regions. However, the literature on education system resiliency in the context of economic development (shocks) is limited (e.g. Moran, 2016; Pinheiro & Young, 2017; Postiglione, 2011), neglecting RHEIs' role in regional resilience.

There is a relatively wide consensus that the presence of universities stimulates economic development and improves the resilience of regions. HEIs have a significant impact on the businesses and organizations of their region (Vaessen & Velde, 2003), opening it up to the wider world. HEIs may serve as the global pipelines bridging social capital, contributing to regional development (Bathelt et al., 2004) and interpreting new ideas, knowledge and technologies. HEIs may also assume the role of experts in local decision-making bodies (Arbo & Benneworth, 2007), act as strategic partners and institutional entrepreneurs (Raagmaa & Keerberg, 2017) and contribute to rural innovation (Charles, 2016).

Typically, resilience (Chapter 1, in this volume) is divided into two main types: (1) bouncing back to a state of normalcy after a crisis and (2) the flexibility to adjust without crossing the thresholds of identity. For regions, *adaptive resilience*, a third type of resilience, is possible (Martin & Sunley, 2015). Hence, we are interested in the conditions that motivate or even force RHEIs to choose their resilience strategy. A RHEI may contribute proactively to the development of its own operational environment, that is, the surrounding region, by acting as an institutional entrepreneur (cf. Benneworth et al., 2017; Cai & Liu, 2020). Institutional entrepreneurs are actors that challenge existing institutions or create new ones (DiMaggio, 1988). However, having the role of a local opinion leader would theoretically lead RHEIs to lock in, assuming a defensive position and losing the strategic vision of the future. Therefore, we attempt to examine whether and under what circumstances RHEIs are sustainable in the long run. We address the following questions:

G. Raagmaa
Tartu University, Tartu, Estonia
e-mail: garri.raagmaa@ut.ee

- How resilient are RHEIs, and what kind of organizational strategies do they use?
- What is the relationship between RHEIs, their locational regions and the HE system from the perspective of resilience?

The answers to these questions are sought by conducting a qualitatively case study on two small RHEIs in the peripheral regions of Kuressaare, Estonia and Seinäjoki, Finland. The case studies are a result of a long-lasting research process in which versatile case study methodologies and data sets have been applied: (1) desk research of policy documents and statistics; (2) data provided by the representatives of RHEIs (e.g. memos, planning documents); (3) semistructured interviews and (4) action research directly involved in the activities of the RHEIs' directors, board members and employees.

The earliest data sets were gathered for both case studies in 2013 as a part of two projects: the TIPS programme[1] in Estonia and ITU research programme[2] in Finland. These data include eight interviews for the Kuressaare case and 11 interviews for Seinäjoki. The interviewees were mainly local HEI leaders, representatives of local and regional authorities and business representatives. Since then, the data have been updated and augmented with a large number of interviews and other written and electronic material up to the year 2019. Some interviews were conducted repeatedly, giving a longitudinal character to the case studies. In the very end of this research process, the manuscript was commented on by two representatives of the case RHEIs to verify and validate our theoretical approach and empirical findings.

[1] Teadus- ja innovatsioonipoliitika seire programm (TIPS) [Research and Innovation Policy Monitoring Program], funded by Estonian Ministry of Science and Education.

[2] Innovaatioympäristöjen tutkimus- ja kehittämishanke (ITU) [Research Programme on Local and Regional Innovation Environments], funded by University of Tampere, Regional Council of South Ostrobothnia, City of Seinäjoki, Into Seinäjoki Ltd, University Consortium of Seinäjoki and Higher Education Fund of South Ostrobothnia.

Theoretical Backdrop

Organizational Resilience and Coevolution in Different Contexts

Here, we construct a theoretical framework to understand how the resilience of RHEIs may be shaped. We begin by outlining organizational resilience, continue with the interaction of RHEI and regions and study the role of the HES. Organizational resilience (OR) is usually defined as the organizations' capability to recover from external shocks. However, this is a narrow view of resilience. More detailed and enriched definitions exist:

> Resilience is the emergent property of organisational systems that relates to the inherent and adaptive qualities and capabilities that enable an organisations adaptive capacity during turbulent periods. The mechanisms of organisational resilience thereby strive to improve an organisation' situational awareness, reduce organisational vulnerabilities to systemic risk environments and restore efficacy following the events of a disruption. (Burnard & Bhamra, 2011, p. 5587)

Here, the emphasis is not only on the individual and sudden shocks in terms of resilience, but attention is paid to incremental changes. Following this reasoning, OR can be understood as organizations' capability to cope with their own operational environment over time. *Coping* does not only refer to surviving or pure adaptation: it also involves the idea of strong agency. Indeed, RHEIs are organizations capable of anticipating the future, preparing themselves for it and shaping their own operational environment. RHEIs may not only interact with other institutions (formal and informal practices), but also proactively create new and modify existing ones (see, e.g. DiMaggio, 1988) because they play an important role in transforming social values and shaping society (Cai & Liu, 2020).

Denyer (2017) created the 'tension quadrant' model on OR based on an extensive literature review (181 academic articles). The model splits OR into behaviours that are defensive (maintaining the *status quo*) or progressive (innovating and taking risks) and those that are consistent or flexible. These four viewpoints form an integral part of the OR 'tension quadrant' (Fig. 10.1). Consistent and flexible behaviours relate to March's (1991) *organizational learning,* where an exploitative type of learning refers to efforts aimed at incremental change and continuity,

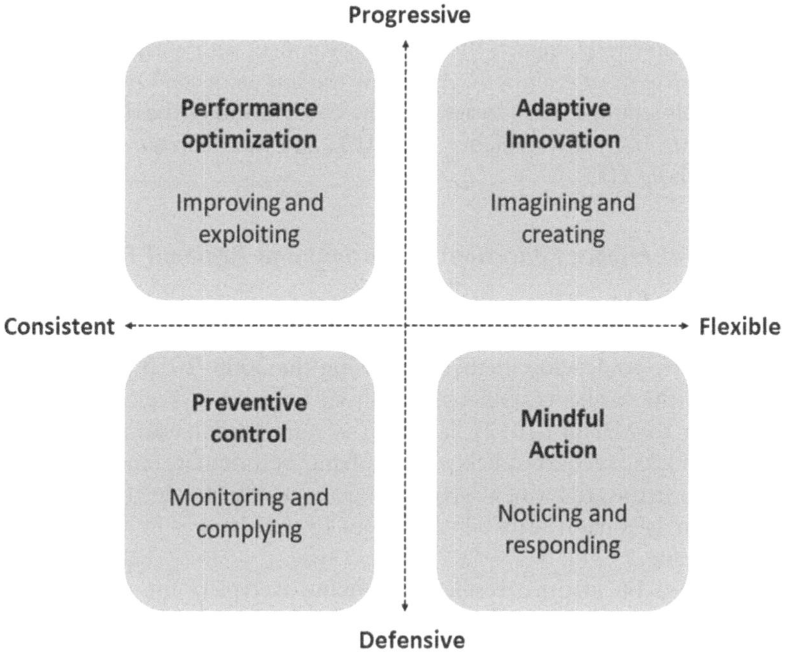

Fig. 10.1 Dimensions of organizational resilience. *Source* Denyer (2017, p. 10)

whereas explorative learning is about seeking new paths aiming at more radical changes and innovations.

Denyer (2017) identified four strategic ways of thinking about OR: *preventative control* (defensive consistency), *mindful action* (defensive flexibility), *performance optimization* (progressive consistency) and *adaptive innovation* (progressive flexibility). A resilient organization utilizes all ways of thinking depending on the situation. Sometimes, it is crucial to defend the integrity of an organization against external interests (Selznick, 1984), and in some situations, a more progressive strategy is called for.

The concept of *coevolution* means that the relationship between agents and their environment is bidirectional. If an agent is merely adapting to changes, the relationship is not coevolutionary. From an evolutionary perspective, coevolution is a matter of series of variation and retention processes (Lewin & Volberda, 1999; Sotarauta & Kautonen, 2007; Sotarauta & Srinivas, 2006). Coevolution calls for agency, which is also an integral part of OR. As Sotarauta and Srinivas (2006, p. 319) stated, *'The co-evolutionary view suggests that both environment and agency are important in the course of evolution'*. Agency is the link between OR of RHEIs, that is, their strategic ways to act, and the coevolution of the determinants constructing both the resilience of RHEIs and their surrounding region and the whole HES.

Regional Higher Education Institutions and Regional Resilience

Regional resilience is a complex phenomenon that determines how a region responds to a shock or disturbance and under what circumstances it will be able to develop further. Following the 2008–2010 global financial crisis, the resilience concept began to be used in regional studies. According to Martin (2012), a region is resilient if it can resist recessionary shocks, recover quickly from them, re-orientate and renew its growth path towards a new growth trajectory. We define the resilience of a region as equal its capability to adapt to the changes in its economic environment.

This kind of adaptive resilience thinking is typical for evolutionary economic geography, which sees regional economies as continuous adapting processes and stable equilibrium states as nonexistent (Martin & Sunley, 2015). This is why so-called bounce-back resilience (see Chapter 1 in this volume) is not easily applied to regions. Regions adjust to new kinds of situations, for example, by creating, diversifying and upgrading industrial paths (Grillitsch & Asheim, 2018). This can lead to changes in regional economic structures like the industrial mix. Therefore, the second type of resilience—an adjustment without crossing the threshold of identity—does not suit regions as such because there is the question of what the 'thresholds' of regional economy are.

A regional economy can go through major changes, and exactly because of this, a region can be called 'resilient'. This is what Martin's (2012) 're-orientation' means. Thus, regional resilience would be a region's capacity to maintain economic performances despite shocks by adapting regional structures and functions; this can also be seen as a 'bounce forward' (Martin & Sunley, 2015, p. 4). Pike et al. (2010, p. 62) studied the mechanisms of regional resilience and found that 'adaptability' is the key issue, which here means the capacity of a region to break free from old paths and ability to find new ones. This also resonates well with

March's (1991) study of organizational learning and its concept of exploration, that is, seeking new avenues and breaking with the past. Bristow and Healy (2014) emphasized that this process of regional reorientation calls for agency.

The components of regional resilience can be divided into five categories: (1) *industrial and business structure*, (2)*labour market conditions*, (3)*financial arrangements*, (4)*agency/decision making* and (5)*governance arrangements* (Martin & Sunley, 2015). These factors explain much of a region's ability to resist and recover from shocks, but also its ability to recognize and benefit from positive changes.

Peripheral regions have many disadvantages compared with core locations. The logic of economy is mostly based on the benefits of agglomerations and accessibility of core regions (Isaksen, 2015). In this respect, the resilience of peripheries faces challenges. HEIs can play a crucial role in shaping regional resilience. Karlsen et al. (2011) and Trippl et al. (2016) pointed out that Nordic peripheries succeeded in compensating for organizational thinness with the institutional thickness provided by public policies. Here, thickness refers to the presence of dynamic clusters and support organizations that can help in developing new industries based on scientific knowledge, while thinness is about the absence of this (Tödtling & Trippl, 2005). There was a policy boom of setting up RHEIs to enrich regional knowledge capacity in many European regions in the 2000s (Hedin, 2009; OECD, 2007). The evolution of RHEI networks in the Nordic countries was the result of several decades of lasting regional and education policy, the resilience of RHEIs and their surrounding regions developing in a coevolutionary manner.

The role of RHEIs in facilitating learning and adaptation processes (Gunasekara, 2006) can be considered particularly vital in peripheral regions characterized by low densities and limited access. Smallness and remoteness can be associated with closeness and kindness—generating rich social capital might be an advantage: capable people with a high knowledge level empowered by high social capital and trust may increase the benefits of a small region. The potentially good and lively community life is often a breeding ground for innovation. In such regions, the quadruple helix model combining HE actors, public authorities, business community and local social community groups may be at the very heart of knowledge-based regional development (Kolehmainen et al., 2016). Peripheries in general—save for one-company towns that might be extremely vulnerable—are less influenced by global shocks that arrive with a delay and in an already modified form. RHEIs located in the peripheries act not only as educators and technology transfer units, but also as institutional entrepreneurs that create new institutions and modify entrepreneurial ecosystem (Raagmaa & Keerberg, 2017; TIPS, 2015).

Peripheral regions are organizationally thin (Tödtling & Trippl, 2005), giving more weight to RHEIs and allowing them to convince local decision makers more easily to implement institutional changes in a shorter time. RHEIs located in small towns tend to be relatively more active in contributing to regional development actions. In addition, regional leadership in policy and business have a significant role in establishing and supporting the development of the RHEI as an initiative maker and funder (Sotarauta, 2014, 2015). However, institutional lock-in and ceasing development are a possible threat because of limited human resources and the pressure of local actors of RHEIs, meaning consequently a much higher role of proactive leadership than institutionally thick well-staffed urban cores.

Regional Higher Education Institutions and the Higher Education System

RHEIs are regional actors, but they are also a part of the national and global HES. Analysing the resilience of an entire HES by using explicitly the concept of resilience appears to be scarce in the literature. Naturally, there is a plethora of studies on the transformation, reforms, change and adaptation of the HEIs and the whole HE system (Stensaker & Benner, 2013; Stensaker et al., 2012; Vukasovic et al., 2012). However, despite different geographical and field-specific traditions and development paths, the university has proven to be very persistent in retaining its basic ideals, such as its knowledge-based nature and open and genuine discourse and interaction (e.g. Rothblatt & Wittrock, 1993). Universities are institutions, not instruments for reaching certain externally set agendas (Olsen, 2007), even if entrepreneurs and even governmental bodies occasionally criticize universities about their rigidity and far less innovative action than society would expect.

Still, as Pinheiro and Young (Chapter 7, this volume) pointed out, in the European context, universities are seen as strategic actors of the knowledge-based economy. These notions call forth the *'Hesburgh paradox'*: how traditional and rigid institutions like universities produce revolutionary change (see Clark, 1983, p. 182). In this light, HEIs could choose a defensive strategy to maintain the status quo. Still, all HEIs are not alike; there are great variations depending on size, age, profile, location strategies and so forth. For example, there is a growing number of 'entrepreneurial universities' (Benneworth & Nieth, 2018; Benneworth et al., 2017; Clark, 1998) aiming to become more adaptive and engaged with public institutions, businesses and civil society. Even the old conservative universities are changing and adapting alongside the changing governmental policy goals and funding conditions, reflecting the more profound changes in economy and society (see, e.g. Tapper & Palfreyman, 2011).

The HES consists of different kinds of HEIs that coevolve together. This holds true for the RHEIs, which are only a small but a particular part of a national HES. Pinheiro and Young (2017, p. 122) defined an HES as *'an emergent, self-organizational, and dynamic complex system where the relations among the actors or agents are characterized as nonlinear, with the relations among system elements and with other systems being co-evolutionary'*. HESs are usually permanent, and thus, it is relevant to interpret their resilience as their capability to adapt in a changing environment without compromising their core essence and values, such as social justice, competence, liberty and national loyalty (Clark, 1983). These basic values may be misaligned or manifest differently in different parts of HESs.

It is also worth noting that there are many kinds of pulling and pushing forces within and among HEIs and within HE systems and policies. Those forces create tensions and result in the coexistence, even coevolution, of multiple, sometimes contradictory, logics. Certain approaches are more dominant than others in certain periods of time. As Pinheiro and Young (this volume) argued, the prevailing European HE policies and systems emphasize short-term efficiency, instrumentalist objectives, rankings and other managerialist practices challenging the resilient nature of universities based on requisite variety, loose-coupledness and slack (see also Pinheiro & Young, 2017). This may not be a good orientation for RHEIs because they do not usually fit into the tight, managerial university moulds because of their distinctive characteristics.

There are few other specific issues in the relation between RHEIs and the whole HES from the perspective of resilience. First, RHEIs are strongly engaged with local and regional stakeholders and needs. However, they are also a part of the whole HES and have ambitions to influence it. On the other hand, RHEIs are institutionally dependent on their 'mother universities', that is, the central administrations of those universities that are responsible for the operations of RHEIs or are members of RHEIs that are network organizations. Therefore, RHEIs have both direct and indirect relations with the ministries and other key institutions within the HES. However, the strategic objectives of RHEIs and their 'mother universities' may differ. Consequently, especially for RHEIs, influencing the whole HES is a delicate balance between their own objectives and their mother universities' objectives.

The second notion relates to the size of RHEIs. Universities have to operate in a rapidly globalizing competitive marketplace (Olsen, 2007), and the recent trends include merging HEIs into larger entities (see, e.g. Välimaa et al., 2014). Large organizations tend to have better resources to face adversities, but small organizations can have other benefits, such as low bureaucracy, effective internal communication, quick decision making and rapid strategic adapting (Vossen, 1998). Hypothetically, choosing a progressive or defensive strategy depends on the size and status of a HEI. Fairly young and small RHEIs can hardly be defensive; instead, they need to be progressive and 'entrepreneurial'. Naturally, this is a simplistic view because the actual lived strategies and strategic practices are context and time specific. Still, it can be argued that when RHEIs are belonging and steered by ever larger mother universities, this becomes a potential source of tensions, and RHEIs should find a way to act within the universities and the whole HES.

Empirical Section

Case 1. Kuressaare, Estonia

Regional HEIs in the Estonian Higher Education System

The Estonian HES is the third smallest among OECD countries. Currently, there are 20 HEIs, including six public universities, one private university, eight state professional HEIs and five private professional HEIs. The universities run six regional units. The number of students reached its peak in 2010 and has been declining because of tightened quality requirements and demographic development in recent years. Estonia is undergoing a period of demographic transition; the domestic HE enrolments are falling, but the number of international students is growing (see, e.g. OECD, 2019).

The development path of the Estonian HES has been eventful because of a number of reforms. There were six national HEIs in Estonia in 1990. Then, demand for market economy professionals increased, and several mainly private HEIs were established. By 2001, there were 49 HEIs that ran 30 regional units outside the old university cities Tallinn and Tartu. There was no national legislation or policy regulating the creation of RHEIs in Estonia; instead, they resulted from agreements between local initiative-takers and the universities. Setting up RHEIs in Estonia was the result of several market-led, societal, governance and leadership-related factors. The process was strongly supported by regional authorities, county governments and/or city governments that lobbied ministries and university rectors (Raagmaa & Keerberg, 2017).

Saaremaa and Kuressaare College
Saaremaa is an island in the Baltic Sea, and with its surrounding islands, it makes up about 7% of Estonian territory and 2% of the population (33,000 inhabitants). The distance from the county seat Kuressaare (13,000 inhabitants) to Tallinn is 217 km, a journey of 4.5 h, including the seaway. Saaremaa's economy is dominated by services, but the share of manufacturing in regional GDP is increasing. The main industries are food, machinery, electronics, rubber and plastics. More than 70% of industrial output is exported. The Development Strategy of Saaremaa County has identified health tourism and small craft building as new growth areas. The latter forms advanced R&D-based industry micro cluster accounting over 90% of the turnover and 80% of the employment nationwide (Sääsk, 2018). Over the last three years, some 150 new highly qualified jobs have been created in companies involved in shipbuilding (Saare Development Centre, 2018).

Kuressaare College of the Tallinn University of Technology (KC), the smallest based on its students numbers, was created in 1999. Saaremaa entrepreneurs were active in the process because they realized that otherwise, they could not employ the necessary specialists. Seven Estonian university colleges started joint collaborative action since 2003, and intensive lobby work with the Minister for Regional Affairs resulted in a national university college programme in 2006. The rectors of six public universities of Estonia signed an agreement in 2008 aiming to develop a network of regional centres of competence (Ülikoolide, 2008). As a result, the EU-financed regional competence centres programme was launched in 2009.

Kuressaare College and Regional Resilience

The regional competence network of Saaremaa, led by Kuressaare College, was created in 2009. Small craft building was agreed to be the most promising area for smart specialization, so the Small Craft Competence Centre (SCC) was initiated (see Reidolf et al., 2011). The purpose was to accumulate and develop related knowhow and provide better facilities to train marine engineers. In parallel, the development of small craft building curriculum started and enrolled its first students in 2010. The proposal for EU funding was approved, and the SCC was officially established as a part of KC in 2011.

Universities were directly communicating with regional businesses when their local staff was conveying knowledge demanded by the community. In return, the (business) community provided feedback and input for education and research activities. At the heart of realizing these mutual benefits were place-based initiatives and intensive regional networking. Making these things happen also called for capable leadership that convinced the community to develop a certain sector with university support. In addition, regional partners had to find additional resources to finance the regional activities of the universities.

In 2014, the new Estonian Regional Development Strategy endorsed cooperation with the universities. Ironically, at this point, regional cooperation was no longer an urgent priority for the universities because they were facing increasing pressure for excellence and competition for enrolling international students and EU research grants. This has been a challenge for RHEIs. Despite this policy mismatch, the network of Estonian regional colleges has had a significant role in increasing the development capacity of different regions (TIPS, 2015). College towns have been growth centres for future-oriented industries because of the accumulation of competences and institutions able to support ongoing industrial transition. KC *progressively* and *flexibly* promotes *adaptive innovation*, and it has a coevolutionary relationship with the region.

Kuressaare College and the Evolving Higher Education System

In 2016, a new Tallinn University of Technology (TalTech) development plan was adopted aiming to optimize its structure. Thus, TalTech merged KC as its smallest unit with the TalTech Maritime Academy in January 2017. The merger was also a potential threat. However, KC and SCC continued receiving support and investments from entrepreneurs and from the local community leaders who convinced the TalTech rector to continue KC and SCC's joint activities as the Centre for Blue Economy. Today, the SCC's main R&D area is marine engineering and vessel hydrodynamics. At the beginning of 2018, TalTech appointed a professor of naval architecture to the Centre for Blue Economy; this was the first Estonian RHEI to open a professorship. In addition, the centre is developing a new specialization on marine bioresources valorization: a product development lab for fish farms and seafood producers. Hence, KC received an opportunity to bounce forward after a risky period.

In small, isolated peripheral regions, the scope of HEI curricula and research activity is usually narrow. KC has focused on the region's potential growth sectors. KC has regional roots and strong links to local businesses and the community but also a close connection with the mother university when defining the regional focus sectors (Keerberg, 2018). This illustrates the creativity of the HEI organization when improving universities' regional contribution 'at a distance', for example, in generating additional finances.

The key message here is that even small peripheral regions generate specific synergy and creativity that help universities deliver useful services to local industries. However, this synergy can be easily disrupted. The KC case can be characterized as a constant fight for survival when convincing local stakeholders, national ministry officials and university headquarters of their future operations. In this coevolutionary process, KC adopted both *progressive* and *defensive* strategies. The future perspective of Estonian RHEIs can be characterized as unclear because of the declining number of students, fragmented local authorities and university management reforms.

Case 2. Seinäjoki, Finland

Regional HEIs in the Finnish Higher Education System

The Finnish HES is based on two complementary sectors: 13 universities and 23 universities of applied sciences. Traditionally, the universities represent a top-down approach because they were owned by the state until 2010 when they became autonomous. Universities of applied sciences are limited liability companies owned mainly by local authorities, and they focus on a bachelor's level of education, research, development and innovation activities with regional stakeholders.

Additionally, there are six (regional) university consortia (UC) mentioned in the Universities Act, which aims to strengthen universities' impact on regional development. Universities see UC as a part of their regional and societal engagement. The central government provides separate funding for them through the coordinating university. The UC were established between 2001 and 2003 in regions with university activities and where there was no university.

South Ostrobothnia and University Consortium of Seinäjoki

Seinäjoki has 62,500 inhabitants, which is one-third of the population of the region. Seinäjoki has been growing, whereas the rest of the region has seen a decrease in the population. The distance from Seinäjoki to Helsinki is 360 km (three hours by train). South Ostrobothnia is a semirural region known for its production of food, metal and wood products. The level of education (tertiary degrees) is one of the lowest among the 18 Finnish regions. The number of companies conducting professional innovation activities and R&D expenditures per capita has been low but growing.

The University Consortium of Seinäjoki (UCS) is located in Seinäjoki, the centre of South Ostrobothnia. UCS was established in 2004 to strengthen the collaboration and provide common services to the universities located in the region; it is coordinated by Tampere University (formerly University of Tampere) because it was the first university that established its unit in Seinäjoki in 1981 (Jumppanen & Riukulehto, 2015; Kolehmainen & Alarinta, 2009), focussing mainly on open university education and some practical development projects. The University of Tampere was initially established as the Civic College in Helsinki; it developed into the School of Social Sciences and was moved to Tampere in 1960 in a wave of regional expansion of HE. In Tampere, it grew quite rapidly and was named the University of Tampere in 1966. In 2019, University of Tampere and Tampere University of Technology (TUT) merged and formed the current Tampere University. Currently, Tampere University has operations in Tampere, Pori and Seinäjoki.

The dual nature of the Finnish HES prevails also in South Ostrobothnia. Seinäjoki University of Applied Sciences (SUAS) has 4800 full-time students and 350 staff members, and it started its operations in 1992. The University Association of South Ostrobothnia was founded in 1960 to enhance HE in the region in the hopes of having its own university. Since then, several universities set up their units in Seinäjoki. Still, in the mid-1990s, there was a rising concern among the central local and regional authorities that the rural and low-educated region was unprepared for the new knowledge economy and innovation policies that were replacing the traditional, more cohesive regional policy.

At that time, the idea of a regional university network emerged. Local and regional development organizations and young academics from the University Association of South Ostrobothnia and university branch units took leadership to carry these ideas forward (Sotarauta, 2015). The strategic conclusion was that the actual problem was not a missing university of their own but rather the lack of competent people and skilled and plausible academic actors (Sotarauta, 2015). Strengthening the university activities in South Ostrobothnia called for innovative actions: developing a new kind of research culture and cooperation between universities, research institutes, enterprises and local organizations. In 2001, the first programme agreement on Epanet network was signed by five universities and local stakeholders, creating a unique partnership between regional authorities and national academic organizations.

The core of the Epanet network is composed of fixed-term research professors who form externally funded research groups. The aim of the network was to create attractive working conditions for talented scholars. One strategic choice was to focus on research and concentrate professorships on nationally new, interdisciplinary and applied fields relevant for both Finland and South Ostrobothnia (Sotarauta, 2015). The goal to establish 12 professorships exceeded in two years. Here, the strong regional cooperation culture was another key issue in the model because the main financiers were local companies, municipalities and public development organizations (see also Kolehmainen et al., 2016). Therefore, the Epanet model is based on several coevolutionary components between RHEI and its locational region.

Establishing UCS in 2004 was both a regional and national venture: it was national legislation initiated and supported by regional actors. University units located in South Ostrobothnia conducted mostly *progressive* strategies (*performance optimization* and *adaptive innovation)* when following Denyer's (2017) typology. The Epanet network, the heart of UCS, has been the major adaptive innovation. In addition, the aim was to secure the existence of the university activities in the region, that is, acting *defensively*. Currently, there are 24 research groups led by professors and research directors. More than 80 private partners and several public bodies are financing the Epanet network. Combining different, mainly regional resources is one of the ways to ensure its sustainability.

As a whole, UCS is a multidisciplinary scientific community of about 90 academics.

UCS and Regional Resilience

It can be argued that Epanet, UCS and Seinäjoki University of Applied Sciences have contributed to the recent development of South Ostrobothnia and Seinäjoki. The relationships between UCS and the local and regional governmental authorities have been close and their strategies well aligned. The key documents here are from the region's side: *South Ostrobothnia's Future Path (*2015*), Tuoreita eväitä Etelä-Pohjanmaalle* (2018) and *Smart and outstanding—South Ostrobothnia's strategy of smart specialization* (2014). Correspondingly, UCS, SUAS and University Association of South Ostrobothnia have their joint collaboration strategy (*Vuorovaikutuksesta vaikuttavuutta*, 2013).

Through these planning processes and documents, the selected HE activities of the region have been profiled even more clearly than before but still hold broad focus areas aligned with the region's industrial and business structure. These regional strategic choices have coevolved in close collaboration between the regional authorities and HEIs. When planning new Epanet professorships, future orientation and support for the renewal of the region are important criteria (University Consortium of Seinäjoki, 2019) from the viewpoint of adaptive resilience.

As analysed above, UCS and its surrounding region have coevolved also in terms of resilience. However, there are also some challenges. During the last years, there has been a debate on the regional demographics, labour market and human capital. UCS has made a strategic choice to focus on research and adult education because SUAS has taken care of the degree programmes. Still, the major problem is the decreasing share of 25–34-year-old people holding tertiary degrees (Regional Council of South Ostrobothnia 2017). This is partly a national problem, but South Ostrobothnia is especially lacking behind, resulting in labour shortages in some key fields of the regional economy. This is not a sudden shock or adversity but a result of many factors; hence, focus of UCS on research and development activities and adult education has been challenged.

In this situation, UCS has taken both *progressive* and *defensive* actions (Denyer, 2017) or *explorative* and *exploitative* actions (March, 1991). On the one hand, it has actively sought new opportunities to expand the educational possibilities, for example, new bachelor's and master's programmes and ways to organize internship periods in the region. These new developments may not be radical as such, but they clearly represent a new phase in the development path of UCS. On the other hand, UCS has held to its core strategy based mainly on research and development activities and strong engagement with the regional stakeholders. In terms of OR as conceptualized by Denyer (2017), it is a matter of *adaptive innovation* and *mindful action* but also *consistency* in terms of the core strategies and activities to maintain their identity.

UCS and the Evolving Higher Education System

The prevailing Universities Act gave the scientific universities increased autonomy in 2010 because they were not owned by the state anymore. However, universities are still heavily dependent on the Ministry of Education and Culture in terms of steering and funding. Finland was hit hard by the global economic crisis in 2008, and the last decade (2010–2020) has been the age of austerity for Finnish HEIs. It can also be labelled the time of 'structural development'. The Ministry of Education and Culture has encouraged HEIs to become internationally more competitive to ensure the quality and effectiveness of universities' research and teaching, to name few objectives (Välimaa et al., 2014, pp. 45–46). It can be argued that the government funding model has played a crucial role in this respect. Namely, the Finnish university funding model is one of the most performance-oriented models in the world (de Boer et al., 2015). On the other hand, Finnish universities are expected to develop both a knowledge-based economy and societal and civic conditions, for example, by reducing poverty, inequality and social exclusion (Kivistö et al., 2019).

Considerable changes have taken place in the Finnish HES over the last decade: some HEIs have merged, HEIs' internal structures have been regenerated and many universities and universities of applied sciences have reduced or discontinued their regional operations and units. The 'structural development' of the Finnish HES continues. The next significant change in the short or medium term might be the convergence of HE subsystems into a more integrated two-pillar model because there are already new kinds of 'university corporations' in which a scientific university owns a regional university of applied science (e.g. Tampere University).

UC have a fairly stable position in the Finnish HES, but they cannot take their position for granted because they represent the most decentralized part of the university system. Currently, the *core value* within the development of the Finnish HES is efficiency, not resilience (cf. Pinheiro & Young, 2017) albeit there are signs of more balanced ways of thinking. However, for many years, it has been more about streamlining the system than cherishing diversity. These ideas have been transferred from the central government and funding bodies to the HEIs themselves. This is natural because the HES is based on certain funding principles set by the central government, and HEIs adjust their activities to optimize funding.

Also, UCS units are constantly under pressure to prove their utility to their mother universities. Therefore, UCS units have made their connections to their mother universities more aligned with their main objectives. In this respect, the high quality of scientific outputs is a key issue. From the point of view of OR, this calls for *progressive-* and *consistency*-driven strategies: the practices of core academic work are developed to optimally utilize resources. However, UCS and other university consortia try to stay original, for example, by being more agile and regionally more engaged as the 'ordinary universities'. It is a matter of *diversity* and *flexibility*. In this way, they can also contribute to the resilience of the whole Finnish HES.

Discussion and Conclusion

Organizational Resilience of RHEIs

Estonian and Finnish RHEI schemes provide an interesting organizational model. University colleges and UC differ from traditional research universities: they are smaller, deal largely with applied studies and have proximate relations to local and regional authorities and business communities; still, they have quite directly subordinated to their mother universities. In addition, Finnish UC have internally diverse network structures. RHEIs are constantly under pressure to prove their relevance and quality to the ministerial and university superiors: the rules and standards have been set and are controlled from outside, even if RHEIs own their local and regional funding and other resources.

In both countries, the intensity and scope of *regional partnerships* depends mainly on local and regional expectations and opportunities because mother universities' interest depends largely on national incentives, steering mechanisms and policies. Local businesses form a specific stakeholder group as the collaborative partners for RHEIs. This is emphasized especially in the Estonian case, even if firms are very important funders and collaborative partners in the Finnish case as well. Support from the local and regional public organizations is also valuable. Especially in Finland, the regional public organizations are strongly committed to support and collaborate with the academic organizations in the region.

The Resilience of RHEIs is Rooted in Smallness

As Vossen (1998) pointed out, small organizations can be agile. The smallest RHEI in Estonia, Kuressaare, has made the best postcrisis progress. In the Estonian case, with a less advanced legislative framework and higher societal dynamism, leadership has played a very vital role in the performance of RHEIs. It has been a constant fight for survival. A small unit can be effective if there is a reasonable labour division: this small unit cannot rely on someone else and can work more intensively because they feel the pressure of the community. Proximity and local buzz also matter (Bathelt et al., 2004), allowing close collaboration and the fast transfer and interpretation of new ideas and knowledge.

Following Denyer's (2017) dimensions of OR, we identify that *progressiveness* and *flexibility* are the most important resiliency strategies for RHEIs. Estonian and Finnish RHEIs and their partner networks have existed for about 15 years, so they are still young institutions whose position in the HES is not completely solid, especially in Estonia, where the whole HES has been more volatile. Innovativeness is required to stay on par with or even ahead of traditional HEIs. However, both cases also show the importance of history: there were several previous higher educational bodies that paved the way for the current HEIs. Even though progressiveness and flexibility are the main characteristics of the OR of RHEIs, there are behaviours that are naturally defensive (e.g. counteracting budget cuts or other clearly negative decisions) or consistency driven (preserving strategic emphasis). It is also notable that both cases show an evolution closer to the traditional HE ideal of the research-teaching nexus (cf. Tight, 2016); the research activities have been strengthened in Kuressaare, and more students will be recruited in Seinäjoki.

RHEIs Being Resilient Between the Region and HES

RHEIs are located at the intersection between the region and the HES. In this position, it is possible to recognize the different components creating the conditions for resilience strategies. Next, our empirical observations about coevolutionary processes between RHEIs, regions and the HE system are summed up. Table 10.1 presents the key components of the relationship of a RHEI and the surrounding region and the RHEI and the entire HE system. Table 10.1 introduces how resilience may appear in these relationships in the fields of governance, resources, structure and diversity, agency and leadership and competence building. These categories are at a very general level and are applied from Martin and Sunley's (2015) determinants of regional resilience and are interpreted in the context of RHEIs.

In sum, to be resilient, to survive and thrive, RHEIs must search for balance between the expectations of their region and the HE system, including mother universities. In this respect, RHEIs are organizations that are constantly facing pressures to adapt their operations. These expectations can sometimes be contradictory to each other, like highly ranked scientific research and applied research in cooperation with local business. In their processes of coevolution, RHEIs also meet a tension between progressiveness/defensiveness and flexibility/consistency. On the one hand, they are expected to provide novelty, but on the other hand, they must secure the continuation of existing functions and support regional industrial structures. The resilience of young RHEIs has been mostly based on progressive and flexible strategies because they have been small and agile. Because they are stabilizing and institutionalizing, they also have more accomplishments to defend.

Table 10.1 The coevolutionary components shaping the resilience of the RHEI, region and HES

Dimensions of coevolution	*Resilient coevolution between RHEI and region*	*Resilient coevolution between RHEI and HES*
Governance	Trusty and reciprocal relationships between the RHEI and the regional public institutions are important for both parties. If the relationship is overly dependent (see, e.g. Kurikka et al., 2018), there is danger of a lock-in situation (Martin & Sunley, 2006) where renewal slows down or ceases	Very hierarchical and managerialist governance reduces the flexibility of RHEIs and the whole HES. More networked and dialogical governance may vary from extreme efficiency to extreme adaptability or robustness
Resources	Municipalities and companies can provide funding for the RHEI alongside university or state funding. RHEIs and their mother universities have competences to attract national and international research funding to the region	The HES is based on certain funding principles and schemes set by the central government (see, e.g. de Boer et al., 2015). It is quite typical that different HEIs will adjust their activities to maximize their funding. Presumably, this reduces the diversity and resilience of the whole HES. RHEIs need to align their activities with the national funding principles and schemes
Competence building	Building competences and increasing human capital is one of the key tasks of HEIs (see, e.g. Vaessen & Velde, 2003). If the educational profile of RHEIs is compatible with the labour needs of the region, this supports regional competence building. In addition, RHEIs, to some extent, depend on the region's labour market because they are specialized employers themselves	Human capital and competences are at the core of the success and resilience of RHEIs and the HES. To successfully conduct key functions, education and research, competences must be built persistently

(continued)

Table 10.1 (continued)

Dimensions of coevolution	*Resilient coevolution between RHEI and region*	*Resilient coevolution between RHEI and HES*
Structure and diversity	The structure and specialization of the regional industry forms the basis for economic development and resilience (see, e.g. Martin et al., 2016). Matching of the industrial structure of the region with the competences of the RHEI benefits them both. The profile of the RHEI can also contribute to the renewal of the region's industrial and business structure to prevent lock-in situations (see, e.g. Benneworth & Hospers, 2008)	From the perspective of system resilience, diversity is key because it helps the system adapt to a changing and complex environment (Pinheiro & Young, 2017). However, there is a natural dilemma between diversity and the efficient use of resources. These notions hold true both for the whole HES and individual RHEIs; indeed, the smaller institutions have only limited possibilities to be diverse
Agency and leadership	Regional actors' attitudes towards RHEIs and their capabilities to lobby for common causes will support making decisions and mobilizing resources. RHEIs can provide insightful people who can generate institutional change and provide their global knowledge networks (see, e.g. Sotarauta, 2015)	RHEIs have quite limited possibilities to affect the whole HES system. Nonetheless, it is a matter of agency and leadership that can reach out from the regional context (cf. Benneworth et al., 2017; Cai & Liu, 2020). Representatives of RHEIs can contribute to the discussion on the regional engagement of universities

References

Arbo, P., & Benneworh, P. (2007). *Understanding the regional contribution of higher education institutions: a literature review*. OECD.

Bathelt, H., Malmberg, A., & Maskell, P. (2004). Clusters and knowledge: Local buzz, global pipelines and the process of knowledge creation. *Progress in Human Geography, 28*(1), 31–56.

Benneworth, P., & Hospers, G. (2008). The role of a university in regional renewal: The case of Newcastle. *Northern Economic Review, 38*, 81–101.

Benneworth, P., & Nieth, L. (2018). Universities and regional development in peripheral regions. In P. Benneworth (Ed.), *Universities and regional economic development* (pp. 1–12). Routledge.

Benneworth, P., Pinheiro, R., & Karlsen, J. (2017). Strategic agency and institutional change: Investigating the role of universities in regional innovation systems (RISs). *Regional Studies, 51*(2), 235–248.

Bristow, G., & Healy, A. (2014). Regional resilience: An agency perspective. *Regional Studies, 48*(5), 923–935.

de Boer, H., Jongbloed, B., Benneworth, P., Cremonini, L., Kolster, R., Kottmann, A., & Vossensteyn, H. (2015). *Performance-based funding and performance agreements in fourteen higher education systems*. Center for Higher Education Policy Studies, University of Twente.

Burnard, K., & Bhamra, R. (2011). Organisational resilience: Development of a conceptual framework for organisational responses. *International Journal of Production Research, 49*(18), 5581–5599.

Cai, Y., & Liu, C. (2020). The role of university as institutional entrepreneur in regional innovation system: Towards an analytical framework. In A. Daniel, A. Teixeira, & M. Preto (Eds.), *Examining the role of entrepreneurial universities in regional development* (pp. 133–155). IGI Global.

Charles, D. (2016). The rural university campus and support for rural innovation. *Science and Public Policy, 43*(6), 763–773.

Clark, B. R. (1983). *The higher education system. Academic organization in cross-national perspective*. University of California Press.

Clark, B. R. (1998). *Creating entrepreneurial universities: Organizational pathways of transformation*. Elsevier Science Ltd.

Denyer, D. (2017). *Organizational resilience. A summary of academic evidence, business insights and new thinking*. British Standards Institution and Cranfield University. https://www.cranfield.ac.uk/~/media/images-for-new-website/som-media-room/images/organisational-report-david-denyer.ashx. Accessed 13 Dec 2019.

DiMaggio, P. (1988). Interest and agency in institutional theory. In L. Zucker (Ed.), *Institutional patterns and culture* (pp. 3–22). Ballinger.

Grillitsch, M., & Asheim, B. (2018). Place-based innovation policy for industrial diversification in regions. *European Planning Studies, 26*(8), 1638–1662.

Gunasekara, C. (2006). Reframing the role of universities in the development of regional innovation systems. *The Journal of Technology Transfer, 31*(1), 101–113.

Hedin, S. (Ed.) (2009). *Higher education institutions as drivers of regional development in the Nordic countries*. Nordregio. https://archive.nordregio.se/Global/Publications/Publications%202009/WP2009_3.pdf. Accessed 13 Dec 2019.

Isaksen, A. (2015). Industrial development in thin regions: Trapped in path extension? *Journal of Economic Geography, 15*(3), 585–600.

Jumppanen, A., & Riukulehto, S. (2015). *Puskasta framille: Viisikymmentä vuotta tekniikan koulutusta Seinäjoella. Seinäjoen ammattikorkeakoulun julkaisusarja B. Raportteja ja selvityksiä 112.* Seinäjoen ammattikorkeakoulu.

Karlsen, J., Isaksen, A., & Spilling, O. R. (2011). The challenge of constructing regional advantages in peripheral areas: The case of marine biotechnology in Tromsø, Norway. *Entrepreneurship and Regional Development, 23*(3–4), 235–257.

Keerberg, A. (2018). Higher education institutions at the periphery of the periphery: Creating sustainable economic development in Estonia. In P. Benneworth (Ed.), *Universities and regional economic development* (pp. 141–158). Routledge.

Kivistö, J., Pekkola, E., Nordstrand Berg, L., FossHansen, H., Geschwind, L., & Lyytinen, A. (2019). Performance in higher education institutions and its variations in Nordic policy. In R. Pinheiro, L. Geschwind, H. Foss Hansen, & K. Pulkkinen (Eds.), *Reforms, organizational change and performance in higher education: A comparative account from the Nordic countries* (pp. 37–62). Palgrave MacMillan.

Kolehmainen, J., & Alarinta, J. (2009). University Consortium of Seinäjoki, Finland: Bringing South Ostrobothnia to the knowledge economy. *Regions Magazine, 273*(1), 17–19.

Kolehmainen, J., Irvine, J., Stewart, L., Karacsonyi, Z., Szabó, T., Alarinta, J., & Norberg, A. (2016). Quadruple helix, innovation and the knowledge-based development: Lessons from remote, rural and less-favoured regions. *Journal of the Knowledge Economy, 7*(1), 23–42.

Kurikka, H., Kolehmainen, J., & Sotarauta, M. (2018). Constructing regional resilience in a knowledge economy crisis: The case of the Nokia-led ICT industry in Tampere. In Benneworth, P. (Ed.), *Universities and regional economic development* (pp. 163–179). Routledge.

Lewin, A. Y., & Volberda, H. W. (1999). Prolegomena on coevolution: A framework for research on strategy and new organizational forms. *Organization Science, 10*(5), 519–534.

March, J. G. (1991). Exploration and exploitation in organizational learning. *Organization Science, 2*(1), 71–87.

Martin, R. (2012). Regional economic resilience, hysteresis and recessionary shocks. *Journal of Economic Geography, 12*(1), 1–32.

Martin, R., & Sunley, P. (2006). Path dependence and regional economic evolution. *Journal of Economic Geography, 6*(4), 395–437.

Martin, R., & Sunley, P. (2015). On the notion of regional economic resilience: Conceptualization and explanation. *Journal of Economic Geography, 15*(1), 1–42.

Martin, R., Sunley, P., Gardiner, B., & Tyler, P. (2016). How regions react to recessions: Resilience and the role of economic structure. *Regional Studies, 50*(4), 561–585.

Moran, K. A. (2016). Organizational resilience: Sustained institutional effectiveness among smaller, private, non-profit US higher education institutions experiencing organizational decline. *Work, 54*(2), 267–281. https://doi.org/10.3233/WOR-162299

OECD. (2007). *Higher education and regions. Globally competitive, locally engaged*. OECD.

OECD. (2019). *Benchmarking higher education system performance*. OECD.

Olsen, J.P. (2007). The institutional dynamics of the European university. In P. Maassen & J.P. Olsen (Eds.). *University dynamics and European integration* (pp. 25–54). Springer.

Pike, A., Dawley, S., & Tomaney, J. (2010) Resilience adaptation and adaptability. *Cambridge Journal of Regions Economy and Society, 3*(1), 59–70.

Pinheiro, R., & Young, M. (2017). The university as an adaptive resilient organization: A complex systems perspective. In Huisman, J. & Tight, M. (Eds.), *Theory and method in higher education research* (Vol. 3, pp. 119–136). Emerald.

Postiglione, G. A. (2011). Global recession and higher education in eastern Asia: China, Mongolia and Vietnam. *Higher Education, 62*(6), 789–814.

Raagmaa, G., & Keerberg, A. (2017). Regional higher education institutions in regional leadership and development. *Regional Studies, 51*(2), 260–272.

Regional Council of South Ostrobothnia (2017). Innovaatiotoiminnan tilannekuva 2017. (Situation Picture of Regional Innovation Activities 2017). https://www.epliitto.fi/images/IKEP%20tilannekuva%2021%2012%202017.pdf. Accessed 13 Dec 2019.

Reidolf, M., Keerberg, A., & Hartikainen, A. (2011). Universities role in the region: The case of Saaremaa Small Craft Competence Centre. In G. Prause & U. Venesaar (Eds.), *University-business cooperation*. Berliner Wissenschafts-Verlag.

Rothblatt, S., & Wittrock, B. (1993). *The European and American university since 1800: Historical and sociological essays*. Cambridge University Press.

Saare Development Centre. (2018). *Saare maakonna ettevõtluse ja ettevõtluskeskkonna kaardistamine ning ülevaade* (Mapping and overview of Saare County entrepreneurship and business environment). https://www.sasak.ee/application/files/6515/6258/9125/2019_06_03_Saare_maakonna_ettevotluse_ja_ettevotluskeskkonna_kaardistamine_ja_ulevaade_.pdf. Accessed 19 Dec 2019.

Sääsk, H. (2018). Eesti laevaehitusettevõtted 2017 (Estonian Shipbuilding Companies 2017). https://www.scc.ee/ee/wp-content/uploads/2019/01/

Eesti-laevaehitusettev%C3%B5tted-2017.-TalTech-V%C3%A4ikelaevaehituse-kompetentsikeskuse-uuring.pdf. Accessed 13 Dec 2019.

Selznick, P. (1984). *Leadership in administration: A sociological interpretation.* University of California Press.

Sotarauta, M. (2014). Territorial knowledge leadership in policy networks: A peripheral region of South Ostrobothnia, Finland as a case in point. In R. Rutten, P. Benneworth, D. Irawati, & F. Boekema (Eds.), *The social dynamics of innovation networks* (pp. 42–59). Routledge.

Smart and outstanding – South Ostrobothnia's strategy of smart specialisation (2014). Regional Council of South Ostrobothnia. Seinäjoki. Accessed 24 Feb 2020.

Sørensen, M. P., Bloch, C., & Young, M. (2016). Excellence in the knowledge-based economy: From scientific to research excellence. *European Journal of Higher Education, 6*(3), 217–236.

Sotarauta, M. (2015). *Leadership and the city. Power, strategy and networks in the making of knowledge cities.* Routledge.

Sotarauta, M., & Kautonen, M. (2007). Co-evolution of the Finnish national and local innovation and science arenas: Towards a dynamic understanding of multi-level governance. *Regional Studies, 41*(8), 1085–1098.

Sotarauta, M., & Srinivas, S. (2006). Co-evolutionary policy processes: Understanding innovative economies and future resilience. *Futures, 38*(3), 312–336.

South Ostrobothnia's Future Path (Regional Development Plan 2040 & Regional Programme 2014–2017) (2015). Regional Council of South Ostrobothnia.

Stensaker, B., & Benner, M. (2013). Doomed to be entrepreneurial: Institutional transformation or institutional lock-ins of 'new' universities? *Minerva, 51*(4), 399–416.

Stensaker, B., Välimaa, J., & Sarrico, C. (2012). *Managing reform in universities: The dynamics of culture, identity and organisational change.* Palgrave Macmillan.

Tapper, T., & Palfreyman, D. (2011). *Oxford, the collegiate university: Conflict, consensus and continuity.* Springer.

Tödtling, F., & Trippl, M. (2005). One size fits all? Towards a differentiated regional innovation policy approach. *Research Policy, 34*(8), 1203–1219.

Trippl, M., Asheim, B., & Miörner, J. (2016). Identification of regions with less-developed research and innovation systems. In Parrilli, M. D, Fitjar, R. D. & Rodríguez-Pose, A. (Eds.), *Innovation drivers and regional innovation strategies* (pp. 39–60). Routledge.

Tight, M. (2016). Examining the research/teaching nexus. *European Journal of Higher Education, 6*(4), 293–311.

TIPS. (2015). The Research and Innovation Policy Monitoring Programme. http://www.tips.ut.ee/index.php?module=32&op=1&id=3683. Accessed 13 Dec 2019.

Tuoreita eväitä Etelä-Pohjanmaalle. Maakuntaohjelma 2018–2021. (Regional Plan 2018–2021) (2018). Etelä-Pohjanmaan liitto. Regional Council of South Ostrobothnia.

University Consortium of Seinäjoki. (2019). Seinäjoen yliopistokeskuksen toimintakertomus 2018 (Annual report of University Consortium of Seinäjoki 2018). https://www.ucs.fi/wp-content/uploads/UCS_toimintakertomus_2018_web.pdf. Accessed 13 Dec 2019.

Välimaa, J., Aittola, H., & Ursin, J. (2014). University mergers in Finland: Mediating global competition. *New Directions for Higher Education, 2014*(168), 41–53.

Vaessen, P.M.M., & van der Velde, M. (2003). University knowledge transfer through social and professional embeddedness: A case study. In R. Rutten, F. Boekema, & E. Kuijpers (Eds.), *Economic geography of higher education: knowledge infrastructure and learning regions* (pp. 87–109). Routledge.

Vossen, R. W. (1998). Relative strengths and weaknesses of small firms in innovation. *International Small Business Journal, 16*(3), 88–94.

Vukasovic, M., Maassen, P., Nerland, M., Pinheiro, R., Stensaker, B., & Vabø, A. (2012). *Effects of higher education reforms: Change dynamics*. Sense Publishers.

Vuorovaikutuksesta vaikuttavuutta. Etelä-Pohjanmaan korkeakoulustrategia 2020 (The Regional HEI strategy of South Ostrobothnia). (2013). Seinäjoki University of Applied Sciences, University Association of South Ostrobothnia, University Consortium of Seinäjoki.

Ülikoolide (2008). Ülikoolide ühiste kavatsuste leping regionaalsete kompetentsikeskuste loomise kohta. (The Agreement of Common Intent of Universities on the Establishment of Regional Competence Centres). Memorandum, Rectors' Conference, Tallinn, 24.11.2008.

Young, M., & Pinheiro, R. (2022). *The post-entrepreneurial University: The case for Resilience in Higher Education. In Pinheiro, R., Frigotto, L., & Young, M. (Ed.), Towards resilient organizations and societies: A cross-sectoral and multi-disciplinary perspective (pp. 179-200). Palgrave.*

CHAPTER 11

Agency, Institutions and Regional Resilience: An Approach from the Basque Region

Edurne Magro, Elvira Uyarra, and Jesus M. Valdaliso

Introduction

Resilience is a phenomenon that has been widely studied in the context of organizations and, in this field, it is normally understood as the capacity to return to a previous 'status quo' after a disturbance. However, in the last decade resilience has been applied to regions as a means of understanding economic development.

E. Magro (✉)
Orkestra-Basque Institute of Competitiveness and Deusto Business School, University of Deusto, San Sebastián, Spain
e-mail: edurne.magro@orkestra.deusto.es

E. Uyarra
Alliance Manchester Business School, University of Manchester, Manchester, UK
e-mail: Elvira.Uyarra@manchester.ac.uk

J. M. Valdaliso
The University of the Basque Country, Bilbao, Spain
e-mail: jesusm.valdaliso@ehu.eus

R. Pinheiro et al. (eds.), *Towards Resilient Organizations and Societies*, Public Sector Organizations,
https://doi.org/10.1007/978-3-030-82072-5_11

In the evolutionary economic geography literature, unlike the meaning of the concept in engineering, resilience does not imply a return to a previous equilibrium point or regional path but the ability of a system or a territory to resist, adapt, respond, recover and/or renew from a shock (Martin, 2012; Evans & Karecha, 2014). Therefore, adaptation and evolution underline the concept of resilience. While adaptation could be seen as a process of change in regions due to unexpected shocks, resilience is the ability of those territories to deal with these changes on a continuous basis (Evenhuis, 2017a). As a consequence, in order to observe and analyse regional resilience it is necessary to adopt a historical perspective as this ability should be seen in multiple episodes (Evenhuis, 2017a).

While the importance of institutions, policies and agency for shaping regional resilience has been acknowledged in recent literature (Boschma, 2015; Bristow & Healy, 2014), this relationship remains underexplored, especially when adopting a historical perspective (Henning, 2019). This is mainly due to resilience being a complex and multifaceted concept, that goes beyond the idea of adaptation. Thus, Boschma (2015) distinguishes between adaptation and adaptability processes, the former related to maintaining regional paths and the latter referred to the creation of new regional growth paths. This distinction is important in order to understand regional resilience as each process relates to very different types of policy rationales and attitudes of the actors involved, namely reactivity and proactivity (Bristow & Healy, 2014).

The notion of shock or disturbance is also another important aspect to understand the concept of resilience, as it can be referred either to macroeconomic fluctuations such as economic recessions or structural changes in the economy (such as deindustrialization). The evolutionary concept of resilience is more adequate to understand how regions respond to the latter ones but also useful for understanding the mechanisms of change delivered to cope with economic crises (Evenhuis, 2017a). Therefore, this chapter will deepen into the different mechanisms of change for a regional economy to develop resilience through exploring the role of policy and agency in the two process of change: adaptation and adaptability. To do so, the chapter adopts a historical perspective to examine how the Basque Country, an old industrial region, has been able to resist, recover and renew itself after different shocks (economic and financial crises) and cope with structural changes in the last forty years.

The chapter first explores the link between resilience and regional policy, with a strong focus on industrial and innovation policies and the relevance of history for understanding regional development. Second, the chapter presents different types of agency that shape institutions and condition resilience. All these concepts will be explored in depth in a regional case that discusses how policy paths relate to different types of regional resilience and disentangle the role of agency in the processes of change.

Regional Resilience and the Role of Policies

In evolutionary economic geography, regional resilience refers to the ability of a region to deal with changes on a continuous basis (Evenhuis, 2017a). Resilience is therefore seen as a dynamic, path-dependent process. This implies that previous regional growth paths condition future resistance to, and recovery from, a shock as well as shape future available paths (Boschma, 2015; Martin, 2012; Martin & Sunley, 2015; Martin et al., 2016; Simmie & Martin, 2010; Webber et al., 2018). The consideration of resilience as a capacity to deal with change needs to be investigated by adopting a historical perspective and by studying the multiple sequential adaptation episodes of a region to shocks, either market, competitive or environmental (Boschma, 2015; Evenhuis, 2017a; Henning, 2019).

Regional economic resilience is a complex and multi-faceted phenomenon. Martin (2010, 2012) distinguishes four dimensions of resilience: resistance (ability to resist a shock), recovery (speed and type of recovery after the shock), renewal (resumption of the pre-shock growth path) and reorientation (towards a new growth path). Recovery can be linked to the classic perspective of organizational resilience (Boinand & Van Eeten, 2014) whereas reorientation is a concept which implicitly requires exploration. As to the factors that explain the resilience of regions, the literature has highlighted the following: the competitiveness and innovative propensity of regional firms, the regional economic structure and knowledge base, knowledge networks, labour market conditions, financial system and institutions such as policy measures, quality of government, governance and social capital (Boschma, 2015; Cortinovis et al., 2017; Crescenzi et al., 2016; Martin, 2012; Martin & Sunley, 2015).

While institutional factors are acknowledged as important in explaining regional resilience, they are still relatively underexplored in the literature. Indeed, Martin et al. (2016) have found a great variation across regions in their resilience towards economic crises in Britain, something that they attribute to regional differences in economic structure and institutions. Although some authors argue that regional policies are not as important as productive specialization (Cuadrado & Maroto, 2016; Eraydin, 2016), there is, in general, a broad agreement around the relative importance of institutions (among which policy measures can be highlighted) and agency in the resilience of regions.

Boschma (2015) makes a distinction between adaptation and adaptability processes underlying resilience, referring to situations where regions maintain previous economic specialization or shift towards new paths respectively. These concepts are not far from the seminal concepts of exploitation and exploration (March, 1991), or from those proposed by the literature of organizational resilience, which distinguishes two types of responses, anticipatory (static) and strategic (dynamic). The former aims at reducing the shock impact, the latter at maximizing recovery and renewal (Annarelli & Nonino, 2016; Billington et al., 2017). The dichotomy proposed by Boschma can be linked to policy responses as it confronts two very different policy rationales and attitudes of the agents involved, namely reactivity and proactivity (Bristow & Healy, 2014). Adaptation and adaptability are also associated to the different types of resilience needed in a region depending on the nature of the shock. Emergencies and macroeconomic fluctuations or recessions might require adaptation but structural changes of the regional economy such as changes in the industrial configuration need adaptability (Evenhuis, 2017a). Nevertheless, these shocks are never isolated as for example economic and financial recessions necessarily affect industrial configurations and regional competitiveness. Therefore, adaptation and adaptability are not necessarily opposed, they can be complementary.

Adaptation and adaptability can be linked to different public policy interventions. A first and broad distinction has been made between reactive policy measures with the aim of supporting the adaptation and resistance to a certain shock, and proactive policy measures, aimed at transforming the existent economy and at creating new growth paths (e.g., measures to encourage adaptability) (Kakderi & Tasopoulou, 2017). Policies that promote social and institutional learning, connectivity and flexibility make regional adaptation to a crisis easier. On the other hand, policies that foster diversity and related variety in the regional economy do not only help to reduce the risk of lock-in but also open up new development paths for the region. It has also been accepted that a governance system with polycentric and multi-layered institutions, which promote public participation and collaboration between the different agents, increases regional resilience (Kakderi & Tasopoulou, 2017). In line with Boschma (2015), Fratesi and Rodríguez-Pose (2016) argue that some factors, such as the workforce skills level or public policies, may provoke short-term adaptation and medium-term adaptability.

However, the literature on regional resilience still lacks a typology of policy measures and instruments. Among the reactive policy measures to adapt and resist, we could find macroeconomic policies (currency, monetary, labour costs) and restructuring policies (aids and subsidies to firms, early retirement schemes...). These policies are usually adopted as a (generally, quick) reaction towards a previous crisis or shock, and are expected to have a short-term effect on the whole regional economy, but they are not very effective on promoting a sustained regional economic development (Landabaso, 2012).

Among the proactive policy measures, we might point to horizontal framework policies (infrastructures, education, energy, internationalization), and to STI and cluster policies (Landabaso, 2012; Nauwelaers & Wijtnes, 2008; Uyarra & Ramlogan, 2012) that attempt to cope with some perceived structural problems or failures in the regional economy or to encourage processes of transformation, such as smart specialization strategies (Foray et al., 2012). In both cases, their expected effects will be observed in the mid to long-term.

We could say that 'reactive policies' (ex-post) attempt to face the *urgent and unexpected* needs of the region, whereas 'proactive policies' (ex-ante) attempt to address some changes seen as *necessary, expected or anticipated*. Regarding the effects of proactive policy measures on the adaptation and/or adaptability of the region, they would depend on the vertical priorities established. They can either reinforce the current economic specialization of the region, or promote an economic diversification, or a combination of both.

Crises and shocks may force the governments to allocate the existing resources towards urgent needs, e.g., the protection of certain groups from their negative consequences (unemployment, firms' closures...); but they can also trigger changes, in the sense that an adverse scenario may facilitate collaboration between agents towards a shared vision and a common goal. Indeed, some broad agendas and strategies for economic development were born in critical junctures of crisis and/or shocks (Valdaliso & Wilson, 2015) as crisis may be windows of opportunity

(Kingdon, 1984; Croenewegen & van der Steen, 2007) or opportunity spaces (Grillitsch & Sotarauta, 2018) for policy change.

Sometimes, policy measures can be framed in broader agendas for action that allocate and distribute resources according to different priorities and to the relative political power of every agent (Campbell, 2010; Mahoney & Thelen, 2009). Agendas cannot be neutral, e.g., they tend to benefit some agents at the expenses of others (David, 2018). Agendas take usually the form of government programmes and are government-led, although its leadership depends on the regional institutional context such as the system's governance and/or the quality of government. Pugalis et al. (2017) indicate that economic strategies, and therefore, agendas themselves, may reflect different dimensions or understanding of resilience, namely resistance, recovery or reorientation, which are link to what the authors conceptualize as conservative, resistant and evolutionary resilience.

Regional Development and Path Dependence

Kakderi and Tasopoulou (2017, p. 1438) argue that resilience must be studied 'within the context of longer run processes of change and policy options' in the region, which are path-dependent. Since Grabher's (1993) seminal work, path dependence has been a concept increasingly employed to explain regional development, initially to account for lock-in situations and, more recently, to explain the different evolutionary scenarios of regions, e.g., why change goes in a particular direction (Henning et al., 2013; Martin, 2010; Martin & Sunley, 2006).

Historical institutionalism has devoted a great deal of attention to the role of path dependence and the mechanisms of continuity and change in social and political institutions and public policies (Campbell, 2010; Kay, 2006; Mahoney & Thelen, 2009; Streeck & Thelen, 2005). Politics is an activity subject to increasing returns and self-reinforcing effects, where the feedback effects of past policy choices shape and condition present and future policy developments (Kay, 2006; Pierson, 2004); and to vested interests of the agents involved, where policy change involves substantial technical, political and expectation costs (Gingrich, 2015; Kay, 2006). Policy measures are not simply short-term reactions to problems or crises. They are framed within shared mental maps, policy paradigms, agendas or discourses that have been previously adopted and maintained by policy communities, and are difficult to change (Baumgartner, 2013;

Kay, 2006). Finally, *agency* and *power* shape the policy process. In the last resort, any policy adopted is a choice made by a government. But this choice is usually the outcome of a complex process of competition, cooperation and negotiation among the key actors involved that may have different interests and objectives (Baumgartner, 2013; Kay, 2006; Mahoney & Thelen, 2009). Indeed, different mechanisms of institutional change can be highlighted from a bottom-up approach, in which actors can reinterpret existing institutional arrangements to a top-down approach in which arrangements are changed by powerful actors (i.e. governments, not only at regional level) (Evenhuis, 2017b). Institutional entrepreneurs, defined as coalitions of different actors (individual or collective) around a common goal (Bristow & Healy, 2014; David, 2018; Martin, 2012), might be able to change institutional arrangements, which is a more powerful source for resilience.

Isaksen (2015) distinguishes among three types of regional paths. *Path extension* is a term which is related to path dependence. It refers to the incremental upgrading of existing industry in a region by maintaining existing technologies, which means adopting an exploitation approach (adaptive processes) (March, 1991). By their side, path renewal and path creation are more related to regional resilience as defined by Boschma (2015) and denote exploration and adaptability processes although to different extent. *Path renewal* takes place when industries shift towards new but related industries and therefore it is a concept linked to related variety (Neffke et al., 2011), which highlights that it is more likely that regional diversification takes place in related activities than in totally new ones. This would be the case of *path creation*, which constitutes a regional shift towards industries totally new for the region or completely new and therefore it reflects an exploration process (March, 1991). This would imply not only the establishment of new firms or industries but also the generation of new knowledge organizations and institutions, including policy. This case is not contemplated in the literature of related variety. Path creation and entrepreneurship are therefore two interrelated concepts, but not only referring to the creation of new industries and firms, also to the creation of new policies and institutions. Indeed, Kakderi and Tasopoulou (2017) argue and demonstrate with a case study that policies that promote social and institutional learning, flexibility and connectivity facilitate new path development and resilience.

Agency, Institutional Entrepreneurship and Resilience

Agency has been acknowledged in the recent literature as one of the key factors shaping the conditions for regional resilience (Boschma, 2015; Bristow & Healy, 2014; Evenhuis, 2017a), including dedicated policies and institutional change. Policies are a form of institution in as much as they are rules for actors that 'can and need to be implemented and that are legitimate in that they will if necessary be enforced' (Streeck & Thelen, 2005, p. 12). In order to understand resilience in regional economies, it is necessary to go beyond a narrow focus on macroeconomic performance of the region and take into account its individuals, organizations, industries and/or clusters, networks and institutions involving multiple agents (firms, workers, associations, RTOs, government and other organizations) (Boschma, 2015; Bristow & Healy, 2014).

The importance of agency in regional resilience is part of a broader intellectual agenda inspired by the idea of institutional entrepreneurship (DiMaggio, 1988; Maguire et al., 2004) that has sought to understand how actors shape the emergence of new institutional arrangements. *Institutional work* is referred to in the literature as the purposive action of individuals and organizations aimed at creating, maintaining or disrupting existing institutions (Lawrence & Suddaby, 2006, p. 215). The literature on institutional work conceives agency as a distributed and temporary embedded process of social engagement, whereby actors both reproduce and transform an environments' structure through the exercise of purpose, imagination and judgement (Emirbayer & Mische, 1998).

Agency is distributed across a multiplicity of actors with different interpretive frameworks involved in different ways at different stages and embedded in networks and emerging pathways (Garud & Karnøe, 2001, 2003). Actors are embedded in social structures and thus shaped by existing institutions, yet able to purposely deviate from them (Garud et al., 2010). It is also inter-temporal because it not only requires the 'capacity to imagine alternative possibilities', but also the ability 'to contextualize past habits and future projects within the contingencies of the moment' if existing institutions are to be transformed (Emirbayer & Mische, 1998, p. 963). Related to this temporal dimension, three different elements of agency have been identified: *iteration*, *practical-evaluation* and *projectivity* (Battilana & D'aunno, 2009; Emirbayer & Mische, 1998). The first element (*interaction*) is oriented towards the past, and describes the 'selective reactivation by actors of past patterns of thought and action' (Battilana & D'aunno, 2009, p. 46). The second *(practical-evaluative)* is the capacity of actors to make practical and normative judgements between alternative possible trajectories of action, in response to emerging demands, dilemmas and ambiguities of presently evolving situations. The third and final element (*projective*) involves an imaginative engagement with the future.

Embedded actors shape and configure new processes and mobilize the past to accomplish their objectives and to create new options for the future (Garud & Karnøe, 2001). They connect the past with the future in the form of visions or expectations, in order to attract interest, mobilize resources, build political networks, develop technical capabilities and legitimize new practices (Croenewegen & van der Steen, 2007; Steen, 2016; Uyarra et al., 2020). The term bricolage has been used to describe social actors purposefully bringing together resources and using what is at hand, and eventually creating the conditions for change and transformation (Campbell, 2010).

Agency, leadership and bricolage are present in regional development literature in the form of accounts of 'regional experimentalism' and synthesized in what Grillitsch and Sotarauta (2020) refer to the trinity of change agency driving regional industrial path development, namely innovative entrepreneurship, institutional entrepreneurship and place leadership. Innovative (Schumpeterian) entrepreneurs are those seeking to mindfully deviate from existing paths and create new paths. Institutional entrepreneurs seek to challenge existing norms, raise legitimacy and institutionalize alternative practices. Place-based leadership, or civic-leadership (Brooks, 2017), involves coordinating efforts and resources to enable new regional development opportunities.

Attention has been given for instance to the role of place-based leadership or place-renewing leadership in supporting resilience of places. Following Bristow and Healy (2014), it is a sort of collective agency that eventually might produce an agenda for action to anticipate and cope with external shocks and unanticipated events. Bailey et al. (2010, p. 462) define 'place-renewing leadership' as 'a form of public–private strategic leadership that empowers institutional or social forms of governance to absorb and adjust (pro-actively and re-actively) to path breaking economic change'. Bailey & Berkeley (2014) examined the role of the West Midlands Regional Taskforce (WMRT) in contributing to the resilience of the West Midlands region in the UK, severely affected by the

2008–2009 economic crisis. They argued that the WMRT played a key role in supporting two dimensions of resilience, in terms of recovery (e.g. by helping maintain key supply chain capacity in place during the crisis) and renewal (helping strategic firms upgrade into higher value activities and diversify into related sectors). Tomlinson and Branston (2014) analysed how the North Staffordshire ceramics industrial district was able to reverse a phase of 'long decline' through purposive adaptation and joint action by local actors, thus arguing that 'there is nothing inevitable about the trajectory of old industrial districts' (p. 502). Brooks (2017) similarly analysed the civic leadership exerted by the Local Enterprise Partnership of the Sheffield city region.

Agency, Institutions and Resilience in the Basque Country

In order to explore the relationship between agency, institutions and regional resilience we employ a case study, with a longitudinal—e.g., historical- and holistic perspective, which fits well with the context-, place- and path-dependent nature of both resilience and the policy process (David, 2018; Flanagan & Uyarra, 2016; Kakderi & Tasopoulou, 2017; Kay, 2006; Navarro et al., 2014; Witt, 2003). Our analysis is based on a broad array of qualitative information: official policy programmes and agendas, reports, academic literature and interviews with the agents involved in the policy process conducted within different research projects developed from 2008 onwards.

The Basque Country is an old industrial region that has experienced a successful economic transformation over the last 30 years, driven by a highly interventionist regional government applying sustained industrial policies aimed at promoting science, technology and innovation, with a strong focus on industry. It is one of the most autonomous regions of both Spain and the EU with competences and self-government in several fields, including tax collection (Morgan, 2016; Navarro et al., 2014; OECD, 2011; Valdaliso, 2015). It belongs to the group of technological advanced regions in the EU, with a strong weight of the manufacturing industry: in 2016 industry accounted for 26.3% of its GDP and 20.1% of employment, percentages much higher than both the Spanish and European average. Its strong industrial base helps explaining another two characteristics: its high R&D intensity and strong export orientation.

This story of transformation goes hand in hand with an increasing resilience of the Basque economy towards the different economic crises the region has gone through, from the late 1970s until today (Birch et al., 2010; Cueto et al., 2017, pp. 71–73; Cuadrado & Maroto, 2016), and can be measured indirectly by its sustained process of catching up and convergence with the EU-15, in GDP per capita terms (see Fig. 11.1). At the sector- and micro-level, Basque firms, clusters and industries have shown, too, a higher resilience than those of other Spanish regions in the last economic crisis (Cruz-Castro et al., 2018; Elola et al., 2013; González-Bravo et al., 2018; Holl & Rama, 2016; Valdaliso et al., 2016; Valdaliso, 2020). Finally, the Basque Country scores relatively high in the quality of government index among European regions (Charron & Lapuente, 2018) and seems to have a good level of social capital (Etxabe & Valdaliso, 2016), two factors that increase regional resilience (Cortinovis et al., 2017).

Following previous works on this issue (Kakderi & Tasopoulou, 2017), our aim is to examine the policy responses given to the main economic crises and structural changes the region has gone through over the last

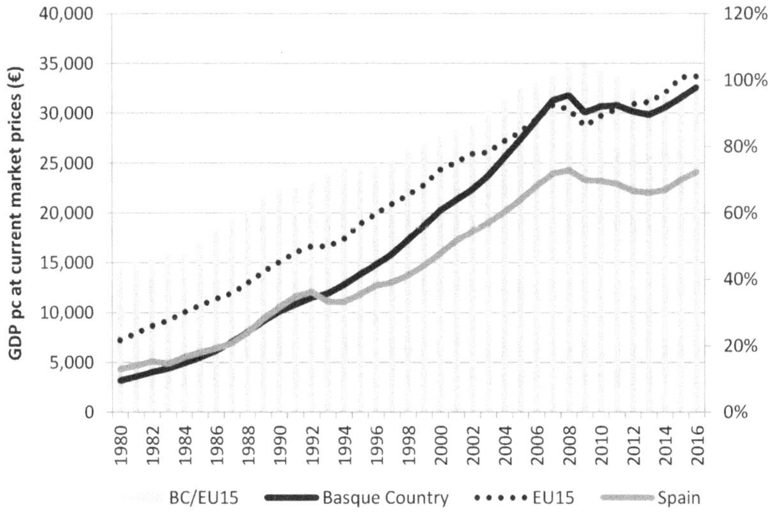

Fig. 11.1 GDP per capita in the Basque Country, Spain and the EU-15, 1980–2016 (*Source* Authors' elaboration from EUSTAT and EUROSTAT)

40 years, the key agents involved and their impact on the subsequent regional growth path. We have considered all types of public policies, from different levels and domains, although only the most important do appear in the Table 11.1. With regard to policy measures, we have made a distinction between short-term reactive policy measures (aimed at resisting and adapting to the crisis) and mid- long-term proactive policy measures (aimed at promoting and/or coping with structural change). The first type would exert an effect on that crisis, whereas the second type could have longer lasting effects on the regional economic resilience that would be manifest, for instance, in the next economic crisis.

However, public policies are not only reactions to external shocks, but they are also embedded in policy processes and dynamics subjected to path dependence, agency and power (Mahoney & Thelen, 2009; Pierson, 2004). In this way, the menu of policies available towards a new crisis is affected not only by the existing policy paradigm in the region, but also by its economic structure and its degree of resilience. Putting it another way, we analyse three pictures (policy responses towards three different economic crises) framed within a single movie (the policy process in the Basque region over the last 40 years).

As important as the policy responses in our chapter are, the key agents involved in the policy process and their behaviour are the primary unit of analysis. The main agents in our case study are the regional government, a few institutional entrepreneurs, and some RTOs (Regional Technology Organizations) and firms. Regarding their behaviour, we follow the typology of Bristow and Healy (2014): they may anticipate, react or transform. We have also attempted to describe the coordination mechanisms of this policy community: networks, coalitions, leaders and leadership.

It should be noticed, nevertheless, that there are other factors that may have an impact on the regional growth path not considered here, such as the evolution of global demand. However, this is a kind of exogenous, taken for granted, variable that affects all the regions within a given economic area with similar levels of openness.

According to the evolution of GDP and unemployment, we identify three major economic crises that can also be observed in other European regions (Martin, 2012): that of 1976–1983, the 1992–1994 years, and the last economic recession of 2008–2015 (see Fig. 11.2). The region has also had to cope with three structural changes: (i) the deindustrialization process that started with the first economic crisis, although only

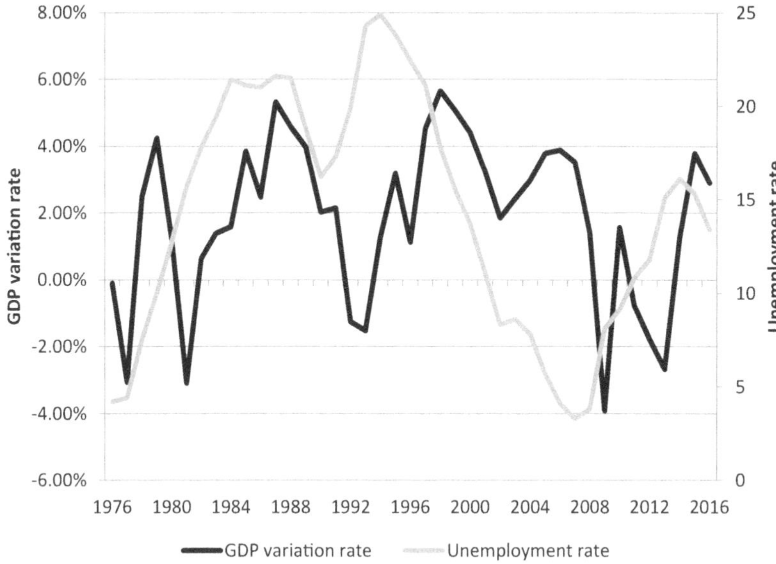

Fig. 11.2 GDP variation and unemployment rates in the Basque Country, 1976–2016 (*Source* Authors' own elaboration from EUSTAT and Caja Laboral Popular [1987] for unemployment, and from De la Fuente [2017] for GDP)

during the last one governments at the different levels—from the European Commission to regional governments—have become fully aware of its implications for the entire economy; (ii) the transition from a closed to an open economy during the 1980s; and (iii) the transition from a factor-driven to a knowledge-driven economy, during the 1980s and 1990s.

Table 11.1 summarizes the history of economic crises, structural changes and policy responses in the Basque Country over the last 40 years. We briefly indicate in the second column their main consequences for the region. The third column presents the policy responses during the crisis and/or in the following years and, if they existed, the government agendas to cope with them. Column fourth identifies the most important agents behind those policies in every crisis; column fifth, the governance mechanism and the dominant behaviour of the key agents; and column sixth, the perceived impact of those policies on the region's subsequent growth and policy paths.

Table 11.1 Economic crises, structural changes and policy responses in the Basque Country, 1976–2016

Crisis (and undergoing structural changes)	*Consequences*	*Policy responses and agendas*	*Key agents*	*Governance, behavior and agency*	*Impact on growth and policy path*
1976–1983: economic crisis and industrial restructuring; radical political and institutional change in Spain	Decrease of GDP Rise of unemployment Disappearance of firms Danger of lock-in due to economic overspecialization Socio-economic instability	Adaptation: • Industrial restructuring, sector and firm-level (subsidies and other aids) (NG and RG) • Industrial promotion (loans, aids…) (NG and RG) • Currency devaluation (NG) Adaptability (RG): • Technology policy (technological upgrading of the existing sectors) • Energy policy (new energy sources)	NG and RG Institutional entrepreneurs (in RG and RTOs) RTOs	Government-led aimed to react Practical-evaluative	Path extension Policy path creation

Crisis (and undergoing structural changes)	*Consequences*	*Policy responses and agendas*	*Key agents*	*Governance, behavior and agency*	*Impact on growth and policy path*
1992–1994: short economic crisis (macro disequilibria); single European market (full openness of the Basque economy): transition from a factor-driven to a knowledge-driven economy	Decrease of GDP Rise of unemployment Disappearance of firms Lack of firms' competences to cope with the advent of the single European market	Adaptation: • Industrial restructuring and promotion (loans, subsidies and fiscal aids) (RG) • Currency devaluation (NG) Adaptability: (new, horizontal policies, RG) • Technology policy (upgrading and diversification into new sectors) • Cluster policy (existing and new sectors, e.g., aeronautics, ICTs) • Internationalization policy • Business change policy (and promotion of new KIBS) • Energy policy (new energy sources) • Urban policy (Bilbao, and new sectors, e.g., creative industries) Agenda: *PGAPI 1991–95*	NG and RG-RDAs (SPRI and EVE) Institutional entrepreneurs (in RG) RTOs Firms	Government-business coalition led by RG aimed to react and transform Interactive, practical-evaluative, and projective	Path extension Path renewal Policy path dependence

(continued)

Table 11.1 (continued)

Crisis (and undergoing structural changes)	*Consequences*	*Policy responses and agendas*	*Key agents*	*Governance, behavior and agency*	*Impact on growth and policy path*
2008–2015: financial and economic crisis and fiscal consolidation Awareness of deindustrialization and its challenges	Decrease of GDP Rise of unemployment Disappearance of firms Fiscal consolidation: budget cuts	Adaptation • Labor market reform and wage cuts (NG) • Reduction of interest rates (QE of ECB) • Small financial support to firms in crisis (loans, aids, RG) Adaptability (policy change and new policies, RG) • Policy change in clusters, internationalization and STI • New policies: RIS3 (Basque Industry 4.0, Energy and Health), diversification and new sector creation (biosciences, cleantechs) Agenda: *PMERE 2014–16*	NG and RG-RDAs (SPRI and EVE) Firms and Cluster-associations RTOs and Universities Other (Innobasque, Orkestra)	Triple Helix coalition with a shared (place-based) leadership (CVCTI) aimed to anticipate and transform Interactive, practical-evaluative and projective	Path extension Path renewal and path creation? Policy path dependence and change

Source Authors' elaboration. PGAPI: *Plan General de Actuación de Política Industrial*; PMERE: *Programa Marco de Empleo y Reactivación Económica*; NG: national government; RG: regional government; KIBS: knowledge intensive business services; RDAs: regional development agencies; RTOs: research and technology organizations.; CVCTI: Basque STI Council

The first economic crisis (1976–1983) hit hardest an economy such as that of Spain, highly protected to foreign competition and scarcely competitive. Old industrial regions such as the Basque Country, which had overspecialized in a small group of sectors (iron & steel, metallic products, machinery and transport material and equipment), faced a real danger of lock-in. To make matters worse, the crisis went hand in hand with a deep and radical political change in Spain, which increased institutional uncertainty, labour mobilization and, in the Basque region, a significant rise of terrorist activities that targeted, among other groups, businessmen and managers. The crisis resulted in the disappearance of hundreds of firms and the loss of thousands of jobs, particularly in the industry (Aranguren et al., 2012; Valdaliso, 2015).

The policy responses adopted were of two types and were led by two government levels. The national government, along with some macroeconomic measures (such as currency devaluation), put in motion industrial restructuring and promotion programmes with the aim of resisting and adapting to the crisis. The Basque government, which had been created from scratch in 1980 (in the context of the new political system in Spain, which gave considerable autonomy and competences to regional governments), adopted some complementary measures of industrial restructuring and promotion over the 1980s, to help the existing sectors to resist, but also started new policies in the fields of technology and energy aimed towards improving adaptability. Behind those new policies was a small group of institutional entrepreneurs that came from the industrial sector and/or a few RTOs, led by the Ministry of Industry, Javier García-Egocheaga. Their dominant behaviour in those years was reactive rather than proactive. In relation to the latter, it was about doing the same things (continuity), but in a more efficient way (*exploitation*, according to March, 1991). During the early 1980s, the first regional government built up an institutional architecture and started a policy path that became reinforced afterwards (Valdaliso et al., 2014).

The second economic crisis (1992–1994) was shorter and more focused but also brought about a decrease in GDP and a significant rise of unemployment. In spite of the economic recovery of the second half of the 1980s and the positive effects of Spain's integration into the EEC (European Economic Community), Basque firms still had several weaknesses that put them in a difficult situation to cope with the new single European market, the most important structural change perceived as such by all the agents in the region. Like in the previous crisis, currency devaluation and industrial restructuring and promotion programs were adopted. However, the Basque government took that crisis as an opportunity space to adopt a broad agenda for change and transformation, to help Basque firms to cope with the advent of the single European market but also to facilitate the transition from a factor-driven to a knowledge-driven economy, centred on industry. In fact, the PGAPI's 1991–1995, led by the Vice-President Jon Azua, who acted as a true institutional entrepreneur (with a lot of political power), explicitly formulated those challenges and envisaged a wide scope of policy measures with the aim of improving what it already existed (path extension) and encouraging the diversification of the Basque economy into new related sectors such as aeronautics, telecommunications, information technologies and knowledge intensive business services (path renewal) (Aranguren et al., 2012; Valdaliso, 2015). The PGAPI agenda reinforced the system's institutional architecture and the policy path taken in the 1980s although allocated some space for change, mainly through layering (Mahoney & Thelen, 2009), e.g., the creation of new institutions and organizations in the system, such as cluster-associations (Valdaliso et al., 2014), alongside existing ('old') arrangements. The regional government continued leading the policy process, although it attempted to get private business involved through the creation of public–private organizations and even by recruiting some individuals from the private sector to political posts in the government.

The policy responses to this crisis and to the structural changes the Basque economy had to cope with traced a policy path and a strategy for economic development that became reinforced over the sustained economic prosperity that lasted up to 2007. In a context of growing budget and plenty of resources, new institutions and organizations (Universities, new RTOs, Innobasque and other agencies, Orkestra, etc.) were added to the system, which became increasingly dense and complex; and the diversification efforts continued towards new science-based sectors such as biosciences, nano- and micro-technologies, with the aim of driving the Basque economy towards a new, knowledge-driven, growth path (Magro et al., 2014; Valdaliso, 2015; Valdaliso et al., 2014). Alongside the regional government and its RDAs, firms and the existing RTOs, new agents such as cluster associations, universities and new RTOs, alongside new government agencies played increasing prominent roles. Policy learning and experimentation helped to transform the system's governance, which became less hierarchical and more participative.

By its length and intensity, the last economic crisis was as important as that of the early 1980s. It also brought about a fiscal consolidation that resulted in considerable budget cuts by the national and regional governments. The macroeconomic policy responses were adopted by the European Central Bank and by the national government (labour market reform). The regional government provided, in the first years of the crisis, financial support to help firms to resist, although not to the same degree when compared to previous crises. The successive Basque governments maintained the broad lines of their sustained economic strategy and policy, strongly focused on industry as the key sector of the Basque economy, but now adopted to the new policy paradigm of smart specialization (RIS3). In this sense, the strong and strategic bet on industry as the core sector of the Basque economy, sustained from the 1980s, allowed the Basque country to resist better—in a European perspective—the danger of deindustrialization with one of the highest shares of industry over GDP of all the European regions (NUTS2). Like in the previous crisis, the regional government saw it as an opportunity to initiate a process of change in some long-sustained policies (clusters, STI [Science, Technology and Innovation], internationalization) and in the institutional architecture and network of policy agents. The budget cuts forced the regional government to concentrate its economic diversification efforts towards three strategic priorities—Basque Industry 4.0, Energy and Health—and to re-design the existing network of cluster-associations and scientific and technological agents (Morgan, 2016; Navarro, 2015).

Overall, policy responses attempted to improve the adaptability of the regional economy and its agents to the new scenario facilitating change and to some extent, anticipating new challenges. The process of policy learning in the previous period and the advances registered towards a more horizontal and participative policy process made possible now a new system's governance with a shared leadership, supported by a triple helix coalition (integrated by the government, RTOs and universities, and firms and cluster-associations), of which the CVCTI or the steering groups of RIS3 priorities were clear proofs.

Discussion and Conclusions

This chapter emphasizes the role of institutions, especially policy, and agency in shaping regional resilience, understood as the capability of regions to resist, adapt, respond recover and or/renew from a shock (Martin, 2012). Adaptation and adaptability processes contribute to resilience as a regional capability to cope with both economic crises and structural changes and therefore need to be studied following a historical perspective (Henning, 2019). This is precisely our contribution with the long-term and holistic perspective we have taken when discussing the Basque case, where we distinguish three main episodes and disentangle the role of policy measures and agency to foster adaptation in the short-term and adaptability in the medium-long term, aiming at creating new regional growth paths as a sign of resilience.

The case effectively shows how policy shapes resilience, but it also highlights that those policy responses are neither single nor simple. Complexity in policy responses is also discussed by innovation studies and sustainable transitions literature under the policy-mix concept (Flanagan et al., 2011; Rogge & Reichardt, 2016) but this chapter goes further by highlighting the importance of combinatorial policy processes (namely adaptive, adaptability or exploitation and exploration), following an evolutionary economic geography view. This supports March's (1991) assumption of the importance of maintaining a balance between exploration and exploitation within a system perspective. Indeed, in this case, the combination of different responses in the three crisis moments shows how policy is context and time specific and denotes path dependence of previous policy paths and influence from governance and power relationships within and beyond the region. Thus, in the three analysed periods policy measures have been combined to foster both adaptation by implementing urgent measures to the shocks and policies aiming at contributing to adaptability have been implemented. It is also important to highlight that the measures directed to foster adaptability over time have led to an evolutionary policy process. For example, technology policy in the first period facilitated the transition towards a knowledge-driven economy in the second period, and this constituted the roots for a strong smart specialization strategy (Foray, 2014) in the last one. These policy responses have facilitated the creation and renewal of regional growth paths coping not only with economic crises but also with economic structural changes.

The case also demonstrates the importance of other types of institutions, such as governance arrangements and agency in regional resilience. It is clear that agency shapes institutions, including policy (Uyarra et al., 2017). The relationships established from the very beginning among different types of actors within the region (regional government, RTOs, firms) and beyond the region (especially national and EU governments) have shaped policy responses. However, the case shows how regional institutions and agency have been the most important drivers for regional adaptability and therefore for regional resilience. This highlights the importance of regional capabilities for resilience, in line with the assumption of Boschma (2015) who underlined the importance of the resilience of different units of analysis within regions (individuals, networks, etc). It is also important to acknowledge the role of institutional entrepreneurs (DiMaggio, 1988) from the very beginning, especially from the regional government. Despite its highly interventionist nature, the regional government facilitated the development of governance mechanisms within the region over time, thus leading to collective agency and shared, place-based leadership (Bailey et al., 2010), which in turn catalyzed regional path renewal and path creation.

In addition, in terms of agency the analysis shows an evolutionary path. The case illustrates how determinant the adoption from the very beginning of a practical-evaluative (approach to cope with emerging demands) is, and especially as the regional government was created from scratch in 1980 and therefore had no pre-existing regional institutional arrangements. But what is also more relevant is that since the first crisis episode the three dimensions of agency were present in the region. Thus, in the 1990s, the *interactive dimension* was present as the policy path taken in the 1980s was reinforced; but a *practical-evaluative* approach was also identified in the form of a diagnosis of the Basque economy and the possibilities and measures to take. Finally, the *projective dimension* arises as relevant because for the first time a sort of vision of the Basque economy is proposed. The projective dimension continued in the last crisis, with the implementation of a regional smart specialization strategy based on related variety and the creation of new growth paths. In addition, the case also denotes the importance of bricolage (Garud & Karnøe, 2003) in times of crises and the ability of regional government to transfer models, practices and experiences from elsewhere to the region (Navarro et al., 2014). All these elements can be signalled as constituents of place-based leadership (Bailey et al., 2010).

Recognizing the complexity of regional resilience and the lack of a single recipe for all territories, the chapter shows the importance of evolutionary processes in both policy measures and agency for regional path development. Furthermore, the chapter highlights a co-evolutionary process (Gong & Hassink, 2019) between policy and agency as both show a reciprocal influence. Policy seen as an evolutionary path-dependent process shapes agency and at the same time, agency influences policy responses. Therefore, there is not a linear causality between policy and agency but a nested institutional context in which the different factors co-evolve and co-determine each other.

Finally, learnings from this chapter could also inform the (organizational) resilience literature more broadly. First, as regards the importance of combining *ex ante* and *ex post* processes (adaptability and adaptation) and keeping a balance between exploration and exploitation processes for resilience. Second, in relation to the importance of agency and leadership for resilience. And finally, in terms of the interplay of institutions (organizations and formal and informal rules of the game) and actors in a co-evolving process of change, which is time and context specific and can lead to mutual reinforcement or mutual weakening outcomes, as described by Gong and Hassink (2019).

Acknowledgements The authors acknowledge financial support from MINECO HAR2016-76198-P (AEI/FEDER, UE), and from the Basque Government Department of Education (IT897-16).

References

Annarelli, A., & Nonino, F. (2016). Strategic and operational management of organizational resilience: Current state of research and future directions. *Omega, 62*, 1–18.

Aranguren, M. J., Magro, E., Navarro, M., & Valdaliso, J. M. (2012). *Estrategias para la construcción de ventajas competitivas regionales. El caso del País Vasco.* Marcial Pons.

Bailey, D., Bellandi, M., Caloffi, A., & De Propris, L. (2010). Place-renewing leadership: Trajectories of change for mature manufacturing regions in Europe. *Policy Studies, 31*(4), 457–474.

Bailey, D., & Berkeley, N. (2014). Regional responses to recession: The role of the West Midlands Regional Taskforce. *Regional Studies, 48*(11), 1797–1812.

Battilana, J., & D'aunno, T. (2009). Institutional work and the paradox of embedded agency. *Institutional Work: Actors and Agency in Institutional Studies of Organizations, 31*, 58.

Baumgartner, F. R. (2013). Ideas and policy change. *Governance: An International Journal of Policy, Administration, and Institutions, 26*(2), 239–258.

Billington, M. G., Karlsen, J., Mathisen, L., & Pettersen, I. B. (2017). Unfolding the relationship between resilient firms and the region. *European Planning Studies, 25*(3), 425–442.

Birch, K., Mackinnon, D., & Cumbers, A. (2010). Old industrial regions in Europe: A comparative assessment of economic performance. *Regional Studies, 44*(1), 35–53.

Boinand, A., & Van Eeten, M. J. G. (2014). The resilient organization: A critical appraisal. *Public Management Review, 15*(3), 429–445.

Boschma, R. (2015). Towards and evolutionary perspective on regional resilience. *Regional Studies, 49*(5), 733–751.

Bristow, G., & Healy, A. (2014). Regional resilience: An agency perspective. *Regional Studies, 48*(5), 923–935.

Brooks, C. (2017). Governance, civic leadership and resilience. In N. Williams & T. Vorley (Eds.), *Creating resilient economies: Entrepreneurship, growth and development in uncertain times* (pp. 125–141). Edward Elgar.

Campbell, J. L. (2010). Institutional reproduction and change. In G. Morgan, J. L. Campbell, C. Crouch, O. K. Pedersen, & R. Whitley (Eds.), *The Oxford handbook of comparative institutional analysis*. Oxford University Press.

Charron, N., & Lapuente, V. (2018). Quality of government in EU regions: Spatial and temporal patterns. *QoG Working Paper Series, 2018*(1), 1.

Cortinovis, N., Xiao, J., Boschma, R., & van Oort, F. (2017). Quality of government and social capital as drivers of regional diversification in Europe. *The Journal of Economic Geography, 17*, 1179–1208.

Crescenzi, R., Luca, D., & Milio, S. (2016). The geography of the economic crisis in Europe: National macroeconomic conditions, regional structural factors and short-term economic performance. *Cambridge Journal of Regions, Economy and Society, 9*(1), 13–32.

Croenewegen, J., & van der Steen, M. (2007). The evolutionary policy maker. *Journal of Economic Issues, 41*(2), 351–358.

Cruz-Castro, L., Holl, A., Rama, R., & Sanz-Menendez, L. (2018). Economic crisis and company R&D in Spain: Do regional and policy factors matter? *Industry and Innovation, 25*(8), 729–751.

Cuadrado, J. R., & Maroto, A. (2016). Unbalanced regional resilience to the economic crisis in Spain: A tale of specialisation and productivity. *Cambridge Journal of Regions, Economy and Society, 9*, 153–178.

Cueto, M. B., Mayor, M., & Suárez, P. (2017). *La resiliencia de las regiones españolas después de la gran recesión*. Consejo Económico y Social del Principado de Asturias.

David, L. (2018). Agency and resilience in the time of regional economic crisis. *European Planning Studies, 26*(5), 1041–1059.

DiMaggio, P. (1988). Interest and agency in institutional theory. In L. Zucker (Ed.), *Institutional patterns and culture* (pp. 3–22). Cambridge, MA: Ballinger.

Elola, A., Parrilli, M. D., & Rabelloti, R. (2013). The resilience of clusters in the context of increasing globalization: The Basque wind energy value chain. *European Planning Studies, 21*(7), 989–1006.

Emirbayer, M., & Mische, A. (1998). What is agency? *American Journal of Sociology, 103*(4), 962–1023.

Eraydin, A. (2016). The role of regional policies along with the external and endogenous factors in the resilience of regions. *Cambridge Journal of Regions, Economy and Society, 9*(1), 217–234.

Etxabe, I., & Valdaliso, J. M. (2016). Measuring structural social capital in a cluster policy network: Insights from the Basque Country. *European Planning Studies, 24*(5), 884–903.

Evans, R., & Karecha, J. (2014). Staying on top: Why is Munich so resilient and successful? *European Planning Studies, 22*(6), 1259–1279.

Evenhuis, E. (2017a). New directions in researching regional economic resilience and adaptation. *Geography Compass, 11*(11), e12333.

Evenhuis, E. (2017b). Institutional change in cities and regions: A path dependency approach. *Cambridge Journal of Regions, Economy and Society, 10*, 509–526.

Flanagan, K., & Uyarra, E. (2016). Four dangers in innovation policy studies—And how to avoid them. *Industry and Innovation, 23*(2), 177–188.

Flanagan, K., Uyarra, E., & Laranja, M. (2011). Reconceptualising the 'policy mix' for innovation. *Research Policy, 40*, 702–713.

Foray, D. (2014). *Smart specialisation: Opportunities and challenges for regional innovation policy* (pp. 25–30). Routledge.

Foray, D., Goddard, J., Goenaga, X., Landabaso, M., McCann, P., Morgan, K., Nauwelaers, C., & Ortega-Argilés, R. (2012). *Guide to research and innovation strategies for smart specialisations (RIS3).* European Commission, Brussels.

Fratesi, U., & Rodríguez-Pose, A. (2016). The crisis and regional employment in Europe: What role for sheltered economies? *Cambridge Journal of Regions, Economy and Society, 9*(1), 33–57.

Garud, R., & Karnøe, P. (2001). Path creation as a process of mindful deviation. In R. Garud & P. Karnøe (Eds.), *Path dependence and creation* (pp. 1–38). NJ, Mahwah: Lawrence Earlbaum Associates.

Garud, R., & Karnøe, P. (2003). Bricolage versus breakthrough: Distributed and embedded agency in technology entrepreneurship. *Research Policy, 32*(2), 277–300.

Garud, R., Kumaraswamy, A., & Karnøe, P. (2010). Path dependence or path creation? *Journal of Management Studies, 47*(4), 760–774.

Gingrich, J. (2015). Varying costs to change? Institutional change in the public sector. *Governance: An International Journal of Policy, Administration, and Institutions, 28*(1), 41–60.

Gong, H., & Hassink, R. (2019). Co-evolution in contemporary economic geography: Towards a theoretical framework. *Regional Studies, 53*(9), 1344–1355.

González-Bravo, M., López, S., & Valdaliso, J. M. (2018). Coping with economic crises: Cluster associations and firm performance in the Basque Country. In F. Belussi & J. L. Hervás-Oliver (Eds.), *Cluster advantage and firm performance* (pp. 245–262). Springer.

Grabher, G. (1993). The weakness of strong ties: The lock-in of regional development in the Rhur area. In G. Grabher (Ed.), *The embedded firm: On the socioeconomics of industrial networks* (pp. 255–277). Routledge.

Grillitsch, M., & Sotarauta, M. (2020). Trinity of change agency, regional development paths and opportunity spaces. *Progress in Human Geography, 44*(4), 704–723.

Grillitsch, M., & Sotarauta, M. (2018). *Regional growth paths: From structure to agency and back* (Papers in Innovation Studies 2018/01, CIRCLE).

Henning, M. (2019). Time should tell (more): Evolutionary economic geography and the challenge of history. *Regional Studies, 53*(4), 602–613.

Henning, M., Stam, E., & Wenting, R. (2013). Path dependence research in regional economic development: Cacophony or knowledge accumulation? *Regional Studies, 47*(8), 1348–1362.

Holl, A., & Rama, R. (2016). Persistence of innovative activities in times of crisis: The case of the Basque Country. *European Planning Studies, 24*(10), 1863–1883.

Isaksen, A. (2015). Industrial development in thin regions: Trapped in path extension? *Journal of Economic Geography, 15*(3), 585–600.

Kakderi, C., & Tasopoulou, A. (2017). Regional economic resilience: The role of national and regional policies. *European Planning Studies, 25*(8), 1435–1453.

Kay, A. (2006). *The dynamics of public policy: Theory and evidence*. Edward Elgar.

Kingdon, J. W. (1984). *Agendas, alternatives, and public policies*. Little Brown.

Landabaso, M. (2012). What public policies can and cannot do for regional development. In P. Cooke, M. D. Parrilli, & J. L. Curbelo (Eds.), *Innovation, global challenge, and territorial resilience* (pp. 364–381). Edward Elgar.

Lawrence, T. B., & Suddaby, R. (2006). Institutions and institutional work. In *The Sage handbook of organization studies* (p. 215). Sage.

Magro, E., Navarro, M., & Zabala-Iturriagagoitia, J. M. (2014). Coordination-mix: The hidden face of STI policy. *Review of Policy Research, 31*(5), 367–389.

Maguire, S., Hardy, C., & Lawrence, T. B. (2004). Institutional entrepreneurship in emerging fields: HIV/AIDS treatment advocacy in Canada. *The Academy of Management Journal, 47*, 657–79.

Mahoney, J., & Thelen, K. (2009). A theory of gradual institutional change. In J. Mahoney & K. Thelen (Eds.), *Explaining institutional change: Ambiguity, agency, and power*. Cambridge University Press.

March, J. G. (1991). Exploration and exploitation in organizational learning. *Organization Science, 2*(1), 71–87.

Martin, R. (2010). Rethinking regional path dependence: Beyond lock-in to evolution. *Economic Geography, 86*(1), 1–27.

Martin, R. (2012). Regional economic resilience, hysteresis and recessionary shocks. *Journal of Economic Geography, 12*, 1–32.

Martin, R., & Sunley, P. (2006). Path dependence and regional economic evolution. *Journal of Economic Geography, 6*(4), 395–437.

Martin, R., & Sunley, P. (2015). On the notion of regional economic resilience: Conceptualization and explanation. *Journal of Economic Geography, 15*, 1–42.

Martin, R., Sunley, P., Gardiner, B., & Tyler, P. (2016). How regions react to recessions: Resilience and the role of economic structure. *Regional Studies, 50*(4), 561–585.

Morgan, K. (2016). Collective entrepreneurship: The Basque model of innovation. *European Planning Studies, 24*(8), 1544–1560.

Nauwelaers, C., & Wijtnes, R. (Eds.). (2008). *Innovation policy in Europe: Measurement and strategy*. Edward Elgar Publishing.

Navarro, M. (2015). Las estrategias territoriales para la transformación productiva. Reflexión desde el caso del País Vasco. *Icade. Revista de las Facultades de Derecho y Ciencias Económicas y Empresariales*, 96, 75–104.

Navarro, M., Valdaliso, J. M., Aranguren, M. J., & Magro, E. (2014). A holistic approach to regional strategies: The case of the Basque Country. *Science and Public Policy, 41*, 532–547.

Neffke, F., Henning, M., & Boschma, R. (2011). How do regions diversify over time? Industry relatedness and the development of new growth paths in regions. *Economic Geography, 87*(3), 237–265.

OECD. (2011). *OECD reviews of regional innovation: Basque Country, Spain*. OECD.

Pierson, P. (2004). *Politics in time: History, institutions, and social analysis*. Princeton University Press.

Pugalis, L., Gray, N., & Townsend, A. (2017). The resilience of growth strategies. In N. Williams & T. Vorley (Eds.), *Creating resilient economies: Entrepreneurship, growth and development in uncertain times* (pp. 160–174). Edward Elgar.

Rogge, K. S., & Reichardt, K. (2016). Policy mixes for sustainability transitions: An extended concept and framework for analysis. *Research Policy, 45*(8), 1620–1635.

Simmie, J., & Martin, R. (2010). The economic resilience of regions: Towards an evolutionary approach. *Cambridge Journal of Regions, Economy and Society, 3*, 27–44.

Steen, M. (2016). Reconsidering path creation in economic geography: Aspects of agency, temporality and methods. *European Planning Studies, 24*(9), 1605–1622.

Streeck, W., & Thelen, K. (2005). Introduction: Institutional change in advanced political economies. In W. Streeck & K. Thelen (Eds.), *Beyond continuity: Institutional change in advanced political economies* (pp. 3–39). Oxford University Press.

Tomlinson, P. R., & Branston, J. R. (2014). Turning the tide: Prospects for an industrial renaissance in the North Staffordshire ceramics industrial district. *Cambridge Journal of Regions, Economy and Society, 7*(3), 489–507.

Uyarra, E., Flanagan, K., Magro, E., Wilson, J. R., & Sotarauta, M. (2017). Understanding regional innovation policy dynamics: Actors, agency and learning. *Environment and Planning C: Politics and Space, 35*(4), 559–568.

Uyarra, E., & Ramlogan, R. (2012). *Cluster policy: A review of the evidence.* National Endowment for Science, Technology and the Arts (NESTA), University of Manchester.

Uyarra, E., Zabala-Iturriagagoitia, J. M., Flanagan, K., & Magro, E. (2020). Public procurement, innovation and industrial policy: Rationales, roles, capabilities and implementation. *Research Policy, 49*(1), 103844.

Valdaliso, J. M. (2015). The Basque Country: Past trajectory and path dependency in policy- and strategy-making. In J. M. Valdaliso & J. R. Wilson (Eds.), *Strategies for shaping territorial competitiveness*. Routledge.

Valdaliso, J. M. (2020). Accounting for the resilience of the machine tool industry in Spain (c. 1960–2015). *Business History, 62*(4), 637–662.

Valdaliso, J. M., Elola, A., & Franco, S. (2016). Do clusters follow the industry life cycle? Diversity of cluster evolution in old industrial regions. *Competitiveness Review, 26*(1), 66–86.

Valdaliso, J. M., Magro, E., Navarro, M., Aranguren, M. J., & Wilson, J. R. (2014). Path dependence in policies supporting smart specialization strategies. *European Journal of Innovation Management, 17*(4), 390–408.

Valdaliso, J. M. & Wilson, J. R. (Eds.). (2015). "Introduction", *Strategies for shaping territorial competitiveness* (pp. 1–15). Routledge.

Webber, D. J., Healy, A., & Bristow, G. (2018). Regional growth paths and resilience: A European analysis. *Economic Geography, 98*(4), 355–375.

Witt, U. (2003). Economic policy making in evolutionary perspective. *Journal of Evolutionary Economics, 13*, 77–94.

PART IV

Taking Stock and Moving Forward

CHAPTER 12

Towards Resilient Organisations and Societies? Reflections on the Multifaceted Nature of Resilience

Mitchell Young, Maria Laura Frigotto, and Rómulo Pinheiro

Introduction

As the chapters in this volume have shown, resilience is a multifaceted and malleable concept that can be fruitfully applied to a wide range of phenomena at all levels of society. At the same time, there is a distinct danger of concept stretching (Collier et al., 1993). In this concluding

M. Young (✉)
Department of European Studies, Institute of International Studies, FSV, Charles University, Prague, Czechia
e-mail: young@fsv.cuni.cz

M. L. Frigotto
Department of Economics and Management, University of Trento, Trento, Italy
e-mail: marialaura.frigotto@unitn.it

R. Pinheiro
Department of Political Science and Management, University of Agder, Kristiansand, Norway
e-mail: romulo.m.pinheiro@uia.no

R. Pinheiro et al. (eds.), *Towards Resilient Organizations and Societies*, Public Sector Organizations,
https://doi.org/10.1007/978-3-030-82072-5_12

chapter, we look at both the extensiveness of the concept, reviewing the range of complementary concepts that have been engaged by the authors, and at how it can be delimited to maintain conceptual distinctiveness and explanatory value.

In the introduction of this edited volume (Frigotto et al., 2022), five questions were identified that address translation issues arising from the resilience concept's importation into the social sciences. The first issue has to do with what type of phenomena resilience entails: is it a characteristic, a capability, a process, an outcome, and/or a philosophy? The second derives from the context of the social realm in which things never return exactly to the original state; there is always an element of change. How can we allow for variance but still keep the concept of resilience separate from other concepts that involve change? The third issue has to do with what drives resilience in the first place. This is generally acknowledged to be some sort of external disturbance, i.e. resilience does not exist ipso facto, but it leaves open the question of how to characterize the triggers that engage resilience and how intense they need to be. The fourth issue has to do with the precise timing of the resilience. Is resilience instantiated as adversity strikes, or can it be before or afterwards? Finally, as we translate from the natural sciences to the social world, we must address the fact that the object of resilience is no longer a material with a clear physical and chemical makeup, but rather something social and often immaterial that can be found at any level of society, from the individual to the system. How can the concept effectively embrace such a broad range of phenomena?

The process of researching and discussing the various cases in this volume has provided several insights on how to frame the concept of resilience as a social phenomenon. Instead of offering a new positivistic definition of resilience, we clarify the concept by delineating it in a similar manner as we would the phenomenon of resilience itself, i.e. by identifying its core elements and its limits or threshold. There are three elements in our understanding of resilience that deal with the key questions stated above: time, essence and adversity.

To begin with, any understanding of resilience must deal with *temporality*. Resilience cannot exist in a single moment but always draws together at least two points in time in which a 'material' or, in our case, social phenomena is compared; i.e. resilience requires that a material at time T2 must recognizably resemble the same material at time T0 despite the adversity that occurred at time T1. The related notion of 'bouncing back' to a previous state, although meaningful in the context of the material sciences, is problematic from a social science perspective where phenomena and contexts coevolve in a dynamic manner and thus cannot revert to a previous unchanged state. For example, as confirmed by many world events, a counter-revolution—even when successful—cannot return a nation state back to the state prior to the initial revolution (Padgett, 2012).

The element of time is thus directly related to the element of *essence*. In the social world, objects simply do not return to the exact same state as before a disturbance, and debating the extent to which they do or do not seems to be particularly futile. The more relevant question is *how much change is possible within the range of resilience?* For resilience to be in play, some sort of essence must continue over time. While a resilient social phenomenon is not exactly the same as before, it is also not entirely different; rather, it must resemble what it was in its previous state. Essence, however, should not be construed as a singular core, trait, or characteristic. Rather, the continuity of essence can be fruitfully understood in terms of family resemblance, a concept that Ludwig Wittgenstein (1968) first used to explain our understanding of the meaning of words. He wondered how we recognize games despite there being no common element to all games. He claimed that there is 'a complicated network of similarities overlapping and crisscrossing: sometimes overall similarities, sometimes similarities of detail' (Wittgenstein, 1968, par. 66). When we talk about the continuity of essence in resilient social phenomena, we mean that the changes brought by adversity or the preparation for it do not impede our ability to recognize the original material. This recognition is not based on a reductionist approach, seeking a core essence that survives, but rather on this broader commonality. The analogy can be slightly adapted for resilience thinking such that the resemblance is like that of a child to his or her adult self.

Finally, we come to the issue of *adversity*. Again, this is not a binary question, but rather one of intensity: how much adversity is required to activate resilience? We argue that in order to qualify as resilience, there must be a level of adversity that threatens the continuity or essence of the material or phenomena at stake. Drawing on the original physics-based origins of the concept, there must be a risk that the material could break and thus change state or identity as a result. At what point does a forest stop being a forest and resemble a quasi-desert as a result of deforestation and climate change (Walker & Salt, 2006)? Again, what 'breaking' means in terms of social phenomena is not readily definable, and our purpose here is not to positivistically define the level of adversity but rather to delineate, that is, to rule out minor adversity as a trigger of resilience.

Returning to the five questions about translation into the social sciences, we see that resilience can be a characteristic, a capability, a process, an outcome, or a philosophy, but regardless of which it is, any phenomena claiming resilience must remain within the limits that delineate the threshold of the concept. Those limits can be understood as threefold: the phenomena should extend over time, maintain a continuity of essence, and deal with serious adversity. In Table 12.1, we summarize the many dimensions, both divergent and intersecting, that appear in the various chapters of this volume. This serves as a guide for the remainder of this chapter as we draw parallels and highlight contrasts between the previous chapters, which can help us to better understand the concept of resilience and identify new avenues for future study.

Comparing and Discussing the Cases Thematically

Structure and Agency

Both structurationists and post-structurationists agree, though in different ways, that structure and agency should be reconciled: structure neither occurs naturally, without human agency, nor is it entirely the product of human agency (Parker, 2010). Structurationist theory, building on Anthony Giddens' work, regards structures as 'dual', by which he means that they are 'both the medium and the outcome of the practices which constitute social systems' (Giddens, 1981, p. 27). In this way, structure becomes inextricably intertwined with agency. Post-structurationists such as Margaret Archer criticize this conflation and argue that a study of structure must analytically distinguish the two, even if they are ontologically inseparable (Parker, 2010). The chapters in this volume provide material to address this debate, and they also explicate a point of commonality, i.e. structures are not only constraining but also enabling. This is possible because they depict individuals as 'knowledgeable' and 'capable of putting their structurally formed capacities to work in creative or innovative ways' (Sewell, 1992, p. 4). This ability to apply knowledge is central to the dimension of novelty and learning that we identified in our theoretical framework for resilience in the introduction to this edited volume (Frigotto et al., 2022).

Table 12.1 Dimensions of resilience in the chapters of this volume

	Unit of analysis	*Publicness*	*Kind of resilience*	*Novelty profiles*	*Temporal dimensions of resilience*	*Theoretical/ disciplinary context*	*Key auxiliary concepts brought to bear on resilience*
Chapter 2	Fire brigade	Public organization, accountable for public safety and rescue	Transformative	Major novelty	Foresight, mechanisms	Organization studies, emergency management	Problem solving and sensemaking
Chapter 3	Individual members of the Austrian Military	Public organization, accountable for national safety and defence	Absorptive, Adaptive, Transformative	Minor, medium, and major novelty	Foresight	Organization studies, high reliability organizations	Exaptation, rule-following, and rule-breaking
Chapter 4	Boilermakers in a naval shipbuilding project	Semi-public company in projects that are publicly funded, serving public defence goods	Adaptive	Medium novelty	Mechanisms	High reliability organizations, sociology of professions	Temporary organizing and occupational identity
Chapter 5	Public agencies responsible for coordination and public transport	Public–private organizations, serving public goods and accountable for safety	Absorptive, Adaptive, Transformative	Minor, medium, and major novelty	Foresight	Organization studies, high reliability organizations	Practice view and teleo-affective structures

(continued)

Table 12.1 (continued)

	Unit of analysis	*Publicness*	*Kind of resilience*	*Novelty profiles*	*Temporal dimensions of resilience*	*Theoretical/ disciplinary context*	*Key auxiliary concepts brought to bear on resilience*
Chapter 6	Public managers in New Zealand	Public administration	Adaptive	Medium novelty	Foresight	Public management, human resource management	Leadership, learning, and micro-management
Chapter 7	Public universities	Public organizations dependent on government support and subject to public oversight, serving public goods	Transformative	Major novelty	Foresight, mechanisms	Complex systems, higher education studies	Loose coupling, slack, and requisite diversity
Chapter 8	Scandinavian universities	Public organizations dependent on government support and subject to public oversight, serving public goods	Transformative	Major novelty	Mechanisms, outcomes	Higher education studies, organizational culture	Identity and legitimacy

	Unit of analysis	*Publicness*	*Kind of resilience*	*Novelty profiles*	*Temporal dimensions of resilience*	*Theoretical/ disciplinary context*	*Key auxiliary concepts brought to bear on resilience*
Chapter 9	Opera houses in Italy	Dependent on public funding and advancing societal culture and values	Transformative	Major novelty	Outcomes	Organization studies, performing arts management	Archetypes and identity
Chapter 10	Regional higher education institutions (RHEI) and their regions	Public organizations dependent on government support, subject to public oversight, and assisting with regional public objectives	Transformative (region), Adaptive (organizations)	Major novelty	Mechanisms, outcomes	Regional studies, organization studies	Coevolution and nestedness
Chapter 11	The region as a composite system	Regional governance, public administration, and organizations within the region	Transformative	Major novelty	Outcomes	Regional studies, organization studies	Agency, coevolution, and path dependency

In each of the chapters of this volume, the authors have dealt with both structure and agency in attempts to analyse resilience across a broad range of social systems and organizations. The chapters differ, however, in how they represent the configuration of structure and agency. In the first part of the volume, we see resilience that emerges from agency in a moment of crisis and resilience that is purposefully institutionalized in structure through deliberative foresight activities. The fire brigade in Chapter 2 is an example of the former. Resilience was created in the moment as the fire raged, and only afterwards did it lead to structuration—via learning—which applied the lessons of what happened in the fire, ex-post, in order to institutionalize a more general form of resilience for dealing effectively with future situations. A similar dynamic can be found in Chapter 4 with the boilermakers in the naval ship construction: resilience becomes institutionalized in the structures of the occupation as a result of repeated interactions and negotiations that were not explicitly aiming to build resilience. Chapters 3, 5 and 6 provide examples of deliberative resilience, i.e. the result of a conscious decision to create structures that enhance resilience. Chapter 5, which looks at public transport and coordination agencies, and Chapter 3, which investigates the Austrian military, describe attempts to shape the structure first so as to ultimately influence the behaviour that happens within it, i.e. making the agents act in a resilient manner. In the third part of the book, we see how structure and agency can be depicted as coevolutionary—e.g. in Chapter 10, at universities within peripheral regions, and Chapter 11, amidst the interplay of regional and innovation systems. In these chapters, the structure and agent are deeply intertwined in a process of mutual adjustment. Specifically in Chapter 10, we see how the region changes the structure of the adversity context within which the university operates as an agent; but at the same time, the impacts of the university's decisions as an actor also change the structures of both the higher education and the regional systems. This dynamic is also seen amidst the interplay of identity and resilience that is central to Chapters 8 (universities) and 9 (opera houses). Chapter 7 takes an approach more similar to those in Chapters 3 and 6, looking at the ingredients needed to cultivate resilience. It argues for the creation of structures that constitutively embed slack, diversity and loose coupling.

Nearly all the cases have used a model of resilience that is based on remaining within a threshold rather than simply bouncing back. The threshold model is particularly attuned to issues of structure and agency, as the threshold is a structural feature within which the agent—be it an individual, organization or institution—operates. However, it would be a mistake to think of the threshold as solely having a constraining function; it also enables the agent's identity and continuity. The threshold demarcates a structural boundary but does not prevent the agent from crossing it. With and against external pressures from other actors and environmental factors, the agent either remains within the threshold or crosses (or is pushed across) it. Typically, the threshold in resilience literature has been depicted as a fixed element; however, we see that it is in fact malleable, shaped both by the actors themselves and other societal forces, which are often a result of the publicness of these actors (Bozeman, 1987, 2004). The model of resilience in Chapter 1 refers to the type of resilience in which change occurs in both the agent and threshold as transformative. Depicting actors and thresholds as both mutually and simultaneously in flux forces us to deal with the complexity inherent in the concept of resilience.

The concept of coevolution, which is addressed explicitly in Chapters 10 and 11, comes from the literature on complex adaptive systems; it observes that the agents in a system do not wait their turn to adapt but are all adapting at once. Evolution then, is not a linear and synchronous process but an emergent one in which different variations succeed based on their fitness to interact with other new variants and the ever-changing environment they create. It should be noted here that when we think about evolution in a social sense, it is not purely random or blind but involves knowledge and learning. It more closely resembles the way breeders attempt to propagate desired phenotypic traits than the natural selection in Darwin's theory. Graham Room (2016) coins the term 'agile actors' to refer to agents in complex social systems that can detect the need for change and adapt themselves. Agile actors are not necessarily resilient, as they may choose to move beyond thresholds, but resilience requires agile actors to manage the coevolutionary pressures from other agents and their environments to avoid crossing a threshold (see Trondal et al., 2022, for a recent discussion linked to the public governance of complexity under turbulence).

Grouping the Chapters on a Novelty and Temporality Matrix

As a means of taking stock of the empirical findings and their future implications, we return here to the elements or overarching principles sketched out in Chapter 1. Each of the empirical cases is plotted along the core dimensions of: *time* (x axis) and *novelty* (y axis). The resulting set of four clusters (Fig. 12.1) can then be analysed in some detail.

Four out of the 10 cases are located within the foresight stage, with the remaining six being evenly split between mechanisms and outcomes. As for novelty, the majority of the cases (8 out of 10) pertain to situations, where either fully (six cases) or partly (two cases), the resilient triggers or drivers were unknown (major), with the remaining cases split between medium and minor levels of novelty. Four of the 10 cases (Cluster 1) encompass more than one temporal dimension. What do these cases have in common, if anything? All of them are public agencies, providing valuable public services and subject to relatively high levels of political and economic interference ('publicness') by external stakeholders such as governments, funders and surrounding communities (Bozeman, 1987). Three of the four cases pertain to higher education institutions (HEIs) operating in increasingly dynamic and volatile environments, laden with national and international competition (for funding and prestige), and

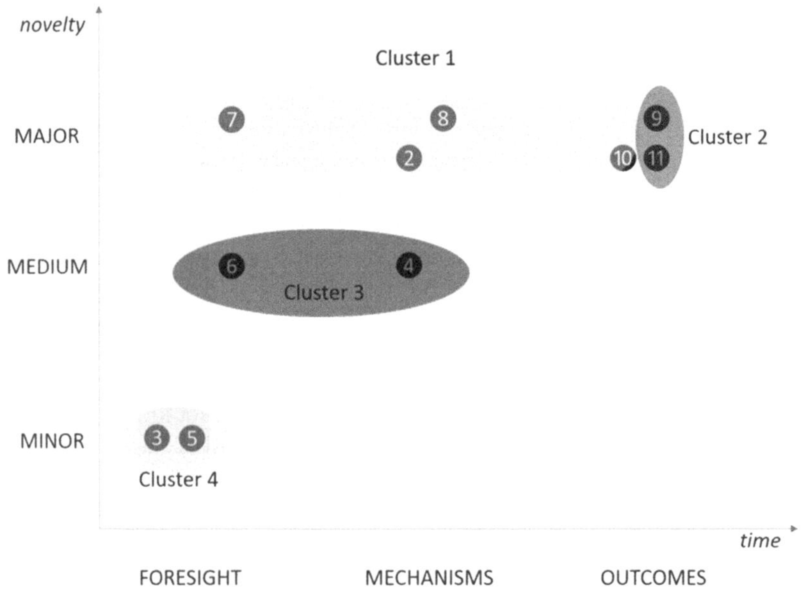

Fig. 12.1 Mapping and clustering the volume's empirical contributions

subject to regulations at the national level and increasingly at the supra-national (e.g. EU) level (cf. Hazelkorn et al., 2018). Studies resorting to systems thinking have shed light on the complexity inherent to HEIs and systems, suggesting that they are deeply embedded or nested in a multiplicity of subsystems (science, economy, culture, polity, etc.), operating at multiple levels of analysis (local/regional/national/global) that, as a result, coevolve with one another (Pinheiro & Young, 2017). Having historically been categorized as resilience organizations by demonstrating the ability to adapt while retaining a sense of identity (Wittrock, 1985), HEIs the world over are now faced with a series of disruptive challenges, testing their ability to absorb externally driven change while retaining a certain degree of internal stability (cf. Tapper & Palfreyman, 2010). The remaining case in this first cluster (Chapter 2) concerns a fire-fighter unit, which belongs to the broader category of high reliability organization (HRO). The latter are notorious for their low tolerance towards embracing risk, given the considerable personal and societal costs resulting from potential disturbances (cf. Sutcliffe, 2011). When it comes to novelty or adversity profiles, the (3) cases involving HEIs face considerable external pressures for change in light of external political and economic agendas (governments and other national and regional stakeholders) associated with creeping 'instrumentalization' (Olsen, 2007). The danger here, from the perspective of internal actors and in the context of the overall resilience of both the HEIs and the higher education system as a whole, relates to attempts by multiple external parties and their vested strategic interests at *co-optation* (Selznick, 1966) of internal goals and functions. Instrumentalization of higher education, studies have shown, tends to focus on short-term imperatives associated with managerialism dimensions like efficiency, performance and responsiveness at the expense of critical long-term aspects (while remaining within a threshold/retaining a sense of identity) such as diversity, autonomy and explorative behaviour (Pinheiro & Young, 2017; see also Pekkola et al., 2021). Finally, one key aspect that binds together the four cases is that for the organizations involved to provide their services to the public in an efficient and legitimate way, they rely on high levels of *trust* or social capital among societal actors (Putnam, 2001), i.e. students, parents and local communities in the case of HEIs, and fellow citizens for firefighters.

As for the remaining (6) cases, which are located within a single temporal dimension, two of these (Cluster 4) correspond to situations where resilience is categorized as an ex-ante process with the corresponding levels of novelty ranging from low to medium to high. The cases in question all pertain to entities centred on ensuring public safety, within the contexts of transportation (Chapter 5) and national defence (Chapter 3). In both cases, resilience is leveraged, on the one hand, in the form of 'rule-following' and 'routine-behaviour'—given the anticipated nature of adversity triggers—and, on the other, by means of 'out of the box' experimentation and/or 'rule-breaking' in light of emerging contextual circumstances where actors are expected to improvise in situ. As a result, in both cases, actors act as relatively autonomous entities or subsystems that are embedded or nested within a larger system of hierarchical interrelations based on multiple feedback mechanisms (Walker & Salt, 2006). Actors operate in highly stressful and volatile situations where the ability to remain calm, i.e. handle emotions and retain a sense of control by acting rationally, plays a key role. By covering a wide spectrum of novelty situations in the context of anticipation or foresight, the cases in question adopt a *processual view of resilience* substantiated with trial and error alongside habituation (cf. Kayes, 2015). This is aligned with the notion that 'the true antecedent of resilience is a cultural infrastructure, an embedded habit, which allows for responding' (Giustiniano et al., 2018, p. 130). What is more, from a dialectical standpoint, these two cases reflect the existing tensions between formal and informal organizing, which are thought to be at the heart of resilience: 'Tensions thus become seen as sources of energy and the dialectical synthesis can be seen as the means of benefiting from the creative energy that the tension generates (Cunha et al., 2002)' (Giustiniano et al., 2018, pp. 131–133).

Cluster 3 is composed of two empirical cases where the levels of novelty are thought to be moderate, representing two specific temporal dimensions: foresight (Chapter 6) and mechanisms (Chapter 4). In the case of public managers (Chapter 6), adversity derives from the ambiguous context characterizing their daily activities in the form of complex tasks and the need to address multiple stakeholders. As rational actors, formal managers devise a series of mechanisms to anticipate or foresee such challenges while attempting to cope with ambiguity and surprise; what Herbert Simon famously termed as pertaining to 'bounded rationality' (1991). Similarly, Chapter 4 describes how boilermakers involved with highly complex and sensitive projects cope with task ambiguity/complexity by drawing upon both tacit and codified forms of knowledge obtained through training and experience (cf. Edmondson et al., 2003) in addition to shared norms and values resulting from professionalization processes (Forsyth & Danisiewicz, 1985). In contrast to the first case where resilience is trigged ex-ante, in the latter situation actors devise mechanisms to overcome challenging and somewhat unexpected situations as they emerge (*in-actus*). In so doing, they enact context-specific learning processes that build upon a combination of the *exploitation* of existing skills and knowledge and *exploration* efforts substantiated on trial and error aimed at reconfiguring cause and effect relationships (March, 1991). Scholars have shown that, when shifting from routine to novel learning situations, factors such as values, identities and collective commitment—aspects intrinsically associated with occupational groups—play an enabling role (Kayes, 2015, p. 17). But, what, if anything, brings together the two cases composing Cluster 3? First, both situations are examples where individual and collective behaviours under novel circumstances are structured around *roles*.

> Roles tell organization members how to reason about the problems and decisions that face them: where to look for appropriate and legitimate informational premises and goal (evaluative) premises, and what techniques to use in processing these premises [...] Each of the roles in an organization presumes the appropriate enactment of the other roles that surround it and interact with it. Thus, the organization is a role *system*. (Simon, 1991, pp. 126–127)

In both empirical cases, managers—as experienced learners—play a crucial role in enabling growth strategies at the individual/employee level by, first, detecting possible failures or challenges and, second, by mobilizing resources to tackle them while supporting their subordinates to explore alternatives to solve novel situations. In so doing, *trust* and shared *norms* play a critically important role, allowing individuals to benefit from sharing knowledge with and learning from one another (cf. Kayes, 2015). Earlier (quantitative) studies centred on the roles played by communication and trust in fostering resilience to cope with surprises like natural disasters, health pandemics and terrorism show a significant positive effect accrued to trust on the internal coordination of crisis communications (Stern & Baird, 2015). In the case of boilermakers, we argue that individual and collective learning (as well as trust) is leveraged by rotating members in the form of temporarily assembled teams (cf. Packendorff,

1995). In the context of organizational learning, March (1991) refers to the importance of employee turnover, particularly in novel situations:

> Rapid socialization of individuals into the procedures and beliefs of an organization tends to reduce exploration. A modest level of turnover, by introducing less socialized people, increases *exploration*, and thereby improves aggregate knowledge. The level of *knowledge* reflected by the organizational code is increased, as is the average individual knowledge of those individuals who have been in the organization for some time. (March, 1991, p. 79; emphasis added)

The potential for conflicts derived from the inclusion of newcomers is minimized since, as an occupational group, boilermakers share a set of professional norms, values, and identities, resulting in higher levels of trust, which in turn foster knowledge sharing and learning, including explorative behaviours centred on finding novel solutions to emergent problems (March, 1991).

Finally, when it comes to Cluster 4, the (2) cases in question, despite being rather different in nature, both pertain to high levels of adversity with resilience mechanisms being trigged following major structural change in their respective organizational fields. They represent circumstances where the systems in question, opera houses (Chapter 9) and autonomous regions (Chapter 11), are deeply embedded or nested in larger societal systems or 'institutional orders' (Thornton et al., 2012), such as the cultural, economic and political spheres upon which they are dependent for both resources (Pfeffer & Salancik, 1978) and legitimacy (Deephouse & Suchman, 2008). In this regard, both cases attest to the ability of their respective subsystems 'to survive and persist within a variable environment' (Meadows, 2008, p. 76). Opera houses, as fiduciary institutions with a life and identity of their own (Selznick, 1996), much like the Scandinavian universities in Chapter 8, required a readjustment of the internal norms and values regulating the subsystem in light of external dynamics and imperatives without resulting in identity loss. In this regard, one could refer to successful adaptation in the context of disruptive environmental change through 'fusion and hybridity' (Padgett, 2012, p. 125), where old (deeply institutionalized) and new (emergent) features, shaping agents' behaviours and identities, were brought together and coexist to some extent (cf. Berg & Pinheiro, 2016). By attaching new (identity) rules to existing ones, the original rules that structured actors' behaviours across the subsystem are gradually adjusted to consider emerging circumstances (Mahoney & Thelen, 2010, p. 16). The Basque case attests to the importance of both *path dependencies* and key *agents* (including policy entrepreneurs) at different levels of the national and regional subsystems (Hay & Wincott, 1998). According to Bucheli and Wadhwani (2013, p. 111), 'adopting a historical approach to studying [the emergence and development of] institutions will enhance our understanding of institutions as a historical process rather than as abstract, reified structures' (see also Padgett & Powell, 2012). Moreover, following Fleming et al. (2012, pp. 537–538), the Basque case confirms the catalysing role played by local institutions in the mobilization and coordination of regionally embedded networks of key agents (universities, forms, government agencies, etc.) working together to enhance adaptability and, hence, the overall resilience of the regional system as a whole.

Towards an Interdisciplinary Resilience Framework for Resilience Organizations and Societies

As indicated at the outset of this edited volume, the concept and phenomenon of resilience first originated in the physical sciences, being subsequently adopted across a wide range of disciplinary fields and their respective epistemological, methodological and theoretical traditions. This, in turn, has led to challenges when it comes to definitions and approaches, most notably as regards comparisons across disciplinary domains. The chapters composing the bulk of this volume attest to this eclecticism when it comes to definitions and conceptualization, but they share a common interest in approaching resilience from a more systemic or holistic perspective. The limited overlap of references among the empirical chapters signals the poor cross-fertilization of resilience studies across research areas, as well as a high specialization of studies in their respective fields. An analysis of such references showed that chapters map onto 114 different references on resilience and that only nine of these are shared between more than one chapter: Lengnick-Hall et al. (2011); Linnenluecke (2017); and Walker and Salt (2006) appear in three reference lists, while Bristow and Healy (2014); Fisher et al. (2018); Folke et al. (2010); Frigotto (2018); Pinheiro and Young (2017); Vogus and Sutcliffe

(2007) appear in two. This overview supports the claim that a stronger interdisciplinary approach to resilience is needed.

A major challenge pertains to the problem of 'conceptual stretching' associated with defining the limits of resilience as a phenomenon (Roe & Schulman, 2008). As highlighted in the edited volume's introduction in Chapter 1, following Giustiniano et al. (2018, pp. 33–37), there are several related resilience constructs such as agility, flexibility and anticipation that are worth taking into consideration. It is often the case in the social sciences that even if we use the same terms, we do not necessarily attribute the same meanings, thus definitions and clarifications are the first necessary step to engage in cross-disciplinary collaborations.

There is an ongoing debate within the scientific establishment about the value of and trade-offs between classic disciplinary-based inquiries and more interdisciplinary ones (cf. Nowotny et al., 2002). One of the arguments defending the latter approach is that it is more suitable to address the multiplicity of 'wicked problems' (Brown et al., 2010) or 'grand challenges' facing humankind, such as climate change, urbanization and rising inequality. This has led to renewed calls for a new mode of knowledge production ('Mode 2') based on collaborations across disciplinary fields in the context of problem-solving and application (Gibbons et al., 1994). Yet, for this to be the case, it is still a requirement for interdisciplinary teams of scientists to be composed of ('Mode 1') basic science specialists in their respective domains if fruitful dialogues are to become a reality (Broto et al., 2009). This is a necessary yet not a sufficient condition for interdisciplinarity to bear fruit, and many other enabling factors need to be present.

According to Klein (2000, p. 7), interdisciplinarity and specialization are parallel, mutually reinforcing strategies: 'The relationship between disciplinarity and interdisciplinarity is not a paradox but a productive tension characterized by complexity and hybridity'. In a more recent contribution on the topic in which the author expands the discussion to encompass transdisciplinary dimensions, attention is paid to the importance of devising a *shared vocabulary* that is conducive to such endeavours (Klein, 2018). In so doing, the author underscores the pivotal relationship between *communication* and *learning*, anchored in socio-cognitive structures for interdisciplinary collaborations that are central to fostering a culture of cooperation and communication. Given the limited scope and ambition of this edited volume, we will primarily focus here on the conditions that are likely to foster integrative, interdisciplinarity arrangements among social scientists in the context of resilience thinking and scholarship.

When it comes to interdisciplinary collaborations, MacMynowski (2007, pp. 8–9) outlines *four* possible scenarios, namely conflict, tolerant ambivalence, mutual identification and cooperation, and transformation. Of these, the last two are particularly relevant in the context of this volume and future initiatives. The scenario characterized by 'mutual identification and cooperation' is one where researchers agree on basic ontological and epistemological underpinnings and analytical structures. However, despite this convergence, the tendency here is to approach research questions from the standpoint of a single analytical framework associated with a specific disciplinary tradition rather than attempting to develop a truly integrative approach that takes into consideration synergies across the various traditions. This aim is achieved in the fourth and most demanding scenario, termed 'transformation',[1] which entails a substantial reorientation and recombination of knowledge claims.

> [Transformation] begins with recognition of a common problem at the intersection of very different conceptual, philosophical, and methodological standpoints. The understanding of the problem, the research design, and the analysis recombine elements from intellectual lineages with little similarity, past cooperation, or shared theory and philosophy [...] Traditional associations with research domains, boundaries, and the distribution of power need to be broken down and transformed. This is a multilevel, intensive reflection and re-creation process. (MacMynowski, 2007, p. 9)

Moreover, for MacMynowski (2007), transformation requires not only a move beyond disciplinary silos but also outside academic walls and isolated projects to engage with multiple knowledge users and other external stakeholders in the spirit of mutually beneficial coproduction and co-creation (Brandsen et al., 2018).

How are we to move from sporadic collaborations towards more integrative approaches anchored in cooperation/identification and/or transformation in the context of resilience thinking and scholarship? For MacMynowski (2007), this entails addressing three important dimensions

[1] It is important to stress that this term should not be confused with 'transformative resilience', which was discussed in the introduction and conclusion of this volume.

or stages associated with interdisciplinary collaborations as an emergent, dynamic, multifaceted and coevolving process (Fig. 12.2). Each stage addresses a set of critical queries that provide the foundation to move to the next stage while acknowledging that the process is non-linear and thus iterative in nature.

The first stage, ***differentiation***, sheds light on a set of epistemological queries centred on how the (new) knowledge is generated. Pertinent questions include, but are not limited to: Is the overall intellectual motivation of the project to predict, to explain, or to interpret? What are the goals of the project? What is the relationship between the subject/object of research and the researchers? What are the aim(s) and purpose(s) of the project? Ideally, the differentiation stage is undertaken at the outset, yet it is also possible to do this at any other stage of the process, iteratively, as research evolves and (new) knowledge is generated and reconstructed (MacMynowski, 2007, p. 10). In the second phase, ***clarification***, participants are to critically and openly discuss the sources and purposes of their

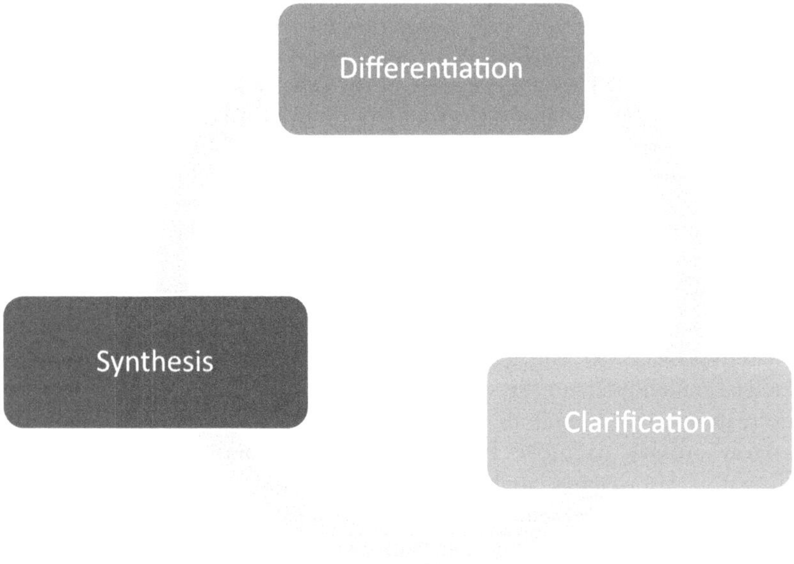

Fig. 12.2 Fostering interdisciplinarity through an iterative process (*Source* Authors' own, based on MacMynowski [2007, p. 11])

different perspectives while addressing questions such as the following: What are the epistemic, rhetorical or normative purposes that are at the heart of differences in perspectives (i.e. potential conflicts) among participants? How are validity, reliability and certainty to be determined? What alternative research approaches (leading to different answers and perspectives) are feasible? Finally, *synthesis* pertains to 'the intellectual fruit after the labour of differentiating and clarifying the research models, concepts, and philosophies at hand' (MacMynowski, 2007, p. 11). Critical queries include: Is it possible to conceive of the subject/object under investigation or research system in a different way? How do the different elements (philosophy, theory, methods) fit together or combine with one another? What gestalt(s) can be created that otherwise could not be if research was undertaken independently within a single discipline or perspective? Finally, as alluded to earlier, the 'process of differentiation, clarification, and synthesis is likely to be an iterative undertaking, repeating itself throughout research design, resolving research problems, interpreting results, and determining conclusions' (MacMynowski, 2007, p. 12).

Based on our experiences, both positive and negative, while undertaking this joint project on resilience with colleagues from different disciplinary traditions and subfields, and regarding future interdisciplinary endeavours centred on a better understanding of the complex and multifaceted phenomenon of resilience within organizations and in society, we offer the following set of recommendations. We conducted two face-to-face workshops over a two-year period with all the participants, and as pointed out above, scholars from different strands need to get to know one another and openly discuss their ontological, epistemological and normative positions. The goal here is not necessarily to reach a consensus but instead to foster awareness and joint understanding of the perspectives and central postulates that drive scientific work and, ultimately, cultivate professional identities. An open, inclusive and reflexive communication process, as was the case with our own project, is likely (though we did not always succeed) to result in joint learning among participants. In an ideal scenario, the former process is anchored in shared socio-cognitive structures, providing a robust foundation for meaningful and sustainable cooperation and, most importantly, identification in the form of a distinct interdisciplinary outlook. Identification, in turn, has the potential to provide the basic foundation for moving beyond traditional disciplinary boundaries, clashes of scientific paradigms, and power structures, substantiated in a shared respect for one another and a fair distribution of authority or influence among the participants. Given the complexity and historicity (temporal dimension) associated with resilience as a social science phenomenon, by 'participants', following MacMynowski (2007), we refer here to all the relevant actors, practitioners included, that both inhabit and have an intrinsic (tacit) knowledge of the structures, mechanisms and antecedents underpinning resilience. Their knowledge and insights are paramount for unveiling hidden structures and underlying processes affecting the behaviours of social actors, individually and collectively. Several empirical chapters in this volume attest to the importance of this partnership between outsiders (researchers) and insiders (practitioners), but we would argue that this mutually beneficial relationship needs to take a more explicit and egalitarian form. All types of knowledge, codified and tacit, are equally valuable in the quest to open the black box associated with resilience behaviour and its direct and indirect effects on individuals, organizations, organizational fields, institutions, and society at large.

Finally, as far as future interdisciplinary studies on resilience are concerned, we propose four possible directions. First, and in light of the fact that, as open systems, all organizations are subject to external forces (Scott, 2003) and that the cases in this volume only included those collective actors characterized as having a high degree of publicness (Bozeman, 2004), future studies encompassing a broader range of organizational types (public, private, hybrid, etc.) and degrees of novelty (low, medium and high levels) could shed light on the extent to which resilience antecedents and mechanisms affect and play out differently across a broader population. Second, the volume's empirical findings lend support to the claim that resilient organizations are, in essence, learning entities—even if they resort to different strategies to learn about themselves and/or their surrounding environments (March, 1991). Future inquiries could, for example, shed light on the key actors, structures and processes associated with different types of learning (and their interactions) at different temporal scales—before, during and after the unfolding of major events triggering resilience behaviours. Third, following systems thinking (Walker & Salt, 2006), there is a need to continue to open the black box associated with nestedness between the micro (agents), meso (organizations) and macro (society) levels of analysis, both within organizations and across organizational fields. Most notably, it is imperative to understand how these levels emerge, coevolve and interact with one another in non-linear ways. Finally, methodologically speaking, future studies should seriously consider adopting both mixed methods (Bryman, 2006) and longitudinal design approaches as a means of capturing the complex and dynamic essence of resilience as a property, process and outcome.

References

Berg, L., & Pinheiro, R. (2016). Handling different institutional logics in the public sector: Comparing management in Norwegian universities and hospitals. In R. Pinheiro, F. Ramirez, K. Vrabæk, & L. Geschwind (Eds.), *Towards a comparative institutionalism: Forms, dynamics and logics across health care and higher education fields* (pp. 145–168). Bingley.

Bozeman, B. (1987). *All oganizations are public: Bridging public and private organizational theories*, Jossey-Bass.

Bozeman, B. (2004). *All organizations are public: Comparing public and private organizations*. Beard Books.

Brandsen, T., Steen, T., & Verschuere, B. (2018). *Co-production and co-creation: Engaging citizens in public services*. Taylor & Francis.

Bristow, G., & Healy, A. (2014). Regional Resilience: An Agency Perspective. *Regional Studies, 48*(5), 923–935.

Broto, V. C., Gislason, M., & Ehlers, M.-H. (2009). Practising interdisciplinarity in the interplay between disciplines: Experiences of established researchers. *Environmental Science & Policy, 12*(7), 922–933.

Brown, V. A., Harris, J. A., & Russell, J. Y. (2010). *Tackling wicked problems through the transdisciplinary imagination*. Earthscan.

Bryman, A. (2006). *Mixed methods*. Sage.

Bucheli, M., & Wadhwani, R. D. (2013). *Organizations in time: History, theory, methods*. Oxford University Press.

Collier, D., & Mahon, J. (1993). Conceptual "Stretching" Revisited: Adapting Categories in Comparative Analysis. *American Political Science Review, 87*(4), 845–855.

Deephouse, D., & Suchman, M. (2008). Legitimacy in organizational institutionalism. In R. Greenwood, C. Oliver, K. Sahlin, & R. Suddaby (Eds.), *The Sage handbook of organizational institutionalism* (pp. 49–77). Sage.

Edmondson, A. C., Winslow, A. B., Bohmer, R. M., & Pisano, G. P. (2003). Learning how and learning what: Effects of tacit and codified knowledge on performance improvement following technology adoption. *Decision Sciences, 34*(2), 197–224.

Fisher, D. M., Ragsdale, J. M., & Fisher, E. C. S. (2018). The importance of definitional and temporal issues in the study of resilience. *Applied Psychology, 68*(4), 583–620.

Fleming, L., Colfer, L., Marin, A., & McPhie, J. (2012). Why the valley went first: Agglomeration and emergence in regional inventor networks. In J. F. Padgett & W. W. Powell (Eds.), *The emergence of organizations and markets* (pp. 520–544). Princeton University Press.

Folke, C., Carpenter, S., Walker, B., Scheffer, M., Chapin, T., & Rockström, J. (2010). Resilience thinking: integrating resilience, adaptability and transformability. *Ecology & Society, 15*(4), 20–28.

Forsyth, P. B., & Danisiewicz, T. J. (1985). Toward a theory of professionalization. *Work and Occupations, 12*(1), 59–76.

Frigotto, M. L. (2018). *Understanding novelty in organizations: A research path across agency and consequences*. Palgrave MacMillan.

Frigotto, M. L., Young, M., & Pinheiro, R. (2022). Resilience in organizations and societies: The state of the art and three organizing principles for moving forward. In R. Pinheiro, L. Frigotto, & M. Young (Eds.), *Towards resilient organizations and societies: A cross-sectoral and multi-disciplinary perspective* (pp. 3–44). Palgrave.

Giddens, A. (1981). *A contemporary critique of historical materialism*. Macmillan.

Gibbons, M., Nowotny, H., Schwartzman, S., Scott, P., & Trow, M. (1994). *The new production of knowledge: The dynamics of science and research in contemporary societies*. Sage.

Giustiniano, L., Clegg, S. R., Cunha, M. P., & Rego, A. (2018). *Elgar introduction to theories of organizational resilience*. Edward Elgar Publishing.

Hay, C., & Wincott, D. (1998). Structure, agency and historical institutionalism. *Political Studies, 46*(5), 951–957.

Hazelkorn, E., Coates, H., & McCormick, A. C. (2018). *Research handbook on quality, performance and accountability in higher education*. Edward Elgar Publishing.

Kane, J., & Patapan, H. (2012). *The democratic leader: How democracy defines, empowers and limits its leaders*. Oxford University Press.

Kayes, D. C. (2015). *Organizational resilience: How learning sustains organizations in crisis, disaster, and breakdown*. Oxford University Press.

Klein, J. T. (2000). A conceptual vocabulary of interdisciplinary science. In N. Stehr & P. Weingart (Eds.), *Practising interdisciplinarity* (pp. 3–24). University of Toronto Press.

Klein, J. T. (2018). Learning in transdisciplinary collaborations: A conceptual vocabulary. In D. Fam, L. Neuhauser, & P. Gibbs (Eds.), *Transdisciplinary theory, practice and education* (pp. 11–23). Springer.

Lengnick-Hall, C. A., Beck, T. E., & Lengnick-Hall, M. L. (2011). Developing a capacity for organizational resilience through strategic human resource management. *Human Resource Management Review, 21*(3), 243–255.

Linnenluecke, M. K. (2017). Resilience in business and management research: A review of influential publications and a research agenda. *International Journal of Management Reviews, 19*(1), 4–30.

MacMynowski, D. P. (2007). Pausing at the brink of interdisciplinarity: Power and knowledge at the meeting of social and biophysical science. *Ecology and Society, 12*(1), 1–14.

Mahoney, J., & Thelen, K. (2010). *Explaining institutional change: Ambiguity, agency, and power*. Cambridge University Press.

Meadows, D. H. (2008). *Thinking in systems: A primer*. Chelsea Green Publishing.

March, J. G. (1991). Exploration and exploitation in organizational learning. *Organization Science, 2*(1), 71–87.

Nowotny, H., Scott, P., & Gibbons, M. (2002). *Re-thinking science: Knowledge and the public in an age of uncertainty*. Polity Press.

Olsen, J. P. (2007). The institutional dynamics of the European university. In P. Maassen & J. P. Olsen (Eds.), *University dynamics and European integration* (pp. 25–54). Springer.

Packendorff, J. (1995). Inquiring into the temporary organization: New directions for project management research. *Scandinavian Journal of Management, 11*(4), 319–333.

Padgett, J. F. (2012). The emergence of corporate Merchant-Banks in Dugento Tuscany. In J. F. Padgett & W. W. Powell (Eds.), *The emergence of organizations and markets* (pp. 121–167). Princeton University Press.

Padgett, J. F., & Powell, W. W. (2012). *The emergence of organizations and markets*. Princeton University Press.

Parker, J. (2010). Structuration theories. Historical development and theoretical approaches in sociology. *Encyclopaedia of Life Support Systems, 2*, 132–175.

Pekkola, E., Pinheiro, R., Geschwind, L., Siekkinen, T., Carvalho, T., & Pulkkinen, K. (2021). Nested hybridity and value definition in public higher education. In J. Vakkuri & J.-E. Johanson (Eds.), *Hybrid governance, organisations and society: Value creation perspectives* (pp. 59–80). Routledge.

Pfeffer, J., & Salancik, G. (1978). *The external control of organizations: A resource dependence perspective*. Library of Congress.

Pinheiro, R., & Young, M. (2017). The university as an adaptive resilient organization: A complex systems perspective. In J. Huisman & M. Tight (Eds.), Theory and method in higher education research (pp. 119–136). Emerald.

Putnam, R. D. (2001). *Bowling alone: The collapse and revival of American community*. Simon & Schuster.

Roe, E., & Schulman, P. (2008). *High reliability management: Operating on the edge*. Stanford University Press.

Room, G. (2016). *Agile actors on complex terrains: Transformative realism and public policy*. Routledge.

Selznick, P. (1966). *TVA and the grass roots: A study in the sociology of formal organization*. Harper & Row.

Selznick, P. (1996). Institutionalism 'old' and 'new.' *Administrative Science Quarterly, 41*(2), 270–277.

Sewell, W. H. (1992). A theory of structure: Duality, agency, and transformation. *American Journal of Sociology, 98*(1), 1–29.

Scott, W. R. (2003). *Organizations: Rational, natural, and open systems*. Prentice Hall.

Simon, H. A. (1991). Bounded rationality and organizational learning. *Organization Science, 2*(1), 125–134.

Stern, M. J., & Baird, T. D. (2015). Trust ecology and the resilience of natural resource management institutions. *Ecology and Society, 20*(2), 1–11.

Sutcliffe, K. M. (2011). High reliability organizations (HROs). *Best Practice & Research Clinical Anaesthesiology, 25*(2), 133–144.

Tapper, T., & Palfreyman, D. (2010). *The collegial tradition in the age of mass higher education*. Springer.

Thornton, P. H., Ocasio, W., & Lounsbury, M. (2012). *The institutional logics perspective: A new approach to culture, structure, and process*. Oxford University Press.

Trondal, J., Keast, R., Noble, D., & Pinheiro, R. (2022). *Governing complexity in times of turbulence*. Edward Elgar.

Vogus, T. J., & Sutcliffe, K. M. (2007). Organizational resilience: Towards a theory and research agenda, in IEEE Proceedings, *International Conference on Systems, Man, and Cybernetics* (SMC), 3418–3422.

Walker, B., & Salt, D. (2006). *Resilience thinking: Sustaining ecosystems and people in a changing world*. Island Press.

Wittgenstein, L. (1968). *Philosophical investigations*. Basil Blackwell.

Wittrock, B. (1985). Dinosaurs or dolphins? Rise and resurgence of the research-oriented university. In B. Wittrock & A. Elzinga (Eds.), The University Research System: The public policies of the home of scientists (pp. 13–39). Coronet Books.

Index

A

Absorptive resilience, 15, 19, 20, 24
Adaptability, 278, 280, 281, 283, 290–293, 295–298
Adaptation, 145, 149, 161, 278–281, 286, 290–292, 296, 298
Adaptive resilience, 15, 19, 20, 24
Administration, 118
Adversity, 308–310, 314, 317, 318, 320
Agency, 278–280, 283–286, 288, 290–292, 294–298
Agile actors, 315
Archetype, 224, 225, 227–231, 233, 235, 238, 240–243
Automatized action, 76, 78, 80–82
Awareness, 7, 18, 19

B

Background knowledge, 66, 71, 74–77, 79–84
Ball-and-cup model, 15, 20, 21
Basque Country, 278, 286, 287, 289, 290, 293, 295
Bounded rationality, 318

C

Case study, 251
Change, 3, 4, 6–8, 10, 13–17, 19–26, 28–30, 32–34
Clark, Burton R., 175, 176, 178, 181–186
Coevolution, 252–254, 257, 268–270, 297, 313, 315
College, 259, 260, 262
Communities of practice, 94, 97, 111, 113
Competition, 174, 175, 179–181, 183, 184
Complex projects, 93, 94, 97, 101, 113
Complex systems, 176, 180, 186, 187
Concept stretching, 307
Contested fields, 202
Continuity of essence, 12, 14, 25, 224–226, 242
Coordination work, 97, 107, 109, 112
Crisis management, 44, 50, 54
Crisis management team (CMT), 118, 123, 128–130, 132, 133, 135

R. Pinheiro et al. (eds.), *Towards Resilient Organizations and Societies*, Public Sector Organizations,
https://doi.org/10.1007/978-3-030-82072-5

Critical junctures, 197, 206, 208, 209, 214

D
Decision premises, 45, 50, 52–62
Degree, 13, 14, 18, 27, 34
Deliberative, 314
Disaggregation, 179
Diversity, 174, 181, 183–187
Drill, 66, 70, 71, 76, 77, 79–84

E
Economic crisis, 286–288, 290–293, 295
Efficiency, 174, 175, 181–183, 187
Emergency, 44–46, 48–51, 55, 56, 59–61
Emergency management, 45, 46, 49–51, 54, 55, 59
Employee behaviour, 145, 148
Entrepreneurial university, 174–187, 186
Essence, 308–310, 326, 327
Estonia, 251, 258, 259, 267
Etzkowitz, Henry, 177, 178
Exaptation, 71, 72, 80–82, 84
Expertise, 68, 78–80
Exploration/exploitation, 319, 320
External stakeholders, 201–203, 210

F
Family resemblance, 309
Finland, 251, 263, 265, 267
Firefighters, 46, 59, 60
Foresight, 12, 23, 24, 31, 32

G
Growth-oriented leadership, 146, 150, 154, 155

H
Higher education (HE), 196, 204–207, 209, 211, 212, 214
Higher education system (HES), 249, 252, 254, 256–259, 261, 262, 265–270
High reliability organizations, 50
High reliability theory, 92, 96
History, 279, 289
Holistic, 4, 8, 27, 34, 35, 224–226, 230, 233, 242
Human resource management, 312
Hybridity, 197, 213

I
Identity, 196–209, 211–215
Identity adaptation, 197, 215
Industrial policy, 286
Industrial safety, 104, 106
Innovation policy, 278
Institutional change, 225, 283, 284, 290
Institutional entrepreneurs, 228, 242, 283, 285, 288, 290, 291, 293, 294, 297
Institutional entrepreneurship, 138
Institutional orders, 320
Institutional perspective, 198
Institutional work, 138, 139
Institutions, 278–280, 282–284, 286, 294–298
Interdisciplinarity, 322, 324
Interviews, 146–149, 153–161

K
Knowledge intensive organisations (KIOs), 144
Kuressaare, 251, 259, 267

L

Leadership, 144–147, 150–152, 154, 157, 160, 161, 163
Leadership development, 151
Learning, 143, 145, 148–150, 152–155, 157, 160–163
Learning entities, 326
Learning, problem solving, 45, 49, 51, 59
Legitimacy, 57, 61, 197, 200–206, 209, 211–215
Line managers, 146
Logics, 228, 241–243
Loose coupling, 175, 182, 186

M

Management, 147, 150, 155, 156, 162, 163
Managers, 99–102, 104, 105, 107–109, 112
Mechanisms, 12, 17, 22–24, 28, 31–34
Micromanagement, 145, 152, 153, 159, 160, 162
Military,training, 70, 73, 76
Mindfulness, 49
Multidisciplinarity, 4, 34

N

Nestedness, 313, 326
Network leveraging, 148–150, 153, 160, 162
New Public Management (NPM), 174, 175, 178–182, 186
Novelty, 12, 14–21, 24, 28–31
NPM, 178

O

Occupational groups, 93, 94, 97–99, 101, 102, 107, 110–113
Occupational safety, 109
Opera, 224, 225, 229–235, 238–243
Opera house, 229, 235, 236
Örebro University, 196, 209, 210
Organisational resilience (OR), 252–254, 265–267
Organizational archetypes, 174, 184
Organizational identity, 196–206, 208, 211, 213, 214
Organizational performance, 92, 94
Organizational resilience, 43–45, 59, 61
Organization theory, 27
Outcome, 7, 11, 12, 14, 15, 17, 22–25, 33, 34

P

Path dependence, 198, 282, 283, 288, 291, 292, 296
Preaptation, 80
Problem representation, 51–55, 59–61
Profession, 225, 226, 229, 230, 238–241, 243
Project-based organizations, 92, 110
Proponents agency, 138, 139
Publicness, 311–313, 315, 316, 326
Public organisations, 146, 150, 162

Q

Qualitative, 73, 251, 286
Quasi-markets, 179, 180

R

Regional development, 250, 255, 256, 260, 262, 263
Regional higher education institution (RHEIs), 249–252, 254–261, 263, 266–270
Regional paths, 278, 283, 297

Regional resilience, 250, 254, 255, 260, 264, 268, 278, 279, 281, 283, 284, 286, 287, 295–297
Relativity, 18, 24
Requisite variety, 185, 186
Resilience, 92–103, 105–107, 110–113, 143–154, 156, 157, 159–163, 196–202, 206, 213–215, 249–257, 264, 266, 268–270
Resilience action, 120, 127–129, 131, 132, 134, 135, 137
Resilience as practice, 118, 120, 121, 128, 137
Resilience frameworks, 118, 119, 123
Resilience proponents, 129, 137–139
Resilience structure, 120, 122, 123, 134, 137, 139
Roles, 44–46, 52, 54–62
Role system, 54, 56, 59, 61
Routines, 66–68, 74, 76, 77, 79, 80
Rule-breaking, 67, 69, 83
Rules, 66–72, 74–76, 79, 80, 82–84

S
Saaremaa, 259, 260
Scales (of resilience), 25
Scandinavia, 204
Schatzki, T., 118–122, 127, 128, 138
Sedimentation, 227, 228, 243
Seinäjoki, 251, 262, 264, 267
Sensemaking, 44, 53, 60, 61
Skill development, 66, 81
Slack, 183, 186, 187
South Ostrobothnia, 251, 262–264
Stability, 5, 12, 14–17, 20, 21, 24, 25, 34
Stabilizing system, 79, 80, 84
Structurationist theory, 310
Systems thinking, 317, 326

T
Temporality, 22
Temporary organizing, 91, 93–98, 102, 110, 111
Threshold, 308, 310, 314, 315, 317
Time, 307–310, 314, 316, 320
Transformation, 227, 228, 231, 236, 238, 241–243, 323
Transformative resilience, 14, 16, 19, 20, 22, 24, 33, 34, 226, 241
Transportation, 118, 123, 125
Trust, 317, 319, 320

U
Uncertainty, 68, 79
Unexpected, novelty, 44, 45, 55, 56
Unexpected situations, 97, 105, 111, 112
Unified actor, 179, 182, 187
Universities, 195, 196, 205, 207–214

W
Work practices, 97, 101, 104, 107, 109

The manufacturer's authorised representative in the EU is Springer Nature Customer Service Centre GmbH, Europaplatz 3, 69115 Heidelberg, Germany. If you have any concerns regarding our products, please contact ProductSafety@springernature.com

Printed and bound by CPI Group (UK) Ltd, Croydon, CR0 4YY
30/09/2026
02225701-0015